Nightmares of the Lettered City

ILLUMINATIONS | Cultural Formations of the Americas

John Beverley and Sara Castro-Klarén, *Editors*

Nightmares of the Lettered City

Banditry and Literature in Latin America 1816–1929

Juan Pablo Dabove

University of Pittsburgh Press

Published by the University of Pittsburgh Press, Pittsburgh PA 15260
Manufactured in the United States of America
Printed on acid-free paper

10 9 8 7 6 5 4 3 2 1

Library of Congress Cataloging-in-Publication Data
Dabove, Juan Pablo.
    Nightmares of the lettered city : banditry and literature in Latin
America, 1816–1929 / Juan Pablo Dabove.
        p. cm. — (Illuminations: cultural formations of the Americas)
    Includes bibliographical references and index.
    ISBN-13: 978-0-8229-4331-0 (cloth : alk. paper)
    ISBN-10: 0-8229-4331-X (cloth : alk. paper)
    ISBN-13: 978-0-8229-5956-4 (pbk. : alk. paper)
    ISBN-10: 0-8229-5956-9 (pbk. : alk. paper)
        1. Latin American literature—20th century—History and criticism.
2. Brigands and robbers in literature. I. Title.
    PQ7081.D2155 2007
    860.9'98—dc22   2006102642

To my wife and colleague,
Susan R. Hallstead

Contents

Acknowledgments

This book would not have been possible without my wife and colleague, Susan R. Hallstead. It owes its existence to her support and encouragement, as well as to her intelligent reading of the manuscript and innate sense of style. The book is therefore dedicated to her. I hope that the product is worth the time and love she devoted to it (and to me).

Nightmares of the Lettered City was conceived in Pittsburgh. Later, I substantially developed the project in Boulder during my first four years there as an assistant professor. Now it returns to Pittsburgh to start another trip. Many people in both cities are to be thanked for making its journey possible. I would like to thank the professors and mentors who transformed me into a Latinoamericanist and a scholar: Mabel Moraña (who gave me the initial opportunity to pursue a graduate career in the United States, and showed me the intellectual and personal challenges of being a Latinoamericanist), Reid Andrews, Gerald Martin, John Beverley, and Alejandro de la Fuente, all at the University of Pittsburgh. It has been an enormous privilege to learn from them, and their legacy will be with me for the rest of my academic career. Also, I would like to thank the friends and colleagues who shared those years with me, in particular Carlos Jáuregui, Federico Veiravé, Susana Rosano, and Ignacio Sánchez-Prado.

The Center for Latin American Studies at the University of Pittsburgh (in particular Shirley Kregar and John Frechione) gave me the opportunity and funding to travel repeatedly to Latin America and Europe to collect data relevant to this research. Also, they provided me (and many, many other hopeful and inexperienced young Latinoamericanists) with invaluable guidance and support. The Andrew Mellon Foundation allowed me to devote a year exclusively to writing. I want to thank Sara Castro-Klarén and John Beverley, editors of the University of Pittsburgh Press series "Illuminations: Cultural Formations of the Americas," and Peter Kracht, the press's editorial director, for giving this book a chance and helping to make it a reality.

In Boulder, colleagues at the University of Colorado's Department of Spanish and Portuguese provided me with a warm and encouraging environment in which to work and live. My friends Emilio Bejel, Peter Elmore, Leila

Gómez, and Luis González del Valle discussed and patiently read this manuscript. Ricardo Landeira, chair of the department, friend, and mentor, gave me the support I needed to work toward my professional and personal goals. Several chapters of this book were conceived and developed in graduate seminars. To the graduate students who participated in them, my heartfelt thanks.

The dedication, generosity, and knowledge of Sean Knowlton, bibliographer for comparative, Spanish, and Portuguese literatures, and of the outstanding staff at the Interlibrary Loan office at Norlin Library (Jane Thomas, Marty Covey, Betsy Gould, and Karen Taylor) were essential to this research, to a degree I do not think they realize. Doreen Delisle, administrator at the Department of Spanish and Portuguese, devoted many hours of patient work to helping me handle all aspects of my professional work. Finally, the Council on Research and Creative Work and the Graduate Committee on the Arts and Humanities at the University of Colorado at Boulder provided me with funding to travel to Latin America and Europe to develop and finish the research for this book.

Introduction
Nightmares of the Lettered City

Anyone who fights with monsters should take care that he does not in the process become a monster. And if you gaze for long into an abyss, the abyss gazes back into you.

Friedrich Nietzsche, *Beyond Good and Evil*

Toward a Cultural Teratology

The Latin American lettered city is haunted by monsters.[1] These monsters turn the lettered city's noble dreams into nightmares. Inescapable and urgent, these nightmares are conveyors of an enigmatic truth. Hence the challenge of the Latin American cultural critic: to reinvent our practice not as the memory of founding fathers (cultural or military ones), heroes, or popular practices (humble albeit respectable) but rather as a sort of cultural teratology. This teratology is diverse. It comprises bloodthirsty bandits that give the rural frontier a hellish quality; rebellious peasants that burn, rape, and destroy apparently without a second (or first) thought; Indians that bind their victims with the intestines of their victim's slaughtered sons; hunger-stricken, harpy-like black females that fight in bloody mud much like dogs—and with dogs—for lard or scraps of animal entrails; disease-ridden immigrants whose deceitful promise of new blood becomes the ominous threat of atavism; prostitutes whose pestilence corrupts the minds and bodies of wholesome family boys—the future of the nation; cannibals; madmen; gays; Jews; communists.

These monsters are formations of the national political unconscious (Jameson 1981), and as such, they are the visible product of transactions between "desire" and "repression." They are floating signifiers (Laclau 1996) that are key to an understanding of the diverse regimes of representation that define national identities. Therefore, this cultural teratology can be thought of as a genealogy of the nation. Instead of reconstructing a multisecular narrative of emancipation, achievement of self-consciousness, and exertion of the potentialities of the origin, I propose a genealogy that will trace the piecemeal cultural conflicts of which national imagined communities are an effect, not a *primum mobile*. In other words, it will specify the ways in which these monsters, understood as identities differing from the man of letters (*letrado*) who is masculine-literate-"white"-proprietor-urban-Europeanized, were less a threat to Latin American national cultures than the secret dynamo that drove their definition. Said genealogy brings to light many of the family ties between heroes and monsters and between the fathers of the nation and its outcasts and many of the dangers that the monsters' furtive lurking in the dark margins comes to metaphorize.[2] These monsters are not the children of a bizarre "Latin" imagination but urgent political responses to real conflicts. One of the most prominent characters within this cultural teratology is the (in)famous Latin American bandit, the dark hero of Latin American rural history.

Bandits

Plateado, bandido, cangaceiro, gaucho malo, llanero, jagunço, bandolero, abigeo, desertor, cabra, vago, malentretenido, insumiso, salteador, fanático, guerrillero, gavillero, agavillado, forajido, malhechor, cimarrón, muchacho del monte, montonero, malandro, Hermano de la Hoja, matrero, malebolo. These are a few among the many names for those engaged in a particularly pervasive form of violence in rural Latin America. Bandits are much more than rural thieves (*ladrones en despoblado*) or cattle rustlers (*abigeos, cuatreros*). Although the figure of the bandit is primarily associated with robbery or an attempt against private property (kidnapping for ransom, blackmailing, protection rackets, cattle rustling, jacquerie), brigandage may comprise such diverse offenses as resisting authority, smuggling, homicide, conspiracy to commit crime, possession of prohibited weaponry, vagrancy, desertion, rebellion, and poaching. Any challenge to state rule could be and frequently was, at one point or another, labeled "banditry." This protean character of the bandit is one of the reasons for its continued political relevance and cultural productivity, and a determination to understand both of these aspects is what gave rise to this book. Bandits and rural insurgents are among the better known characters in Latin American history, from Tupac Amaru to Emiliano Zapata and Che Guevara through, of course, Pancho Villa (all four labeled as bandits at one point or another in their careers). However, little has been done outside the realm of historical studies to examine in a comprehensive fashion (beyond particular cases or particular regions) the ways in which banditry has been depicted in elite discourse, and how this representation has been crucial to the constitution of Latin American national cultures as we know them today.

Although I draw upon the works of Adolfo Prieto, Josefina Ludmer, and Nina Gerassi-Navarro, I intend for this book to fill a void in Latin American cultural criticism. This work is particularly timely because in the academic and political agendas of Latin American studies, the inquiry into the interactions between elite culture and subaltern culture occupies a central position.[3] As such, part of my goal in writing this book was that it would be relevant beyond literary criticism. I want it to be read as part of a series of studies that map foundational tropes in Latin American national cultures of the nineteenth century. Indeed, the exploration of the symbolic mechanisms of construction and negotiation of identities—Latin American "fables of identity" (Ludmer 1999, 470)—has led to important works in the field of cultural and literary studies that have "tried to articulate the foundational period of national literatures with the nation-state process of formation and institutionalization in Latin America, trying to focus on the complex process of mediations and representational strategies through which social actors try to define themselves" (Moraña 1984, 42). The contention of this book is that the rural rebel labeled a bandit by the state was among the foremost cultural Others of Latin American modernity. As such, it is essential to our understanding of the form that said modernity assumed, as well as its contradictions and shortcomings.[4]

As John Beverley states, the bandit (together with the Indian or the runaway slave) was the "main demoniacal force in the liberal epic" of the nineteenth century (1987, 102). The meaning of this statement is twofold. The bandit-as-demon (a topic that the European gothic novel took quite literally, as in the case of *The Manuscript Found in Saragossa*, by Count Jan Potocki) can mean the bandit as "adversarial force" of liberal discourse. Additionally, through the form of possession, the bandit is regarded as the evil, hidden "driving force." This ambiguity points to the constitutional split of the bandit trope and its changing relationship to hegemonic identities.[5]

As an adversarial force, the bandit as Other is essential in the constitution of the citizen as Self. As Jean Baudrillard points out, "Power exists solely by virtue of its symbolic ability to designate the Other, the Enemy, what is at stake, what threatens us, what is Evil" (1990, 82). The cultural history of Latin American banditry amply proves this postulate. The letrado elite excluded certain rural practices and rural subjects. This exclusion certainly had a crucial material dimension, since "bandits" were targeted for suppression, but it was at the same time a rhetorical one, since it was made possible by the mobilization of the trope of banditry.[6]

This labeling played an integral part in the legitimation of an elite-led project of nation-state building in Latin America and thus was a defining feature of the Latin American historical experience. As Miguel Ángel Centeno brilliantly proves, Latin America "lacked [the] identification of an external enemy that encouraged the development of a national identity. As far as state elites are concerned, the greatest threat to their power has not come from competing elites across the border, but from the masses below. . . . The enemy of 'la patria' was not perceived as the nation next door, but as those in the population who threatened the social and economic status quo" (2002, 90). Banditry is born as a trope when, from the state's viewpoint, popular illegalities are represented as crimes and its subjects as criminals (Foucault 1975, 83, 292).[7] This labeling is faced with resistance (cultural or otherwise) from below, which is why, in the protracted debate on the existence and nature of social banditry, it has been hard to reach a concrete definition of what the bandit does (that is, the exact nature of his offense). The bandit is not the thief, the smuggler, the poacher, the cattle rustler, or the vagrant. There would be no banditry without one of these offenses, however, and since no particular action is deemed banditry, any action could be (and was) deemed banditry, a catchall word used much in the way that "terror" is currently used in the United States. Because of this, Gilbert Joseph states that the term belongs to the "metalanguage of crime" (1994, 160).

This impossibility of defining banditry once and for all would account for the conspicuous absence of banditry as a codified offense in penal codes, in spite of the fact that we find the term everywhere in literary works, journalistic sources, travelogues, and memoirs. Mid-nineteenth-century Mexico was, by all accounts, the golden age of Latin American banditry. In certain areas, gangs numbered in the hundreds, waging war much like regular armies, celebrating unofficial treaties with governments and controlling significant tracts of territory (Vanderwood 1992). One would imagine that legislation would reflect this situation, since banditry amounted to a formidable challenge to state building. However, in the Mexican penal code of 1871, the brainchild of liberal penal thought, banditry is not defined as a crime (Vanderwood 1992, xxxv). Actually, the very word banditry does not appear at all in the more than three hundred pages of the code. Different offenses associated with banditry do indeed appear (such as highway robbery [*robo en despoblado*], association to commit crime [*asociación para cometer robo*], kidnapping for extortion [*plagio*], and rebellion), but banditry does not. Similar situations are found in other Latin American penal codes of the nineteenth century.

In any case, it is safe to say that a bandit is he who maintains through his actions (which may not form part of a conscious "political program") his "right" (usually uncodified) to engage in certain practices that collide with a legality-in-the-making that portrays such actions as out-and-out crimes. Since banditry is the name for a conflict revolving around representation, it does not name an essence but an identity in constant flux. Banditry is the product of the encounter between a hegemonic effect of identification (Laclau 1996, 3, 6) and popular illegalities. Each appearance of the bandit in the text of a culture is the trace of a conflict, "not the majestic unfolding of an identity but the response to a crisis" (Laclau and Mouffe 1985, 7).[8]

Rafael Muñoz, author of *¡Vámonos con Pancho Villa!* (1931) and one of the best writers of the genre called the novel of the Mexican Revolution, offers an excellent example of banditry considered as a mark and a signifier. After being defeated by the Carrancista general Álvaro Obregón, the División del Norte (Villa's famous army) was a shadow in constant flight and was limited in resources and human support. In fact, the División del Norte was no longer an army; it had become a "gang." Tiburcio, the main character of the novel, is loyal to Villa to the bitter end (until death), and unlike so many others, he refuses to desert his chief. Tiburcio muses,

> And now, what are we? . . . Tiburcio's mind plunged into an abyss.
> —We are bandits.
> All of us? No! But there is a sign that makes us all the same, a mark that distinguishes us from the rest of humankind, a sign that separates and stops us. We are bodies destined to the gallows. Once we are rounded up, once we are captured, we are going to die. Those of us who do not get away will hang from the trees. Anyone who sees us there will rejoice upon discovering the sign, the word branded on our foreheads. Not all of us are bandits, but those who are captured will not have time to say it, or even to implore clemency. (Muñoz 1931, 110)

With a lucidity arising from his utter hopelessness, Tiburcio realizes that he and his fellow fighters have become bandits. They are bandits indeed, but not because they are more violent, greedy, or corrupt than before. Tiburcio realizes that banditry is a mark (*señal*), a word that sets them apart from the rest of humankind. (After the defeat, Villa, formerly the "Mexican Napoleon," becomes a bandit who is hunted down like a wild animal, and as such he hides in a cave to lick his wounds.) Being bandits is not something that they do; in this case, they are just running away from their enemies and living off the land much like they did before. Instead, it is an identity effect embedded in a political conflict, a position before the law, like the outlaw in the Anglo-Saxon tradition (Prassel 1993).

I mentioned that the bandit-as-demon was also a driving (possessing) force. As such, it shows the lack of suture in the tissue of the social body. That is, it exposes the precarious and contested character of all dominance and all identity. Tiburcio clearly realizes that banditry is not a practice but a "mark" (a signifier) branded on a practice and as such, it brings the practice under the gaze of the state. Therefore, contingency, or the lack of a "natural" relationship between mark and practice, is its defining character. There was nothing that Tiburcio or Villa did differently to cause their demotion from liberators to bandits. What was different was their position in a precarious interplay of forces.[9] However, for the same reason that the bandit trope marks what needs to be excluded, subordinated, or suppressed, it also marks what escapes the material and symbolic control of the elite. It is what exceeds its paradigms. This excess denaturalizes the hegemonic identity and its mechanisms of representation, since it shows the fissures that tear it. As an "imagined" identity the bandit is a testimony of domination as well as of resistance and of the anxiety that such resistance triggers within the elite. Therefore, the bandit can embody the mythopoetic power of the elite, as well as the mythopoetic capabilities of what Pier Paolo Portinaro refers to as "savage powers" (1999, 11), Michael Hardt and Antonio Negri (2004), as "constituent power," or Baruch Spinoza as the "multitude."

The bandit trope is, within the text of Latin American culture, both the product of and the arena for the struggles between the lettered city and the various social sectors that challenged its dominance. Banditry defines, in a contingent, ever-changing fashion, the identities of the adversaries within this struggle. In Latin America, banditry defied what Michel Foucault called "the rule of optimal specification" as the cornerstone of the semio-technique that defined the modern approach to the "power to punish." This rule, as Foucault reconstructs it, states that "for penal semiotics to cover the whole field of illegalities that one wishes to eliminate, all offenses must be defined; they must be classified and collected into species from which none of them can escape. A code is therefore necessary and this code must be sufficiently precise for each type of offense to be clearly present in it" (1975, 98).[10]

Banditry is crucial in the constitution of the paradigms of bandit/citizen and outlaw violence/state violence. At the same time, however, it is what makes those paradigms unstable and ultimately untenable. Therefore, our reading of the vast literary tradition dealing with banditry in the so-called "long nineteenth century" will always be twofold and traceable to Derridean deconstructionism. To begin, we should identify the operations through which the letrado, in specific conflicts, carries out a mapping of the social terrain in which the opposition between lawful and outlaw violence is the defining feature. In addition, we should show the ways in which this very opposition is interdicted and erased (again, in the Derridean sense) and how letrado thinking is brought to its own limits.

The bandit is perhaps the most important in a series of *dramatis personae* that in postcolonial Latin American culture function as frontiers between "domains of sovereignty" (Chatterjee 1993, 6). This character is particularly fit to embody the many unresolved ambiguities of Latin American modernity. As such, an in-depth examination of the bandit trope would allow us to "write into the history of modernity [i.e., Latin American modern culture], the ambivalences, the contradictions, the use of force, and the tragedies and the ironies that attend it" (Chakrabarty 1997, 288).

In addition to being a problematic juridical figure, the bandit is a literary, historical, and scientific figure that makes conflict visible within the social realm. This conflict has an economic basis, but it goes well beyond this notion. The vast plains of Venezuela (*llanos*) and Argentina (*pampas*) offer important cases in point. Transforming the Venezuelan *llanero* bandit and the Argentine *gaucho malo*, respectively, into totalizing metaphors for the whole rural population was a strategy the elite used to intervene in a multi-secular struggle for the appropriation of resources (wild cattle and horses). This metaphor also highlighted alternative concepts of property (the liberal-landowner concept versus the traditional community-oriented concept of the seminomadic hunter-shepherd), alternative concepts of violence (the state monopoly on violence versus the individual ownership and administration of it), and alternative concepts of citizenship, community, and rights. Following this "original" scene of formation of the bandit trope, many quarrels in Argentine or Venezuelan culture were depicted (i.e., narrated) using the rural bandit as "conceptual persona" (Deleuze and Guattari 1991). Banditry is thus what Josefina Ludmer has termed a difference effect between two orders in conflict and reciprocal transformation (1988, 16). As a difference effect, the bandit trope appears initially from the state gesture of expulsion. It is important to remember that the etymology of *forajido* is precisely *salido afuera*, whereas that of *bandido* is not thief, but rather *proscripto*, from the Italian *bandir* (Corominas 1954, 487), and that the canonical lexical definition is that of the *"fugitivo llamado por bando"* (*Diccionario de la Real Academia Española* 1992, 260). The *Tesoro de la lengua castellana o española* (1611) makes this connection even closer. It includes the notions of *bandido* and *bandolero* within the entry *bando*, defined as "the proclamation ordering a criminal who has dropped out of sight to appear before the authorities." From this derives the use of the names *bandidos* and *bandoleros* (*el pregón que se da, llamando a algún delincuente que se ha ausentado, y de aquí se dijeron "bandidos" y "bandoleros"*) (Covarrubias Orozco 1611, 162).

The proclamation or bulletin (*bando*) was not initially intended to be read to the bandit, who would have been busy running away from the looming gallows. It was meant for those who were not bandits, for those who did not (openly) support them, and for those who obtained a collective identity vis-à-vis that Other who was just (symbolically) "thrown out." ("Cast aside," "thrown down," or "thrown out" are some of the etymological meanings of "abject," past participle of the Latin word *abicere*.) Therefore, the bandit was the occasion for a state-lettered performance of exclusion (the reading of the proclamation or bulletin). This performance creates a public sphere. The axes of this public sphere are the letter (the written document that enforces the law) and the state (the public official who reads the proclamation). Its exterior limit is precisely the bandit, lurking frightened or defiant in the neighboring countryside.

However, this image is an oversimplification since the bandit is never a simple criminal. Popular appropriations of the bandit appear in ballads, yarns, and oral traditions (e.g., *corridos, folletines*, and *cordel* literature in Mexico, Argentina, and Brazil, respectively). These appropriations transformed the outlaw into a hero for communities that resisted the advance of capitalism as well as the diverse forms of coercion and disruption that it implied. In these cases, bandit narratives are a form of negative reciprocity (as defined by James Scott) that allows a given community to voice a desire or a challenge without risking a reprisal. These popular appropriations of the bandit figure belong to an intermediate zone between public transcript and the hidden transcript (see Scott 1990).[11] Bandit narratives are thus public performances that are admitted only with suspicion and apprehension by elites. An excellent example of this in-between, dangerous condition is the cultural war that erupted in turn-of-the-century Argentina around bandit narratives known as *folletines criollistas* (see Prieto 1988) or the recent widespread debate on the banning of *narcocorridos* in Mexico (Wald 2001), both of which are forms of popular expression considered out-and-out incitements to crime.

Although the cases presented above may give the impression of a false ideological purity, elite-concocted tropes or popular appropriated tropes are rarely mutually exclusive options, since the bandit lives and preys on his victims at a crossroads. Often, the brigand figure stands for changing military, political, or cultural alliances between popular sectors and the elite, examples being the gaucho genre in Argentina or the regionalist and social novel in Brazil (e.g., the works of Jorge Amado). In other cases, bandit narratives may represent what Raymond Williams in 1991 termed the "selective appropriation" of traditions of rural insurgency (e.g., the novel *Astucia* by Luis Inclán on tobacco smugglers in Mexico known as the "Brothers of the Leaf").

A remarkable illustration of this complex dynamic is the figure of Jesús Malverde, the "angel of the poor." Jesús Malverde's existence is still debated, but tradition has it that he was a peasant bandit from the Mexican state of Sinaloa. He met the fate of most peasant bandits: capture and summary execution. Also, like many peasant bandits, he posthumously became an object of popular devotion. He is now the patron saint of drug dealers (*el narcosantón*), and the Culiacán chapel dedicated to him is cluttered with votive offerings (*exvotos*), some bearing surnames that appear in the police chronicle: Quintero, Gallardo, Félix, Carrillo. According to legend, the initials "R.C.Q." on one of the engravings bear witness to a donation by none other than Rafael Caro Quintero, a Mexican drug lord (Wald 2001, 616–24). Malverde thus connects multiple cultural lines. On the one hand he connects the traditions of insurgency deeply embedded in local culture, such as the stories on Heraclio Bernal, a.k.a. "El Rayo de Sinaloa" (who is remembered, as is Malverde, in corridos, legends, and old wives' tales across Mexico), with the new Mexican American culture.[12] (Malverde is well known—just like the narcotics that are cultivated in or transported through Sinaloa

—in Los Angeles or Chicago as well as in Culiacán.) In addition, Malverde connects popular traditional Catholicism with modern icons of consumption and mass culture. Furthermore, he ties the old rural *corrido de bandidos* or *corrido de valientes* to the postmodern urban-rural *narcocorridos* hip among Mexican and Mexican American youth affiliated with the culture of violence. Finally, the example of Malverde shows the "deep Mexico," with its intact myth-producing capacity, juxtaposed against the postmodern, "for-export" image of Mexico.

Another outstanding example of the bandit figure playing on both sides of the divide is the cultural history of Joaquín Murieta, described by Ireneo Paz, one of his early biographers, as "the most celebrated California bandit," a phrase that became the subtitle of the first novel about Murieta. The story of Murieta is paradigmatic in its incidents, since it pertains to a particularly relevant contact zone (Pratt 1992) and since it came to represent the conflict-ridden frontier between the United States and Mexico in the immediate aftermath of the U.S.-Mexican War in 1846–1848. As such it was mobilized by Anglo Americans, Mexican Americans, Europeans, and Latin Americans alike. Murieta also offers a rare case study of the Latin American bandit whose cultural career spans from the 1850s to the present. There are countless variations of Murieta's biography, but most agree on some basic facts. Murieta was a hard-working, American-friendly Mexican miner and rancher in California shortly after its conquest by the United States. In spite of his intentions to advance in the newly formed Californian society, he falls prey to endless abuse by Anglo Americans. He is forcibly displaced from his claim; his brother is lynched after a false accusation of horse stealing; his sweetheart is gang-raped. Murieta is driven to a point at which he vows revenge against all Americans, and, in classic social bandit fashion, he becomes an avenger set out to right wrongs. However, he wants to right not only the wrong done unto him but also the injustices committed against his "kind": the Californios and Mexicans under American rule. In some versions of the story (see Paz 1904), Murieta is even portrayed as a leader with the long-term goal of leading a general uprising of Mexicans and Californios so as to return California to Mexico.

Murieta was the first and most prominent in a series of Mexican American outlaws that includes Tiburcio Vázquez, Gregorio Cortéz, Juan N. Cortina, and Eligio Baca and whose last individuation in this series is the legion of drug dealers, both big and small, of the Mexico-U.S. border who have become heroes in the epic of the *narcocorridos*. Murieta's head—decapitated, displayed in freak shows, later lost in some bizarre turn of history—is a macabre metaphor that for Richard Rodriguez represents Hispanic California's violent and suffering past (Rodriguez 1992).

In spite of this lurid story, scholars now agree that Murieta never existed (Leal 1999; Thornton 2003). He was born of both fear and greed: the Anglos' fear as they faced the violence of Mexican rebels and outlaws and the greed of the California Ranger Harry Love and his men. The rangers invented Murieta to justify the killing of a Mexican whose name will be forever a mystery and to claim the reward money offered by the state of California for the capture of the bandit(s) that roamed Calaveras County (Leal 1999, 14). Maybe there were several men who could have been Joaquín Murieta; maybe there was no such person at all. For some, Murieta is a fiction written into history by the state of California and the Anglo American press in order to label as criminal the threat (more or less imagined) of an interclass alliance between Mexicans and Californios struggling for land, cattle, and mining rights in Southern California (Leal 1999, 2; Jackson 1955, xxiv). The first example of the unruly Mexican bandit (later termed "greaser"), Murieta was a tool in a campaign of counterinsurgency, land occupation, and cultural discrimination that encompassed the whole Southwest, as evidenced in the sad history of the Texas Rangers (the infamous *rinches*) and the cinematographic stereotype of the greaser (Woll 1987).

Murieta was far more than a badge of infamy upon Hispanics in the United States, however. He was "stolen" by Hispanics from the Anglos as bounty in a cultural war that is still raging. After the popularization of his figure by Cherokee American writer John Rollin Ridge (a.k.a. Yellow Bird) in the novel *The Life and Adventures of Joaquín Murieta, the Celebrated California Bandit* (1854), Murieta embodied several types of heroes: a popular hero in the corrido tradition ("El corrido de Joaquín Murieta"); a cultural hero of Hispanidad versus Anglo culture in Ireneo Paz's *Vida y aventuras del más célebre bandido sonorense Joaquín Murieta* (1904); a class hero in Pablo Neruda's *Fulgor y muerte de Joaquín Murieta, bandido chileno injusticiado en California el 23 de julio de 1853* (1966); an anti-imperialist hero in Antonio Acevedo Hernández's play *Joaquín Murieta* (1938); a totalizing icon of the "Chicano nation" in Rodolpho "Corky" Gonzales's epic poem *I Am Joaquín* (1967); and finally a model for Chicano resistance in Oscar "Zeta" Acosta's *The Revolt of the Cockroach People* (1973).

On the opposite side of this cultural war is Bruce Thornton's excellent book *Searching for Joaquín* (2003). Thornton argues that the mobilization of the image of Murieta by Chicano militants and intellectuals implies a fundamental fallacy: their denial of the fact that the Murieta myth was avidly consumed by Anglos and people of many different ethnicities alike (a statement that he backs up with an impressive amount of scholarship). For Thornton, Murieta embodied the nostalgia for a simpler, more bucolic California in the face of accelerated transformation and social tensions and not the battle cry of a humiliated Hispanic California.

This enumeration, lengthy as it is, does not take into account the countless repetitions, perversions (e.g., Zorro) and plagiarisms of Murieta's history in the novel, drama, and cinema of both the Americas and Europe, in Spanish, English, and French.[13] Like Martín Fierro, the *desperado* contemporary of Murieta at the other end of the continent, Murieta "can be everything for everybody, because he is capable of almost endless repetitions, versions, perversions" (Borges and Guerrero 1954, 537). Thus, on one side or the other of the social divide—from *El periquillo sarniento* (1816) by José Joaquín Fernández de Lizardi to Mexican hip-hop—narratives on banditry serve to map essential segments of the heterogeneous discursive and geopolitical space that we call Latin America.[14]

The Bandit Debate

The classic definition of banditry was coined by Eric Hobsbawm in 1969 in the first edition of his book *Bandits*.[15] Bandits "are peasant outlaws whom the lord and state regard as criminals, but who remain within peasant society, and are considered by their people as heroes, champions, *avengers*, fighters for justice, perhaps even leaders for liberation, and in any case men to be admired, helped and supported. This relation between the ordinary peasant and the rebel, outlaw and robber is what makes social banditry interesting and significant. It also distinguishes it from other kinds of rural crime" ([1969] 1981, 17). Bandits are subjects of rural violence that are perceived as a threat to the state's monopoly of legitimate violence because they either enjoy (or are perceived to enjoy) more or less voluntary support from a group beyond the gang itself or they share (or are perceived to share) certain values with a larger community. Because of this support, they go beyond mere criminality.[16] Although obtaining a "booty" is always a paramount goal, it is not the only one. It is essential that the bandit be recognized by the rural community, by the state, or by a sector of the state as a bearer of violence (or what the state considers to be violence).

Unlike the social bandit, the criminal does not know any affiliation beyond his gang. The criminal may be employed by someone, but this relationship belongs to the market of violence—and it implies violence as a commodity—and therefore cannot be properly termed an "affiliation." The bandit's group of affiliation can be extremely diverse: peasantry, small to large landowners, family or patronage networks, ethnic groups, alliances across class and/or regions, or combinations of all of the above. These alliances are never, at least from a Hobsbawmiam point of view, "subcultures," but rather they are part of a fully developed rural culture. They vary greatly in their solidity and capacity to withstand time and challenges and stand more or less successfully against and beyond the state definition of politics, since they do not have state takeover as their main goal, unlike other forms of peasant insurgency, such as the Marxist-inspired guerrilla of the twentieth century.

This relationship between bandit and group of affiliation opposes state law and may be a principle of legitimacy for the use of violence based upon nondominant codes (oral or traditional: family ties, patronage, neighborhood ties, etc.) or in heterodox appropriations of dominant codes (property or conceptions of authority belonging to political systems already extinct, religious syncretism, etc.). Therefore, the bandit's capacity to claim a particular kind of sovereignty and/or extract resources from civil society on a more or less regular basis (sometimes in collusion with, sometimes in opposition to analogous efforts by the state) is just as important—if not more important—than the existence of desired valuables. In the ideal model of social banditry, the material or cultural solidarity between bandit and community of affiliation is the feature that separates the bandit's actions from mere criminality. However, Alan Knight, one of the most prestigious supporters of the social banditry model in the Latin American case, points out that the distinction between bandits and criminals, although analytically relevant, is extremely problematic when confronted with historical facts and specific cases, because it is highly relative in time and space. Latin American bandits inhabited fluid and changing situations, unlike, for example, the Irish rapparees of the seventeenth century, who practiced robbery following pre-existent and well-defined distinctions between friend and foe (Catholic Irish/Protestant English). In Latin America, the social bandit of one region is the criminal of another. The social bandit of today, enjoying widespread peasant support, is the criminal of tomorrow, opposed by the same peasants who once may have supported him (Knight 1986, 2:354–55). This fluctuation returns us to our initial assertion of the impossibility (and the ultimate inappropriateness) of providing a positive, essentialist definition of banditry, or of deciding, once and for all, if a certain peasant rebel is a criminal or a social bandit. It is only possible to analyze bandit narratives as ephemeral, conflict-embedded effects of difference.

In Hobsbawm's initial formulation, epidemic social banditry is opposed to endemic banditry, permanent in all rural societies to the point of becoming a sort of natural fact of life. As an example of endemic banditry, in Akira Kurosawa's film *Seven Samurai* (1954), a wailing female peasant enumerates the evils that plague peasant existence. In no particular order, she mentions taxes, draft, war, drought, famine, and bandits (the last being the theme of the movie). Epidemic banditry, on the other hand, occurs in contexts of accelerated social transformations, such as the one occurring in Mexico toward the end the colonial period, with its collateral effects on population growth, land scarcity, inflation, and increased trade and opportunities for robbery (Taylor 1982, 56). In this case, it is a form of both resistance and adaptation to the advances of commercial agriculture and the modern state. It could also be a symptom or product of a generalized crisis (e.g., revolution, war, or dynasty change) in the legitimacy of an established order. Relevant historical examples include banditry during the French Revolution (see Andress 2000), during the European Thirty Years' War (see Danker 1988), during the Mexican Revolution (see works by Knight as well as Frazer 1997), during the war for Cuban independence (see Perez 1989), or in Republican China (see Billingsley 1988). Epidemic banditry could also respond to ecological changes such as droughts or to crop failures (see Archer 1982, 68).

Hobsbawm took up the notion put forward by Friedrich Engels, who regarded criminality as a form of "primitive protest" (1845, 149, 242–43, 309), and adopted Fernand Braudel's idea that banditry was an "incomplete revolution," that is, a revolution carried out by a group lacking class consciousness in a landscape of widespread peasant rebellions in the Mediterranean Basin (1949, 738–39). According to Hobsbawm, banditry, mafia, millenarianism, and labor sects are all forms of "primitive rebellion." He includes in the spectrum of "primitive rebellion" all archaic or pre-political peasant movements that depend upon the material and cultural resources of the peasant communities whose universe they express or defend (hence the social character) but that are doomed to extinction with the advent of modernity (Hobsbawm [1969] 1981, 10; 1973, 20).

Hobsbawm identified four varieties of social bandit: the noble robber (e.g., Robin Hood), the avenger, the haiduk (or what Christon Archer aptly called "guerrilla bandit"), and the expropriator.[17] In Latin America, the "guerrilla bandit" (Pancho Villa, Manuel Lozada) and the avenger (Lampião, Juan Moreira) were the most prominent examples of the social bandit. However, Latin American literature is also well populated by noble robbers, even if they are not the most prominent figures in national imaginaries. Among the better known bandits are Fiero Vásquez, champion of the indigenous community of Rumi in *El mundo es ancho y ajeno* (1941) by Ciro Alegría; Lucas Arvoredo in *Seara vermelha* (1946); and Lampião in *Capitães da areia* (1937) by Jorge Amado; "Ñato Eloy," Chilean brigand and popular poet killed by police in 1941 (and hero of the 1960 novel *Eloy* by Carlos Droguett); Heraclio Bernal from Sinaloa and Chucho el Roto, heroes of corridos and countless novels and movies; the Argentines Mate Cosido and the Velázquez brothers (from El Chaco province); and Vairoletto (from the dry pampas [*pampa seca*]) and the bandits who lead the Andean *comuneros* in their struggle against the abuses of the Cerro de Pasco Corporation in Manuel Scorza's *Redoble por Rancas* (1970). To my mind, however, the most clear-cut example of the noble robber is the commendable Tuerto Ventura in *Los días terrenales* (1949) by José Revueltas (1914–1976). Ventura, a cattle rustler and indigenous community leader, represents the dreams for justice of "Acamapichtli or Maxtla, of Morelos or Juárez" because of his face, scarred by violence. The charismatic leadership of this bandit had no limits since "everybody loved him, and everybody was ready to plunge with him from a cliff" (1949, 14).

Some scholars, without flatly denying the relevance of the "social bandit" model, understand particular occurrences of epidemic banditry as struggles that revolve around different lines of conflict. For Pat O'Malley (who researched the case of the Australian bushranger Ned Kelly) banditry is a form of class struggle between the rural proletariat and rural bourgeoisie. Even though such struggle happens outside the channels of institutional politics, it still happens in a fully formed class society and not, as Hobsbawm proposes, in a context of transition toward capitalism (O'Malley 1979, 494–

99). Other scholars, such as Ralph Austen (for the African case) or Alberto Flores Galindo (for the Andean case) consider banditry a form of racial struggle whereby banditry is part of a larger dispute over economic resources or political predominance, where class is not necessarily the most relevant category of analysis (Austen 1986; Flores Galindo 1990). Fernando Ortiz, for his part, considers banditry in Cuba a byproduct of runaway slavery (*cimarronaje*). Therefore, he does not deem it a phenomenon related to the displacement of "traditional peasants" by sugar plantations (since "traditional peasantry" was nonexistent in Cuba). Rather, he regards it as a phenomenon of resistance with its origin in the plantation system itself, which is to say he understands banditry not as a phenomenon triggered by the transition toward capitalism but as a byproduct of rural capitalism (Ortiz 1995, 190).

In the latest edition of his book *Bandits* (2000), Hobsbawm acknowledges the existence of social banditry in history before the rise of capitalism, as in the case of rural societies that resisted the advances of other rural societies (e.g., sedentary peasants raided by nomadic shepherds or rural communities resisting the advances of rural empires). He also points out that banditry can thrive in late capitalism, such as the contemporary banditry associated with the demise of nation-states, Afghanistan, countries that comprised the former Yugoslavia, and Chechnya all being examples (Hobsbawm [1969] 2000, 9).

Postnational, globalized banditry is also analyzed by Steven Sampson (2003) vis-à-vis the contemporary process of reformulating the nation-state. In Sampson's account, this new form of banditry articulates the conflicts in a globalized arena, whereby banditry interacts and competes for sovereignty not (or not only) with traditional nation-states but also with nongovernmental organizations (NGOs), international peacekeeping forces, mercenary private security outfits, and so forth. He mentions "northern Albania, eastern Bosnia, sections of Kosovo, the northern Caucasus [including Chechnya], [and] large portions of Africa" as places where the fragmentation of traditional political units (e.g., communist states) are "hot spots" for this new form of insurgency (2003, 314).

In some cases, banditry is not really a symptom of a crisis (a meaning embedded in the term "primitive rebellion"). Rather, it may be part of a process of negotiation either among segments of the elite or between rural elites and sectors of the rural poor. For Hobsbawm, Ethiopian banditry offers a case in point: it did not emerge as a sign of crisis; rather it was an accepted venue of political competition for positions within the political order and was therefore integrated into the social fabric. Ottoman banditry, as superbly analyzed by Karen Barkey (1994), represents a rather different case. In the seventeenth-century Ottoman Empire, bandits entered into complex arrangements with Ottoman rulers. Under this arrangement, bandits did not challenge the centralizing efforts of rulers; rather they became timely allies in these efforts. In this way, bandits were able to mollify threats of peasant unrest, which in the Ottoman Empire were kept to a minimum when compared to similar situations in other regions of the Mediterranean Basin. As a final example, in northeastern Brazil the *cangaceiros* functioned as retainers for landowners (*coronéis*) or as the fighting force in decades-long family feuds, and they were an accepted and appreciated way of conducting politics in the absence of a strong state presence.

Hobsbawm's model continues to inform many recent and current approaches to the problem. Examples include Gonzalo Sánchez and Donny Meertens's *Bandoleros, gamonales y campesinos: el caso de la violencia en Colombia* (1983), Knight's *The Mexican Revolution* (1986), Ana María Contador's *Los Pincheira: un caso de bandidaje social: Chile, 1817–1832* (1998), and Hugo Chumbita's *Jinetes Rebeldes: historia del bandolerismo social en Argentina* (2000). However, in the Latin American context, critiques of Hobsbawm's model are abundant. The so-called revisionist school flatly denies any social character to banditry (the main thrust of Hobsbawm's model). This line of thought is brought forth by the remarkable volume *Bandidos,* edited by Richard W. Slatta (1987), which was intent upon discussing (and debunking) Hobsbawm's thesis as applied to the Latin American case. Revisionism objects to the very existence or at least relevance of the bandit-peasant link, which is essential in the "social" character of banditry. In earlier editions of *Bandits* (1969, 1972, 1981), Hobsbawm tended to emphasize this horizontal link, based on material and cultural commonality and solidarity, either real or symbolic (vis-à-vis the landowning classes or state officials). It is in this way that banditry may become a forerunner of full-fledged class struggle (hence the "primitive" in "primitive rebellion"). Revisionists such as Paul Vanderwood, for Mexico, or Linda Lewin, for Brazil, deny this link and emphasize the vertical alliances that bandits forged and preferred. These vertical alliances could cross class lines (as in the case of patronage networks), or they could link bandits and landlords or local politicians, thus denying the "social" content to banditry and making it synonymous with out-and-out criminality or even with one of the means of landowners' social control. For Vanderwood, banditry is a means of upward social mobility or an alternative to accepted means of profit, as he defines bandits as "mainly (but not only) self interested individuals and their followers who found themselves excluded from the possibilities and opportunities, not to mention the benefits, of society at large, and who promoted disorder as a lever to enter a system reserved for a few" (1992, xv). Literary examples of these vertical alliances between bandits and landlords, designed to keep subalterns in check, are present in two of the most important novels of twentieth-century Latin America: Juan Rulfo's *Pedro Páramo* (1955) and Jorge Amado's *Terras do sem fim* (1943). In the first case, the local landlord (Pedro Páramo) recruits (literally buys) a band of insurgents who had come with the original intent of plundering his hacienda. Instead, he puts the group under the command of his own retainer, the trusted Damasio, a.k.a. *El Tilcuate*. While officially revolutionaries, these guerrilla-bandits have the unofficial task of protecting Páramo from any possible advances by the real revolutionaries. In Amado's case, the bandits (*jagunços*) are the essential manpower that allows the landowners to maintain and increase their holdings, either by violently dispossessing (and sometimes assassinating) peasants and smaller landowners or by fighting against other large landowners. In both cases, banditry is a means of social mobility. *El Tilcuate* is given a ranch and cattle as a payment for his loyal services, the jagunços earn many times the pay of regular rural workers, and they are entitled to certain deferences both by their masters and their subordinates.

A number of critiques of Hobsbawm's model focus on the paramount place that he assigned to oral testimonies or literary reconstructions of past bandits as he put together his model. This debate relates to another one involving the remarkable uniformity of banditry as it appears in songs, tales, and written testimonies. This uniformity is an essential element in Hobsbawm's model. An important question in this debate then becomes, Should this uniformity be considered a trait of banditry per se, as emanating from peasant culture, or should it be considered *a posteriori* reconstruction by intellectuals? Revisionists deflate the value of Hobsbawm's oral and literary sources, and they stress the importance of police and court records, which they regard as more reliable.

This critical current of historical thought, sometimes a little too intent upon refuting Hobsbawm's model, has indeed produced some of the most important case studies in the field.[18] Revisionism considers banditry as just another form of criminality. (Paul Vanderwood even coined an expression counter to "social bandit": the Mexican "profiteering bandit.") Its social effects, if any, are not (as the legend goes) emancipatory; quite to the contrary, banditry favors the status quo since it may become an alternative way of climbing the social ladder and an informal instrument of elite control of the peasantry. For revisionists, banditry is, in the final analysis, compatible with the interests of the elite.

Rosalie Schwartz makes another good point against the "social bandit" model in her analysis of Cuban banditry. She opposes Louis Perez's take on Cuban banditry, which closely follows the "social bandit" model. Schwartz, investigating class origins and regional patterns of nineteenth-century Cuban banditry, shows that banditry was more intense in the most developed regions of Cuba and that the bandits were far from being destitute peasants; rather they were sons of somewhat well-to-do ranchers and small landowners. Thus, as Schwartz explains, banditry in the Cuban case lacked any true "social" (in the Hobsbawmian sense) thrust and much more closely resembled the profiteering banditry mentioned by Vanderwood (Schwartz 1982, 1989).

The distillation of this critical current can be summarized in the deliberately terse definition provided by Slatta: "Banditry is the taking of property by force or by the threat of force" (1994, 76). It should be noted that this definition limits banditry to robbery, as conceived, for example, during the seventeenth century in *The Third Part of the Institutes of the Laws of England* (1634): "'*Robbery* is a felony by the Common law, committed by a violent assault, upon the person of another, by putting him in fear, and taking from his person his money or other goods of any value whatsoever'" (Coke quoted in Spraggs 2001, 1). The attack on property, as mentioned before, is a key element in the definition of banditry, but a definition limited to that aspect leaves unexplored several factors crucial to the understanding of banditry.

The first factor is that, until the twentieth century, "property," in the Latin American context, was not an obvious and unequivocal concept. Indeed, the concept was undergoing profound transformations. The bloody struggles between liberals and conservatives in core zones of the region were an expression of this phenomenon, because the ancestral corporative rights of the peasant communities and of the Church were being challenged by the new liberal concept of individual property. Even less clear was the concept of property in frontier zones such as both banks of the Río de la Plata or the Venezuelan llanos. In these regions the claim to property was not established before the struggle. To impose a certain notion of property rights was the ultimate goal of the struggle, since cattle (*cimarrones* or *orejanos*) often did not have a clear proprietor (Storni 1997). Therefore, "crime against property" was not a crime that was easily defined.

Secondly, as Centeno summarizes the situation, Latin America, with the exception of the income related to foreign commerce, did not have a fully functioning central tax system for most of its postcolonial history (2002, 6). This lack of a revenue base made state support for armies and police forces practically impossible. Due to this fact, "the taking of property by force or by the threat of force" was one of the main activities of all armies and state armed forces well into the twentieth century. The only differences between banditry and army expropriations were the scale of plundering as well as the inherently dubious state sanction of the army's actions. Therefore, unless we agree upon the fact that Slatta's definition applies to most armed forces throughout the "long nineteenth century" (something that would not be completely far-fetched, as the Mexican Revolution shows), one cannot accept Slatta's definition unequivocally.

In 1968 Roberto Carri analyzed the case of the Argentine bandit Isidro Velázquez (who thrived in El Chaco province in the 1960s), and he offers the opposite critique of Hobsbawm. (He does, however, recognize the fundamental soundness of Hobsbawm's model.) Carri acknowledges the "social" character of banditry but resists its definition as "pre-political." For Carri, the term has an unavoidable Eurocentric connotation because pre-political means diverging from what qualifies as politics (e.g., party politics, unions, NGOs, etc.) in a European (or Europeanized) perspective. Instead, he prefers the term "pre-revolutionary," which endows the bandit with a fully political character or at least gives a political aspect to the community's perception of the bandit's actions. In Carri's model, the bandit is not considered primitive, although his actions are not yet fully articulated as a revolutionary awareness. Thus, Carri's position was an early expression of the third position in the banditry debate. This position was adopted by historians specializing in Latin America who incorporated the contributions of Ranajit Guha (1983) and James Scott (1985). Gilbert Joseph, Daniel Nugent, Florencia Mallon, and Rosalie Schwartz, among others, do not examine banditry as mere criminality or as a rudimentary form of peasant resistance but as a form of peasant politics fully articulated into a peasant consciousness. In their approach, banditry belongs to a continuum of resistance that runs from gossip to open rebellion.[19] The Venezuelan historian Lisando Alvarado also provided an early formulation of this position when he proclaimed that the brigands of the Federal War "were not the predecessors of the February Revolution, but the revolution itself" (quoted in Matthews 1977, 168).

Furthermore, these scholars focus their epistemological and ethical concerns on the impossibility of translating peasant conceptions of politics into a nationalist-statist notion of politics. Both can negotiate and even collude, but they remain essentially heterogeneous. A revealing literary illustration of this distance between forms of lettered national politics and peasant politics is the despair of the pro-Indian engineer Fernando Ulloa, the main character in *Oficio de tinieblas* (1962), a novel by the Mexican writer Rosario Castellanos (1925–1974). Ulloa does not understand why the Chamula Indians, whom he helped to rebel, now wander aimlessly in the mountains pillaging haciendas instead of attacking the cities, hunting down landowners, and organically promoting an agrarian agenda. This situation highlights the fact that the political struggle is also (and in some cases mainly) a struggle to define the dominant conception of what will be understood as "politics" (Lechner 1995). Banditry has not only an economic meaning but also a cultural, identity making meaning for peasants and for those implicated as bandits.[20] This affirmation of identity is a key component of all popular bandit narratives and has found expression in literature as well. *Gringo viejo* (1985), by the Mexican writer Carlos Fuentes, offers a good example. In this novel, the revolutionary gang of Tomás Arroyo plunders and meticulously destroys a hacienda. Only one room of the hacienda escapes their fury: the hall of mirrors. For these guerrilla-bandits, the mirrors of this Chihuahuan Versailles allow them their first opportunity to see the image of their entire bodies. Arroyo confesses,

> Not my men. They had never seen their bodies in full before. I had to give them that great gift, that feast: now, look at yourselves, move about, lift your arm, you, dance a polka, get even for all the dark years in which you lived blind toward your own bodies, groping in the dark in order to find a body—your own body—so alien and silent and distant as all the other bodies that you were not allowed to touch, or that were not allowed to touch you. They moved in front of their own reflection in the mirror and the spell was broken, gringuita. (Fuentes 1985, 119)

A no less dramatic example can be found at the other end of Latin America. The *sapukay* is the distinctive yell uttered as a sign of joy or defiance, and it is characteristic of the rural populations of the Argentine northeast (Corrientes and Chaco provinces). In 1967, the region's state police attempted to ambush Isidro Velázquez, the famous bandit of the region. When he was about to escape from his pursuers, he could not help but utter his cry of defiance and contempt: "the last sapukay." This act of pride made him a target and ultimately led to his demise. Had he not cried out, he might have slipped away. This act of rebellion and affirmation of his identity vis-à-vis state violence is celebrated in Argentina to this day in the very famous *chamamé* (a genre of popular music) entitled "El último sapukay," by Oscar Valles.[21]

Thomas Gallant has proposed a new notion of banditry with a twofold goal: to mediate between those who, like Hobsbawm, link epidemic banditry with the transition to capitalism and those, like O'Malley, who emphasize the presence of epidemic banditry in fully developed agrarian capitalist economies (e.g., nineteenth-century Australia and the post–Civil War American Midwest); and secondly, to mediate between those who see in banditry a clear political thrust and those who see in it an exclusively economic motivation (Gallant 1999).

In order to accomplish the first goal, Gallant turns to Emmanuel Wallerstein's model in *The Modern World-System* (1974), arguing that it is fruitless to limit critical research to the development of a single, all-encompassing model of banditry. Instead, Gallant proposes that several models must be devised according to the different societies in which they emerge: core societies (such as England), semiperipheral (such as O'Malley's Australia), and peripheral societies (such as Ethiopia, the nineteenth-century Balkans, or northeastern Brazil, Hobsbawm's favorite cases). In order to accomplish the second goal, Gallant coins the apt expression "military entrepreneur" (following Anton Blok's Sicilian "violent entrepreneurs" and Volkov's "violent entrepreneurship" in Russia), thus capturing the ambiguous relationship between banditry and the law (sometimes enforcing the law, sometimes breaking it), and banditry and economic profit. He explains that "by 'military entrepreneur' I refer to a category of men who take up arms and who wield violence or the threat of violence as their stock in trade. I use 'military' here not in its contemporary common connotation of a national army, but in an older, more ambiguous form referring only to the use of arms and weapons. They are entrepreneurs in the sense that they are purveyors of a commodity—violence. They may act in the employ of others or as agents in their own right" (Gallant 1999, 26). The notion of violence as a commodity has the particular advantage of helping us to avoid a common intellectual mistake: that of speaking about violence as if it were a purely negative notion. This mindset was the target of Hobsbawm's critique of the liberal notion of violence in his essay "The Rules of Violence" (1973).

My position is less about the history of banditry per se. I am concerned more with the history of its representation within selected national cultures. This depiction is always a site of conflict and contested meanings where the state struggles with urban and rural sectors of civil society to impose particular agendas through the "invention" of banditry. From this point of view, and without giving in uncritically to the much-reviled (and often misunderstood) postmodern "textualism," I maintain that the representation of banditry is as important as banditry itself. Furthermore, the distinction between these two elements is frequently difficult to perceive. The dispute on meaning as being central to the definition of banditry appears even in Hobsbawm's classic definition, in which the double perspective (the state's view versus that of the peasantry) is what makes banditry relevant for social history.

We know that the lexical meaning of *bandido* implies a state performance: the calling by proclamation or edict. The dramatic (semiotic) element is not accidental, and, as Foucault (1975) illustrates, it is one trait that existed well before the penal reforms of the eighteenth and nineteenth centuries, and it lasted long afterward. Imperial Rome offers an interesting example. One of the punishments reserved for bandits was to force them to take part in theatrical representations of a historic or mythological nature. The character played by the convicted bandit died at the end of the play. The twist in this case was that the death was not a special effect or a dramatization: the actor-executioner really executed the bandit on stage (by crucifixion or exposure to bears) when the plot so indicated (Harries 1999, 151). Today, the punishment of criminals is something shrouded in secrecy, at least in Western culture. Cheering, awe-stricken crowds no longer gather to witness executions. However, what if not theaters of law are the many *Cops*-like reality shows (including its Mexican counterpart, *Policías*) in which the drama of crime and punishment is reenacted time and again, for the thrill and education of an eager public?

Focusing on this dramatic metaphor is not arbitrary; it emphasizes the element of performance involved in any act of domination. Thus, by focusing on bandit narratives as performances of domination I connect this study with those on state formation, in which, as Philip Corrigan puts it, "Key questions then become not *who* rules but [also] *how* is rule accomplished. . . . No historical or contemporary form of ruling can be understood (1) as or in its own discursive regime or image repertoire terms; (2) without investigating the historical genealogy, archaeology, origination (and transmutation) of those terms as *forms*" (1994, xvii–xviii, emphasis in original).

This dramatic component was clearly present in Latin America. Although rarely reaching the extremes of punishments meted out in Spain, where bandits such as Jaime el Barbudo were quartered and fried, Latin American bandits were not simply executed: they were hanged from conspicuous trees, publicly shot, decapitated or quartered, exposed at crossroads, in markets, on pikes, on fences, in squares, and even photographed in order to obtain maximum publicity from the punishment. This very public form of execution can be called a "theater of law" (Blok 1998, following E. P. Thompson 1975, 105) through which dominant classes symbolically restore or confirm their dominance after it is called into question by the bandit. These dominant classes also establish a counterpoint between the body of the bandit and the body of the sovereign (under the species of his armed officials).[22] The theater of law is what Alfredo Ebelot called a "good end" when referring to the death of a bandit of northeastern Argentina, "understanding by this word an ending that satisfactorily conciliates our hunger for adventure with our instincts of security" (1889–1890, 105).

Without overextending the application that Blok gave to the notion, I maintain that the theater of law comprised a continuum of symbolic practices that encompassed both scaffold and poem and that was clearly intended as a "pedagogy of terror" (Salvatore 2001, 310). The collusion of the theater of law and banditry has given the West its most important symbol and story. I am referring to the Cross of the Passion that joins the highest order—God—and the most abject—the robbers (*latrones*) through the infamous punishment that Roman law reserved for the worst class of criminal that the *Digesto* defined. Robbers were condemned to death by exposure as part of the theatrical version of state-sponsored terrorism of which Rome was so fond (Shaw 1984). The second major trope of Christian morality, the martyr *ad maiorem gloria Dei,* originated in another of the punishments reserved for brigands: death in the circus arena, devoured by wild beasts.

Perico, the rogue protagonist of *El periquillo sarniento,* by José Joaquín Fernández de Lizardi (1816), understands the inner workings of the theater of law very well. Perico redeems himself of his many vices and crimes when at a crossroads (literal and metaphorical) he sees the rotten corpse of Januario, an old friend and accomplice. Januario was executed as a brigand chief. Perico understands that this meeting has not occurred by chance but is a "lesson" (416) that "Januario, although lifeless, loudly announces from that tree trunk" (417). Fittingly, Perico reacts by composing a sonnet (417), thus showing the live link between legislating (*legislar*) and reading (*leer*) (González Echevarría 1990). This relationship between letrados and bandidos took an even stranger turn (because of its extreme literality) in 1910, when the poet Salvador Díaz Mirón (1853–1928) was commissioned by Porfirio Díaz to direct the persecution of Santana Rodríguez Palafox, a.k.a. "Santanón," a bandit who roamed the sugar producing areas of Veracruz. *El imparcial,* the newspaper of porfirismo, instituted a column entitled "The Bard and the Bandit" (*El bardo y el bandolero*) devoted to these rocambolesque series of events, as part of the celebrations of the nation's centennial (Barrera Bassols 1987).

Banditry and the State

> A new ruler is always stern.
> Prometheus, referring to Zeus, *Prometheus in Chains*

Banditry and its relation to the state constitute a topic that goes to the core of Latin American identity since it has been argued repeatedly that the Spanish *conquistadores,* the founders of one of the most formidable and enduring empires the world has ever witnessed (and of the social formation now called Latin America), were little more than bandits (Hobsbawm 2000, 42). In fact, nineteenth- and twentieth-century literature and historiography, perhaps picking up on the Lascasian theme in which conquerors are persistently deemed cannibals and impious plunderers, abundantly express this motif: from Félix Varela's *Jicoténcal* (1826), the first Latin American historical novel, to romantic novels (Miguel Cané's *Esther,* from 1858) to positivistic criminology (Julio Guerrero's *La génesis del crimen en México,* from 1901) to modernist essays (Leopoldo Lugones's *El imperio Jesuítico,* from 1904), to indigenist novels (Mauricio Magdaleno's *El resplandor,* from 1937).

In any case, in nineteenth-century Latin America a central feature of the desire called modernity was the constitution of nation-states enjoying sovereignty and territoriality, instead of segmentarity (i.e., a low reach of the administrative political center, thus creating internal frontiers) and heteronomy (discontinuous control over the territory) (Giddens 1985, 16, 53, 65, 160). The successful constitution of the nation-state implied at least two conditions. In the first, there would exist a monopoly on both ownership and allocation of violence, resulting in control of populations and resources vis-à-vis multiple forms of private violence. The states that stemmed from the independence wars in Latin America did not meet this condition since they were, as Centeno puts it, "fragments of empire" and not unified states (2002, 25). This situation was not unique since traditional states—city-states, agrarian empires, feudal orders, absolutist states—or empires such as the Spanish empire did not have the capacity to hold a territorial monopoly over violence (Giddens 1985).[23] Perhaps most importantly, these political syntheses did not construe their relationship with violence in terms of a monopoly in a continuous and perfectly (or sufficiently) delimited territorial realm (Tilly 1975b, 27; Giddens 1985; Thomson 1994, 9). The elite intent on nation-state building, modernization, and social engineering agendas made monopoly of ownership and allocation of violence a priority against groups that either actively resisted that monopoly or that wanted to negotiate from a position of force. Thus, the expropriation of the means of coercion from individuals, groups, and organizations within the territory that the state claimed as its own was (and in some cases still is) a matter of contention.

The second implied condition consists of a social consensus on the legitimacy of the monopoly on ownership and allocation of violence. This consensus is reached through the imposition and validation of narratives that would make the expropriation of violence by the state "natural" and "necessary." Social narratives are crossed by hegemonic practices in which it is possible to find a disciplinary/pedagogical impulse (Leps 1992). It is in this sense, as Dennis K. Mumby points out, that these narratives are forms of social control and spaces from which an image of the social takes shape and naturalizes itself. In this book, naturalization follows Stuart Hall's definition: "a representational strategy designed to *fix* difference, and thus *secure it forever.* It is an attempt to halt the inevitable 'slide' of meaning and to secure discursive or ideological 'closure'" (1997, 245, emphasis in original).

Among these hegemonic practices, literature was one of the most important during the nineteenth century, at least from an axiological point of view. In general terms, this is the theoretical position from which I address literature: as a legitimating tool for the state monopoly of violence but, at the same time, as a place where inevitably the contradictions and impossibilities related to that monopoly surface now and again. (In this volume, "literature" is understood in the broad use of the term pertaining to the nineteenth century, which included criminological treatises, journalistic pieces, and doctrinaire essays as well as a novels, poetry, and drama.)

Throughout the long nineteenth century, bandits had a constantly changing role in the drama of the nation-states and the latter's struggle for the monopoly of violence. At times, bandits were able to place their significant means of violence at the disposal of the central government, as was the case of the Plateados of Salomé Plasencia, who sided and fought with the Liberal Party during the Mexican wars of reform. It was also the case of the bandits who became part of the rural police in porfirian Mexico and the core of the famous Rurales. This collusion prompted Vanderwood to coin the term *bandit-Rural* in his book *Disorder and Progress*. Conversely, bandits were a mighty force in containing efforts toward centralization. In some cases, banditry hindered and even prevented the functioning of state offices or the convening of legislative bodies (mid-nineteenth-century Mexico is the best example). It was in this role that bandits acquired their most popular image.

Under other circumstances, the bandit gang could itself become a state-like organization or influence the state in a very definite way and thus become a model of political organization for later generations. A paramount example of this situation is Pancho Villa's governorship of Chihuahua, which Alan Knight described as "institutionalized social banditry" in his classic work, *The Mexican Revolution.* Another case is the agrarian legislation devised by José Gervasio de Artigas, the founding father of Uruguay who began his career as an outlaw and cattle smuggler in the northern frontier of the Banda Oriental (present-day Uruguay). Yet another is the popular revolution of José Tomás Boves, a royalist *caudillo* of the Venezuelan plains who recovered the Capitanía General de Venezuela territory for Fernando VII of Spain in 1814. The less illustrious cases of the Plateados of Morelos, of

Manuel Lozada in Tepic, or of Inés Chávez García in the Bajío (all of these in Mexico) could also be mentioned. Perhaps even more illustrative than these examples is that of Antônio Conselheiro and his jagunços. Conselheiro established a fully functioning, autonomous, and prosperous community (by northeastern Brazilian standards) in the remote Bahian *sertão*. The authorities of the fledgling Brazilian republic clearly understood the implications of the success of this "opting out," and the consequence was a massacre that still haunts the Brazilian national imagination.

A brief discussion of the Argentine *gauchos* will give us a clear idea of how this "naturalization" of state violence functions. In narrative, essay, and journalistic works (mainly *La guerra gaucha* [1905] and *El payador* [1916]) Leopoldo Lugones (1874–1938), an organic intellectual of the Argentine oligarchy at the peak of its power, turned the gaucho, or vagrant Argentine outlaw, into "the prototype for the modern-day Argentine" (1916, 66), the only Argentine epic hero (1916, 170). Lugones regarded *El gaucho Martín Fierro* (1872) and *La vuelta de Martín Fierro* by José Hernández (1879)—the two-part poem that best told of the misfortunes of the gauchos at the hands of state (in)justice—as the Argentine equivalent of Homer's *Iliad* in its role of expression and promotion of nationhood (Lugones 1916, 163–88). However, the epic interpretation of this bandit narrative is based upon two types of forgetting. First, the gauchos did not have a clear notion of nationhood in the modern (i.e., Lugonian) sense of the word that equated nation with nation-state. The fatherland (*patria*) was most commonly the *pago*, that is, the county, or the province at best, as many of these narratives show (Guerra 2003, 32; Salvatore 2003, 128; de la Fuente 2000), or it intersected with partisan identities in such a way as to make partisan affiliation more important than nationality (Halperín Donghi 2003; de la Fuente 2000). Also, the modes of political affiliation corresponded more closely (although not completely) with the patron-client model than with the republican model of the citizen in arms. In the second forgetting, the gaucho, as a challenge to the state's monopoly of violence, was outlawed, dispossessed, jailed, used as cannon fodder, and forced into labor by the same landowning and commercial elite that would later elevate him to an heroic status. To place the *gaucho malo* as a prominent figure in the state pantheon is to build it upon paradoxical foundations: the state is paying eternal homage to those whom it purposefully eliminated in order to achieve its monopoly of violence, "founding the nationality with their blood" (Lugones 1916, 81) and then expropriating the voices of these victims in order to sing the patriotic songs of the centennial of the May Revolution (the main thrust of *La guerra gaucha*). This forgetting, as Benedict Anderson points out (1983, 1992), is represented as a "reassuring fratricide," crucial in the construction of the nation as imagined community. In Lugones's case, then, the bandit was utilized as a *dramatis persona* in letrado fables of self-legitimation and the legitimation of his class against the "zoological tidal wave" (*aluvión zoológico*) of immigrants from Central Europe and the Mediterranean Basin, which had begun to threaten the hegemony of the landowning oligarchy. To oppose this new enemy, Lugones did not hesitate in calling to duty the old enemies who were now newly discovered brothers. He did this by inventing a selective tradition that allied the current masters and old subalterns (gauchos) against the new subalterns (the European immigrants).

Banditry developed another relationship to state-making when the threat of banditry was used as an excuse to increase state centralization (or to stage a coup within internecine elite struggles). The repression of banditry was used as an instrument of legitimation for the establishment of forces of direct control over regions and individuals. Several historical examples spring to mind: the "Santa Hermandad" in medieval Spain was created with the overt purpose of finishing off the bandit epidemic that was a collateral effect of civil war, but it was actually conceived by the Catholic kings primarily as part of an effort to create a centralized state, erect a royal monopoly of violence, and strip local lords of power (Lunenfeld 1970; Storni 1997, 75). In eighteenth-century rural Mexico the "Tribunal de la Acordada" and in the second half of the nineteenth century the Rurales were not only a police force but also tools used by the executive branch of government to bypass such institutions of control over the use of violence as the Audience, the courts of law, and the congress, and to balance the power of regional elites or disaffected corporations such as the army (MacLachlan 1974; Vanderwood 1992).[24]

This paradox, in which banditry comfortably plays both sides of the law, appears time and again in Western political thought. Writing in *The City of God* in the fifth century, Saint Augustine of Hippo wonders,

> Justice removed, then, what are kingdoms but great bands of robbers? What are bands of robbers themselves but little kingdoms? The band itself is made up of men; it is governed by the authority of a ruler; it is bound together by a pact of association; and the loot is divided according to an agreed law. If, by the constant

addition of desperate men, this scourge grows to such a size that it acquires terri-tory, establishes a seat of government, occupies cities and subjugates peoples, it assumes the name of kingdom more openly. For this name is now manifestly con-ferred upon it not by the removal of greed, but by the addition of impunity. It was a pertinent and true answer which was made to Alexander the Great by a pirate whom he had seized. When the king asked him what he meant by infesting the sea, the pirate defiantly replied: "The same as you do when you infest the whole world; but because I do it with a little ship I am called a robber, and because you do it with a great fleet, you are an emperor." (1998, 58)

In the Greek novel bandits are a staple of the narrative (much as in the later Gothic novel). In *The Adventures of Leucippe and Clitophon* by Achilles Tatius, the same word used for "king" is used for "bandit chief" (βασιλέα). Theory on the state, from so-called conflict sociology (proposed by Randall Collins) to contemporary philosophy (e.g., Gilles Deleuze and Felix Guattari) has picked up on this trope of the collusion between banditry and state-making. Charles Tilly, in his pathbreaking work "War Making and State Making as Organized Crime" (1985), considers the nation-state to be very similar to a protection racket. In this and other works, Tilly places banditry in a "continuum of state-making" whose "defining feature . . . is the extent to which control over the use of force is concentrated in a single organi-zation." In his view, then, there is not a difference of quality but of degree between the rural Sicilian mafia, banditry, the nation-state, and empire (1975a, xx–xxiii).[25]

The risk of this intertwining and eventual conflation of banditry and the state made it even more urgent for Latin American elites to impose a limit between these two forces, in order to create the conditions and scene for the foundation of a nation-state. If the nation is, as Anderson maintains, an imagined community, then "imagined" necessarily means "knowable"—stretching Williams's notion (1973)—and as such it asks for a strict demar-cation of its symbolic limits. Much of the fictional literature written on the Mexican Revolution may be understood as an attempt to draw these limits, to draw distinctions between the bandit, the true revolutionary, and the corrupt representative of an oppressive state (who also calls himself a revo-lutionary), in order to understand the Revolution as either the inaugural event of Mexico as a modern nation or an opportunity forever lost. Some early works (e.g., *Los de abajo*, by Mariano Azuela, first published in 1915–16) as well as some later ones (e.g., *El corrido de Juan Saavedra*, by María

Luisa Ocampo, from 1929), show that these distinctions are difficult and at times even impossible to make.

Thus, the most dangerous challenge posed by banditry was not chaos or what passed for chaos in the eyes of the elites.[26] The most dangerous challenge was symbolic. In its most developed forms, banditry did not challenge a law or a right but rather the state as law-giver and ultimate source of legitimate violence (what Vanderwood called the "idea of banditry" as opposed to its reality). Using the distinction proposed by Walter Benjamin between law making violence and law maintaining violence (1921, 283), I am inclined to say that banditry presents the state with a form of violence that, just like that of the state, creates law, albeit of a different nature (that is, one that is local and oral). Its presence challenges not only the letter of the law but also the position of enunciation that supports it (i.e., the judge as origin of the sentence, the lawmaker as the origin of the law). This distinction has of course the ambiguous nature of any statement concerning banditry. The challenge that banditry poses, not necessarily in a self-aware fashion, and that may be (and usually is) only the perception of the state (unlike modern Marxist guerrilla warfare, where that challenge is deliberate) is a cause of deep uncertainty and repulsion by the lettered city. In fact, the scene of the personal encounter between the letrado and the bandit is a motif in and of itself in Western narratives. The tone of this encounter ranges from the warm brotherhood between bandit and lawyer in Alexandre Dumas's *Les Frères corses* (1844) to the happy acquaintance in which bandits and letrados hit it off through mutual respect (as in Don Quijote's encounter with Roque Guinart on the outskirts of Barcelona or Rob Roy's enduring and efficacious protection of Francis Osbaldistone during his northern adventures in Walter Scott's novel) to the somber destiny of the letrado in Antonio Di Benedetto's *Zama* (1956), who has his hands cut off by a bandit.

Aside from these trusting or anxious fantasies, the real and theoretical collusion between banditry and state formation during the nineteenth century called for the ferocious repression of banditry. The *Ley número 19 sobre jueces de camino y persecución de ladrones en despoblado*, passed in Mexico in 1852, established that the penalty for robbery with violence or the threat of violence was death, regardless of the amount stolen or whether violence was actually exerted. In the *Ley general para juzgar a los ladrones, homicidas, heridores y vagos*, also from Mexico (1857), a clear distinction is established between rural robbery (*robo en despoblado*), punished with the death penalty, and urban robbery, punished with hard time. Banditry deprived the culprit of the rights and guarantees derived from citizenship. From the times of the Acordada, brigands were subjected to special tribunals that held summary trials without appeals, pardons, or amnesties, and the usual sentence was immediate execution (Vanderwood 1992, xxxiv–xxxv).[27]

The forgoing of the rights entailed in citizenship in the case of bandits was even a matter of pride for state officials. Ernest William White, in *Cameos of the Silver-Land, or the Experiences of a Young Naturalist in the Argentine Republic* (1881), tells us the following about his experience in San Juan: "Until the present Governor assumed office, the city suburbs lay at the mercy of a gang of highwaymen. As lawless and daring, but not so merciful, as Dick Turpin: black-mail was levied and submitted to by all travelers, under pain of death, so that at last, locomotion beyond civic bounds became well-nigh impossible. . . . [T]he Governor issued the order to his soldiers. 'Go out, capture and slay those ruffians without benefit of clergy!' and forthwith ten of them slept and San Juan became as peaceful as quackerdom [Quakerdom]" (396).

For Domingo Faustino Sarmiento, an Argentine intellectual and father of the famous civilization versus barbarism binarism, bandits were "enemies of humankind" and to kill them on the spot, without due process, was a "natural right" previous to laws and constitutions:

> A man, because of revenge, rage, or any other cause, kills another man, just like because of need or deprivation he steals something. This is a common crime, with a name, a place, and a jurisdiction. Banditry targets anybody outside cities and the protection of the law. Banditry victimizes not a particular individual, but everybody, society as a whole, the human race as a whole. The highway robber has as his backdrop the desert and the mountains, and in order for travelers to be safe it is imperative to declare that the robbery outside urban areas is a crime against humanity [*delito contra la humanidad*] and that the culprit is outside the common law. This is why nations are expected to turn over famous bandits, even though there may not be extradition treaties. A pirate on the sea and a bandit on land are outside the law and can be killed, *put to death,* by anybody, anytime. This is at the same time natural and public law, which supersedes any constitution, and therefore these constitutions cannot annul it. (1899, 206)

Sarmiento is following a well-established tradition, one that has been clearly stated in colonial legislation, as follows:

> We order and command that any criminal or highway robber who roams the countryside as part of a gang, robbing highways or populated areas, and who hav-

ing been called by a proclamation . . . does not appear in front of the judges [be] declared an incorrigible and publicly condemned rebel, and we allow that any person . . . freely offend, kill or catch said criminal, without fear of any reprisal . . . bringing him in front of the court dead or alive [having either] dragged them, or hanged, or quartered and exhibited on the roads or places where he committed his crimes. (*Tomo tercero de autos acordados, que contiene nueve libros, por el orden de títulos de las Leyes de recopilación*, Madrid, A expensas de la Real Cía. de Impresores i libreros del Reino, 1775, 3:405, in Solares Robles 1999, 144–45)

Sarmiento suggests that banditry is not a problem to be solved within the institutions created and regulated by law because it touches on the problem of the origin of law itself. The distinction between bandit and lawful citizen is the primal scene where the distinction between human and nonhuman takes place. In this scene, defined by law making violence, the division that gives origin to the social takes place, thus defining the locus and possibility of legitimate (human) association. Literature repeatedly echoes this primal division. For example, Guillermo Prieto (1818–1897), a Mexican writer and liberal general, wrote a series of romances on Manuel Lozada, a bandit of Tepic. The most important is "Grande y chispeante romance de las dos furias (Rojas y Lozada)." In this poem Lozada is a Fury, a monster, a wild beast, a miasma bubbling up from the social mud, and a satyr, as well as the hallucination of a disturbed mind, a demon, and a natural wonder. For Prieto, Lozada is not a human product embedded in a specific social situation fighting a human fight. He is beyond (or before) the human and the social since he is alien and he preceded the social contract. In the case of Lozada, the state as the embodiment of the social contract is charged with the explicit task of erasing him. However, paradoxically enough, if the bandit is a monster, the most important metaphor of the state (that of the leviathan) also makes the state a biblical, inscrutable monster. This metaphorical contamination, in which monstrosity can be the interior or the exterior of the social, lies at the core of my investigation.

Bandit Narratives

The purpose of this book is to reflect upon a number of narratives produced throughout the nineteenth century following the numerous articulations (a term defined by Laclau and Mouffe 1985, 105) of the bandit trope as an arena of negotiation and conflict for the imagining of the nation-state and its "others" in Latin America. I am particularly interested in the representation of banditry (or any form of peasant insurgency called banditry) by the letrado elite as a decisive and urgent expression of the desires, contradictions, and conflicts that define the "heterogeneous Latin American modernity" (Herlinghaus 2000). We now recognize that banditry was key in the definition of some of the founding paradigms in Latin American national development (e.g., civilization versus barbarism, order versus chaos, modern liberalism versus colonial corporatism, city versus country capitalism versus pre-capitalism, free market versus socialism), and Sarmiento seems to give expression to this intuition in a particularly forceful way. While speaking of the decisive showdown that would embody (and resolve) the Argentine riddle, he says, "In my opinion, a war that is possible (and even desirable, if our fatherland cannot be spared that evil) is a war that would pit freedom against *caudillaje,* a war that would have strategy and military science on the one hand and banditry [*bandalaje*] and compulsive rural insurgency [*alzamiento compulsivo de campañas*] on the other; a regular army on the one hand and irregulars wearing the red *chiripá* on the other; civilization in the means on the one hand and barbarism in the ends on the other" (1852, 301).

As Hall points out, "The nation state was never simply a political entity. It was always also a symbolic formation—a 'system of representation'" (2000, 38). Thus, we must pay attention to the ways in which the European-minded, lettered, Creole, male, urban elite depicted, through literature, a form of nonstate rural violence in societies that were at that moment overwhelmingly rural, illiterate, and nonwhite and followed rules of life that differed markedly from those of the dominant culture. By maintaining this focus, we can reconstruct a crucial segment of that "system of representation" and of the conflicting conditions under which modernity took hold in Latin America.

The term "bandit narratives," which I use throughout the book, refers to the vast corpus of writing that deals with bandits or with forms of peasant violence called banditry. This corpus comprises novels, short stories, criminological treatises, essays, poems, and film. Beyond specific differences concerning each format, the narrative form is common to them all, and they share a paradigm of representation that I attempt to outline. Bandit narratives are, to my mind, an essential part of the theater of law, and they take the form of an allegory of the violent constitution of the nation-state. I follow Fredric Jameson's proposal in the opening pages of *The Political Uncon-*

scious when he disavows the distinction between cultural texts having a political resonance and those devoid of it. For Jameson, this false distinction is "a symptom and a reinforcement of the reification and privatization of contemporary life" (1981, 20), a political fact itself. Angus Fletcher maintains that there is an inherently political character in all literary allegories, since they enact "a conflict of authorities" (1964, 22), while Gordon Teskey shows the nexus between allegory and state violence in the cultural history of the West (1996, 137–38).

The relationship between allegory and theater of law is captured with eerie precision in the anecdote of Remirro de Orco in *The Prince* (1513) by Niccolò Machiavelli. (I am following, to a certain extent, Teskey's superb account and interpretation of the scene.) Cesar Borgia had commissioned Remirro to pacify the Romagna, which he did at the price of extreme cruelty and the loss of Borgia's popularity and prestige. In order to regain the goodwill of the citizenry and to placate any discontent, Borgia ordered Remirro to be secretly abducted. One fine morning, Remirro's body appeared at Cesena Square chopped in half, a bloody knife by his side. "The ferocity of this scene left the people at once stunned and satisfied," Machiavelli recounts (22). This ferocity did not reside exactly in the quartered body but rather in the bloody knife. The knife was not (and could not have been) the murder weapon, since a knife does not easily cut a human torso in half, bone and all. Soaking the knife in blood and setting it by the corpse was an intentional plus of meaning, an indication that in that death there was a message and that the message went beyond treason and punishment: it was an allegoric staging of the power and the violence of the sovereign (Teskey 1996, 137–38). Bandit narratives are like that bloody knife: they are at the same time traces and signifiers of state violence, documents of culture as well as of barbarism, similar to the "cultural treasures" of which Walter Benjamin speaks in "Thesis on the Philosophy of History" (2006).

Doris Sommer (1991) proposes allegory as the privileged signifying mode of nineteenth-century Latin American writing (or at least of narrative). Sommer's central thesis is that love that crosses racial, class, linguistic, or legal boundaries was a metaphor with which the lettered city depicted its utopia of national integration, or conversely, its malaise regarding the lack thereof. Jameson, in his article "Third-World Literature in the Era of Multinational Capitalism" (1986), argues that the national allegory does not belong to a differentiated fictional corpus of a specific period but that it is a feature pertaining to literature of the so-called third world (69). This idea has triggered numerous criticisms and revisions, some of which are quite powerful.[28]

At the same time, Sommer's approach can be criticized on several grounds, in particular because there is no theoretical attention paid to violence being as important a signifier as romance (even when violence is occurring within romances). It may be argued that romance was her focus, but then we would be forgetting that many (perhaps most) foundational romances are to some degree mixed with violence, and that violence is therefore the other side—an inseparable element—of the national romance.

I agree with Fletcher when he indicates that beyond allegory as a specific literary genre, all fictions have an allegorical component to a certain extent. He distinguishes between allegory and allegoresis, the latter partially independent from the author's intentions and based upon the act of reading (1964, 4, 12). I offer several arguments in favor of the notion that "national allegory" is continually productive. In Latin America a certain brand of literature finds its political dimension in the erasure of the distinction between public and private, or the symbolization of the former in the terms of the latter. (Nineteenth-century literature is exemplary of this fact.) In addition, the literary allegory does not necessarily imply a closure of meaning in favor of a pre-existent ideology. Quite to the contrary, allegory can question that ideology, thus distinguishing allegory from pedagogy. This is the meaning of allegory as it is put forth by Marthe Robert in her reading of *Kafka,* or by Benjamin in *The Origin of German Tragic Drama.* Also, the national allegory has a self-referential dimension that has to be read as an interrogation on its instance of enunciation—a questioning of the role of the "national letrado." Finally, many of the cases I analyze locate the problem of rural violence in a specific region (e.g., the northeastern Brazilian sertão, Morelos or Jalisco in Mexico, the pampas in the Río de la Plata region, or the Venezuelan plains). However, as Gerald Martin points out (1989), the region in Latin American literature does not function as a strictly subnational unit but rather as a national or supernational trope. Thus, the pampas in *Facundo o civilización y barbarie* by Sarmiento (Argentina, 1845) or the Arauca Valley in *Doña Bárbara* by Gallegos (Venezuela, 1929) are metaphors of Argentina or Venezuela as well as of a Latin America torn apart by the conflict between civilization versus barbarism. This link is created by means of the national allegory.

Time Frame

This book analyzes representations of banditry during the long Latin American nineteenth century, running roughly from late colonial times to the late 1920s. This period marks the incorporation of Latin America into global markets based upon an export-led growth model (Bulmer-Thomas 1994). This model, which had a clear colonial precedent, was imposed toward the middle of the nineteenth century and secured the hegemony of a commercial and/or landowning class that obtained maximum political and economic benefits from it. This so-called neocolonial pact (Halperín Donghi 1997) implied a peculiar model of capitalism focused on the production of agrarian commodities for global consumption (e.g., sugar, wheat, coffee, cocoa, beef, and bananas), highly concentrated landownership, and a modestly centralized state. Such an arrangement progressively expanded legal and judicial systems, economic and administrative infrastructures, national armed forces, and police that coexisted easily with less prestigious institutions: debt peonage, the company store (*tienda de raya*), restrictions on peasant mobility, forced military service, and out-and-out genocide. It also coexisted with precapitalist modes of production such as the Indian community in its role as a provider of cheap labor (Mallon 1983). The dual process of state building and establishing a particularly ruthless mode of agrarian capitalism implied struggles and negotiations between local, regional, and national elites. It also implied pitched struggles between elites and popular sectors intent upon preserving landownership or autonomy (Joseph and Nugent 1994, 3). It is rather easy to see how the bandit trope acquires particular relevance during a period focused on land and population control.

The Great Depression marked the end of this period as well as the beginning of the so-called crisis of the neocolonial pact as a model of growth. Even when banditry and rural unrest persisted well after this period (up to today, as Sendero Luminoso in Peru, the endless Colombian civil war, and the zapatism of the Chiapas region exemplify), all of these expressions are qualitatively different from the phenomenon that I examine in this volume. From the mid-1920s on (or later, depending on the case), most expressions of peasant unrest and its representation were inspired (or were charged with being inspired) by Marxism, which determined to varying degrees the self-perception of the participants, the relations between rural and urban insurgency, and the cultural character that the whole process acquired. This political movement adds a whole new dimension to the "bandit problem," and therefore any analysis of post-1920s banditry should form part of a different project. Also, from the 1920s onward, the social landscape in rural Latin America (particularly, the presence of the state) was more or less established along lines fashioned by the elite, dramatically changing the ways in which agrarian struggles were fought. Banditry thus changed its place in the political and cultural arenas.

The reader will note that I devote little attention to the Mexican corrido, the Brazilian *literatura de cordel,* the Río de la Plata *payada,* or the Argentine *folletín criollista,* which are the cultural expressions that first come to mind (in part, due to media popularity) when one thinks about Latin American banditry. My decision to focus on the elite perspective of banditry was based upon both methodological and theoretical motives. This perspective of banditry in cultural discourse (as different from police and court reports) has received scant attention, although there is a well-established body of scholarship on the elite perspective on urban criminality. Moreover, to analyze corridos or folletines from a purely textual perspective (the only one available to those with professional training as literary/cultural critics) would betray their political-cultural specificity, thus creating a mere spectral counterpoint between popular and lettered culture. The political dimension in these art forms is lost in formal textual analysis, since they exceed the protocols that characterize literature (and upon which literary criticism methodologies are built). In some cases, the political dimension is distorted in a mere folklorization. (There are, however, brilliant works, such as Daus 1982, that engage in textual analysis of popular culture.) Corridos, *cantigas*, and popular songs require specific multidisciplinary analyses that take into account highly local contexts (e.g., communities of production and interpretation, migration patterns of styles and motifs, complex interactions between popular, high, and mass culture). An additional difficulty is that many of these expressions deal with transient entities that are sometimes not even well defined—an advancing army, a famous trial or execution, an election, an assassination—thus making the need for a grounded and detailed analysis even greater. A classic example of this approach is found in Américo Paredes's *With His Pistol in His Hand: A Border Ballad and Its Hero* (1958). Paredes analyzes the "Corrido de Gregorio Cortés," exploring its deep connections with the struggles on Texas' southern border during the first half of the twentieth century. Other examples are Adolfo Prieto's examination of Argentine *folletín criollista* in *El discurso criollista en la formación de la Argentina moderna* (1988), Candace Slater's study of the *literatura de cordel* in *Stories on a String* (1989), or Elijah Wald's *Narcocorrido* (2001).

Furthermore, even though "popular" and "elite" are entirely relative terms and are constituted through mutually modifying conflicts and negotiations (and I am aware of the fact that this important factor in the cultural dynamics will not be part of the analysis), they do not always have the same periodizations, they do not operate within the same units, they do not follow the same protocols of representation, and they are not inhabited by the same narratives. (For example, Villa and Artigas were suppressed or distanced from elite discourse for decades, which allowed for their flourishing in popular and mass culture.) In any case, an analysis of popular depictions of bandits would require not only another book to consider the large number of examples but also to cover the method, theory, chronology, and the political and cultural conflicts involved. I am confident, though, that what I have lost by denying each of my analyses a more grounded examination I have gained by providing insight, for the first time, into a cultural phenomenon encompassing the entire continent.

My focus is bandit narratives from Argentina, Mexico, Venezuela, and Brazil. Of course, epidemic banditry was not restricted to these countries; Cuba during the wars of independence, the Andean region during the post-independence period, and twentieth-century Colombia had more than their fair share of large-scale banditry. However, in the four previously mentioned countries, a tradition of bandit literature had a prominent place in the national literary canon and in the larger national imagination. This is not as apparent—so far—in the other countries of Latin America.

The texts considered in the following pages will not be organized chronologically or by national traditions. Rather, each part groups a number of case studies according to their different takes on banditry vis-à-vis the national projects: the bandit as Other, the bandit as instrument of critique, and the bandit as devious brother and as suppressed origin.

Part I examines cases in which banditry is addressed as the unequivocal demon of national, modernizing projects and the suppression of the bandit is a paramount (and essential) moment in the narrative. I devote this part to analyzing foundational texts of Latin American culture such as the picaresque novel *El periquillo sarniento* (1816), by José Joaquín Fernández de Lizardi (1776–1827); the essay *Facundo* (1845); the doctrinarian piece *El Chacho: último caudillo de la montonera de los Llanos* (1867), by Domingo Faustino Sarmiento (1810–1888); the novel *El Zarco* (1885–1888), by Ignacio Manuel Altamirano (1834–1893), as well as criminological works by Raimundo Nina Rodrigues and Julio Guerrero's *La génesis del crimen en México* (1901).

Part II examines cases in which banditry is mobilized as part of variously oriented critiques of the modernizing path that Latin American countries were following toward the second half of the nineteenth century. This part is devoted to the novel *Astucia: el jefe de los Hermanos de la Hoja o los charros contrabandistas de la Rama* (1865) by Luis Inclán (1816–1875); the Venezuelan novel *Zárate* (1882) by Eduardo Blanco (1839–1912); the celebrated poem *Martín Fierro* (1872/1879), by José Hernández (1834–1886); as well as *Juan Moreira* (1879), the hugely popular serial novel by Eduardo Gutiérrez (1851–1889); and *Alma gaucha* (1906), the play by Alberto Ghiraldo (1874–1946), who rewrites *Martín Fierro* by fashioning his main character as an anarchist *avant la lettre*. The last chapter of this part deals with the novel *Los bandidos de Río Frío* (1891) by Manuel Payno (1810–1894).

Part III examines the role of banditry as the suppressed origin of the national community, a tropic use that takes the ambiguity that characterized the bandit figure to an extreme, since it includes and puts tension on the two previous uses of the bandit figure. Because of this, the first chapter of Part III is devoted to perhaps the most complex work of the corpus, *Os sertões* (1902), by Euclides da Cunha (1866–1909). In addition, this part examines *La guerra gaucha* (1905) and *El payador* (1916), both by Leopoldo Lugones (1874–1938), the novel *Los de abajo* (1915) by Mariano Azuela (1873–1952), the essay *Cesarismo democrático* (1919) by the Venezuelan Laureano Vallenilla Lanz (1870–936), and finally *Doña Bárbara* (1927), the novel by Rómulo Gallegos (1884–1969).

The conclusion of the book summarizes some of the main topics visited throughout these pages and establishes a number of categories that I consider useful for further analysis.

Part I

The Foundation of National Identities

The Bandit as Other

1

El periquillo sarniento

Banditry as the Non Plus Ultra

Lasciate ogne speranza, voi ch'intrate.
> Dante Alighieri, *Inferno*, on the evening of Good Friday in the year 1300

El periquillo sarniento (1816) by José Joaquín Fernández de Lizardi is Don Pedro Sarmiento's autobiography. Don Pedro was a redeemed rogue, proprietor of a sizable rural estate in San Agustín de las Cuevas, Mexico, and an exemplary *pater familias*. On his deathbed, Don Pedro penned the history of his life since childhood, from his initial evil ways to his timely redemption. He intended his narrative to be an object lesson for his offspring (ownership, fatherhood, and the sacredness of the written word comprised the ideological tripod on which this project was based).[1] Since the narrative was written *in articulo mortis,* a friend edited the text. That friend, "El Pensador Mexicano" (Lizardi's journalistic pseudonym), added a foreword and footnotes. The narrative spans from the second half of the eighteenth century to the mid-1810s.

El periquillo sarniento's status as the first Latin American novel is still debated.[2] When viewed as a novel, it has an obvious picaresque matrix (Leal 1974; Van Praag-Chantraine 1979; Compton 1997). Since the picaresque is, almost by definition, an urban genre, *El periquillo sarniento* has been read as a totalizing critique of the expiring colonial regime and in particular of its eminent institution: the lettered city (Rama 1984; Vidal 1985; Moraña 1997a; Dabove 1999). Perico (Don Pedro) indeed scoured almost all colonial social spaces, from the extremely low-class gambling house and inn (*arrastraderito*) and the humble Indian shack to the palace of the Creole aristocrat.[3] He tried his hand at all trades and professions: university student, seminarian, notary, professional beggar, professional gambler, barber, civil servant, secretary, personal assistant, sacristan, soldier, priest, physician—and this list is far from complete. He became familiar with outrageous wealth as well as with the most abject poverty, where a blanket amounted to substantial capital. In this journey, he painted a sober picture of an expiring colonial society from Acapulco and the Philippines to Veracruz. This critique, as "decolonization of discourse" (Vogeley 2001), seems to serve multiple purposes: the presentation of the economic utopia in the bucolic set-

ting of San Agustín de las Cuevas (Franco 1983); the totalitarian utopia of
the Island of Saucheoufú (Leal 1977; Ruiz-Barrionuevo 1997); or the letrado
utopia of the father-letrado passing down his teachings to his sons and by
extension to citizens of the future (Dabove 1998).

As a jack-of-all-trades, any walk of life seemed suitable to Perico. There is
a void however, a subject position that he did not (and could not) occupy
even though he had the opportunity: he was never a bandit. At the beginning of the fifth and last volume of the narrative, after yet another vertigi-
nous turn of fortune, Perico finds himself dispossessed of all earthly belongings. Disenchanted with life, he looks for courage in some cheap liquor and
attempts suicide. Down on his luck, he even fails at that (5:2–5). When leaving the city in shame, Perico is found by his old accomplice, Aguilita, de-
spondently walking along the Río Frío highway. Unlike previous acquain-
tances who failed to help—or even recognize—Perico when he was down on
his luck, Aguilita offers him the opportunity to join his prosperous band of
highway robbers (5:9–13).[4] Perico declines this offer and suggests that cowardice was behind his decision. But since his situation is rather dire (he was
reduced to begging), he agrees to participate in the enterprise as an auxiliary, thus not venturing to the highways or actively engaging in robbery
(5:25–28). He stays with the band and witnesses its endeavors until its
eventual demise.

There are no "moral" reasons (that is, reasons explicitly given in the novel
to elucidate the character's actions—what Gérard Genette called "motivation") that fully explain why Perico could not become a bandit. Moral values
were for Perico, at best, part of a performance, never something to which he
became seriously attached. Actor was another thing Perico never was, but
this would have been redundant: the entire fictional world was for him a
performing stage. His actions provided plenty of evidence for his lack of regard for moral values. In his decades-long career as a rogue, Perico was guilty
of his mother's and his first son's deaths; he was involved in the embezzlement and forgery of public records (3:3–31); because of his malpractice as a
(false) medical doctor he caused the deaths of many patients, both Indians
and Creoles (3:116–33); he broke his contract as a barber's apprentice
(3:31–45); he attempted to rape his estranged wife, whom he had previously
abandoned to her own destiny (3:191–231); he committed sacrilege (3:232–
62) and gambling fraud (2:52–109). In all these instances Perico showed a

remarkable nerve, courage, a capacity to simulate, and a lack of remorse (which also shows that his excuse of being a coward had little basis). In addition to all this, he did not mind stealing in the least: robbery in itself was not a frontier he feared crossing, since he did it repeatedly. Therefore, the somewhat enigmatic nature and importance of Perico's not becoming a bandit is crucial to our interpretation of the novel.

Fernández de Lizardi's exclusive emphasis on the urban milieu (starting from his selection of an urban genre—the picaresque) is less self-evident than what it may seem. Urban criminality (and plebeian lack of morals in general) was indeed an old source of preoccupation and anxiety for colonial authorities (Viqueira-Albán 1987), and the last decades of colonial rule were no exception (Haslip-Viera 1999; Lozano-Armendares 1987). But the urban crowd was never a clear and present danger to the colonial elites, either because of its unruliness or its insurgent sympathies (Scardaville 2000). Banditry, on the other hand, was at the very eye of the hurricane. Outlaw activity was endemic in central and western New Spain during the entire colonial period (Martin 1957; Bernaldo de Quiros 1933), but toward the end of the eighteenth century the problem was compounded by an increase in population, commerce, and transit (thus increasing the opportunities for highway robbery). Moreover, agrarian pressures elevated the number of vagrants and landless, disgruntled peasants who turned to banditry to eke out a livelihood or to channel their grievances (Taylor 1982, 1988). The problem acquired epidemic proportions after 1810 with gangs (*gavillas*) increasing both in number, size, frequency of attacks, and boldness. From an average of five members, the gavillas jumped to an average membership of fourteen, and in some cases they soared to several hundred (Taylor 1982, 47; MacLachlan 1974, 105; Archer 1982, 71). The breakdown of colonial authority brought about by the Hidalgo rebellion dramatically intensified this process through the collusion of banditry and *independentista* insurgency into a hybrid form for which Christon Archer coined the term "guerrilla-banditry" (Archer 1982). Of course, the vice regal administration and its supporters routinely labeled all insurgents as "bandits," thus denying them political status, as can be seen in, among other places, the "Reglamento Político Militar" issued by Viceroy Calleja (Hamnet 1986, 59–66; Archer 1982, 60; Van Young 1997).[5] This denial of political character had frightening consequences when guerrilla-bandits met their punishment: "a summary trial followed by a swift execution delayed for just the four hours needed to prepare a decent

Christian death: soldiers then hanged the bullet-ridden bodies along roads or at the entries of towns" (Archer 1982, 77).

The situation was indeed confusing. On the one hand, there were old and new gavillas that took advantage of the general disarray of the viceroyalty to maximize profit, what Paul Vanderwood famously termed "profiteering bandits" (Vanderwood 1992; see also Vanderwood 1987). On the other, there were also gavillas closely connected to the insurgency and whose leaders boasted authentic or usurped military commissions from insurgent leaders (Taylor 1982, 36; Van Young 2001). Other cases were much more difficult to classify, since loyalty to the insurgent cause did not hinder the quest for profit or indulgence in cruelty (and of course, all military units—royalists as well as insurgents—routinely lived off the land, further blurring the line between army provisioning and profit making). The most famous of these cases was without a doubt that of Agustín Marroquín, a bandit-turned-revolutionary whose exploits as well as his ruthlessness achieved national visibility (as Eric Van Young notes, for a time every highway robbery in the Valley of Mexico was ascribed to him). Like Julián Villagrán, a bandit named Commander General of the North, or Chito Villagrán, a field marshal of the insurgent army, Marroquín became part of Hidalgo's inner circle. He played a crucial role in the Guadalajara executions of December 1810, was captured in Saltillo with Hidalgo as the chief of his escort, and met a similar fate at the receiving end of a firing squad (Archer 1982; Van Young 1997).

When it came to outlaw violence, this lack of clear-cut definitions made the question of banditry ever more urgent, since a war was being waged against an ambiguous enemy. Thus, an important question arises: is Fernández de Lizardi ignoring the most pressing issue of the time (maybe because of censorship)?[6] Or, as I propose, is it precisely the marginality of the bandit episode in *El periquillo sarniento* that bespeaks its importance? Is it possible that this brief moment is enough to illuminate the whole text? There is a crucial clue that allows us to begin answering this question. Perico's stint among the bandits (which resembles in some aspects Lucius's stint among the robbers in the form of an ass, in Apuleius's *Metamorphoses*) was not lengthy. Nonetheless, this short episode is the turning point of the narrative. After it, Perico begins in earnest his reformation into a respectable citizen, father, and proprietor. The fact that the bandit episode happened when he was thirty-five years old, that is, "nel mezzo del cammin della vita," only adds symbolic relevance to the episode, making it a sort of descent into Hell (coupled with the ascent into the Paradise of citizenship).[7] Banditry in the novel is then an impossible limit to cross, as well as a turning point.

While the picaresque cycle had a limit in banditry, the agrarian utopia that followed it found its limit in rural insurgency. In fact, Don Pedro had to realize his assets and move to Mexico City to protect himself and his family from the insurrection (5:140). The narrator only indulges in very general reflections on the insurrection (mainly quotations from classical authors) because, as he stated, "it is extremely dangerous to write about this in Mexico in the year 1813" (5:140). Therefore, it is not difficult to postulate that one limit (banditry) plays into the other (insurgency). We can indeed argue that banditry is the image through which the narrator indirectly embodies his perception and evaluation of what is otherwise impossible to talk about (except as an outright condemnation). The unspeakable, of course, is the insurgency. I am not suggesting that Fernández de Lizardi was a royalist supporter, a thorny issue in and of itself (see Spell 1971). What I propose is that he silently appropriated a state-sponsored trope ("insurgency as banditry" [see Van Young 1997]), which was originally promoted as part of its "prose of counterinsurgency" (Guha 1983, 1988), and he put it to a different use: it served as an artifact to depict the conflict by dehistoricizing it and to pass judgment on the possibilities of popular insurgency as an alternative to the colonial order.

Upon first inspection, the bandit society in which Perico participated lacked any hellish quality. Unlike urban society, divided according to the logic of *homo homini lupus* and in which the rogue is condemned to alienation and radical solitude (Maravall 1987, 245), bandit society in *El periquillo sarniento* is depicted as a true community, one whose hallmarks are a common sense of belonging and the absence of internal conflicts. The bandit world is not devoid of violence, of course, since a certain practice of violence is what defines this world as banditry. But in a mechanism uncannily similar to violence in modern nation-states, this violence is exerted only against external enemies (in this case, travelers, the "human prey"). This is indeed the cornerstone of the gang's internal coherence. Unlike Mexico, where greed was the passion that governed all characters, thus making community impossible in a landscape of *bellum omnium contra omnes*, in Río Frío there was no personal greed (although collective greed defined them, of course), and, in a "primitive communism" of sorts, Aguilita authorizes the collective use of the booty according to the needs of each member of the community (5:31–32).

During Perico's picaresque urban cycle no one is what he or she appears to be. In Río Frío, on the other hand, no one can pretend to be what he or she is not. Of course, all gang members lie about what they have been before becoming part of the band, but once incorporated into the Río Frío gang, their sincerity and loyalty toward the gang are beyond question, and there is no gap between essence and appearance. This unity stems not so much from a moral choice as from the fact that since the written word has little prestige and everyone's identity lies in what they do, there is no gap between performance and being. As such, any fraud is immediately discovered (e.g., when Perico pretends to be a doctor [5:39]).

In Mexico City not all human destinies are equal. There is a strict and continuously enforced stratification along race, class, gender, and occupational lines. Río Frío, on the other hand, can boast of the most perfect "organic solidarity" (Durkheim 1893), one in which there is an efficient and egalitarian division of tasks and even lazy and useless Perico can find a place. Río Frío, far from a hellhole of vices and unchecked passions, is a "happy Arcadia" (5:33), a veritable *locus amoenus* where there is no unmet need, no alcoholism (5:24), and no racial stratification or even gender conflict, since free love prevents marital oppression and jealousy (5:33).[8]

Still, the novel celebrated the disappearance of this arcadia through the intervention of a deus ex machina, the Acordada. (This deus ex machina character is further emphasized by the fact that by the time Fernández de Lizardi published *El periquillo sarniento*, the once fearsome Acordada as the agency in charge of rural security no longer existed [MacLachlan 1974, 106–107].) This arcadia had to disappear because it was built upon perverse foundations. Wildly successful, Río Frío's society was, however, outside the law as defined by Lizardi's trilogy (fatherhood, ownership, written word). Río Frío's organization lacked patriarchal principles and thus lacked a symbolic center that would serve as a guarantee for its perpetuation. (We should remember that it was precisely the feebleness of the law of the biological father that thrust Perico into the life of a rogue.) Even though Río Frío was a society ruled by men, all bandits shared women and possessions "like brothers" (5:33). Thus, the gang was a false image of a family and indeed a false image of a society, since the prohibition of incest seemed not to bear upon it. Unlike the nineteenth-century family metaphor that reaches its peak in the romantic novel (heterosexual, exogamic, centered on its perpetuation through reproduction), this family consists of incestuous brothers without fathers. Therefore, it is not an institution whose law ensures its continuity (hence the absence of children in Río Frío) but a Freudian primitive horde in the interregnum without law, after the murder of the father and before the erection of the totem (Freud 1912–1913). This gavilla is even more disturbing as a brotherhood since its members all belong to different races (Pipilo is a mulatto, Aguilita is Indian or mestizo, Januario is white), thus making fatherhood even more uncertain, even more absent as a law and as a principle of order and representation. (This is indeed an old motif: in *Las tres justicias en una,* by Calderón de la Barca, banditry and rebellion against the father are twin moments in the perdition of Don Lope.) The bandit gang is a community that not only lacks a totem (for Fernández de Lizardi, fatherhood is the symbolic order that ensures authority in its relation to writing, since the memory of the community is a memory of the father), but it is one that cannot have a totem, since its members do not even share a common father. Therefore, the "happy Arcadia" shows itself to be a perverse, deceiving image of society that masks a fundamental, horrific chaos: the absence of written law (for the letrado elite, the rule of a different, subaltern law—clearly at work in Río Frío) equals the utter absence of any law.

As a rogue, Perico carries his colorful panoply of offenses under the symbolic guarantee of the colonial order. Indeed, he needs the colonial order to thrive. By trying to eke out a living as a false physician, a false notary, a false barber, a false priest, and a false nobleman, Perico has to advocate the social prestige and relevance of each of these subject positions. Therefore, even when it comes to criminality, roguery is not a true challenge to the material and symbolic orders upon which colonial society is based (or it is a challenge of a completely different nature). Roguery is, rather, an unsanctioned and punishable way to obtain advantages that work from within the colonial system. Thus, not only is the rogue not a rebel, but his actions are a form of symbolic reduction of those of the true rebel, whose performance does openly contradict dominant values (Maravall 1987, 438–39).

The bandits of Río Frío whom Perico reluctantly joined committed crimes in their own name, as bandits who addressed their victims as such. Of all the rascals and criminals that densely populate *El periquillo sarniento,* bandits are the only ones who do not negotiate with the state in any way; they never try to disguise what they are nor do they attempt to appropriate any of the state's symbolic guarantees. They openly act as what they are. This openness is a direct challenge to state rule, and it is treated as such.

Thus, the closure of the bandit episode is an allegory of the foundation of the state as both a power holder and a conceptual community defined in letrado terms. The first movement is the expropriation of organized violence from society. This happens in three concurrent moments: the destruction of the bandit gang, Perico's selling of the pistols to the lieutenant of the Acordada, and the fearsome "theater of law" provided by Januario's corpse. (Januario is a Creole, *gente de razón*, like the most fearsome bandits of the independence era, the Anayas and the Villagráns [Archer 1982, 74], so in his case the "theater of law" has an even more sobering effect.)

The ambush that destroys the band (5:44–46) is the fatal blow that the state, in the form of the Acordada, deals to the only form of organized violence that actively competes with it throughout the narrative. (Violence pervades the entire narrative, but its perpetrators never become an effective, well-organized armed body, except in the case of the bandit gang, which competes with the state for armed control of the highways.) Even though the band as an organization is destroyed, it symbolically survives in Aguilita's pistols, the weapons provided for Perico's first (and ultimately failed) incursion in the field (5:42). Perico, understanding the risks of carrying the guns, disposes of them in a not so insignificant fashion: he sells them to an officer of the Acordada with whom he happens to share an evening and who fell "in love" with them at first sight (5:53). The purchase signifies the transfer from private to public ownership of a commodity that the state covets: not the pistols, but the violence of which the pistols are a metonymy. As with most dealings between society and the state, the transfer masks itself as a coercion-free transaction (in this case, a market transaction). However, it is not a coercion-free transaction, since it is essentially Perico's fear that motivates it.

Immediately after this transaction, Perico is faced with the spectacle of the enthronement of state law. At a crossroads, Perico sees a body hanging from a tree:

> I approached [the body] in order to examine it more carefully; but what would be my reaction when I realized that that deformed corpse was my old and unfortunate friend Januario? My hair stood on end, my blood curdled; I could not speak, as if my tongue was knotted within my throat; my forehead was drenched with

cold sweat, and having lost my nerve, I was about to fall from the horse. . . . But God wanted to help my fainting spirit, and making an extraordinary effort of bravery, I tried to recover myself little by little from the bewilderment that oppressed me. . . .

I confirmed more and more my resolution to change my ways, and seeking to profit from the lessons that the world gave me and reap a moral benefit from men's evil ways and adversities. (5:53–54)

This body is not just a memento mori, in the style of the *Danza de la muerte*, where Death addresses the living, reminding them of the inevitable and universal fact of death. This corpse has a precise and urgent meaning, and Perico is able to "read" the message that the state (not Death) has written on Januario's body, which has been punished in the customary fashion (Archer 1982, 66; Van Young 2001, 168). He is even able to gloss it in the sonnet-epitaph that he writes "before the law," on the fatal tree from which the corpse was hanging: "But today, from that pole from which you are hanging / You advise me to mend my ways. And I notice / That I should listen to you, because you satisfy me / Preaching well from beyond the grave" (5:55).[9] The state publicly exerts and exhibits its violence upon the body of the bandit, and it is this violence that interpellates and creates the citizen as a disciplinary subject. Not surprisingly, immediately after this episode Perico enters into a round of church-sponsored spiritual exercises, thus drawing the episode to an end, whereby Perico is completely redeemed (5: 57ff.). But the closure of the bandit episode has an added significance. It is the point where the narrative space closes itself, where the anonymity of the colonial metropolis becomes a familiar space and, therefore, all the characters reunite and Don Pedro finds Roque, Pelayo, Anselmo, Andrés, Jacobo, Tadeo, the Chinese, and Don Antonio.

The bandit society is then the image of an alternative society without a lettered city at its center. This, for Fernández de Lizardi, equals a society without a center. The bandit society is one in which the sacredness of the written word is absent, the institutions that rely upon the written word are absent, and alternative, subaltern knowledge rules. Banditry, for Lizardi, is the image of a society organized and ruled from below, *ex nihilo*, lacking the principles that lie at the very origin of the process of state making. Clearly, even though Fernandez de Lizardi's idea of the role of the letrados has changed from the immediate colonial paradigm, there are deep continuities in the way in which he still considers the letrados to be those who imagine the community and who define the meaning and criteria for belonging to said community. There is an emblematic scene that puts the bandit and the letrado face to face, in which the narration identifies the difficult position of letrados when faced with subaltern insurgency: when invited to join the gavilla, Perico tries (as usual) to talk his way out of the predicament, with classical quotations and brilliant arguments. But the sarcasm of the bandit cuts to the chase: "Well, Perico, look at how much you know! But with all your knowledge you are naked. We know much more than you do" (5:30). This presentation of a society where the written word has no privileged status is far from the liberating utopia of a return to nature. Quite to the contrary, it serves as the reductio ad absurdum of any political project that relies on agency from below: it is a condemning depiction of the "Other rebellion" (Van Young 2001) that was threatening to shake the foundations not only of colonial order but also of letrado order as such. By destroying this "Other rebellion" in effigy (Januario's rotten corpse hanging from a tree), Fernández de Lizardi "closes the alternative paths within modernity that had refused to concede their powers to state authority" (Hardt and Negri 2000, 96).

This answers the first question asked at the beginning of this chapter: why could Perico not become a bandit? As we saw, a society without written law at its center is not a society but the diabolic mimicry of one. Active participation in it would have irreversibly polluted Perico. So the narrative walks a thin line. Perico cannot be a bandit, but he has to be a witness to bandit society in order to assess the fate of this experiment. Like European ethnographers and travelers who found themselves stranded among "primitives" (and it is important to remember how nineteenth-century narrative was predicated upon an ethnographic matrix [González Echevarría 1990; Pratt 1992]), Perico has to witness the horrors of incest and cannibalism. But he cannot indulge in these forbidden pleasures. Doing so would preclude any possibility for a narrative, since he would have "gone native" and quit his privileged locus of enunciation: he would have ceased to be a letrado, a westerner, an ethnographer, and he would have monstrously colluded with this Other.[10] Perico cannot cross the line into banditry, because if he were to do so, there would be no "redemptive" moment, no fatherhood, and no narration. The legal status of bandits emphasized that they were beyond redemption, on the other side of a line across which one could not return; they were unable to seek sanctuary in churches (MacLachlan 1974,

70–71) and were unable to benefit from routine royal pardons, just like regicides, sodomites, blasphemers, and priest killers (MacLachlan 1974, 82). But Perico also has to witness the demise of bandit society at the hands of the Acordada, since it is this "pedagogy of terror" (Salvatore 2001, 310) that will transform all living experiences into transmissible letrado cultural capital. The lessons that he can impart to his offspring have as a condition the lesson that the state taught him through Januario, which transformed the raw experience of the Outside (banditry) into letrado wisdom.

The presentation of banditry in Fernández de Lizardi's novel shows an impossible alternative to the colonial order: the alternative that the popular insurgency was proposing to Mexico, the danger of sovereignty from below that made Lizardi share Iturbide's project of "independence from above" (Anna 1990). The bandit gang is thus Lizardi's take on "subaltern consciousness" as an active challenge to the state, a commentary on José María Luis Mora's assertion on the risks of sovereignty ("Discurso sobre la independencia del Imperio Mexicano") when it is reappropriated by the constituent power: "The ignorant populace, persuaded that it is sovereign, and lacking precise ideas that would determine, in an exact fashion, the meaning of the word 'nation,' has come to believe that any gathering of individuals belonging to the human race, without other qualities or circumstances, should be called 'nation.' These are erroneous concepts, which are bound to fan the flames of discord and civil war!" (Mora quoted in Palti 1997, 105).

2 *Facundo*

Banditry and the State as Nomadic War Machine

> En la República Argentina han sido innumerables los ejemplos de gauchos
> alzados y montaraces; encarnan, puede decirse, la historia del país en sus
> primeras décadas de vida independiente.
>> Paul Groussac, "Calandria," *El viaje intelectual*, 1904

> En una carta a un amigo de infancia en 1832, tuve la indiscreción de llamar
> bandido a Facundo Quiroga. Hoy están todos los argentinos, la América y la
> Europa, de acuerdo conmigo.
>> Domingo Faustino Sarmiento, *Recuerdos de provincia*, 1850

In 1833 a young Charles Darwin (1809–1882) visited Juan Manuel de
Rosas's army campaign headquarters by the Río Colorado. Rosas, Argentine
strongman from the late 1820s until 1852, was engaged in a war against the
Indians that would earn him, in the eyes of his all-too-ready admirers, the title "Hero of the Desert." It was indeed a milestone in his career as stern ruler
and "Restorer of the Laws." The caudillo impressed Darwin favorably. In his
travelogue, Darwin called him an "extraordinary character" who seemed to
be using his influence over the country "to its prosperity and advancement"
(1839, 65). This sympathy did not extend to the caudillo's men, "a villain-
ous, banditti-like army . . . never before collected together" (64, 91). This
gang-like assortment of "mixed breed, between Negro, Indian and Spaniard"
(64) was not devoid of a somewhat terrifying charm: "[A]t night, when [the
banditti-like soldiers in the Rosas army] were sitting around the fire, and
playing at cards, I retired to view such a Salvatore Rosa scene. They were
seated under a low cliff, so that I could look down upon them; around the
party were lying dogs, arms, remnants of deer and ostriches; and their long
spears were stuck in the turf. Further in the dark background, their horses
were tied up, ready for any sudden danger" (100). The analogy between
Rosas's army and a gang of bandits is for Darwin little more than a commonplace literary hyperbole well suited to the exotic surroundings.[1] Plus, by
quoting Salvatore Rosa, the seventeenth-century painter whose images of
bandits and forbidding landscapes were well known, Darwin was linking the
Argentine rural scene to European classical art. The bandit metaphor served

as a representational device that, far from removing the gauchos from Western intelligibility, rendered them easily accessible for an educated European public. Both Darwin and *El periquillo sarniento*'s Perico were witnesses to the terrors and lurid charms of banditry. Darwin was more fortunate, however. Unlike Perico, who experienced a world turned upside down, where his condition of letrado ensured him a subaltern status and put him on the verge of losing himself, Darwin could keep both a material and an intellectual distance from banditry. As an object of contemplation and reflection, banditry did not pose political or epistemological problems for him.

For his part, Domingo Faustino Sarmiento probed much deeper and in a more dramatic fashion into the meaning of the analogy between the bandit gang and the rosista army. Unlike Darwin, Sarmiento was not detached from the scene of violence and abjection. He was indeed the *victim* of that violence, as shown in the episode of the vicious beating he suffered at the hands of the Mazorqueros that opens (and originates) *Facundo* (1845, 4–5). In *El periquillo sarniento*, the letrado made a descent into the hell of outlawry without being interdicted (outlawed) himself. This experience of the limits (without *le pas au-delà*) was the cornerstone of the formation as father/proprietor/letrado that would enable Don Pedro to put together an image of a social whole (the autobiographical narrative itself) from a position of epistemological privilege. In *Facundo*, to the contrary, the letrado is interdicted and expulsed ("abjected"): after the beating, Sarmiento is forced into exile. This banishment is more than a reversal in political fortune: it is an incomprehensible scandal since interdiction equals a loss of epistemological privilege in which the tables are turned and the criminal association (the Mazorca) has the power of both interdiction and interpretation.[2]

Facundo, understood as an urgent attempt to explain the Sphinx-like Argentine reality (see the book's foreword, "Advertencia del autor"), had to conjure up the ghost of the outlaw (Facundo) who had the key to the answer that Sarmiento lacked ("You know the answer to the secret: reveal it to us!" [7]). The outlaw knows the solution to the enigma of the nature and forms of the (dis)organization of rural violence, which is crucial in explaining how a law without power (the Unitarist Constitution of 1827) was overcome by a power without law (Rosas ruling for almost two decades with the Suma del Poder Público [Sum of All Public Powers] and no Constitution). An explanation of the origins and development of rural outlawry would in turn explain the scandal of barbarism. The scandal is the fact that outlawry had been able to accomplish a task that civilization could not even begin: a "Unitarist government" (203) of national scope.

The bandit trope is the discursive device through which Sarmiento was able to fully develop the doctrinaire and political consequences of the distinction between civilization and barbarism, the cornerstone of the mythology of exclusion (Shumway 1991, x) upon which the imagined community called Argentina was built.[3] The bandit trope is therefore a privileged tool through which Sarmiento defined and positioned his Others, from the monster José Gervasio de Artigas (Sarmiento 1885) to the monster Ángel Vicente Peñaloza (1867, 400) to the monster Juan Manuel de Rosas (1845, 9). In this effort, he would have a long and illustrious Latin American following, since more than three-quarters of a century later he would still inform many scholars' visions of banditry from the earlier Euclides da Cunha to Pedro Baptista (*Cangaceiros do nordeste,* published in 1929) and Gustavo Barroso (*Heróes e bandidos,* published in 1918).[4]

For Sarmiento, the bandit metaphor had a specific epistemological value that allowed him to go beyond the limitations of the Unitarist exiles when conceiving the Rosas phenomenon. Still trapped in an aesthetic-political imagery pertaining to a classical era, these exiles conceived Rosas as a bloody tyrant who prolonged King Fernando VII's rule (and style). As such, Rosas was perceived as an heir to Spanish despotism and depicted as the "murderer" of the May Revolution, a popular allegory at the time.[5] The imagery was rather predictable, though politically ineffectual. For Sarmiento, Rosas's triumph was not the enthronement or the restoration of a tyrant (as in the case of the European Restoration)—an analogy that had many followers in liberal historiography, as late as José Ingenieros's *La evolución de las ideas argentinas*—but the appearance of a completely new phenomenon.[6] Sarmiento's Rosas was a monster, "half-woman," "half-tiger" (1845, 9), not only because of his supposed cowardice or the lust for blood that, for Sarmiento, characterized his rule, but because he was a "Sphinx" that posed "the riddle of national organization" (9). "Monstrosity" here names the epistemological difficulty of conceiving a particular system of domination: one that is anarchical but that exerts an unheard-of micropolitical power over the population (the terror, the red badge, the ever present picture of the Restaurador, the constant fear of denunciation, the theatrical style of retaliation against enemies). It is an authoritarian system, but at the same time

"until the end of the Colony brigands were not perceived as a serious threat to a social order whose center was in the city and that paid little (if any) attention to what was happening in rural areas" (Fradkin 2005, 4), by the 1810s the situation began to change. On the one hand, the new pressures exerted on rural areas by the urban revolutionary elite, as well as the reluctance by rural folk to mobilize resources such as cattle or to be mobilized themselves to fight the elite wars, revived an old perception among the elite that rural Buenos Aires had a truly lawless nature (for this perception, see Rodríguez-Molas 1968; Slatta 1980, 1983; Fradkin 2005). On the other hand, the nature of the conflicts made the differences between professional robber and marauder, the federal *montonero,* the peaceful *paysano* who—drafted against his will—opted for the life of a deserter, and the gaucho exerting his ancestral rights to unchecked mobility and the slaughter of unclaimed cattle and horses almost impossible to ascertain. This confusion was intensified because in many cases the same subject successively or simultaneously occupied several of the aforementioned positions before the law.

In this context, the "retroversion of sovereignty to the people" for which the patrician Jacobin Mariano Moreno pleaded took a very different meaning. "People" ceased to be a euphemism for the Creole elite and acquired far more threatening meanings, as Esteban Echeverría would acknowledge years later in *Ojeada retrospectiva* (1846) and superbly embody in fictional form in *El matadero* (1871).[8] *Caudillismo* was the name applied to this phenomenon that haunted the letrado imagination for decades to come, since it implied a departure from the undivided constitutionalist faith of early revolutionary times and a challenge to the elite leadership of the new order.[9]

Initially, the proper name given to this phenomenon was José Gervasio de Artigas. For Sarmiento, Artigas was the first and foremost in a less-than-illustrious "lineage of bandits." There was even a price on his head; a decree dated February 11, 1814, issued by Director of the United Provinces Gervasio Posadas, offered a reward of six thousand pesos for Artigas, dead or alive. From *Facundo,* in which banditry was a product of the peculiar lay of the land, to Sarmiento's later work (in which banditry had a racial component since it was one more unfortunate consequence of Indian heritage), Artigas was above all a bandit (1885, 210, 211, 215, 217–20) and a true product of the preeminent bandit territory, the Banda Oriental (1885, 131, 204–206), where "the virus of general confusion" originated and contaminated the rest of the area (1885, 206). Prominent in this lineage were Francisco Ramírez,

Facundo Quiroga, Juan Manuel de Rosas, Ángel Vicente Peñaloza, and Ricardo López Jordán.

Sarmiento traced a homogeneous line that went from Artigas to Peñaloza. However, caudillos had widely divergent visions with regard to key questions. Land tenure was the most telling example. Whereas Artigas's *Reglamento de tierras* (1815) privileged the distribution of land plots and cattle to free blacks, zambos, Indians, and poor paysanos, Rosas favored the system of the large ranch (*estancia*), the foundation of the socioeconomic order of modern Argentina (Lynch 1981). Artigas, Jordán, and Peñaloza in fact considered their leadership an alliance with poor rural populations or small landowners (de la Fuente 2000). Rosas and Estanislao López, who never forgot that their legitimacy was based among these classes, were still staunch defenders of the rights of the large landowners (being large landowners themselves), and in most cases they opposed the traditional vindications of rural populations (Salvatore 2003). In fact, the "immortal brigand" Rosas was a formidable hunter of cattle rustlers and vagrants (Lynch 1981).

Like Pancho Villa a century later, José Gervasio de Artigas is indeed a most striking example of bandit-turned-legitimate sovereign. Like Villa, Artigas began his career as a social bandit, and during his outlaw stint he acquired superb knowledge of the terrain as well as unique martial skills that served him well. It was also during this time that Artigas built enduring relationships with the Indians and paysanos who populated the frontier, and it was when he acquired the enormous prestige that made him an invaluable ally for the Buenos Aires junta during the initial struggles of the independence wars, as well as a fearsome enemy later. From the perspective of the urban elites of Buenos Aires and Montevideo, his outlaw career was an enduring badge of infamy. In fact, it was responsible for the beginning of the "Black Legend" that lasted well into the second half of the nineteenth century. The cornerstone of this legend in Uruguay was Feliciano Sáinz de Cavia, whose pamphlet published in 1818, *El Protector nominal de los pueblos libres, D. José Artigas, clasificado por el Amigo del Orden,* exposed Artigas as the "New Attila." This pamphlet was followed by Francisco Berra's *Bosquejo histórico de la República Oriental del Uruguay.* Sarmiento draws upon the negative image promulgated by the "Black Legend":

> Who was Artigas?, many contemporaries have asked themselves, astonished at his power, without asking who gave him that power.

> Artigas . . . is a brigand [*salteador*], nothing less, nothing more. Thirty years of practice murdering or stealing by himself, murdering or capturing or smuggling on behalf of the Spanish government, giving doubtful titles to command the group of Indians stirred by a political revolution, and among whom is engraved the name of Artigas as a bandit chief, of Artigas as [the] person in charge of exterminating them, of Artigas as the caudillo of an entire country in arms. (Sarmiento 1885, 215)

Unlike Pancho Villa, Artigas did not enter the outlaw life by fleeing an encounter with an unjust system that preyed upon the downtrodden. To the contrary, he belonged to a traditional family of the Banda Oriental (if something like that can be said of an area of recent settlement: his grandfather was among the original settlers of Montevideo). He voluntarily abandoned the career to which he seemed to be destined (the church) to engage in rural labor in the frontier area that lay between the Spanish and the Portuguese dominions (this voluntary option for the countryside and its inhabitants would later be the foundation of the Artigas cult). Smuggling was prominent among those rural endeavors because the sale of cattle between the two colonies was tightly regulated. (This regulation was nominal, however, since illegal commerce was rampant; hence the enduring image of the Banda Oriental as bandit country [Storni 1997, 154].)[10] Artigas became the chief of what at times was a very large band of smugglers (around two hundred, according to some sources), and, as in any frontier pursuit of that kind, he had routine clashes with state officials intent upon disrupting smuggling. Following a well-known pattern of outlaw becoming lawman, he became toward the end of the eighteenth century captain of the Blandengues, who were in charge of maintaining rural order. His taking on this role did not mean there had been a fundamental reversal of his affiliations or procedures. The initial core of Blandengues that Artigas recruited comprised bandits, smugglers, and vagrants. During his stint as Protector de los Pueblos Libres, that core continued to be a close ally, at least when it came to military decisions.

Also unlike Villa, who has been charged (perhaps justly) with lacking a national vision, Artigas had a clear vision of what he wanted for the United Provinces of the Río de la Plata (and for the constituent Banda Oriental) in political, economic, and cultural terms. Artigas was a staunch proponent of a faithful version of federalism, in which each political unit (provinces and pueblos within provinces, either cities, towns, hamlets, or Indian villages) would be endowed with true sovereignty, not subordinated to the dictates or centralist aspirations of either Buenos Aires, the main city-port of the former viceroyalty, or Montevideo, the main city of the Banda Oriental (Frega 1998, 102). By the same token, he envisioned an economic arrangement that was not dictated by the economic imperatives of the city-port. He proposed integration into international commerce by prioritizing the development of indigenous industries (both manufactured goods and agricultural products), in particular those of the interior provinces and the provinces of the Paraná/Uruguay basin, his base of power (Reyes Abadie 1974, 220). Finally, he conceived a rule that was sustained by the rural populations with full citizenship, whose cultural capital was not to be suppressed but organically incorporated as a cornerstone of the national project (Torres 1997, 2000; Frega 1998). Of course, these three postulates had as their core Artigas's aforementioned agrarian project, which envisioned a wholesale and equitable distribution of land among the poor inhabitants of the Banda Oriental so that they could put it to productive use, thus avoiding both land concentration and land misuse (Chumbita 1999).

Artigas's insurgency brought to the fore what for the liberal mind was to be the infamous *montonera* and the particular form of war waged by Río de la Plata "bandits." Indeed, the word montonera had its origins in the Banda Oriental during the independence wars. According to Daniel Granada's *Vocabulario rioplatense razonado* (1890), the groups of gauchos among which Artigas lived were called *montones,* hence the name montonera, which was applied to the cavalry groups that followed the caudillo (Granada quoted in Benarós 1961, 32–33). Historian Ariel de la Fuente seems to agree with this origin of the word (1998, 276).

For Sarmiento the conception of the montonera as the outlaw's natural mode of organization served the purpose of genetically explaining the scandalous fact that the "immortal bandit [Rosas], the estancia owner of Buenos Aires" (1845, 67), made the montonera into a "system of legislation applied to letrado society" (67). This in turn would allow Sarmiento to differentiate between the state proper (associated with the written word and hence, civilization) and the false state (associated with oral culture; hence, barbarism).[11] Through the perceived alliance between the rural multitude and the caudillo, and their descending upon the city, for Sarmiento the state itself became a montonera, a bandit gang, and a nomadic war machine (Deleuze and Guattari 1980). In both Lizardi's and Sarmiento's cases the bandit trope served to depict the phenomenon of rural lawlessness. While in *El periquillo sarniento* Perico the rogue moved from the city to the countryside—where he found banditry as an image of insurgency and as an alternative mode of social arrangement that threatened the letrado order symbolically but not materially—in Sarmiento the countryside has moved into the city to forcibly replace urban social arrangements. Sarmiento wants to explain the fearful reality of what in Fernández de Lizardi was—up until that point— only a threat. Moreover, while Darwin draws a clear difference between the statesman (Rosas) and his "banditti-like army," in Sarmiento both instances are just nuances of the same phenomenon.

In *Facundo,* "bandit" is the name for a *contradictio in terminis:* the very expression "rosista state" as a political oxymoron and a fearful reality that Sarmiento cannot deny.[12] Allow me to clarify my assertion of this "becoming-gang" of the state. In "Decreto del gobernador de Salta alzándose con el poder" (1851) Sarmiento recounts how Governor Saravia established, without either the consent or the knowledge of Salta's lawmakers, an extraordinary tax on foreign imports. Saravia also extended his own enjoyment of extraordinary powers (among them, the power to levy taxes). The levying of taxes is traditionally an act of the state. But for Sarmiento it is better described as an act of banditry because it is violent, arbitrary, and unchecked by any of the mechanisms or institutions established by the law. He also considers it banditry because it extracts resources from a society that did not validate—through its representatives—either the taxation itself or the powers that gave the authority to establish it:

> The second, third, and fourth articles of the famous decree can be summarized as follows: all imports from Chile and Bolivia are free for pillaging.
>
> The first and fifth articles are reduced to this: the governor, not having the acquiescence of the current Legislative body, assumes power and shall kill anybody who resists his will.
>
> These two decrees are as old as the world. They have been put in practice by men that put themselves outside the law, bandits and highway robbers.
>
> The *alzado* declares that a 25 percent tax will be paid up front in cash at the moment of the commodities being introduced, and the confiscation of the goods and discretionary penalties are to those who introduce commodities while trying to dodge this arbitrary arrangement. It is the classic "Your money or your life!" [¡*La bolsa o la vida!*] of all highwaymen! (Sarmiento 1851, 221)[13]

In his celebrated work, *Las catilinarias* (1880–1882), Juan Montalvo, another great Latin American prose writer of the nineteenth century, did the same thing as Sarmiento when he tagged the dictator Ignacio Ventimilla as a brigand chief. But Sarmiento went further than just dubbing the ruler a robber-chieftain. Were he just doing that, Sarmiento's trope would presuppose a split between a violent, illegitimate state and a passive, victimized civil society that the statesman/robber dispossessed through force. But Rosas's case is more complex since he was not a tyrant but an undoubtedly popular ruler (and Sarmiento knew better than to deceive himself about this). Thus, Sarmiento uses the bandit trope to condemn popularity as a source of legitimacy outside the law. For the rosista regime, legitimacy was indeed one of its main concerns (Myers 1995, 19; Salvatore 2003), and the law (Rosas being the "Restorer of the Laws") was a powerful signifier in rosista discourse (Myers 1995, 77). Federalism claimed Republican values for itself and blamed the Unitarists for unlawfulness, as shown in *Rasgos de la vida pública de S.E. el Sr. Brigadier General D. Juan Manuel de Rosas,* commissioned and published in 1842 by the Buenos Aires Chamber of Representatives. In this document, an event outside the law (the execution of Manuel Dorrego in 1828) serves as the founding event of rosista mythology. Through the trope of banditry (and its privileged military form, the montonera) as the specific mode of rosista domination (the *"sistema americano"*), Sarmiento is able to cancel rosista legitimacy because his use of the bandit trope denies the federalist population of the countryside and of the *orillas* the status of "the people" (and of "general will" in the Rousseauistic sense). Sarmiento demotes the population to a gang. Without turning to the bandit trope, Echeverría does the same in *El matadero* when he denies the federalists the status of people and depicts them as *la chusma,* a semihuman mob. Banditry takes the place of civil society in the desert of the pampas (it is the simulacrum of civil society that the pampas generate), and by this, the entire state-formation process in Buenos Aires is vitiated and thus nullified. This process duplicates the collapse of civil society into the discursive realm of the state that was attempted and, to a certain extent, accomplished by Rosas (see Myers 1995).

Sarmiento's thought had a notorious romantic imprint. In romantic Europe, however, the genealogy of the nation-state was imaginarily traced to a polity, the *Volk*, as a "principle of cultural unity of the body politic" (Svampa 1994, 89). Sarmiento (in a typical postcolonial predicament) posed the very destruction (material or cultural) of that *Volk* as a condition for the birth of the nation-state. Sarmiento identified legitimacy in the exertion of violence and authority with a law that was undoubtedly associated with the order of the letter. Thus, he denied the principle of "popular sovereignty" put forward by Moreno (because of the risks of which rosista rule was a powerful reminder) and replaced it with the sovereignty of a literate class with an exclusive relationship to European values and knowledge. The first step in denying the *Volk* as the principle of cultural and political homogeneity and, concurrently, as the self-legitimation of the man of letters as mediating instance between European knowledge and the knowledge of the other (Ramos 1989, 19) is the invention of the desert as an absolute beginning and, simultaneously, as a void of society.[14]

This fable of the pampas as a desert and of the desert as the breeding ground of an unruly crowd of *gauchos malos* is a politics of the landscape (Area and Parodi 1994; Andermann 2000) at the service of an idea of the city as the only source of state building and the exclusive seat of sovereignty. It is supported by the link between material necessity and the birth of the moral-political community.[15] In the pampas, however, the situation was rather anomalous: "men are scattered without forming a society," and the exceptional qualities of soil and water, the superabundance of cattle, and the temperate climate created a widely scattered population "free from any necessity" (Sarmiento 1845, 57).[16] These circumstances, for Sarmiento, were a dubious blessing that voided any need for commerce, industry, or education and prevented any shared interests or enterprises. With these circumstances, society as a collective venture disappears in its most advanced form, the municipality (31), and even its most degraded form, the tribe, in which at least a principle of authority and a traditional moral code survive (30–31).[17] In the pampas, so as to ensure the somewhat productive occupation of the land, it "has been necessary to dissolve any association" (30). "Society has completely disappeared" (31), and in its place "a monstrous kind of association" has appeared, a "nonsociety" where "any type of government is impossible: the municipality does not exist, law cannot be enforced, and civil and penal judges have no means to catch criminals" (31). This nonsociety lacked a state primarily because it lacked a civil society that would have made such a state necessary; the only place where people gathered or at least shared the same physical space was the general store (*pulpería*). For Sarmiento this was an "assembly without [any] goal of a public nature and without any social interest" (58). The pulpería was not a significant market for capital goods, for labor or commodities, because the gaucho had all the necessary skills to provide for almost all his personal or work needs, and he had cattle and nature to provide all necessary resources (57). But if the pulpería was not a marketplace, neither was it an agora in which necessity-free men would have disputed values or priorities. The pulpería was a place of reunion, but at the same time it was a "disassociation" (56) lacking both *res publica* (31, 35) and a "moral collective body" in Rousseau's terms. Without association or common good there are no markers upon which to build a reputation or to tell one man from the next (work skills, money, virtue—all of these are meaningless in the pampas). The only prowess is courage, and therefore the knife fight and the unmotivated duel are the sole base upon which to build a reputation in rural society.

The pulpería as a microcosm of the pampas is an accumulation of singularities without "organic solidarity" or division of labor: a multitude. Thus, we find again the motif that we saw in the work of Fernández de Lizardi: a group that is a diabolic simulacrum of the real body politic. In this unique pseudorurality, common life is regulated by a single value: violence as the foundation of an oral reputation.[18] As Sarmiento explains,

> It is not my intention to persuade anybody that murder and crime had always been a ladder for promotions. However, we can count in the thousands the brave men who have ended up as unknown bandits; and we can count in excess of several hundreds the ones who owe their position to those acts. In all tyrannized societies great natural gifts go to waste in crime; the Roman *genio* that conquered the world is nowadays the terror of the Pontino lakes, and the Zumalacárregui and the Spanish Minas are found by the hundreds in Sierra Leona [*sic*]. Man has a need to develop his strengths, his capabilities and ambitions, and where there is no legitimate means to do so, he creates his own world with its morals and its laws, and he takes pleasure in showing that he has been born a Napoleon or a Caesar. (1845, 59)

In the tradition of Western political thought, from Aristotle to Hegel, the state is where man becomes moral through his internalization of Right, what Hegel called "the ethical state" (Melossi 1990, 46–48). It is within or through the state that morals are imposed as the rule of law. The state depends on an instance in which interior sovereignty is located (the de jure aspect of sovereignty) and from which the coercive power of the state stems (the de facto aspect of sovereignty). In the path of the United States' model (the one that Sarmiento prefers, just like most early Latin American constitutionalists), state sovereignty is vested in the constitution. In the countryside, however, the formation of state institutions cannot hide its violent nature (without even the fiction of consensus implied in the constitution), and the state does not appear as a differentiated sphere, which is one of its essential features in modern societies (Oszlak 1982, 19). Therefore, the state is a simulacrum, a gradation on a singular scale of violence. The judge is a gaucho malo himself (somebody who excelled at the pulpería knife duel, which served as the foundation of this mimicry of the public sphere) leading other gauchos malos: caudillo and/or malefactor are variations of the same identity in a continuum of relations based on force: "In this society, . . . in which the culture of the spirit is useless as well as impossible, where municipal affairs do not exist; where the public good is a word without meaning, because there is no public, the man eminently endowed makes an effort to stand out for himself and adopts for that the means and ways that he finds available for him. The gaucho, then, will be a criminal or a caudillo, according to the direction that the winds blow" (Sarmiento 1845, 60). Local authority does not arise out of an instance that eliminates or expropriates private violence in order to create a commonwealth, only to return it under the objective form of authority and right (as postulated in Hobbes's *Leviathan*). Quite to the contrary:

> *To repress heartless people, judges even more heartless are needed.* . . . Before any other quality, valor is needed: the terror and awe that his name inspires are the most powerful of the punishments that he applies. The judge is, naturally, some famous [gaucho malo] *of old times,* who has been reduced by age and family to a more orderly life. It goes without saying that the justice that he administers is completely arbitrary: his consciousness and his passions guide him, and his sentences are without appeal. . . . The judge makes himself obeyed because of his reputation for fearful audacity, his authority, his judgments without due process, his sentences being supported on a "because I order so," and his punishments invented by himself. (61, emphasis added)

This was the order of the pampas, compared to the order of the cities. For centuries, these two orders coexisted in mutual ignorance, since this coexistence of two different societies (61)—city and countryside, the rule of law and the rule of the strongest—was also a coexistence of two different temporalities: the nineteenth and the thirteenth centuries (55). This parallelism was, however, severely compromised by the independence wars, when the city legalized the rustic authority of the caudillo. Thus, the city sanctioned a power holder that it did not create; it acknowledged a form of legitimacy heterogeneous to legality. This legitimacy finally superseded legality. That is why all caudillos, according to Sarmiento, were originally rural commanders (*comandantes de campaña*) appointed from the city. Artigas is a perfect example since, in Sarmiento's own words, he was a "fearsome smuggler until 1804 [*sic*], the year in which the civil authorities from Buenos Aires gained him for their own cause and made him serve . . . the same authorities that he had fought right up to that time" (66).

Facundo Quiroga, on his part, entered political life by mediating the feud between the Ocampo and Dávila clans (93). And of course, Juan Manuel de Rosas was named by Buenos Aires to be *comandante de la campaña,* a position from which he launched his political-military career (61).[19] The analogy that Sarmiento offers for this "state suicide" is quite telling: "In the same fashion, the papal authority enters into negotiations and makes concessions to bandits, to whom it gives official positions in Rome, thus stimulating brigandage [*vandalaje*] and creating a safe future for it. In the same fashion, the Sultan gave to Mehemet-Alí the rank of Egyptian pasha, only so that he would be recognized as the hereditary king, in exchange for not being overthrown himself" (61).

By sanctioning as political authority what was previously outlaw leadership, the city elevates banditry to the stage of national politics (61). (Sarmiento emphasizes that there is no transition between rural culture and montonera life.) Over time, the montonera infuses the army with its spirit and exerts the monopoly of violence. This transition occurs not because of a mandate of law but because the montonera is "a representation of physical force and of everything that the plebes had in the way of strength, everything that the instincts of the masses could offer in terms of belligerence and aggression, everything that popular delinquency had in the way of audacity and impulsiveness in blood crimes" (Ramos-Mejía 1907, 106). The montonera does not put violence at the service of the constitution, the development of productive forces, or an increase in the population and social wealth; rather, the only aim of the montonera is mere ransacking.

So, for Sarmiento the knife duel as social interaction is the foundation of the montonera and, in turn, of the rosista state. This concept is not completely unheard of in nineteenth-century political theory. Carl von Clausewitz in his classic, *On War,* conceived of war as a "duel on an extensive scale"

([1832], 101). The difference is that in Clausewitz, war is a means toward political ends.[20] For Sarmiento's Rosas, war is the end, and therefore, there is no difference between means and ends, as there is no difference (one carefully laid out by Clausewitz [121]) between people, army generals, and politicians. (Rosas conflated the three but not under the guise of the citizen in arms.) This conflation goes to the core of Sarmiento's characterization of rosismo: Rosas's state is a nomadic war machine that springs from a criminal association: "The Argentine Republic is organized, today, as a war machine that cannot stop working, without annulling the power that has absorbed all social interests. Finished in the country, the war has already moved outside it" (Sarmiento 1845, 233). As Ricardo Salvatore explains (2003), the rosista state was indeed organized around war needs, and it exerted constant pressure on the countryside, extracting manpower, cattle, and resources. ("The true industry of the Tyranny was the war budget" [Sarmiento quoted in Salvatore 2001, 46].) This impression was further confirmed by travel writers such as William MacCann, Francis Bond Head, and Charles Darwin. Juan Bautista Alberdi, on his part, stated in *El crimen de la guerra*, "In spite of its unique and happy uniformity, South America is the classic land of war, to a degree that it is now the normal state of affairs, a kind of government, assimilated to such a degree with all aspects of its current life, that no one even conceives of the fact that war could be a crime" (1870, 237).

The association between banditry and nomadism appears in *Facundo* with Quiroga's entrance into the narrative, when he is running away from the law because he has committed murder. In this episode, he inhabits an empty territory (79). To call the rosista army "nomadic," however, may seem erroneous, since its constituency was firmly rooted in Buenos Aires province and since it was sustained by an economic base that was far from nomadic. However, for Sarmiento "nomadic war" has two meanings that do not necessarily refer to aimless wandering. First, it is not a war whose meaning is conceived and directed from a city but one that inversely uses the city as a medium. Secondly, there is no goal of state building. Therefore, this war does not have an end and does not even belong to history as the narrative of the gradual coming-of-being of a political synthesis whose teleology is the liberal nation-state (Palti 2004, 529).

Rosas's animosity toward high-ranking veterans of the independence wars was well known and recorded by Sarmiento. Sarmiento understands this animosity not as a personal dislike but as the conflict between war-making and state-making principles. Quiroga's brief career in San Martín's army is an example. He could have ranked high among the glorious veterans of the independence war (like LaSalle or Paz), but he never ceased to be a gaucho malo whose take on war was essentially different. (The same is said of Artigas, who "could have been the Bolívar of the South had he given up his outlaw ways" [Sarmiento 1845, 17].) As Sarmiento explained (or imagined), Quiroga was not indifferent to the idea of independence from Spain, but he hated the disciplinary, soul-taming apparatus that was synonymous with the military: "The rebellious soul of Quiroga could not endure the yoke of discipline, the order that prevailed in the barracks, or the lengthy wait for promotions. He felt a call to be a leader, to appear by a single strike, to create for himself and by himself, in spite of civilized society and in hostility toward it, a career in his own fashion, *associating bravery and crime, government and disorganization*" (83–84, emphasis added).

Montonera and army are different when it comes to their respective efficacy. In Sarmiento's view, however, they could be distinguished according to the decisive political-semiotic problem of representation, that is, what each one represents and the way in which each one can be represented. Félix Frías points precisely to this when he quotes Víctor Cousin: "Give me the military history of a nation, and I can retrieve all other elements of its history" (1945, 44). Frías also claims to be able to tell the difference between two enemy camps in the civil war according to how they wage war.

According to Sarmiento, the montonera does not fight for anything but itself. The montonera (and it is important that the montonera as a whole be considered more important than its components, the individual fighters) engages in a type of war that is completely intransitive. This seeming self-interest is not related to greed or bellicose instincts but to the fact that the montonera as war machine conflates what for Clausewitz are distinctly separate entities: the political objective and the military target (Scavino 1993).[21] The rosista army wages war not in order to build an empire or even to crush its enemies but in order to continue waging war. At this point Sarmiento joins an old and established line of Western thought. Indeed, the man of war whose call to arms is not limited by the statesman and who does not fight to conquer states but rather uses the state as part of his own war machine is an old fantasy/anxiety in Western thought. Men of war from Attila, Tamerlane, and Tamburlaine to Wallenstein and Hitler have provoked such anxieties. (In "Anotación al 23 de agosto de 1944," Borges rooted this anxiety in the "mental and moral impossibility" of explaining such characters [1974, 1:102].) In several of these cases, such as Tamburlaine's, banditry was the trope used to explain this disturbing hubris in which the state apparatus of capture is captured itself (see Marlowe's *Tamburlaine the Great*, c.1590). The unrestrained war machine (of which Walter Benjamin's "great criminal" is a smaller-scale example) is the more threatening manifestation of what Benjamin called "law-making violence." The unrestrained war machine "emancipates" itself from the state and even shows how the supposed state privilege on the declaration of war is really dependent upon the nomadic war machines. This manifestation exposes the lack of "founding power" of the state act of "declaring war" as a secondary moment vis-à-vis the war machine.

The montonera does not represent either city or countryside: it does not defend locales or ideologies or systems of production outside the realm of the montonera itself. Sarmiento considered the inscription "Religión o Muerte" in Quiroga's banners preposterous, especially since, for him, Quiroga was a "*condottieri* [here we find Wallerstein again] who would defend a cause with the same ardor with which he would support the opposite one" (1867, 327). However, if the montonera does not represent the city or the country, neither does it lend itself to representation (depiction) through the forms of knowledge contained within the city (maps and manuals), since it fights using peasant knowledge and techniques. The montonera understands space in a different fashion than the regular army, since it does not have a "front" and a "rearguard" and since it does not defend a city, a defined perimeter, or a line of supplies. It is, to a certain extent, indifferent to the distinction between victory and defeat. Defeated in one place, it disbands according to a plan laid out beforehand, only to gather and reappear in another locale. A telling example of this baffling perception of the montonera by letrados is the different accounts of the same armed encounters that Sarmiento in *El Chacho* and Eduardo Gutiérrez in the Peñaloza saga offered. What for Sarmiento are continual defeats (according to him, the Chacho is a general who never won a single battle) are for Gutiérrez impeccable victories. The historical record is not severely compromised here, only the narrator's perspective. Gutiérrez narrates from the montonera's point of view, from which the notion of "battle" is quite irrelevant.

Even when it wins, the montonera never loses its local uprooted character (Sarmiento 1845,15). The bandit gang rules a territory, but only through military occupation and never as a true sovereignty that may expand its realm. Territorial sovereignty as a feature opposes traditional states (which exert an imperfect or null control outside of "core areas") to nation-states that ideally exert an effective and homogeneous control over all the extension of territory and any one of the citizens (Giddens 1985, 3–4). Because of this feature of territorial sovereignty, the state ceases to be surrounded by frontiers and comes to have borders with other sovereign states, which accounts for the birth of the nation-state as a necessary part of a system of nation-states. In the case of the rosista federation, however, the opposite is true: the city becomes a frontier and the desert overtakes the national territory (Sarmiento 1845, 185). Because of banditry, the distinction between city and countryside disappears; most of Sarmiento's biography of the adult Quiroga narrates the ransoms, the plundering, and the abuses to which Quiroga subjects the cities of the western and central provinces. Because of these abuses, the city loses its symbolic status and reverts to wilderness (*despoblado*). The bandit is he who robs in the wilderness. According to Sarmiento, Quiroga's montonera or gang *produces* the wilderness (like Attila's hordes).

"Banditry," when the term is applied to the federation system, names a policy of pillaging that is simultaneously erratic and systematic. The bandit gang is a system of sacking in order to extract resources from society, but its only argument for doing so is coercion, not the formation of a common-wealth (like the state that Sarmiento wishes). Tax collection is, in republican states, a limitation on property rights imposed by government. But this limitation, to begin with, acknowledges property rights as a necessary foundation of society. Plus, this limitation ensures its citizens the enjoyment of other rights, and it can only be used in a frame of juridical security. No taxation without representation: the classic formula of American liberal democracy subordinates the extractive capacity of the state to an acknowledgment of the rules of the political game that ensures representation and respect for common interests within civil society (Oszlak 1982, 20). The contributions to the federal cause, when forced and when not balanced by state services, become robbery, and the state reverts to its *Ur*-form: organized crime, banditry. (The flip side of this coin would be other acts of organized robbery such as the wholesale confiscations of Unitarist property whose subsequent distribution was used as a tool for building support in both city and country.)

In *Facundo,* the epitome of the modern army is General José María Paz. Unlike the montonera, the modern army is transcendent in the sense that the relationship between physical environment and conceptual filiation transcends the visible. The army fights in the countryside, but it does not belong to it. It belongs to the city, a place it represents. It does so not only because of the ideology or convictions of its officers and soldiers. The army is the city transformed into a war machine, with its maps, blueprints, battle formations, artillery calculations, supply lines, hierarchies, uniforms, and presses. The army is the law in motion, and in this sense, it has an importance far beyond the armed encounters: it is a veritable citizen producing machine (Centeno 2002).

Juan Lavalle, the *unitario* general who together with Lamadrid and Paz staunchly fought Rosas, made the fatal mistake of believing that the urban, civilized character of an army resided only in the political convictions of its members. He thought that he could fight for the city, but as a gaucho, so not only was his enterprise materially doomed (nobody fights better as gauchos than the gauchos themselves), but it was also doomed in symbolic terms. Lavalle's becoming a gaucho preempts the cause he was fighting for, since the cause was not only defended by the army but it was *embodied* in it. Something similar can be said of Lamadrid, whose blind bravery occluded the pursuit of a strategy, that is, fighting for the city as a citizen.

Facundo begins with the invoking of Quiroga's ghost. Ghosts roam the earth, gothic fiction teaches us, when they must tend to unfinished business. This unfinished business almost invariably has to do with the tragic circumstances of their deaths. So, if Quiroga is invoked, it is because the meaning of his assassination is unclear, and in this assassination lies the answer that Sarmiento looked for throughout *Facundo.* There are two possible meanings of this assassination, which eerily resembled a stagecoach robbery. On the one hand, Quiroga's assassination in Barranca Yaco could be the replacement that enabled the montonera to continue functioning as a nomadic war machine. Rosas, in Sarmiento's account, had Quiroga assassinated because the latter began to harbor constitutional beliefs and started the transition (like Vallenilla Lanz's democratic Caesar) from gaucho malo to statesman. "In *Facundo,* after having defeated the Unitarists and dispersed the Ph.D.s [*los doctores*], the idea he harbored before entering the fight reappears: his decision to make a bid for President and his belief in the need to put order in the affairs of the Republic" (Sarmiento 1845, 186).

On the other hand, Sarmiento gives an additional meaning to Quiroga's assassination. If Quiroga is considered a statesman, it is because the energies of the nomadic war machines were by definition finite, and sooner or later they would exhaust themselves. Thrown into an endless effort against Bolivia, Brazil, the Banda Oriental, Chile, England, and France, Rosas would eventually run out of men, or resources, ideologues, and alliances. This depletion would result in the return of civilization. "The gauchos, the plebes, and the gangsters support him? Well, he will extinguish them: his armies will devour them" (Sarmiento 1845, 235). So, another substitution is conceivable, not the one in which one Tamerlane (Quiroga) is replaced by another, shrewder and more clever (Rosas), but one in which the process that Rosas bloodily interrupted in Quiroga is allowed to run its full course and the bandit chieftain indeed becomes a statesman: his name was Justo José de Urquiza, in whom Sarmiento put his hopes for a time.

In reality, things would be much different. Exhausted in Buenos Aires (exhaustion that Sarmiento records in *Campaña en el ejército grande*), the montonera would rise again in its very cradle, La Rioja. And this time Sarmiento himself would be charged with finishing and bringing the provincial state to fruition. This time he would do so under the deep vacant gaze of a beheaded Peñaloza.

3 El Chacho
Banditry and Allegories of Legitimation

Los *lores* del desierto . . . pretendían ahora reivindicar con Rosas, que la mejor
constitución es el cuchillo aplicado a las gargantas por el bárbaro rudo de las
campañas, o las clases bajas organizadas en bandas armadas.
    Domingo Faustino Sarmiento, *El Chacho*, 1867

En Chile, el salteador es un salteador, por tal es tenido, que él mismo se da por
tal. De este lado de los Andes, el que tal profesión ejerce, es un salteador y un
partidario de algo o de alguien, con lo que toma aires de jefe de bando o caudillo.
    Domingo Faustino Sarmiento, "Muerte de Guayama," 1879

During his tenure as governor of Argentina's San Juan province
(1862–1864), Domingo Faustino Sarmiento commissioned some work on a
picture of Ángel Vicente Peñaloza (a.k.a. El Chacho, 1799–1863), taken several years before in Valparaíso, Chile. The work to be done on the picture of
Sarmiento's obstinate enemy (who was keeping the La Riojan countryside in
a constant state of rebellion in spite of the best efforts of liberal officials and
military forces allied with the *porteños*) consisted of some retouching in order to prepare it for international distribution. In the new version, a *chiripá*
and a sword would be added to Peñaloza's figure, and a horse would now appear in the background (Luna 1966, 172). Gaucho attire, a horse, and a rustic sword (but not the illustrious saber of the independence warriors), as opposed to European clothing and firearms, were for Sarmiento the features
by which barbarism became visible on the body (Hallstead 2005).[1] The gaucho malo depiction of one of the last genuine federalist peasant leaders and
one of the last bastions of federalism in retreat after the Battle of Pavón and
the political defection of Justo José de Urquiza in 1861 not only expelled
Peñaloza from the political field but made his struggle another instance of
rural criminality, mere *vandalaje* (the Americanism that Sarmiento preferred). It also deprived him of any political clout or citizen rights, and it
made him a body ready to experience the extremes of state retribution. This
meant, after his defeat in 1863, treacherous assassination, mutilation, be-
heading, and public exposure of his head on a pike (see Luna 1966, 182, for
a sympathetic account of Peñaloza's last moments). We have to admire the
sheer modernity of Sarmiento's operation with the photograph, which an-

ticipated some of the worst habits of twentieth- and twenty-first century totalitarian rulers as well as of democratic, security-obsessed ones.

Adding gaucho attire and a sword as indicators of outlawry and as metaphors for barbarism amounted to more than mere propaganda. From the
perspective of the letrado elite—whose spearhead was Sarmiento—this
technique was not deceptive. Ariel de la Fuente mentions how "the political
struggles of the 1860s allowed the provincial authorities, as well as the officials from the national government, to use the word 'gaucho' as a synonym
for 'bandit.'" He also mentions that using "gaucho" as synonym for bandit
was derived from the generalized Federalist sympathies of the rural populations. This equation reached a point where Unitarist authorities began to
use the word "bandit" to refer to all Federalists (de la Fuente 1998, 272).
Therefore, for Sarmiento to see and to make seen the bodies of the rural
folks as bandits and of Peñaloza as gang chief (1867, 301) so as to justify liberal disciplinary action or extermination is only to reunite the truth, as expressed in laws, with visibility. The falsification—as Sarmiento would have
termed it—had happened previously, when Chacho did not appear as a bandit but as a general of the national army (which Peñaloza legally was).[2]

El Chacho presents itself as a continuation and culmination of the historical drama whose opening scenes were enacted in *Facundo*. There is a striking
commonality: both are biographies of popular caudillos from their origins to
their bloody endings. Both are triggered by the assassination of the said out-
law-caudillo, and both revolve around the assassination as a reality and as a
symbol within the political conflicts of the time. However, there is a no less
dramatic difference: the assassination of Peñaloza belongs to Sarmiento's
record, not (like Facundo's) to his enemies'. Ordering or allowing (the historical record is not clear) Peñaloza's execution after his defeat and surrender in Olta was an act that followed Sarmiento the rest of his political career
(we can see its shadow in the 1875 senate debates, after Sarmiento's presidency, in which the topic was still hotly discussed). Even beyond the grave,
this act was Sarmiento's badge of infamy; at the one-hundredth anniversary
of Chacho's assassination, many of the myriad statues featuring Sarmiento
were meticulously vandalized (Luna 1966, 165).[3]

El Chacho, the work in which Sarmiento recalls his political and military
campaign against Peñaloza, is then a text oriented toward controversy and
defense. In it some of Sarmiento's central views are played out, since the
text is, above all, an "allegory of legitimation" (González Echevarría 1990).

This "allegory" occurs at two levels. On one level *El Chacho* attempts Sarmiento's legitimation before the law. At this level, Sarmiento addresses himself to an authority, in this case public opinion, to "establish [his] own precarious and often contested protestations of civil and political being through language" (González Echevarría 1990, 59). Just like in *Facundo*, Sarmiento is at the center of the scene of violence, but, unlike *Facundo*, in this instance he is not the victim but the deliverer of the state's retribution. As in Fernández de Lizardi's depiction, Sarmiento's depiction of Peñaloza's montonera as mere highway robbery deprives peasant insurgency of political status. By doing this, Sarmiento was legitimizing both the counterinsurgency campaign that he launched from San Juan and its bloody epilogue. He weaves himself into both *Facundo* and *El Chacho*, and this self-depiction is central to his political-literary vision (González Echevarría 1990, 113–14). But in *El Chacho*, his self-depiction is the very site of contestation, since his own position before the law was at stake as he was answering charges against himself (not formal criminal charges but ones that threatened to tarnish his reputation and historical legacy). Therefore, the distinction between political insurgent and common bandit was far from an exclusively theoretical one, because it was essential in deciding if his own acts qualified as acts of state with overwhelming doctrinal and historical precedents or as outright murder. This position as carrier of the state's retribution is also crucial to the argument here, since it puts the bandit and the letrado/statesman face to face.

Detailing Sarmiento's convoluted explanations of the conflict between San Juan and La Rioja is unnecessary. Suffice it to say that the final conflict between Chacho and San Juan had its origins not in a political dispute (Sarmiento denied Peñaloza all political or institutional status and did not acknowledge any other motive for his actions except theft) but in an alleged case of banditry: "In November [1861] a gang of vagrants [*una partida de vagabundos*], deserters or highway robbers of those that found asylum in the llanos left the area and, heading toward the Lagunas de San Juan, sacked the house of the Justice of the Peace, taking with them horses and cattle, and snatching from a caravan of mules the goods that it was transporting from Buenos Aires. They also robbed and left two French travelers naked and, after viciously beating them, carried them together with the bounty to the Llanos. This was aggravated highway robbery" (1867, 326).[4]

Chacho pardoned and released these highway robbers. By doing so,

Chacho—an ad hoc military authority—assumed judiciary faculties and therefore denied the division of powers, dogma of the Liberal creed. With this gesture, which offered state protection to criminals (for Sarmiento, La Rioja was a mere "asylum to cattle rustlers and vagrants" [1867, 324]), La Rioja ceased being a state, and the counterinsurgency campaign was now directed against a "robber's den, whose presence threaten[ed] the inhabitants, and where there [was] neither government nor police" (341). The subsequent war was considered a "police operation" (*guerra de policía*, 391) against the gang leader (*jefe de bandas*) Peñaloza (301) and his fellow robbers and highwaymen (*ladrones y salteadores*), "without giving them the honor of considering them political opponents, nor elevating their depredations to the rank of rebellion" (341). Once Peñaloza surrenders at Olta, trusting the guarantees that have been given to him, he surrenders his knife and disbands his men. He is immediately executed with spear, knife, and rifle. His corpse is profaned and beheaded, and his head is exhibited on a pike for public display. (Sarmiento's extreme gesture was almost simultaneously replicated at the other end of the continent, when, in 1861, Marcelino Cobos was beheaded and his head sent to Mexico [quoted in Altamirano 1901, 105]). According to Sarmiento, this measure was nothing more than the standard, legitimate procedure for dealing with highway robbers: "Chacho . . . died in a police operation, where he was apprehended, and his head was put on a pole in the theater of his depredations. This is the law and the accustomed form for executing a waylayer" (1867, 391). He also explained that "[g]uerrillas, since they are outside the protection granted by governments and armies, are outside the law, and can be executed by military chiefs in the field. Notorious waylayers are outside the law of the nation and outside municipal laws as well, and their heads have to be exposed at the sites of their crimes" (397).

On another level *El Chacho* attempts Sarmiento's legitimation as state maker. In discussions of Buenos Aires province in the pre-Caseros period, the word "banditry" named the anomalous process in which the provincial state developed as a nomadic war machine that prolonged, on an international scale, the unruliness that characterized the lack of civil society in the Argentine plains. "Banditry" named the anomalous collusion of the margin and the center, of the outlaw and the lawmaker. In *El Chacho*, written in the post-Caseros, post-Pavón context, "banditry" bespeaks the effective impossibility of state formation in a province such as La Rioja, where the presence of nonstate violence was overwhelming (de la Fuente 2000). These permutations of "banditry" have to do with the topics upon which Sarmiento is reflecting: the geographic, economic, and symbolic extremes of the national project. Buenos Aires was (and is) the richest province in the region and has a more developed state (Halperín Donghi 1972), while in La Rioja, the poorest province, the state was almost nonexistent well into the second half of the nineteenth century.[5]

This wealth and governance differential was not the only counterpoint between provinces that ran throughout Sarmiento's text. *El Chacho* was intended to present a counterpoint between San Juan (where Governor Sarmiento credited himself with erecting a state from scratch) and La Rioja (where popular insurgency prevented this task). This counterpoint was essential in the ideological definition of Unitarists of the interior provinces, a different incarnation than the Unitarists of Buenos Aires but one that converged with them in some ways. The latter supported a utilitarian, centralist ideology that was beneficial to the political and economic interests of the most powerful and self-sustaining province (due to the huge revenue base from the Buenos Aires customs house).[6] The Unitarists of the provinces (Sarmiento among them) believed that the interior provinces' lack of economic and political viability (with few exceptions) justified the dismantling of provincial sovereignties (the nucleus of the Federalist ideology) as a means of ensuring that federal funds would be available for the construction of a state (de la Fuente 2000, 20).

For Sarmiento, in the northwestern provinces the state never became a reality, whereas in the littoral provinces the state was born in an anomalous fashion (as in *Facundo*). The revenue base in La Rioja was so weak and the material resources so insignificant that its capacity to monopolize violence was almost nil (de la Fuente 2000, 20). Thus, the bandit trope applied to Peñaloza does not name the becoming-gang of the state (as in the rosista federation); instead it names the impossibility of the state and the irreparable confusion that occurs in a province where a gang of cattle rustlers can mobilize more men than the entire provincial militia and a landowner, more resources than the entire provincial state. Eduardo Gutiérrez, in his celebratory multivolume saga of the rise and fall of Peñaloza (*El Chacho, Los montoneros, El rastreador,* and *La muerte de un héroe*) narrates the beginnings of Chacho's popularity in Guaja. The episode that launches him into a career as a defender of the downtrodden is a classic tenet of social bandit narratives:

he defended a peasant from the abuses of a state official (narrated in *El Chacho*). The genre-mandatory fight with the posse—which appears in so many of Gutiérrez's novels—is the focus of the episode.[7] Gutiérrez is unable to grasp the paradox that Chacho fought a posse that may have been the entire La Rioja provincial militia.[8] The difference between bandit and rebel (so important in Sarmiento's argument) is, from the point of view of the state, irrelevant, and Chacho's montonera dominance does not imply the collapse of a state order because that order was, in fact, almost irrelevant to the economy of violence in the La Riojan countryside.

In Sarmiento's narrative, San Juan was close to this state of affairs at the beginning of his administration. (It was his first position in an executive office, and it provided him with his first opportunity to prove his vision, even if in a "microscopic theater" [Botana 1994, 42].) In both provinces, banditry ran unchecked (Sarmiento 1867, 301), the state was a fiction, and civil government was almost inconceivable (319, 376). Both provinces had to be put in order from the ground up (319). The fundamental difference in Sarmiento's narrative is that San Juan is run by Sarmiento himself (who was elected governor "by acclamation" [318], in an odd return of civil society to the scene) and the national army and the local elite are allied with other provincial elites (e.g., Tucumán, Santiago del Estero), while La Rioja is ruled by Chacho and his alliance of peasants and small landowners. Sarmiento's fable is the face-off between a legitimate (legal) principle of state making (San Juan, supported by the national army and national resources) and a band whose "situation in the Argentine Republic, with its character and means of action, was that of the Arab tribes of Algiers, receiving from each new government the investiture and closing its eyes to the raids that they have conducted to steal the cattle from some other tribes" (301). At this level, *El Chacho* works as a negative exemplum, a cautionary tale on the risks of popular sovereignty. So Sarmiento writes *El Chacho* as an attempt in legitimation on yet another level: Peñaloza is the nemesis of Sarmiento himself, the counterfigure, the position in relation to which Sarmiento legitimizes himself not as the letrado that imagines nations (as with the exiled letrado of *Facundo*) but as the letrado who builds states. The letrado-statesman and the bandit are the two poles of the national project in the interior provinces, their respective conditions of possibility and impossibility. Therefore, the counterpoint letrado versus bandit/popular caudillo in Sarmiento bespeaks the virtues of the Unitarist (or Liberal, as it was called at the time) agenda for the interior provinces. From similar initial circumstances (in both cases the devastation of the civil wars that made the state a fiction), diverging processes ensued, putting the Unitarist-letrado-statesman (Sarmiento himself) in stark relief against the backdrop of the Federalist-illiterate-bandit (Peñaloza).

This legitimation of his position as state maker serves a more ambitious purpose: Sarmiento postulates himself as the one who single-handedly closed the cultural gap that divided Argentine culture. Peñaloza's execution is the suture in this cultural chasm. This act of historical reparation (the unfinished task of the Unitarists of yore) is the end of an era for Sarmiento. Sarmiento called Peñaloza a "megaterium" as well as a "glyptodont" (400). Like the sphinx metaphor discussed in the case of Rosas, these metaphors embodied the inscrutable character that peasantry had for Sarmiento, in spite of his boisterous explanations (400). Also, the metaphors using prehistoric (and extinct) animals embodied the same temporal paradox as Quiroga, since both were representatives of one of the temporal poles that characterized Argentine heterogeneity, with two noncontemporary societies living side by side. In his narrative, Sarmiento postulates himself as the temporal axis around which the national project revolves. There is a telling episode that will serve as an example. In *El Chacho*, Sarmiento recounts how the news of the last Chacho rebellion, which put an end to the treaty of La Banderita, reaches San Juan the same day that news arrives from Buenos Aires, Chile, and Paris announcing the success of various projects of economic development (mines, roads, railroads, smelters, machinery) (335–36). News from the past and news from the future reach him, the man of the present, at the exact point where the conflict that left its imprint on Argentine culture converges. In *Facundo*, permitting this convergence between civilization and barbarism was a fatal mistake made by the city: the *comandante de campaña*, as Sarmiento pointed out, was little more than a bandit chief. In San Juan in 1863 the struggle between the two temporalities had a different outcome because there was a difference: this war was in the hands of the letrado who was in firm control of the war machine. (Sarmiento devotes a great deal of the book to explaining his allegedly paramount role as director of the war against Peñaloza, even though he remained in San Juan the entire time, and Paunero, Sander, and Irrazábal actually managed the war [337–84].) This image of the letrado as warrior cancels the opposition between a law without power (Rivadavia and the Unitarists blinded by European ideologies and legal niceties [374]) and a power without law (Rosas, Quiroga, Artigas, and Peñaloza). Thus, Sarmiento himself becomes (imaginarily) a reenactment of Paz, so to speak (381), and by doing so, he cancels Argentine heterogeneity: the past disappears, and the city finally imposes its will on the countryside.

Therefore, the execution of Peñaloza is a foundational act, and it has, as Sarmiento himself majestically relates, a double character. It is a political act since he orchestrated it as director of war. At the same time, however, it is a pre-political act, since it is the act that cancels an era and inaugurates the time and the imaginary enclosure in which "politics" proper can begin. In this respect, it is an "illegal" act. But it is illegal because it is the enforcement of a law that is previous to and more important than any other law. In "Salteadores y montoneras bajo la ley militar" this concept is explained in detail. The text deals with the execution of Segura, another montonero-bandit, by Zavalía, a federal appointee to rule San Juan during Sarmiento's presidency. The charges against Zavalía were similar to those directed against Sarmiento, since Zavalía executed a rebel without due process. Sarmiento defended the execution in a spirited fashion with the following argument. The constitution did not speak of highway robbers or montoneros (204), but this omission was not because they fell under the provisions of regular penal law. It was for a more essential reason. The constitution was a founding document, but it was oriented by "eternal truths" that the constitution only enforces (205). One of these eternal truths is the nature of the bandit vis-à-vis society. Banditry, continues Sarmiento, is not a common offense. It is a crime that it is directed "against everybody, against society, against the human species" (206). Therefore, bandits are not to be dealt with by the police (police deal with law breakers, not with those outside the law (206]) but instead by the military (207): "[T]he brigand is the chief of a gang[;] the organization of this gang assumes an army-like form and it is therefore subjected to the laws of the armies" (207). However, the military is to deal with them in a special fashion. A bandit gang is an army-like organization. But behind an army proper there has to be a nation-state, or a province, or an organized party, or at least a periodical that articulates a clear program (209–10). This background is the guarantee that the fighting force is an army proper and as such is entitled to be respected by the enemy, if defeated.[9] If none of these symbolic anchors exists, there is no army proper, only a bandit gang, and as such the fighting force has no rights whatsoever and its members "can be put to death by anybody, anytime" (206). Sarmiento is emphatic: "[T]his natural law . . . is previous to any constitution and no constitution can abrogate it" (206).

The execution of the illiterate Peñaloza was fully justified. He was the leader of "a conspiracy of unknown ringleaders, of ignorant masses that stir dully in the rural areas, of the lowest urban social rings, without ideas, newspapers or audible spokespeople [*órganos audibles*]" (328). Since Peñaloza's montonera did not represent anything and did not act within the coordinates of letrado representation, it was a gang of mere bandits and as such was repressed.

The execution was thus a founding act because the caudillo-bandit not only did not belong to the political community but also did not belong to the human community, and his suppression provides the opportunity for the constitution of a human community. For Sarmiento, the human condition only exists within a commonwealth regulated by law. This commonwealth relegates the Hobbesian *homo homini lupus* to the past. At this point, it would be convenient to remember that, for Aristotle, *barbaroi* were excluded from *oikumene*, the human community (Sorensen Goodrich 1996, 10). Sarmiento only draws on the extreme consequences of this classical perception. As such, then, the distinction between bandit and citizen is for Sarmiento the matrix of all other social distinctions. This is why Sarmiento objects to any negotiation (the ones established by Mitre, for example) with Peñaloza. In the Liberal vision, the state is the common arena of negotiation and regulated conflict (Oszlak 1982, 19). The bandit is an enemy of the state (understood not only in the institutional sense just mentioned but also as "the laws that rule a society"), and therefore the bandit is a case apart, intractable, and can be dealt with only by the firing squad. The "bandit" in *El Chacho* is not a metaphor devised within the state order but one that constitutes this order since the bandit must be suppressed for society to be constituted. It precedes human law, and it is through that "natural law" in which bandits may be killed on the spot that human becomes synonymous with civic. "In Italy," Sarmiento writes, "the brigandage of the Abruzzos was not included in the constitutional plan, just like the Argentine *montonera* would never lend itself to any form of compromise [with civilization]. They are both negations of society itself" (1867, 400).

The execution was illegal because there were no laws validating it, only the universal "eternal truths" that preexisted any political organization. Because of this, the suppression of the bandit is fundamental to the constitution of the rule of law. It is an act exterior to state law, and as such the state is not the subject of the act. Indirectly, Sarmiento extricates himself from the legal quagmire by putting the debate in a completely different scenario, one in which he does not have to answer to the legality of his actions because the law is secondary vis-à-vis this action. Thus, the letrado is the statesman, but he is also what comes before the state (and thus before the statesman). The assassination of the bandit directs Sarmiento's writing toward an inhabitable place. So, if Peñaloza is a monster of the past, to a certain degree, so too was the letrado/warrior, who lived within/without the law, at a crossroads of temporalities. The letrado is the reverse of the bandit because he was his enemy united by a secret (their own status outside the law) and denied community. This is the greatness and tragedy of Sarmiento that still makes him the most important nineteenth-century letrado and the very definition of the contradictions of the Latin American lettered city.

4 | O Cabelleira

Cangaceiros, Sacarocracy, and the Invention of a National Tradition

Fecha a porta, gente
Cabelleira vem
Matando mulheres
Meninos também
    Anonymous, Pernambucan lullaby

É um deus todo poderoso o deus-assucar
    Franklin Távora, *Lourenço*, 1881

O Cabelleira (1876) by Franklin Távora is the fictionalized biography of José Gomes (a.k.a. Cabelleira or Cabeleira, as later editions preferred), a brigand (*cangaceiro*) who roamed the Pernambucan sugarcane area of Brazil during the last third of the eighteenth century. The narrative spans from his childhood to his repentance, capture, and later execution on the scaffold in Recife. Contrary to what has been asserted (see Cartwright 1973, 12), this is not the first work of Brazilian fiction that features a bandit. Among the antecedents are *O Índio Afonso* (1873) by Bernardo Guimarães (1825–1884) and *Til* (1872) by José de Alencar (1829–1877). However, Távora's *O Cabelleira* is indeed the first novel in which a cangaceiro is the focus of a literary project of (intended) national relevance. In this respect, *O Cabelleira* is an inaugural novel. The cangaceiro was the other frontiersman who haunted the Brazilian cultural imagination besides the *bandeirante*, another wandering character (Chandler 1978).

The bandeirante has two opposing roles in Brazilian culture. He was hailed as a democratic warrior as well as derided as a violent promoter of slavery and oppression. He was the icon of an expansive nation sporting an aggressive brand of capitalism but was also considered the reason for the lack of Brazilian accomplishment. He was the flawed version of the North American pioneer (Clementi 1980, 145–47; Vianna Moog 1954). A contemporary example provides a microcosmic example of how the cangaceiro has an even more deeply conflicted or divided reputation than the bandeirante. An article in the summer 2001 issue of the popular magazine *Veja* announced that "Lampião is alive!" thus raising doubts about the death of Brazil's most important cangaceiro, who was famously killed in 1938 in an ambush in Angicos. And *lampião* was alive indeed; the article revealed that more than half of the population of the northeastern *sertão* (the dry interior area encompassing portions of Bahia, Sergipe, Alagoas, Pernambuco, Paraíba, Rio Grande do Norte, and Ceará) lacked electrical services of any kind, so they used *lampiões* (oil lamps) for home lighting.

That same month in 2001, the fashion and lifestyle magazine *Trip para Mulher* devoted an article and photo essay to the "*cangaço* style." Under the title "Caboclo Making Fashion Headlines," the article stated that "even without any idea of what it would become in today's fashion world, the *cangaceiras* had a sense of style and set trends." Dadá, the wife of the cangaceiro Corisco and, according to the article, *arbiter elegantiarum* of bandits around the sertão, enjoyed wearing strong colors in daring combinations, provocative embroidery, and leather accessories. The Forum brand launched its fall/winter 2001 collection imitating the designs, patterns, colors, and fabrics used by Dadá. Leather and gabardine were invaluable, we imagine, for cruising the *caatinga* (forest of thorny shrubs and stunted trees) of São Paulo or Rio de Janeiro.

These two examples touch on the extremes of the Brazilian culture for which the cangaceiro was a metaphor: infamous poverty (lack of electricity and running water) and the struggles that this dispossession triggers (the local cultural capital siphoned off by the elite in order to transform it into a commodity with an edge in the global market, much like the Rio carnival, allegedly frequented by vast numbers criminals and visited by anxious tourists who later do not dare leave their hotels by themselves). Between both extremes there is a history of violence and material and symbolic struggles that even the complacency of *Trip para Mulher* cannot avoid. Amid the magazine's fashion pictures, there is a small black-and-white picture of an old lady branded on the cheek with the initials *JB*. The letters stand for José (Zé) Bahiano, the black legend of Lampião's gang, who branded women for (alleged) sins against modesty. The fashion world cannot incorporate this violence into its narrative, although it belongs to the same symbolic universe as the harmless leather accessories. As such, it remains an isolated, strange, colorless body in a colorful display: out of place, out of time. The inscrutable character of this violence is what prompted, since the nineteenth century, the many attempts to decipher it. Rural violence (with the cangaço as its most visible expression) was indeed the mirror in which successive definitions of Brazilian modernity as well as its critiques contemplate themselves so as to define themselves. This is true from the nationalist-sacarocratic project of Franklin Távora and the positivistic criminology of Raimundo Nina Rodrigues to Jorge Amado's Marxism, well into the twentieth century and beyond. But, as Euclides da Cunha's *Os sertões* (1902) brings to the fore with unsurpassed force, violence in the parched interior region of the Northeast (that is, *sertanejo* violence) was a tricky mirror in which the distinctions between original and reflection, between the modernity of the plantation and the premodernity of the gang, between "us" and "them," always ran the risk of disappearing.

The northeastern part of Brazil comprises at least two distinct regions: the humid zone close to the coast (*tabuleiro* and *agreste*) and the semidesert interior zone (*sertão*).[1] Since the beginning of Portuguese colonization, both areas developed in a complementary fashion. The first was dedicated to sugar production for overseas markets and was worked by slaves, while the sertão was devoted to cattle ranching and subsistence farming. The ecological, socioeconomic, historical, and racial differences between both zones prompted Federico Pernambucano de Mello (1985) to make a distinction between two types of northeastern banditry: banditry of the sugarcane area (*o cangaço no verde*) and banditry of the sertão (*o cangaço no cinzento*).

Until the second half of the eighteenth century, the coastal area was the most economically dynamic area of the colony (in addition to having the capital, Bahia, later moved to Rio de Janeiro). Portuguese preference for coastal settlements, the concentration of economic activity, and the ease of communication resulted in a significant imperial presence in the coastal areas. Crown officials, church dignitaries, commercial houses, and military officials remained in the littoral, where cities such as Salvador, Recife, and Olinda flourished. The pattern of land tenure gravitated toward concentration, which determined the characteristics of banditry in the area. Until the emancipation of slaves in 1888, the area did not have features of social banditry nor was it linked to disputes between families or clans (as was the case in the sertão). Banditry existed in the classic mode of professional banditry or *cangaceirismo profesional* (Mello 1985), in which independent bands pilfered for profit (much like Vanderwood's "profiteering bandits"). Cabelleira was the foremost representative of this variety. Unlike banditry of the arid zone, the *cangaço no verde* never reached epidemic proportions and never created an icon of the stature of the Brilhante brothers, Antônio Silvino,

Lampião, Sinhô Pereira, or Corisco (all representatives of the *cangaço no cinzento*). As Cámara Cascudo pointed out, "The agricultural cycle of sugarcane [as opposed to cattle] could not have produced the cangaceiro" (quoted in Mello 1985, 88).

We might find Távora's archeological or folkloric "rediscovery" of a little-known cangaceiro of the eighteenth century somehow disconcerting.[2] Pernambuco, Bahia, Ceará, and Sergipe at that time had their share of bandits (at the time that Távora published *O Cabelleira*, Jesuíno Brilhante, the most important Brazilian bandit of the nineteenth century, was in his prime). However, Távora's choice was crucial, since through the bandit, the author tells a story whose main concerns are not rural insurgency per se but the sugar economy and its community making power (i.e., its power to co-opt peasant rebellion and put it to good use). Through this focus, Távora invents a genealogy for the nation whose forefathers were not bandits but the embattled nobility of colonial Pernambuco.

As previously mentioned, *O Cabelleira* had an inaugural place in Brazilian literature. The letter-prologue in which Távora formulated the program for the "Literature of the North" (of which this novel is the first in a series of three) is considered the foundational manifesto of northeastern regionalism (Candido 1969, 300; Aguiar 1999, xviii).[3] As such, it opened one of the most dynamic cycles in Brazilian literature, one that included *O grande sertão: veredas* (1956) by João Guimarães Rosa (1908–1967), perhaps the most important Brazilian novel of the twentieth century. In his manifesto, Távora postulated that, like politics, literature has a geographical nature that cuts across national lines (1876, 12). This brings to the fore what for Távora was the need for at least two differentiated literatures within the larger rubric "Brazilian literature": the then dominant "Literature of the South" (its fin-de-siècle model being Joaquim Maria Machado de Assis [1839–1908]) and Távora's proposed "Literature of the North."[4] This dislocation implied a particularization of what, until then, passed for national literature, where the South ceased to be either the showcase for the nation or the privileged position of enunciation from which the nation could be depicted and interpreted. At the same time, the "Literature of the North" implied an inversion embedded in a hegemonic project that would be continued well into the twentieth century: the affirmation of the North as the repository of nationhood. This goal was achieved through a twofold strategy. First, Távora affirms the difference and preeminence of the North when compared to the "contamination" of the South by the "invasion" of immigration and modernity (12). Then he moves on to affirm the representative character of the Northerner as the true Brazilian (something that, in the future, would deeply resonate in Euclides da Cunha's view of the *caboclo*, an inhabitant of rural Brazil, particularly northeastern Brazil, who claims a mixed racial heritage comprising varying degrees of Portuguese, Indian, and African ancestry).

The dislocation sprang from a conflict: the relative decadence of the sugar producing North (and of Pernambuco—Brazil's main exporter of sugar during the nineteenth century—in particular) versus the thriving (and rapidly modernizing) coffee producing South and the many tensions (economic, political, and cultural) arising from this fact. After 1830, coffee officially became Brazil's main export item. The relative decline of sugar (though production totals were in fact on the rise) was determined by a conjunction of factors. The Caribbean sugar plantations (especially those in Cuba) produced more than their Brazilian counterparts because their soils were of better quality, the Cuban plantations had more modern production techniques, they were located closer to the North Atlantic consumer markets (in particular the United States), and they benefited from political advantages in terms of exchange. Another factor was that the international price of sugar was down as a result of excess production beginning in the second half of the nineteenth century. Also, Europe, traditionally an importer of cane sugar, began to produce and even to export beet sugar, which dramatically reduced demand in a key market. In addition, hard currency gained from the sale of coffee (prices for which were on the rise, while sugar's prices were down) overvalued Brazilian currency, thus reducing the purchasing power of sugar exporters and further depressing their place in the national economy. Finally, the creation of a financial structure (needed for investment in an increasingly competitive line of production) led landowners to become more and more dependent on bankers from the South (Eisenberg 1974; Burns 1993, 150–55).

Thus, the "Literature of the North" had a specific and deliberate class content. It has to be read as an attempt to vindicate both the historical mission of the sugar producing landed oligarchy (*sacarocracia*), which in the northern countryside had a long lineage (e.g., the Silveiras and the Távoras, families that had settled the area centuries earlier [Aguiar 1997]), and its continued relevance on the national stage. This mix of dithyramb and elegy to the sugar producing universe is intoned by the narrator of *O matuto:*

> It seems that an all-out war against sugarcane in the North is in the making. In order to carry out this plan—the destruction of the blessed plant—they use the wholesale cultivation of coffee as an instrument in the interior of the provinces where until now mostly sugarcane was planted.
>
> It makes me sad, my friend, to witness any indication that the culture of the sugarcane is going to be substituted by the culture of a different plant. . . .
>
> In my eyes, sugarcane is not a plant, it is a magical and picturesque being. . . .
>
> To the Northerner, the sugar mill (*engenho*) is the representative of timeless and glorious traditions. The Pernambucan, in particular, is born contemplating with friendly eyes those large buildings that are like our feudal castles. The sugar mill is like the seigniorial manor of the North. The nobility of the country began with it; it does not know another abode. The sugar mill has a prominent place in the most important pages of the history of the Empire. Its importance is legendary, historical, and holy.
>
> And now they want to substitute the sugarcane with coffee! . . .
>
> A secret and consoling voice, dispelling my fears, tells me quietly that you, most beneficial plant—banner of the independence and richness of the Pernambucan, in spite of any conspiracy against you—will not disappear from our plains, from our hills, from our valleys and slopes. (1878, 78–80)

The vindication of the *latifundio* and of a particular class rule is not expressed in economic terms. It is disguised as the defense of a tradition that does not belong to the sugar baron alone. Távora highlights the *cultural* aspects, that is, the solidarity across classes that sugar production is supposed to create and the sugar patriarchy's capacity to put together a true community based upon relationships of reciprocity. (It should be remembered that this happened in the midst of the debates over the abolition of slavery.) The cornerstone of this true community has a name: the "bosom of Abraham, of paternalism that was a cherished tradition in the rural homes of yore" (Távora 1878, 81). Távora's literature is then a conservative defense of a particular class arrangement (and a model of social interaction between classes), the only one in which community is possible: a community where the very origin of Brazil, both as idea and as reality, can be traced.[5] In addition to that, this return to the eighteenth century was, if not the return to a golden age of the North, at least to a time when the area had significance in national and even international terms. This vindication will have a long heritage, reaching as far as *Menino de engenho* (1932), the first novel by José Lins do Rêgo (1901–1957) and the works by Gilberto Freyre (1900–1987), son of the declining sugar patriarchy who brilliantly attempted a vindication of sugar culture (see *Casa-grande & Senzala: formação da família brasileira sob o regime de economia patriarchal* [1933] and *Sobrados e mucambos: decadência do patriarcado rural e desenvolvimento do urbano* [1936]).

This is why it is not surprising that "Literature of the North" characters are not noblemen or writers but bandits and sertanejos and that this literature's themes are not eclogues of sugar cultivation but traditions of violence.[6] The focus on the poor population of Pernambuco is an indirect legitimation (from an artificial "below") of elite violence and of its capacity for disciplining and educating a community perceived to be in the process of decomposition because of market forces. (That this is an artifact of legitimation is evident in the fact that Távora omits any serious portrayal of the violent relationship that is key to the sugar mill world: slavery. Even though the novels happen within sugar plantations, slaves are very marginal to the narratives, except when they are despised because they defend with less-than-commendable enthusiasm their masters against their enemies or because they betray their masters just when they are about to be set free.)

O matuto (the second book of the Literature of the North) gives us one possible resolution to this ideological fable: it is the story of a would-be bandit who is co-opted by the capture apparatus (to use the phrase of Deleuze and Guattari) of the sacarocracy and who becomes a hero of a multiclass, anticolonial, antimarket epic. Lourenço was a bandit *in fieri*, a vagrant orphan whose evil tendencies ran unchecked. At ten, he was already a feared and tenacious thief, a "wild beast" (Távora 1878, 29) with "tiger entrails" (57) who had murdered his infant brother and set fire to his foster mother's house (27). He was a good candidate to be a successor to "O Valentão-da-Timbaúba," the bandit who populated the fearful yarns of the mule drivers who gathered in Pasmado (11–20). Caught while trying to steal, Lourenço was forcibly adopted as a son by Francisco, a *lavrador* or sharecropper on the Bujary sugar plantation (22–30).[7] The transformation of Lourenço into an honest peasant did not progress as expected, however, since he kept returning to his old ways. This downward spiral was interrupted only by the sugar harvest, whereby the spectacle of agrarian society in action deeply impressed the young *matuto*. But this cessation of his antisocial behavior was not the mere awakening of an ambition to become a plantation master. It was a true epiphany, the experience of a communion with sugar culture (80–90) in which the powerful "Sugar God" revealed itself. This epiphany, in turn, meant the reterritorialization of Lourenço's nomadic violence into just violence, "owned" and oriented by the interests of the benevolent sugar producing patriarchy. He became an *agregado* (a landless peasant who lives on a plantation in exchange for work, manpower, or services) of *colonel* João da Cunha and, later on, was the master's efficient and obstinate henchman and soldier during the War of the Mascates. He was loyal even after his master's demise.

The War of the Mascates (an intra-elite conflict in eighteenth-century Pernambuco that pitted Portuguese commercial interests in Recife against local landowning interests centered in Olinda) as presented in *O matuto* and *Lourenço* is then an allegory of Távora's contemporary milieu. The colonial conflict translates easily into an all-too-familiar nineteenth-century conflict, with one landowning oligarchy being threatened in its political preeminence (its economic preeminence already lost) at the hands of a class with "inferior" origins—newer but much more dynamic and undoubtedly better connected in the circuits of global capitalism. Thus, the intra-elite competition of the War of the Mascates is depicted as an anticolonial struggle in which the damage done by Portuguese business leaders to the Pernambucan noblemen is a wound to the emerging nation. (In *O matuto* the noblemen are considered proto-nationalists or, as in the case of the younger ones, nationalists *tout court* whereas the mascates are supported by an unfair and decadent metropolis.) This conflict parallels the situation of the North with respect to the "internal colonialism" of the new metropolis, the new coffee producing oligarchy (Eisenberg 1974). [8]

In addition to being an exalted defense of both a particular rural arrangement of affairs and the relative position of this arrangement in the national landscape, the Literature of the North was a legitimation of the intellectual organic to that class. As a man of letters who lived most of his life in a semi-periphery, Távora seeks to make himself (like Sarmiento in *Facundo*) the privileged mediator between the center (the Rio de Janeiro court) and a differentiated cultural tradition; thus Távora would be the one person capable of putting the "popular Muse of the North" in written form (1878, 306). [9] As such, he proclaims the North as being refractory to all attempts at understanding it when those attempts are not arising out of a true bond of belonging (e.g., Europeans or Southerners): "[A] lot has been written about

Pará and the Amazonas from the time of their discovery to the present. What is the value of all those writings and travel narratives? Almost none" (6). In the same brazen fashion Távora indicates that the only acceptable judgment of his novel should come from the Pernambucan critical establishment (*critica Pernambucana*) (7).[10] In this way, the Literatura do Norte will become both a northern "archive" (see Higgins 1995) and an exclusive, self-legitimating position of enunciation (see Candido 1969, 303). Its only immediate competition would be the almost contemporary *O sertanejo* by José de Alencar.[11]

O Cabelleira narrates a story that, at least at the beginning, is the alternative to *O matuto*. Cabelleira is not the bandit who redeems himself just in time and who becomes a soldier of the sugar latifundio; rather, he is literally a nomadic "crime machine" (1876, 69). Cabelleira was a "free" brigand without ties to any segment of rural society, except his *coiteiro*, the tavern keeper Thimoteo.[12] Out of terror, Thimoteo provides refuge for Cabelleira, who while still a teenager beat Thimoteo's common-law wife to a pulp (40–43). (Northeastern cangaceiros, on the other hand, were usually tied to long-standing family feuds, or at least they had an important degree of participation in them, since this involvement granted them sorely needed protection [Mello 1985; Queiroz 1968].)

Cabelleira lived the life of a cruel and irredeemable bandit until he found Luiza, his long-lost childhood sweetheart. He found her while trying to kidnap and rape her (Távora 1876, 97–105), and she forced him to quit banditry (*cangaço*), get rid of his weaponry, and embrace Christian virtue (228, 240). In spite of this transformation, his enemies did not give him quarter and finally caught him under the direction of the regional militia chief (*capitão-mor*) Cristóvão de Hollanda Cavalcanti. Cabelleira, at the time of his apprehension, was already well advanced on a path of redemption, a fact that was noticed by his former persecutor, the *capitão-mor* whose wife Leonor had tried, without success, to gain a pardon for the bandit (280). Unmovable, the colonial judicial system sentenced Cabelleira to death. The final scene of the novel (Cabelleira's execution by hanging), far from a spectacle of terror, a theater of the law, becomes an apotheosis and a martyrdom in which the monster turns into the moral hero of the crowd. Through this unity of feeling vis-à-vis the redeemed bandit, the crowd in turn becomes a people who assume a collective identity when positioning itself against the decision of the colonial state.

Cabelleira became a bandit because his father (himself a bandit) had cor-
rupted him (69–88) and forced the young matuto to abhor his original "soft
nature and benevolent heart" (69). This good nature, remarks the author,
could have taken him not to the scaffold but to the hero's pedestal. But the
paternal metaphor is more than a moralistic point on education policies
within the nuclear family. Biological or adoptive fatherhood becomes truly
parental authority when it is linked to the wider social order. Joaquim is a
bad father and Francisco is a good one, not because (or not only because)
Joaquim is a tiger who, driven by his "cannibalistic passions" (1876, 16), enjoys evil for its own sake while Francisco is a matuto of adamant honesty,
but because Joaquim is a free agent in rural society. As such, he is unrelated
to the universe of the sugar mill. It is this lack of ties that makes Cabelleira a
monster, an incomprehensible, almost supernatural being (216). This is why
he, having had the opportunity to become the "Pernambucan Cid or Robin
Hood," becomes instead an outlaw who has to be put to death for the education of the populace (16). His record is indeed telling: he murdered (stabbed
and shot) two children in cold blood because he (erroneously) suspected
them of having involuntarily deprived him of part of a bounty (48–50); he
attacked and robbed Gabriel, a very loyal aide who helped him get away from
a governor's posse (61); he stole money from Thomas da Encarnação Costa e
Lima, Recife's model bishop, money that was destined for victims of
drought and plague (60); he raped, kidnapped, and beat defenseless women
to death (41–43, 101–105); and he killed elderly women (103). He is, literally, "a wild beast" (68), a "human animal" (19), a "tiger" (45), and a cannibal
(145) who has gone beyond all accepted and even conceivable codes of rural
violence. Indeed, Cabelleira will go down in history (together with Cundurú)
as the proverbial bandit who was also a sociopath, a kind of Gilles de Rais of
the sertão (Barroso 1918, 148).

In *O matuto,* this development of the young, unattached matuto warrior
into a full-blown brigand is pre-empted by the revelation of the Sugar God,
who enlisted him in the legions of its followers. Since this does not happen
in *O Cabelleira* (Cabelleira is unable to work [1876, 221]), a different path
should be followed, in which the suppression (not the co-optation) of the
bandit's violence is the key to the narrative. Given the inefficiency of the
colonial armed forces and security forces when left to their own devices
(1878, 57), there are only two social classes able to oppose Cabelleira's violence: the small landowners and rural folk who are victimized by Cabelleira

and his gang on the one hand and, on the other, the *coronéis* (literally, colonel, which in northeastern Brazil was a landlord who often enjoyed political and/or military appointments). The allegory that the novel develops concerning the relationships between violence and state formation will completely change depending on which class the novel presents as appropriate for the task.

In the first case, Liberato seems to fulfill all of the requirements as Cabelleira's worthy adversary among the rural rank-and-file. As a descendant of Henrique Dias, black hero of the war against the Dutch, from whom he inherited his land (1876, 114), Liberato belongs to a warrior tradition. He has the material resources to wage war since he owns a small *fazenda* by the woods where the bandits have their *couto* (hideaway); he has prestige as an independent farmer in possession of prime land (he could have been the poster child for rural middle-class prosperity [111]); and, finally, he has the motive (his brother Gabriel helped the brigands to avoid capture, and in return, they killed him [68, 116]).

Liberato's martial enterprise is an attempt to put together a mechanism of social control from below, based on the enthronement of the rural oral code (one that claims reparation for Gabriel's death). It is a warrior tradition that does not necessarily conflict with the elite one, although it certainly competes with it (Liberato—notice the connotation of the name—never seeks elite alliances.) He fails spectacularly because he falls short in building support among the neighboring peasants (117) and is ultimately betrayed, defeated, and killed (119–22). Liberato bears the marks of his class (peasant) and of his race (black), and, as such, the novel dooms him to fail as an efficient (and therefore legitimate) principle of state building.

The *capitão-mor* Cristóvão de Hollanda Cavalcanti, on the other hand, can boast a similarly illustrious warrior genealogy: he is the son of a landowner (of the same name) who fought for the rights of the Pernambucan gentry during the War of the Mascates (209). It is his class position (he is the owner of the Petribú sugar mill), however, that makes him the most logical choice to become the primary state builder from the region (the *Ur*-nation). But his ability to achieve what Liberato (or the Portugal-appointed governor) was unable himself to achieve—the capture of Cabelleira—does not mean the complete disowning of peasant violence because the patrimonial order is conceived as a consensual one. Therefore, Hollanda Cavalcanti triumphs also in forging an alliance (like in *O matuto* and *Lourenço*) with the peasantry's oral code. Cabelleira is captured because he was tirelessly persecuted and later discovered and denounced by Marcolino, a peasant (261). Marcolino was obsessed with Cabelleira's capture, not because he wanted to see the state's justice done but rather because he wanted to clear his name of the shadow of cowardice, especially after an encounter with the brigand tainted his reputation to the point of making him the butt of some slanderous rural rhymes (226, 248, 254). The fact that the written law is enabled and inhabited by the heterogeneous oral code of honor and revenge (249) does not speak of the impurity of state making. Quite the contrary: Marcolino's hubris (the novel calls it "madness" [259]) is wisely channeled in a "productive" direction: oligarchy-centered state building. Marcolino successfully followed the path that Liberato failed to recognize. Liberato attempted to become an axis of violence (organizing and allocating collective violence), and, as such, he built his own patrimonial order so as to enact his vengeance (his posse was composed of members of his extended family [117, 138]). He was not recognized as a legitimate power holder, and hence, he was betrayed (118–19). (It is important that Liberato's demise is due not to class struggle but to intra-class treason. This naturalizes the massacre as pertaining to the "natural order of things," not to political determinations: Liberato brought his fate upon himself.) Marcolino allowed his violence to work along the lines demarcated by the patrimonial order, and then he retired with honor, even glory (278). The fable shows how the patrimonial order is able to happily co-opt nomadic violence working outside itself. And when it is unable to co-opt it, it is able to destroy it.

However, Cabelleira's persecution and capture have even deeper repercussions in Távora's Pernambuco. Before, the woods just outside Recife were unknown to and undominated by the state. It was a place where anomalous individuals tested other social arrangements. Essentially they were a true frontier, one of which "nobody knew the nooks" (57), a space in which bandits were sovereigns since their knowledge of the woods was unsurpassed (247).[13] Unlike other works on the sertão, in which there is not a stark opposition between the *mata* (woods or jungle) and the manor (the case at hand being Alencar's *O sertanejo* and Alfredo d'Escragnolle Taunay's *Inocência*), in *O Cabelleira* the mata is supplementary to the rural order and hinders its consolidation.

In the enterprise of eliminating Cabelleira, the state truly occupied this frontier: in a single day, the entire coastal zone of the province from Alagoas to Parahyba was isolated from the interior by a continuous line of armed military forces. All the matas within this area were simultaneously searched inch by inch (205); hence, territorial sovereignty ceased to be a claim and became a reality. Not by chance, the last encounter between Cabelleira and his persecutors happened not in the woods but in a sugarcane field (that is, not in nature, but in culture). The officials did not evict Cabelleira from the sugarcane field. In a gesture full of symbolism, the slaves—protected by soldiers under the orders of the *capitão-mor*—cut down the entire field; this is an unsurpassed metaphor of the state's homogeneous domination over land and of the link between sugar and the patrimonial order. Cabelleira thinks that the "blessed plant" will give him refuge and sustenance like a "maternal bosom" (268). Instead, the cane field becomes a trap. This is so because the protection of sugar can only be reached within the medium of the patrimonial order. (This is why Sugar is revealed to Lourenço during the harvest, when the plant becomes a commodity for the benefit of the landowning class). In any other case, the same plant becomes deleterious, and the same ritual (the sugar harvest) becomes a punishment.

The effort to eliminate Cabelleira serves as a decisive transition in collective identities. The only two modes of actualization of collectivity occur at the beginning of the novel where the crowd is subject to mass passions (either the superstition of the religious processions or the irrational fears of collective flight from the bandits). Similarly, the events of the collective include natural catastrophes such as drought or smallpox epidemics (34, 100) or events concerning metropolitan politics such as the war with Spain or curses like Cabelleira himself (215).[14]

The enterprise to eliminate Cabelleira symbolically cancels Pernambuco's situation of dispersion and lack of population, and it creates a synchronic "general will" that becomes a hierarchical political body. These changes occur since the coordination of the persecution creates a public sphere, a realm of local problems, in which all inhabitants participate outside of coercion and beyond their particular interests. Thus, they evolve from inhabitants to citizens of a political unit that the novel does not yet call "Brazil." The development of this collective will logically sets the stage for the major development of the novel: the (symbolic) demise of the colonial state, replaced by the new political body as an articulation of landowners and the "people." Again, the body of the bandit is crucial, since it is the point of articulation around which, on the one hand, the legitimacy of rule is going to be fought and, on the other, the alliance between the landowning class and the "people" is going to be sealed.

Cabelleira's repentance in Luiza's honor is a reversal of problematic credibility. Even less credible (but with ever firmer ideological motivations) is the coup de théâtre when, immediately after being caught, Cabelleira ceases to be everyone's nightmare and starts being everyone's darling: his dignity and his bravery impress his captors: "With rare exceptions, there were almost no families, from Recife to the high sertão who had not been robbed of a dear member by the knife or the gun of the terrible killer" (207). Even fewer, however, "were the ones whose eyes did not overflow with tears when they saw the unhappy youngster bound by an ignoble chain" (281). Even the soldiers who caught him now regret having done so (285), and in a strange turn of events the *capitão-mor* is the first one to change his mind when it comes to the unfortunate bandit.

That the apprehension of the bandit is an allegory of the social order is clear in an enigmatic gesture. When apprehended, Cabelleira becomes what he has never been: a humble peasant respectful of social hierarchies. As such, he performs the immemorial ritual of class acknowledgment in rural societies: he takes off his hat (276). In jail it is this transformation that allowed Cabelleira to become a sort of adoptive son for the *capitão-mor* and his wife, in lieu of his perverse biological parents (288). The only one unable to perceive that the prodigal son of the gentry has returned to the fold is the colonial administration. The governor and the court—depicted in the novel as detached morally (293) and physically (297) from colonial society—refuse to understand Cabelleira's redemption.

Thus, Távora establishes a difference within the colonial state: the captain as an alternative principle of state formation is doubly legitimized with respect to the peasantry (with which he formed the alliance that allowed for Cabelleira's capture) and the metropolitan administration (which he opposes when its decisions are unjust [288–89]). This is exactly the same formal and ideological scheme that we saw in the case of *O matuto* and *Lourenço*, in which the mascates' rebellion places the *senhores de engenho* in the position of those who legitimately exert local rule against "colonial absolutism" (180).

The death of Cabelleira then, is not the reaffirmation of the rule of law but an injury inflicted upon a people no longer affiliated with the Empire (of Portugal). This is shown in the double death presented to the reader: the death of Cabelleira and the death of his mother, who passes away in the bosom of the people: "In the midst of the multitude [of spectators] this death scene was simultaneously replicated in another form. In the arms of some folk women, most certainly poor, Joana had just breathed her last breath. [Upon witnessing her son's death] her heart had instantly exploded out of pain" (299). The whole scene has a Christ-like quality. This is so not because Cabelleira is depicted as a savior (although to a certain extent he is, since the community of the believers in the gospel of the nation coalesces around the event of his death), but because, just like Christ, he is the victim of violent state retribution and is executed by a despotic colonial power as a bandit (just like Christ), with two other bandits (Joaquim and Teodosio) by his side (299). Like the drama of the crucifixion, his mother suffers by and with him.

The death of Cabelleira is a performance of the theater of law, but within this performance Távora overwrites another drama: a theater of delegitimization of a law that transforms it into one of barbarism "that fills humankind with horror, and covers with shame and mourning, like so many other, the history of the colonial period" (299). The voice of the narrator disguises itself as the voice of the people and condemns this "juridical crime" (301), a crime that can only be evaluated as such from the vantage point of another law in the making, that of Hollanda Cavalcanti and his class, the law of the Ur-nation. The death of the bandit is then the consecration of the law of the patrimonial order. The execution at the same time shows his capacity to punish and his ability to forgive. Thus, the fable vindicates its capacity to create a cohesive community in cultural, political, and economic terms, the precursor of a true "ethical state." This, for Távora, would put Brazil on the path to true national consolidation. In his eyes, this consolidation was something that the elites of the South, in their pursuit of modernization, were destroying.

El Zarco

Banditry and Foundational Allegories for the Nation-State

My trade is retribution—vengeance is my calling!
Karl von Moor, bandit chief in *The Robbers*, by Friedrich Schiller

Ignacio Manuel Altamirano (1834–1893) is considered a founding father of Mexican national culture, and his literary production is understood as a culmination of nationalistic literature. In his writings the vindication of the "national intellectual" is decisive as an exclusive interpretative instance, a mediation able to achieve a synthesis between a "universal" idea of culture and the diverse economic, geographic, cultural, and ethnic elements that comprised the problematic Mexican nation (Giron 1976). In this project of a synthetic "national narrative," the novel, as the "Bible of the nineteenth century," would have a central role. It would define models of behavior capable of restoring the social cohesion and system of authority that the fall of the old order had destroyed and that was impossible to rebuild until well after 1867 (Palti 1994, 87).[1]

El Zarco (posthumously published in 1901) is Altamirano's most famous novel.[2] Together with the celebrated novella *La navidad en las montañas* (1871), *El Zarco* best illustrates Altamirano's moralizing and utopian intent, since it expresses his ambiguous adherence to the principles of "developmental liberalism" (Knight 1985, 61) and since it represents an attempt at conciliation and overcoming the contradictions and impossibilities of the liberal project that ravaged Mexico during the nineteenth century. But unlike *La navidad*, where this conciliation has a pacific, Arcadia-like setting that makes the threat of violence carried by the narrator (a military representative of the triumphant Liberal order) irrelevant, *El Zarco* conjures up the most fearful ghosts of the liberal imagination: the Plateados. The Plateados, who peaked in the mid-nineteenth century, were a group of gangs that fought with the Liberals during the Three Years' War and, when improperly rewarded after licensing, raided central-south Mexico for several years.[3] They were especially fearsome since they gathered bands numbering up to a thousand men (Vanderwood 1992, 8). Even though they were ruthless, they tended to have a business-like approach to their activity. Instead of focusing on stagecoach robbery (like the more popular and romanticized Río Frío bandits), they secured a more stable revenue base through extortion of towns, commercial enterprises, or hacendados, all of whom had to pay sizable sums and offer the bandits hospitality and support. (Lampião of Brazil, more than half a century later, would have the same modus operandi.) This was the only means to avoid either property damage or the feared fate of the *plagiado* (victim of a kidnapping): abduction for ransom, which implied enduring unimaginable tortures and the likely prospect of death (Vanderwood 1992, 8).

The Plateados were far from rebellious peasants on the run. Through sheer size and firepower, they became de facto rulers (or at least influential forces) in certain areas, boasting wealth, social standing, and prestige. Their superb riding gear and attire, both silver studded (hence the name Plateados), were emphatic symbols of this position in a society that, on the one hand, "lacked well-developed institutions for exchange and legitimate means to profit" (Vanderwood 1992, 8) and, on the other, could not impede the existence of the alternative, unlawful means for exchange and profit. The Plateados' celebrity status reached a point in which their image was appropriated by their purported enemies, the Rurales (Vanderwood 1992, 54).

The Plateados then had a particular place in the liberal imagination because they were unlike most contemporary bandits. For example, bandits such as Heraclio Bernal, Chucho el Roto, or Santanón were renowned as rebels and resistance fighters against the encroachment of the nation-state and its values during the porfiriato. The Plateados, on the contrary, impressed the collective imagination for the opposite reason, namely "their group power and haughty regional control. The *Plateados* were admired more as stern rulers than as troublesome subjects" (Vanderwood 1992, 90). Also admired as a ruler was Manuel Lozada, who established an unorthodox experiment in the form of a peasant republic in Tepic (Meyer 1984, 1989). However, Lozada's ethnicity and his political project (which called for a high degree of autonomy for Indian communities) made it easy for the porfirian intelligentsia to unequivocally label him a "barbarian."

The Plateados came to define a model of Mexican masculinity (Vanderwood 1992, 91). Because of this reputation they continued to haunt the state-minded letrado class. Almost fifty years after their insurgency, the zapatistas of Morelos (who were certainly not bandits) had to bear the comparison (and the affiliation) as a badge of infamy in the slanderous 1912 pamphlet by Popoca y Palacios: *Historia del bandalismo en el estado de Morelos: ¡ ayer como ahora! ¡1860! ¡1911! ¡Plateados! ¡Zapatistas!* I contend that the Plateados continued to occupy letrado consciousness because they challenged the state on its own terms. *El Zarco*, then, must be read as a fable in which all collusion between the Plateados and the state is erased and the Plateados as a group must be crushed for the nation-state to emerge. But this legitimating fable is different from Sarmiento's *El Chacho*, which seemingly has a similar purpose. In *El Zarco*, this task is not in the hands of the letrado-warrior, as a representative of the civilizing ideals of the metropolis. In *El Zarco*, it is civil society itself that rises to the task of eliminating bandits. In this task, there is an alliance between civil society and state and between center and periphery that is central to the ideology of the novel. In Sarmiento's work, the erasure of the bandit would not have been possible without the letrado. In *El Zarco*, the letrado role (played by Juárez in the novel) is more complex. On the one hand, he comes second since civil society organizes itself against the bandit without the intervention of the letrado. On the other hand, however, it is incumbent upon the letrado to make a crucial political decision: to decide (upon rather contingent grounds) that the counterinsurgents were not bandits themselves. The relation between violence and the state is then one of an *alliance* that captures violence but does not completely overwrite it.

El Zarco has been deemed, quite rightly, a "foundational romance" since, just like in *Clemencia* (1869), the other great novel by Altamirano, love that crosses and conciliates racial lines is a trope of the constitution of the nation as an integrative imagined community (Sommer 1991; Schmidt 2000). *El Zarco* is indeed the story of two romances. The first is the romance between Nicolás, an Indian ironsmith of the Atlihuayán hacienda who personifies all liberal civic virtues, and Pilar, a mestizo orphan living in the household of Doña Antonia, owner of an orchard and a small plot of land in Yautepec, Morelos (at the time part of the State of Mexico).[4] The second is the story of the ill-starred passion that Manuela, Antonia's daughter, harbors for Zarco, the irresistibly good-looking captain of the Plateados.[5] (The motif of the fateful, mistaken love for a bandit is a staple of the European gothic novel. Examples that come to mind are Marguerite in Matthew Lewis's *The Monk* and Madame Cheron's love for Montoni in Ann Radcliffe's *The Mysteries of Udolpho*.)

At the beginning of the novel these two romances are mismatched. Nicolás hopelessly and prudishly loves Manuela, but she scorns him against the wishes of her mother because he was a "horrible Indian" (Altamirano 1901, 120) and a "poor artisan" (119). Instead, she had many a secret rendezvous with Zarco, whose moonlight-bathed chivalric figure seems the embodiment of a Romantic imagination (135–39). Manuela is, in fact, a reader of European romantic novels, a sort of Madame Bovary of the *tierra caliente,* and therefore her attraction to Zarco is all too natural. But just like in the case of the other Bovary, her fantasy—that here also entails a very risky political option—ends up being lethal. Manuela elopes with Zarco, and the pain of her escape ultimately kills her mother (238). In addition to this tragedy, her escape is a fiasco. Very soon, she experiences the disillusion before the not-at-all-romantic reality of the Mexican rural bandit (249–58). Zarco, enraged because of Manuela's contempt, her resistance to participating in bandit society, the (correct) suspicion that Nicolás has become his rival in Manuela's too volatile heart (301), and Nicolás's role in the bandit persecution, plots to kill the ironsmith (332). But instead, Zarco falls under the swift and stern justice of Martín Sánchez Chagollan (334), the rancher who had become a bandit hunter in order to avenge the death of his family at the hands of the Plateados (303). Manuela dies by Zarco's side, of sheer passion (334). Pilar and Nicolás, on the other hand, marry and live happily ever after.

This is a love story. But the world depicted is split between citizens and bandits, and this divide defines the conditions, the identities, and the spaces in which romances will prosper, wither, or come to a disastrous end. The fact that the world is depicted in the novel as split is a precondition of the utmost ideological momentum: before the integration of difference (the foundational romance of the mestizo, liberal, capitalistic nation), the erasure of what is radically different and embodied in the bandit (the insurgent, premodern, anticapitalistic hybrid) is essential. This makes the romance somehow redundant (analytical, in logical terms) because it is only the ritual of symbolic incorporation of the already incorporated. Thus, the destruction of the bandit gang is the real political stance of the novel, since it is what allows for an imaginary a posteriori re-foundation of the national project. This re-foundation happens in a twofold fashion. On the one hand, it allows for the re-creation of the state as a new contract between people and rulers, as the conciliation of regional conflicts, and as the expropriation of control over violence. On the other hand, it allows for the re-foundation of the family as a privileged space of citizenship that replaces the genealogical model from the colony with the liberal generative model. Similarly, it permits the class and race alliance between Nicolás (an acculturated Indian, belonging to a sort of rural working-class elite) and Pilar (a Creole with a small landholding).

Homi Bhabha points out that Romanticism inaugurated the modern metaphor of landscape as an exterior form of national identity (1990, 295). This metaphor is relevant in Altamirano's work because it encompasses sociability and territory, nature and culture in a totalizing fashion. This is one of the reasons for Altamirano's admiration for Jorge Isaacs's *María,* hailed as the Spanish American novel par excellence.[6] In Altamirano's work the landscape trope functions in a problematic way because it is the testimony of an almost unsolvable duality: the Mexican rural landscape is not the idyllic locus of uncorrupted, timeless, and picturesque traditions but rather the stage of bitter, violent struggles over land, money, and power. Because of this, the landscape in *El Zarco* is split: on the one hand it is the "model" and, on the other, it is the model's reverse. Each landscape has an opposite relationship with the law and, through the mediation of the law, with the national project.

Yautepec is the dwelling of responsible and hard-working citizens, a group of small landholdings that grow citrus for outside consumption. The nature of the fruit produced in Yautepec is not ideologically insignificant. It is a Mediterranean fruit, not an American one. The landscape itself bears witness to this alien admixture: it is half American, half Mediterranean. Both the economy and the nature of the city itself (through the naturalizing metaphor of the landscape) appear to be happily, harmoniously transculturated.[7]

Yautepec represents the cohesive and harmonious Mexican "imagined community" that is egalitarian in economic and racial terms (there are no "pure Indians" [Altamirano 1901, 101]). Yautepec's economy is overwhelmingly modern: there is no subsistence agriculture, the agrarian system works in a monetary goods market that is integrated into the national economy (98–99) and free from the corporative and economic hindrances of the past —represented by the Church, the hacienda, and the indigenous community that is relegated to the mountain slopes. Yautepec is (or could be) an arcadia that would be, at the same time, a capitalist utopia (Escalante 1997, 191).

Even though the novel highlights the fact that the population is "hard work-ing" (Altamirano 1901, 100), labor is never depicted in the novel (thus em-phasizing the Arcadia character, the *otium* as opposed to the *negotium*). Only two dimensions appear in the novel when Yautepec is depicted: the domes-tic sphere (Antonia's house and the house of Pilar's uncles), and the public-civic sphere (the Major and the citizens gathered in Assembly and the mar-riage of Pilar and Nicolás).

Yautepec could be a capitalist utopia, but at the beginning of the novel it certainly is not. Yautepec is, in spite of its potential, in a dismal state. This utopia does not come to fruition because of socioeconomic contradictions in Yautepec itself. There is no mention of an exploited rural proletariat, of the problematic effects of economic integration into the national system, or the way large landowners were dispossessing the peasantry (which was indeed happening in the real Yautepec).[8] The contradictions are projected toward the exterior, under the form of banditry, and they are territorialized in Xochimancas, the Plateados' hideout.

Xochimancas is the exterior because it is beyond the reach of the state. Xochimancas, just like Lizardi's Río Frío, is reached only through traveling a labyrinth (249). But the metaphor here has a dramatic reach: from the state's gaze, the entire Mexican geography is a labyrinth since state power was illusory outside most cities. "Labyrinth" bespeaks the lack of difference between the "interior," where the state claims exclusive sovereignty (here, illusorily), and the "exterior," where force is the only means for gaining respect. (In the novel, the army has to protect travelers as if they were [or because they were] traveling in a foreign and hostile land [132, 206]). Con-versely, the Plateados do not act like guerrillas in enemy-dominated terri-tory. They go into battle and have flags, marching bands, and cannons as if they were a standing army. In fact, they are better equipped than regular armies. (The miserable condition of the army column that traverses Yaute-pec is a paramount example; see, e.g., chapter XIII, "El comandante.") This war machine is funded with highway tolls and a taxation system that bur-dens neighboring haciendas (105, 118, 245), and it is aided by an extended network of auxiliaries in both the country and the city, as well as allies in po-litical circles (114, 131, 245, 297, 319). They have a well-run "production" system based on bleeding their kidnap victims (*plagiados*) white (288). (The production metaphor applied to the plagio is reinforced by the fact that the captives are "stored" in the same place where sugar used to be stored at the hacienda.) They even have accepted symbols of shared identity, such as the silvery ornaments that gave them their name, Plateados (140–41). For all practical purposes, the Plateados are a state, and they include in their alternative territoriality all that is opposed to the institutions and bourgeois discipline that the liberal project supports.

This situation may be better understood by thoroughly examining Xochimancas, a pre-Columbian town and later a *tierra caliente* hacienda that became a bandit hideout. Even though it is close to Yautepec, it is also infinitely distant, since only the bandits know the way. This makes it heterogeneous to the national space. However, Xochimancas is also heterogeneous to itself. Unlike Yautepec, the place of miscegenation and racial uniformity, Xochimancas is a realm of confusion and juxtaposition without hierarchy. It is also a place of sexual confusion where brides are kidnapped, marriage does not exist, and women are held in common and available to all (286).[9] There is no regulation of social spaces, no bourgeois domesticity, no private sphere (257). The chapel of the hacienda is used as kitchen, storage space, and stall (256), a pandemonium where riches and rags accumulate without any principle of organization; the altar in the chapel is used as a bed, not for sleeping but for the deflowering of stolen virgins. The hacienda's main hall, the center of hacendado life, is the place where the gang holds its grotesque mimicry of high society (291), preferring high society dances (such as the waltz) to the popular *jarabe*. In contrast with Yautepec, where *mestizaje* (either racial or cultural) is a harmonious reality, Xochimancas is a hodgepodge of races without racial hierarchy. This heterogeneity is replicated in the lack of organic solidarity between the bandits. Manuela dreams of the gang and the hideout as a Bohemian forest (as in *The Robbers,* by Schiller) or an English Sherwood Forest (in the Robin Hood saga), where the captain would be a moral leader held in the highest regard. But she comes to realize that there were no hierarchies or loyalties among the bandits (see chapter XXI, "La orgía").

In fact, bandit sociability presents an inversion or disorientation of normal sociability. This type of sociability is depicted as "chaos" (the ball is an "orgy" [275]), but it is possible to imagine a "bandit perspective" on this view: the purposeful desecration of multisecular symbols of authority and rural oppression. It should not be forgotten that Zarco was a hacienda peon himself, and the high moment of his career occurred when his former master performed the same service that he himself used to perform: holding horse reins (in this case those of Zarco) (169). In the same fashion, Manuela's seduction can be viewed from Zarco's perspective as the breaking of long-established lines of division (according to class) in rural society: when he was a hacienda worker, Zarco saw Manuela as an impossible dream (171). In *El periquillo sarniento*, the orderly nature of Río Frío hides the unapparent chaos of a human aggregation not ruled by any parental or letrado principle. In Xochimancas, the chaos is the most apparent element. Xochimancas is a world upside down, a countertheater of the poor, the image of hierarchical rural Mexico in an inverted mirror (thus its horrific effect in the letrado's conscience). Manuela's mistake is then not having regarded the bandits as "men who have made robbery their particular line of trade" (247) but having clung to her letrado perceptions (the "noble robber" image), which she acquired vicariously. She is a traitor to her class, and there is no doubt about that. But what was fatal, in her case, was that she remained in between the two conflicting orders.

The bandit's hideout is also a meditation on the legacy of colonial rule. Xochimancas was a flower growing field before the Conquest, a slave-worked tropical hacienda later, a ruin, and finally the Plateados' headquarters (see chapter XIX, "Xochimancas"). Banditry is thus the closure of a historical cycle, a process of degradation that began with the colony (Cruz 1993–1994, 83).

This cleavage in the physical space is replicated in the characters Nicolás and Zarco. Their differences are put into starker contrast by the fact that their initial point of departure was the same: the hacienda, where both were workers. While Nicolás represents an image of the socially ascendant rural proletariat who is economically and ideologically integrated into the project of agrarian capitalism, Zarco opts out of this enterprise.[10] The significant point is that this opting out (as with Manuela's opting out of her gender role) is equated with crime, not with class struggle (Nicolás being living proof of the inconsequential character of class struggle: he ends the novel as part of the gentility [*gente decente*], as a leader of his community).[11]

A split in the landscape, however, as a metaphor for a split in the social body, is a strong means of making this social body intelligible. The situation of loss at the beginning of the novel is more radical because it is one of an absence of limits. Once again, the romance is a major metaphor. Antonia wants Manuela to marry Nicolás, an Indian. Manuela rejects this class and race alliance. In reneging on her obligations to her family and eloping with her lover, Manuela crosses the garden wall that encloses family, work, property, and definite gender roles and separates them from the exterior (this garden has clear biblical resonance as the Garden of Eden).[12] In so doing, she crosses over to crime. When the sentimental choice is a metaphor for the political one, Manuela's election is not a bad choice of husband but a fatal political mistake. However, it is important to note that this personal trespassing is possible because of the previous transgression at the national level. The ill-starred personal encounter between Manuela and Zarco was only possible because of an earlier national transgression: the conversion of bandits into liberal storm troopers during the Three Years' War whereby the bandits became legitimate Liberal warriors who inhabited the public sphere as heroes.[13] In fact, Manuela falls in love with Zarco after a Liberal victory, when the winners of the day paraded in the streets of Cuernavaca (166). Manuela correctly points out that plagio was introduced not by bandits but by political factionalists (247), and the novel shows how armies behave just like bandits, plundering, and living shamelessly off the land and off honest citizens, executing only to instill fear (see chapter XIII, "El comandante"; also Vanderwood 1992, 28). This mistake (both Manuela's and Juárez's) provoked a confusion of legalities, a collusion between banditry and national politics that is crucial to the drama since the novel is at the same time its presentation and its symbolic cancellation and brutal corrective. The death of Zarco before a firing squad (with Manuela by his side) provides the possibility of "burying" (literally and metaphorically) a past of ambiguous compromises as a condition for a future without divergences.

Banditry is the condition for the existence of the family as a privileged form of social identity, since it is the family's exterior and threatening Other. By the same token, it is the dissolution of the "natural" family (Manuela's treason) that allows for the family's re-foundation on new ground. When Manuela elopes, Antonia acknowledges her own closeness with Pilar, the inheritor of her values and ethics and the person who tends to her on her deathbed (see chapter XVII, "La agonía"). On her deathbed, Antonia makes Nicolás her son since her last words are "Nicolás! My son!" (238). This is a political fact, since the marriage of Nicolás and Pilar is a metaphor of the formation of a modern civil society. As the novel says, it was a family celebration, but the entire population was part of it (327). The scene of the marriage as private/public occasion returns us to the landscape trope since the flowers that embellish the ceremony are orange and lemon blossoms (328).

They are flowers of production (they will be fruit, Yautepec's commodity), of citizen work, and of transculturation, as opposed to the roses that Manuela favors (109), which are ornamental flowers of seduction and loss.

Finally, consider Martín Sánchez Chagollan. This character is the one who cuts through the Gordian knot of violence. Martín Sánchez is a character built around a structural duality: offense/revenge. He was a rancher until the Plateados razed his ranch and killed his family (303). From that moment on, his life was an undivided desire for revenge (revenge is his motive, not justice, as the narrator points out [307]).[14] This structural duality is typical of the avenger, a variety of social bandit. The novel confirms this. In his role of bandit hunter, Martín Sánchez moves about like a bandit himself: secretly, at night, with a posse that has a sinister and imposing appearance (311). When it comes to his military strategy, he defeats the bandits because he acts like one in many respects. He terrorizes peasant communities to the point of (unofficially) prohibiting silver ornaments (312), he imparts justice not sanctioned in any written code (307), he is cruel to the point of horror (308), and he acts as an "Angel of Death" (308). His biography is, in fact, a bandit one, but reversed. The state did not dishonor him, turning him into a bandit, but the bandits affronted him, turning him into a vigilante first and a state official later.[15]

The history of Martín Sánchez exhibits the transformation of the sign of violence in two steps. First, a private revenge becomes a collective revenge ("from avenger of his family he had turned into a social avenger" [307]). Later, this communal violence becomes state violence, in the memorable meeting between Martín Sánchez and Benito Juárez, who legalizes Sánchez's actions (323). This dialogue represents an act of reciprocal empowerment. The legality that Juárez gives to his actions thus transforms Sánchez's unlawful violence into state violence and allows him to disguise what it "really" is: a private revenge, not much different from that of the Plateados. However, if Juárez endows legality, Sánchez endows legitimacy, since Juárez is recognized from "below" as the one who can allocate and regulate violence. None the less, this scene of double recognition, apparently without rest or fissures, is still problematic. In spite of what the novel says ("the law of public health arming honesty with the lethal lightning bolt" [326]), Sánchez *first* becomes bandit hunter and *later* obtains legal sanction. When Sánchez Chagollan goes to see Juárez, his position in relation to the state is still shaky, and it is as shaky as the Plateados' relationship; he was, in many respects, an outlaw just like them (without the powerful supporters within the state that the Plateados did have). However, Juárez needs him, and he thus co-opts a violence that the president does not own or even allocate (Sánchez Chagollan would not act differently, with or without Juárez's blessing: Juárez only relabels the actions, now calling them state retribution). Juárez does this through a decision (in the Schmittian sense) not grounded in the nature of the violence involved. In fact, the Plateados, up to that point, had been equally (if not more) useful to Juárez than Sánchez Chagollan had been (remember that the Plateados fought alongside the Liberal González Ortega, who later betrayed them [168]). The state, far from being the sovereign that originated violence, or expropriated it, is a third party that allies itself with one of the contenders in a field of struggle where each agent uses its portion of force. It is from this *contingent* alliance that the state is born as a false totalization of the social (in class, race, and also, very importantly, regional terms: the capital [Mexico City] with the state of Morelos).[16] One of the fundamental operations of this totalization (which also plays to the cherished liberal myth of its civilian origins, detached from the professional military) is to show that it is "natural" and "necessary," since it is a reaction to unjust violence and it emanates from contractual needs of society, thus closing the distance between law and justice.

The birth of universal law through violence means that all differences disappear in a homogeneous citizenship corroborated by the state: Nicolás is the model citizen, protected on his wedding day by Sánchez Chagollan. This is the condition of the last level of meaning: the novel itself is both the new epic poetry of the nation-state and the new agora of the citizens' abstract assembly. Its paramount example is the war against the Empire. The novel is set in the period between the Three Years' War and the Intervention, the last one a fight that the nation as a whole will fight (and one whose ideological riddles will be developed in *Clemencia*, Altamirano's other great novel).

The deaths of Zarco and Manuela are a metaphor of the death of the past in order to make room for a future of clear-cut features. The marriage of Pilar and Nicolás is a metaphor of the birth of civil society. The meeting of Juárez and Sánchez is a metaphor of the birth of the state. The last scene ties all three of these metaphors into a single, complex scene. Nicolás and Pilar marry at the office of the justice of the peace and at the church (thus conciliating Catholicism and liberalism). After the wedding banquet, they depart toward Atlihuayán. Zarco plots to kill Nicolás during the trip. Sánchez finds out and ambushes Zarco's gang. The nuptial procession, the bandits, and the bandit hunters meet at a crossroads (the place where state justice was deployed, in the form of the hanging body of the bandit). The happy couple witnesses the death of the evil one by the decree of the state. The bandit's death, as well as that of Manuela—the stranded woman—is the propitiatory offering that the state, through Sánchez Chagollan, makes to the new class and race alliance. It is a sort of wedding gift from Sánchez Chagollan as surrogate father: just like in *El periquillo sarniento,* in *El Zarco* there are no fathers (which equals chaos). The point is, always, to find a masculine/paternal principle that will fill the void. This also serves as a memento of the violence that is the condition and foundation of any given institution. With this terrifying symbol, the novel ends.

6 | Criminology
Banditry as the Wound of History

In spite of its somber, sometimes ominous tone, turn-of-the-century positivistic criminology was an undivided celebration of the status quo.[1] This celebration had a precise purpose: to move social conflict away from the political realm. Criminology did not deny the existence of conflicts within societies. Quite to the contrary, it brought them to the fore and shed a lurid light upon them. But it denied what I, together with Ernesto Laclau, would call its political character, that is, the historical contingency of the determinations bearing upon the conflicts, of the identities playing them out, of the dynamics in which the struggles were decided. By resorting to what José Ingenieros called cognoscitive monism—the postulate that both social and natural phenomena could ideally be described by the same set of principles, such as evolution, the progressive internal differentiation of organisms (Ingenieros 1910, 13)—these phenomena were explained away (or were expected to be explained away) through laws analogous to those of the natural sciences. Thus, criminology transformed conflicts in natural phenomena under the rubrics of atavism, criminal character, hereditary vice, or character flaw. The teleology of these explanations was, from Mexico to Argentina, the liberal-oligarchic state.

The various discursive practices that revolved around the topic of crime were a festive generic and theoretical hybrid that should be inscribed (in spite of the fact that criminologists abhorred this inscription) in the tradition of the Latin American national essay. In fact, criminology appropriated the epistemological privilege accorded to natural sciences, without abiding —as Robert Buffington correctly points out—by any of its restrictions, let alone developing a coherent theoretical foundation for their practice (Buffington 2000, 39–40). This leaning toward essay was more pronounced because, as many of its practitioners bitterly pointed out, the practice of empirically grounded social science was impossible in Latin America because of the lack of data gathering venues that would have made the practice possible as well as the institutional anchorage that would have given criminology a clear-cut status as a differentiated discursive practice (Guerrero 1905a, 7). Therefore, in spite of the perceived competition and struggle with traditional intellectuals, criminology should be viewed as another instance of the lettered city, in its multisecular battle for epistemological privilege.

Criminology was capable, however, of articulating practices and subjectivities to the signifier that marked them for exclusion, forcible exile, or outright extermination; this signifier was crime. The fixation of meaning by which popular illegalities were framed as crimes appeased the cultural anxieties born out of demographic and cultural fluxes of Latin America at the turn of the twentieth century, where modernity was changing the social landscape in unexpected ways and posing unheard of challenges to the position of the letrado elite.[2] Thus, the trope of crime gave a precarious legibility to an increasingly blurred map of the social realm.

Social and cultural historians devoted to criminology, either when interested in its relationship with policy making or in the conceptual and narrative aspects of its constitution as a discursive practice, link it predominantly with urban crime and policy making in the cities and also see it as part of a reflection on incarceration and discipline (see, among other examples, Guy 1991; Salessi 1996; Picatto 2001; Aguirre 2005). There are strong reasons behind this emphasis, since accelerated urban development was one of the primary features of the period and the locus of elite anxieties. However, it should not be forgotten that the original scene of criminology puts a bandit and a letrado face to face. When Cesare Lombroso was famously examining the skull of the Italian bandit Vilella he discovered the middle occipital fossa and the hypertrophy of the vermis in the criminal brain, and he saw, "lighted up as a vast plain under a flaming sky, the problem of the nature of the criminal—an atavistic being who reproduces in his person the ferocious instincts of primitive humanity and inferior animals" (quoted in Jones 1986, 83). Therefore, in order to recuperate the founding political gestures of criminology, we should step back from urban crime and address how criminology studied rural banditry. I contend that the "problem" of banditry took criminology to its own epistemological limits and made its practitioners able to experience, even to think, outside of its own practice and determinations.

"Lucas da Feira": Identities Out of Place, or Africa in Brazil

The adoption of a Lombrosian thesis by criminalists, the medical establishment, and policy makers in Latin America surpassed the success that the Lombrosian school had in Europe itself, where the Lombrosian approach never ceased to be challenged or resisted, either by competing schools of thought or the legal establishment (Leps 1992). Gilbert Joseph suggests that "as in Italy, Latin America's weak states found in Lombroso's concoction of anthropology, biology, medicine, and law a compelling rationale for monitoring, categorizing, disciplining, and centralizing control over still-fragmented and regionalized populations" (Joseph 2001, xv). Buffington (2000), Dain Borges (1993, 2001), and Picatto (2001) complement this suggestion by arguing that Lombroso (or fin-de-siècle European science in general) provided a theoretical framework through which it was possible to codify racial difference as a difference "before the law" and enact policies that were at the same time overly racialized but not "racist," since science provided the alibi to safely pass otherwise problematic value judgments.

In Brazil, one of the most respected representatives of this discipline was Raimundo Nina Rodrigues (1862–1906), the enthusiastic publicist for Lombroso's criminal anthropology. Nina Rodrigues was one of the most famous and orthodox practitioners of anthropometry as promoted by the Italian school, and he founded the Escola Bahiana of criminology. A small testimony to his importance was his being the recipient and analyst of the head of the charismatic Antônio Conselheiro after his body was unearthed and his severed head was paraded on a pike in the homecoming celebration of expeditionary forces upon the fall of Canudos in 1897. Nina Rodrigues presented the (disappointing) findings of his examination in the essay "A loucura das multidões," and he kept the head as a curio in the School of Medicine of Bahia. The relic eventually disappeared in a fire (Nina Rodrigues 1939, 131–35; Levine 1992, 184). Surprisingly enough, Nina Rodrigues failed to name the parading of a human head on a pike among the symptoms of collective madness (something that Euclides da Cunha, one of his readers, would ambiguously do [1902, 515]). His criminological work, as this episode shows, had several problematics at its center: the (lack of a) constitution of a true national subject, the transformations brought about by the emancipation of the slaves, the Canudos trauma, the European migration to the southern part of the country, and the economic crisis of the last decade of the nineteenth century and the authoritarian military government of the 1890s.

Nina Rodrigues's work bore the racist imprint that dominated the thought of the social sciences during the nineteenth century, a counterpart to the "Age of Empire," the high moment of European colonial expansion, and its concomitant medicalization of positivistic social thought. Within this paradigm, mixed race (*mestiço*) equaled "degenerate," an assertion that he argues at length in "Os mestiços brasileiros" and *As raças humanas: a responsabilidade penal no Brasil* (1894).[3] Indeed, racial interpretations of Brazilian banditry were very common in turn-of-the-century literature. The only two cangaceiros who were unequivocally deemed "noble robbers" were Antônio Silvino and Jesuíno Brilhante. Both were white or passed as white. As described by Antonio Fernandes in *Os cangaceiros*, Silvino "was blue-eyed, tall and broad-shouldered" (Días Fernandes 1914, 8), whereas Jesuíno Brilhante was, according to Rodolfo Theóphilo, blond: "His hair, of a reddish blonde, matched perfectly his eyes, which had the same color and were slightly squinting. The white skin with many freckles matched the hair color beautifully" (Theóphilo 1906, 19).

Along these lines, Nina Rodrigues wrote a series of essential articles published in French and Italian criminological journals. They were posthumously compiled by Arthur Ramos according to Nina Rodrigues's plan, in order to put together what we know as *As collectividades anormaes*. Along with *Os sertões* (1902) by Euclides da Cunha, the book is one of the preeminent examples of Brazilian positivism. Both books were written when the illusions of republican liberalism were facing ferocious resistance and showing their darkest sides. *As collectividades anormaes* devotes itself to—among other topics—the examination and condemnation of the two most important forms of nonstate violence that characterized the "long nineteenth century" in the northeast: the militant millenarianism of Antônio Conselheiro and his *jagunços* (discussed in his articles "A loucura epidêmica de Canudos" and "A loucura das multidões") and endemic banditry (discussed in "Lucas da Feira").The short essay on Lucas da Feira was to be the first installment of an entire treatise on criminal associations in Brazil, but Rodrigues's death prevented the project from coming to fruition. The essay opens with a seemingly off-topic statement (one that Euclides da Cunha will echo): "[W]e can only speak of a Brazilian people from a political point of view. From a sociological or anthropological viewpoint, a long time will elapse until we can consider Brazil as having a homogeneous population" (Nina Rodrigues 1939, 153). This lack of homogeneity and hence of political coherence is due to the undeniable plurality of Brazil, with "races that live together without mixing" (153). From this fact, Nina Rodrigues infers that "few human populations would be able to offer the Italian criminological school a most bril-

dity and racial mixture" that Gustavo Barroso attributed to all northeastern bandits (1912, 98). In Nina Rodrigues's account, Lucas was morally well above his milieu. "He was truly a superior black" (160) who comprised all the features of the romantic good robber. Generous and loyal, he did not turn in his accomplices, even when under torture (160); he never attacked his masters like a resentful runaway slave (161); he only killed in extreme circumstances (although, when forced to do so, he did it in a barbaric fashion); and he only killed traitors (162). Whenever possible, he robbed only people who did not belong to the area or people whom he did not know; thus, he tried to keep his band on amicable terms with his original community (162). Moreover, far from being asocial, he was able to establish regular commercial relations with prominent members of the local community (160).

Lucas was then not an *uomo delinquente,* to use Lombroso's term. But he was still an outlaw who admitted "having killed more than twenty people, having stolen on numerous occasions, kidnapped and raped more than six girls, etc." (158). (It is surprising that Nina Rodrigues is silent about what made Lucas a gory celebrity: after sexually assaulting his female victims, he tied them to trees, spread honey all over their naked bodies, and abandoned them to be devoured by ants [Coelho Fontes 1999, 11].) If Lucas's banditry is not inscribed indelibly in his body or his actions, it is because his criminal mark does not have to do with nature but with culture. As Josefina Ludmer proposes, crime is a "difference effect." In Lucas's case this difference effect has to do with the fact that he is out of place. The yearning for command, the brave arrogance that in Africa would have made him a "monarch" (160) or a founder of states in Brazil tossed him into a life of banditry (159). It made him gallows fodder and the figure against which the state built its legitimacy. But it did not escape Nina Rodrigues's attention that the conflict in which Lucas was involved had nothing to do with the nature of the violence that he meted out but rather that it was only a matter of conflicting perspectives on the same violence (something that he tried to explain away with the distinction between intrinsic and extrinsic crime): "Lucas is a criminal for us, the rest of the Brazilians who live under the clout of European civilization. In Africa he would have been a brave warrior or a renowned king" (162–63). This oscillation between criminality and ruler resonates in the appellation of the two most important bandits of the northeast: Antônio Silvino, called the "governor of the frontier" (Governador do sertão), and Lampião, celebrated as "king of the bandits" (O Rei dos Cangaceiros).

But Lucas was not in Africa. He was—ominously for those who imagined themselves living "under European civilization"—in Brazil. And it is from this being-out-of-place (understanding that the letrado elite determined which was the "proper place") that banditry is born in Nina Rodrigues's essay as the figure (rhetorical, but also penal) of the conflict when two or more collectivities claim the same territory. Nina Rodrigues, who quotes *L'Ethnographie criminelle* by Armand Corre, understands the intrinsic link between colonialism and banditry, in which banditry is the spark that illuminates the struggle between colonial castes and renders it intelligible. Lucas would have been a completely different thing in Africa. He would have inhabited another extreme: not extreme marginality, but extreme power or glory. (Ricardo Palma, in the *tradición* "Un negro en el sillón presidencial," narrates the story that would complement Nina Rodrigues's: the story of the black bandit Escobar, who briefly occupied the presidential chair in Lima. To the actual astonishment of witnesses and narrator, he behaved better than most postcolonial presidents.) At this point, Nina Rodrigues's logic faces an insurmountable obstacle. What he does not say, what he cannot say, is that the clash of perspectives that makes Lucas a bandit and not a father of states is not gratuitous. The existence of two cultural orders in the same territory is not natural but instead is motivated by powerful historical forces of which Lucas is only an effect. Lucas would be living in Africa, and he would be a king, if the needs of the sugar economy had not propitiated the slave trade that brought his parents, like so many others, across the Atlantic.

Nina Rodrigues's positivism is then an attempt—in what Roland Barthes (1957) called mythical fashion—to hide as nature (either race or psychology [Nina Rodrigues 1939, 163]) what was history (slavery). But the attempt failed, and banditry made visible the constitutive heterogeneity of society, the existence of two claims to the ownership of legitimate violence: Lucas versus the Bahian or Brazilian state. At the same time, the essay hides the historical character of that heterogeneity, thus changing the sign and shifting the responsibility for that violence. This take on banditry attempts to hide the fact that this heterogeneity is the product of modernity itself, not a vestige of premodern circumstances (Schwarz 1995, 278). The violence of the sugar economy based upon a slave workforce (the original violence that brought Lucas's parents across the Atlantic) becomes secondary, defensive violence. State violence is fashioned as the violence of the law that protects its prerogatives (and those of law abiding citizens) against the hubris of the bandit. Thus, Nina Rodrigues erases a link that for Lucas may have been essential: the link between the state and the slave trade.

The bandit's violence marks the undeniable gap between Europe (under whose codes live those whom Nina Rodrigues represents) and Africa (under whose codes live Lucas and the "abnormal collectivities," that the slippage of Nina Rodrigues's prose now shows as "collectivities," since there is an unrecoverable split in the norm). But this distancing between Europe and Africa (which is also an encounter: the reunion of Europe and its culture through Africa) has a name: Brazil. I am not aware of a more vivid testimony of this perception, of this disorientation when faced with the violence from below than the letter that Colonel José Américo Camelo wrote to the Barón de Jeremoabo. Américo Camelo (one of the most stubborn local adversaries of Conselheiro, one of those who lived "under the clout of European civilization") *no longer knew where he was,* since the "bandit" Conselheiro had become a statesman and Brazil revealed itself as Africa. Writes the colonel, "[S]ince we do not have government any longer in this unhappy land [Antônio Conselheiro] is now more powerful than Napoleon. I am not Brazilian any longer. The greatest insult that someone can heap upon me is to call me Brazilian. Today, I am considered and I intend to naturalize myself as African" (quoted in Novais Sampaio 1999, 97).

Lucas is an identity out of place, and his lonely presence in the backlands acquires a tragic stature when, through banditry, he can not only terrorize the backlands but also interdict an entire body of European knowledge and silently exhibit the wound of slavery upon which Brazil was founded. Lucas is out of place, maybe. But Nina Rodrigues's acumen manifests itself precisely at the point where it shows its limits: when he faces the fact that he and his ideas are no less out of place and that the placid scientist and the fearsome bandit share a common destiny of solitude and estrangement.

Hordes, Tribes, Gangs, States: The Dilemmas of Sovereignty in Julio Guerrero's *La génesis del crimen en México*

Julio Guerrero was part of an entire generation of intellectuals who took upon itself the task of justifying the historical necessity of the porfiriato. This was done through the differential appropriation of European criminological science. Carlos Roumagnac, Francisco Martínez Baca, Manuel Vergara, Miguel Macedo, Luis Lara y Pardo, and Rafael de Zayas Enriquez were the most important among these intellectuals, with positions encompassing all branches of the newly developed Mexican state, from the medical establishment and the university to the police, the army, and the judiciary. The porfirian establishment reciprocated, granting recognition to the new discipline in both intellectual and institutional terms.[4]

Upon first inspection, Guerrero's *La génesis del crimen en México: estudio de psiquiatría social* (1901) is exemplary in its positivistic bent. The purpose of the volume, as stated by the initial chapters, was to discover and explain the physical laws that would account for criminality in modern Mexico. This project would remove any significance from crime as social conflict, thus making state intervention to suppress crime not a political act but, as the porfirian elite preferred to call it, "administration."[5] Guerrero begins with the well-known postulate of the struggle for life as the scientifically determined law governing interaction between all living things (v). In orthodox fashion, survival of the fittest and adaptation to the environment are considered necessary corollaries of the previous postulate (v–vii). Crime is thus defined within this logic as the expression of differential evolutionary periods within society (vii), in which criminal activity (and its repression) is the conflict between those who, better prepared for the struggle for life, are evolving more successfully and at a more rapid pace, and those who are lagging behind because their weaker constitutions (due to heredity) make them more prone to succumb to the enervating influences of the environment (vii–viii).

Guerrero researches two general factors that account for these constitutional problems (thus providing a physical grounding to Mexican criminality): atmosphere and land (*territorio*). When it comes to atmosphere, Guerrero's approach is quite sophisticated, in particular when confronted with contemporary rudimentary approaches to climatic determinations, such as that of Francisco Bulnes (*El porvenir de las naciones hispano americanas ante las conquistas recientes de Europa y los Estados Unidos* [1899]), who subscribed to the centuries-old hypothesis of the inferiority of tropical countries. For Guerrero, Mexico's central plateau has a unique set of climatic characteristics, such as aridity, thin air, heat, unpredictable rain patterns, lack of major rivers, and excessive sunlight. The multisecular influence of these factors on populations (from blood oxygenation and muscle response to psychology) is, for Guerrero, responsible for the peculiar character flaws of the Mexican: laziness, sullenness, aggressiveness, lack of respect toward others, lack of planning for the future, lack of trust in the virtues of work, verbal incontinence (*glosolalia*), and compulsive gambling (*ludopatía*). These character flaws (*taras caracteriológicas*) are the origin of the staggering number of blood crimes in the Federal District. Moreover, the unpredictability of climatic changes also created a particular worldview based on a misperception of relations of causation, a misperception that Guerrero called either *teísmo meteórico* or *meteorismo teológico* (62–63), that is, the belief in the divine causation (hence, inscrutability) of climatic phenomena. This belief—transformed in a stoic, fatalistic attitude in the face of history—encompasses the entire Mexican historical experience, from Cuauhtémoc to Juárez (63).

Climate as a determinant of social behavior (something that had been already postulated by Montesquieu as well as Rousseau) served the canonical positivistic purpose of eliminating or strongly interdicting the notion behind all "theological" or "metaphysical" ideas of criminality, that of free will (the notion of which is embedded in the Mexican penal code of 1871, which defines crime as the "voluntary violation of a penal law, by doing what the law prohibits or not doing what the law commands" [*Código Penal para el Distrito Federal y Territorio de la Baja-California*, 4]).[6] In this interdiction of classical criminology he joins Zayas Enriquez, author of *Fisiología del crimen* (1885–1886), as well as Francisco Martínez Baca and Manuel Vergara, who wrote *Estudios de antropología criminal* (1892), even though their etiology was more related to organic factors (such as brain or skull malformations).

Land, the second factor Guerrero believed to affect criminal behavior, poses different theoretical problems for him. The unique cornucopia shape of Mexico and the enormous distances (aggravated by rains, vast deserts, or forbidding mountain ranges) were formidable obstacles throughout history to the formation of a fluid network of communication between different areas of the country (64–74). This difficult topography generated a particular brand of human being, with unique psychological characteristics. But it was decisive at another level: during what Guerrero calls the "pre-railway era," land was an insurmountable obstacle to the viability of a nation-state, not only because the communications necessary for running an administration were almost impossible, making political organization "theoretical and laughable" (79), but also because isolation implied that "each region . . . was in a different phase of evolution" (78).

At this point, Guerrero's argument changes direction because his "study on social psychiatry" becomes a study on the *historical* possibilities or impossibilities of the state as the privileged subject of Mexican history, and

Guerrero's criminological reflection becomes a historical narrative, encompassing the entire colonial and postcolonial Mexican experience (in a way similar to what the Argentine José María Ramos Mejía and José Ingenieros did in *Las multitudes argentinas* and *La evolución de las ideas argentinas,* respectively). This amplification of the topic takes his logic to an extreme where he finds himself in a landscape removed from the initially intended one. I depart from Buffington's assessment that this type of oscillation pertains to the pre-paradigmatic condition of Mexican criminological reflection (2000, 41) as well as the generalized eclecticism that characterized Mexican criminology.[7] I would argue that, at least in Guerrero's case, this oscillation pertains to the logic of his true problem, which is not crime in and of itself but the flawed process of constituting a Mexican ruling class, one able to exert hegemony over the nation. This flaw is for Guerrero the ultimate cause of crime in Mexico. By shifting to this political-historical approach, Guerrero moved away from science and reinstalled politics at the center of his reflection. It is this conception of the political as a discursive struggle and the historical as a cultural struggle where legitimacy equals contingent hegemony.

Guerrero discovers this problem, but for him it is hardly a reason to celebrate, since he is reintroducing what porfirian intellectuals detested, which is a deterritorialized conception of politics (without a natural link to the letrado elite). For Guerrero, with his porfirian sensibility, this reintroduction is a risk when not an out-and-out catastrophe. Thus, the problem of the genesis of crime is the same as the problem of the modern state and its achieving a monopoly of violence. Again, this monopoly of violence has two aspects: the physical expropriation of the means of violence from civil society and the imposition and validation of narratives that made this expropriation "natural" and "necessary." Territorial morphology (and hence territorial constraints) hindered both attempts in post-independence Mexico, when the conditions of the independence war and the intrinsic flaws of the new rulers (unacquainted with Mexican territory) were unable to achieve the monopoly of violence. But above all the new rulers were unable to replace the Church as the spiritual (cultural) ruler of the Mexican nation. As Guerrero puts it, "The paramount duty of any government is to last. But due to the difficulties in communications faced by all Mexican governments that preceded the current one, all were condemned to failure and fall" (103).

Spanish domination was more a moral than a military one. None of the new rulers who vied for power during the pre-railway era had the feudal loyalty, the catholic obedience of society, or the large army they would have needed to adequately replace the Spanish imperium. These rulers also lacked the necessary elements to establish their authority throughout the still embryonic nation. In particular, many lacked the basic knowledge needed to replace the Spanish imperium, since they knew little about the country they were attempting to govern (104). In this context of material and cultural collapse, a completely different conception of crime appears, one that it is not organized around race (as in the ideas of Carlos Roumagnac), or class (as in the works of Macedo or Verdugo), or weather (as in the writings of Bulnes), or craneometry, craneoscopy, cerebroscopy, or morphology (as advanced by Martínez Baca and Vergara). This new notion of crime is not even focused on the urban environment. In this novel conception, history enters the narrative in an unexpected fashion. Laziness ceases to be an atmospheric predetermination and becomes a feature of the reserve workforce, a byproduct of internal migrations unleashed by the continuous state of post-independence rural insurgency. Furthermore, the concentration of the population in cities (also a byproduct of rural insurgency) generates endogamy and modes of marriage and coupling that in turn cause birth defects, deformities, and hereditary illnesses that will later generate crime. Guerrero turns the order of causation upside down. Crime does not threaten the cohesion of the state; rather, it is the lack of cohesion of the state (a lack whose embodiment is insurgency) that engenders crime.

Under the single rubric "crime" we can find then two different types: crime that *transgresses* the law and crime that *destroys* or *creates* law. (I am appropriating Walter Benjamin's distinction here.) The first type is a problem for the state. It had to develop educational, urban, hygiene, and security policies able to control the violent proclivities of the "little people" of the Federal District who reacted to the stimuli of the environment not by adopting healthy lifestyles (proper alimentation and exercise) but by consuming strong stimulants like tobacco, chocolate, pulque, and coffee. The second conception of crime poses the problem of the body politic or, as Guerrero prefers, the problem of the imperium (103). Neither conception of crime is detached. To the contrary, the first one depends on and derives from the second, because, in fact, the first is an atavistic, relatively harmless residue of the second.

The first conception of crime is the idea of crime under porfirian rule. It is the residue of chaos within order. It may be a bloody type of criminality, certainly, but one that lacks any real potency to tear apart the fabric of society. The second compels Guerrero to return to the original scene of chaos: the independence wars. Reduced to its most terse expression, Guerrero's thesis can be read as follows: the War of Independence, like the collapse of the Spanish imperium and the end of the cultural unity of the viceroyalty, is the genesis of chaos of which crime is only an isolated symptom.

From this perspective, the War of Independence was a catastrophe. On the one hand, it was a necessary catastrophe since it was a crisis implied in the evolution from the theological to the next level, the metaphysical stage. However, it is immediately after the Córdoba agreements sealing Mexican independence (1821) that Guerrero locates the watershed that returned Mexico—via atavism—to the original scene of the struggle between Aztec cannibals and Spanish bandits. This watershed is the legitimation crisis (Habermas 1973), which accompanied the demise of theology as the only general belief system that supported as a coherent whole what was, in fact, impossible to sustain (200). (Vanderwood calls this general belief system "the aura of the King.")

At this point crime abandons its racial, class, linguistic, or cultural marks and becomes a problem that has to do exclusively with a legitimation crisis within the ruling class, in particular the letrado elite, what Guerrero called *los profesionistas superiores*. The lack of familiarity with the terrain (and hence, the lack of knowledge of the human varieties produced by this terrain) determined a complete dissociation between constitutionalist ideology and reality, which was at the root of the "administrative lyricism" and the collapse of authority that began with Iturbide and ended with Lerdo de Tejada. In his criticism of early liberals, Guerrero makes clear the stark difference that Marxism, decades later, would pose between ideology and hegemony (Williams 1977, 110).

The concept of crime as transgression is the occasion for Guerrero to indulge in his deft naturalistic prose. The concept of crime as collapse of hegemony, and as regression to a state before the law, offers Guerrero the opportunity to rehearse his biblical voice where the downfall of the state equals the end of the world and the bandit is the rider of the apocalypse:

> In more than four thousand military encounters the land was turned upside down with the tumulus of the fight, and piles of bloody corpses have fertilized the growing fields of the country's valleys. . . .
>
> At the highway crossroads, at mountain passes, at river fords, gangs of out-

laws sprang up robbing carriages, wagon caravans, and mule trains. Putting a pistol to the chest of their victims, the rebels forced the hacienda administrators to give money, jewelry, cattle, or seed as forced loans. The bandits tied them, in their presence they raped their daughters and wives, and beat and humiliated their bloody bodies lying in their offices. . . .

Population that in the times of Dr. Mora numbered eight million people did not amount to six when the French invaded, according to the estimates of Jourdanet. More than half a million square kilometers of national territory were lost, innumerable towns disappeared, frontier towns became cattle ranches or shanty-towns, and of many others only burned walls and scattered boulders are left. People ran away from villages to cities, but even there they did not find refuge from robbers, because in broad daylight and sporting firearms, the robbers held up houses, palaces, churches, and convents. . . .

The biological annihilation reached animals, hindering individual nutrition and species selection and improvement. People became smaller and thinner. . . . horses were less robust, donkeys were weaker, and cattle and pigs slimmer. . . .

Even plants felt the effects of the devastating hurricane of this cursed war. The vegetables of the Valley of Mexico were less savory, fruits were less sweet, and flowers lost luxuriance and fragrance. The breath of desolation that spelled death to the scattered remains of the Colony penetrated even to the calices of flowers and, at the same time, poured out men's lives in rivers of blood and killed the vigor and the reproductive ability in flowers' pollen (228).

Not only does Guerrero not eliminate the political from his consideration of crime, but—via the pathetic fallacy just quoted extensively—he *generalizes the political*. However, this generalization implies the return of the violence of the multitude (what Antonio Negri called the "constituent power" [1992] 1999). For Guerrero, this is the beginning of a process of decomposition that returns the state to its horrendous truth of brigandage:

The anarchic effect of these movements is perfectly symbolized in the series of decreasing rebellions that followed the Acordada uprising of 1824. Zavala rebelled against the War Minister who had just been elected President of the Republic. During that rebellion all the commercial establishments located in the Parián were plundered. Melchor Múzquiz rebelled against Zavala; Colonel Gil Pérez in Puebla rebelled against Múzquiz; and the Seventh Regiment that was in charge of guarding the transport of $2,000,000, under the orders of Gil Pérez, rebelled against its superiors and sacked the bounty. (211)

The eclipse of the state as an active agent is what causes the "return of the repressed" under the guise of regressive types in the eras of vandalism. But this regression does not have an exclusive racial reference. If, among the Indians, the priest of Huitzilopotzli reappears, then in the Creole version the Spanish brigand—the military adventurer just released from the jails of Córdoba or Sevilla—reappears (247). The return to the past is the nomadic band (Huns, Bedouins, Tuaregs, Ethiopians), the war machine, or, as Guerrero favors, "military banditry," where violence becomes its own principle of rationality and reproduction. This nomadic band, at one extreme, claims legitimacy as a state making factor, but on the other, it is just a plundering gang.

Thus, Guerrero faces the problem of deciding upon which foundation to reestablish statehood. He decides to set the nomadic war machine against another machine: the train. The railway connects the land to transport troops who would end military banditry, and it segments the land in order to make it available for production, ownership, and taxation. The train cancels the smooth space of the insurgency. It claims the territoriality expropriated by the gang for the state and centers this territoriality in the city for the needs of global capital. The assemblage of the army/railway/telegraph is, according to Guerrero "the most perfect machine ever conceived by man to transform a multitude of isolated populations into a strong and homogeneous state" (199). Also (as Guerrero states elsewhere), it is a means to end the rule of military banditry as the form par excellence of premodern war and as the enemy of modern capitalism (1905b, 8).

But this assemblage is successful only if it is animated by the soul of ideology. Thus, what Guerrero understands as social psychiatry is not the common positivistic idea of abnormal psychiatry but rather the study of the cultural bases for the legitimation of rulers, and *La génesis del crimen en México* is a treatise on the building of hegemony. This is why the body of the book, surprisingly, is not devoted to criminals but to the Catholic Church, the only successful experiment so far in constructing hegemony in Mexico. But in porfirian Mexico, where the Church no longer played this key role within society, that task pertained to a particular social group, the *letrados científicos* as producers and supporters of the ideology around which a modern society would coalesce. Porfirio Díaz, Guerrero stated, was able to suppress banditry and build a nation from a colony (1905a, 13) out of a shapeless accumulation of fiefdoms ruled by political bosses (*cacicazgos*) (1905a, 14). But this was done without a radical transformation of the languages of power; therefore it was empirical and not destined to last. In fact, Guerrero's project becomes an analysis of the class to which he himself belongs, and the assessment is similar to the one that he applies to the Mexican lower classes: if in one case the Mexican citizen is affected with verbal incontinence (*gloso-lalia*), the Mexican intellectual is affected by a similar disease of undue attachment to grand-sounding words (*glosología*). On the one hand there is a language without reality making capabilities (Liberalism), and on the other there is a reality maker (Porfirio Díaz) that lacks a language. That gap can be bridged by the constitution of a modern (not Arielista) elite. The password of that ideology is "science," but its use resembles more of a dogma, governed by a principle of differential distribution, in which science does not perform the liberal role of universal emancipation but the cohesive one of cementing hegemony. Science is the new letrado Church, through which the relationship between letrado and national project is reestablished as a double gesture of restoration and expropriation of the political. This establishes Guerrero's unique place within Latin American positivism. The task for the Mexican intellectual is to develop the language of power (1905a, 18) as a mechanism for producing reality (what early Liberals lacked). The ownership of this language will be the realm of politics, a realm that becomes restricted politics (or as Pier Paolo Portinaro prefers, "high politics"), away from the generalized politics of insurgency ("low politics"), Guerrero's military banditry.

Part II

Between Conservative Nostalgia and Radical Politics

The Bandit as Instrument of Critique

7 | *Astucia*
Banditry and Insurgent Utopia

> The bandit may appear at a critical point where the reigning emperor has reached a crisis of legitimacy. . . . The bandit is less a positively constructed alternative form of power than the symbol of what the emperor should be. He is an *imperator* "manqué."
>
> Brent Shaw, "Bandits in the Roman Empire"

Astucia, el jefe de los Hermanos de la Hoja o los charros contrabandistas de la Rama: novela histórica de costumbres mexicanas con episodios originales, by Luis Inclán (1816–1875), was published in 1865. Today it is considered a key work in nineteenth-century Mexican literature, although often for the wrong reasons. In order to recover the political value of the novel, it is important to detach the novel from the state-sponsored nationalist populism that promoted it as a happy repertoire of *la mexicanidad,* as if Inclán's work were a forerunner of *Allá en el Rancho Grande* (1936), by Fernando de Fuentes (1894–1958). This nationalist appropriation, however, is not without reason. As we will see, in the trope of the charro–social bandit, Inclán convoked all the motifs that would later crystallize in porfirian and revolutionary nationalism. But at the same time, Inclán moved radically away from these models because he did not make the nation-state the final cause of the bandit's politics. *Astucia* inscribes itself in an alternative space of intelligibility, and while the novel occasionally converges with the nation-state, or is "captured" by it, it does not belong to the nation-state.

It is precisely for this reason that *Astucia* is an outstanding case study to open this part, which is devoted to the appropriations of the bandit trope that function as a direct critique of the political-cultural dimensions of modernity. Without limiting themselves to the exhausted, commonplace lionizing of the noble robber à la Robin Hood (attempts in that direction rank among the most notorious fiascos in Latin American literature), all of the works in this part use banditry as cultural artifact in a critique geared toward the political and cultural synthesis that was on its way to becoming dominant in Latin America. In *Astucia,* as well as in the other works discussed in part II of this study, the borders between bandit and letrado projects are porous, and the trope's mobilization shows internecine conflicts and cultural wars within the letrado elite, as well as widely diverging conceptions on the issue of rural violence (or outlaw violence in general) vis-à-vis nation-state formation.

Astucia can be divided into three parts: the first comprises the adventures of Lorenzo Cabello (a.k.a. Astucia), who is chieftain of the Brothers of the Leaf (Hermanos de la Hoja), the tobacco smuggling band in Santa Anna's Mexico.[1] In particular, the novel details the gang's long-standing feud against the Resguardo, the armed outfit that upholds the state monopoly.[2] Astucia sports all the classic features of the social bandit. He begins his bandit career because a representative of the state (a tax collector [*alcabalero*]) wrongs him. In addition, his values are the same as those of his community, with which he never loses contact and in which he is never seen as a criminal. He uses economic as well as military means to help the poor, the weak, and women, and he kills only when doing so is unavoidable. He also has a superb, almost perfect knowledge of the terrain in which he operates. Finally, he is invulnerable, and he can be defeated only through treason, which ultimately happens when an auxiliary of his band gives the Resguardo a hint about the whereabouts of his gang, which in turn allows the Resguardo to execute a fatal ambush of the Brothers of the Leaf (Inclán 1865, 400).

After this defeat, facing the pressing need to support his family and those of his fallen brothers, Astucia sets himself up as chief of public security and autocrat of the Quencio Valley ("the Valley") in Michoacán.[3] There, he creates a kind of parallel state entirely distinct from the Mexican state: it is legitimate, meticulously honest, and impeccably efficient. This act of becoming a statesman is not a redemptive radical change in moral condition as in *El periquillo sarniento*. Astucia was not a criminal but a social bandit, a condition unknown to Fernández de Lizardi and other authors analyzed earlier. Social bandits do not redeem themselves; they only abandon the highway, so to speak. In addition, the principles that regulate the very existence of the Valley as a body politic are built upon the cultural capital of the former bandit gang, as emblematized in the mottos "All for one and one for all" (*Todos para uno, y uno para todos*) and "With cunning and wisdom one can take advantage of any situation" (*Con astucia y reflexión se aprovecha la ocasión*). Legality (that of the state of Michoacán) and legitimacy (that of Astucia's rule) seem to reconcile toward the end of the second part of the novel, when Astucia has an interview with the governor of Michoacán—who happens to be his father-in-law (note the similarity to *El periquillo sarniento*).

characters. In Novo's work, Lencho abandons his father and home because he wants to know Mexico, and the voyage is a metaphor of Lencho's becoming a citizen. In Inclán's text, the space of the novel is never called Mexico. In spite of the fact that it is read as a "most Mexican" (*mexicanísima*) piece of prose, to use Mauricio Magdaleno's superlative (1948, 85), or as a "treasure of the language and a mural of Mexican customs and manners," according to Esther Martínez Luna's (2001) most Cervantine expression, "Mexico" has a notoriously scant presence in the novel. For example, the word "Mexico" is rarely uttered or referred to. This is not because Mexico has such an overwhelming presence that any mention of it is unnecessary, as in the *Q'ran* of "El escritor argentino y la tradición" (1932, in Borges 1974), where "Arab" does not need to appear as a represented object because it is what originates the representation. It is not that Inclán is a sort of "naive poet" (Schiller 1795–96) whose closeness to his community hinders him from giving it a name. (Novo would be, from this perspective, the "sentimental poet.") In the novel, quite to the contrary, "Mexico" as it was constituted toward the mid-nineteenth century was the enemy. Mexico was the state that negotiated with criminals to make them Resguardo officials and persecuted honest ranchers (158). Mexico was the corrupt and treacherous Alcabala officials (66, 334). It was the unceasing uprisings (*pronunciamientos*) that gave political stature to common criminals (347). It was the dizzying change in governors (466), and it was the city from which nothing good ever came and whose most conspicuous representatives were the former prostitute Amalia la Bulli Bulli (194) and M. F. C., the student who rapes Mariquita (320).

However, this departure from state-sponsored nationalism does not imply that Inclán neglects the problem of the nation. It means that he defines it according to a different set of parameters. *Astucia* tries to solve the liberal dilemma of the cultural and political incorporation of the peasant and the rural inhabitant in general, beyond the doomed alternative between forced assimilation to European sociability or violent suppression. Through the trope of the charro–social bandit, Inclán sets (within the limits of elite discourse) the conditions for the homogenization "from below" of the Mexican cultural space, a "popular liberalism" of undeniable force during that time although barely articulated at the letrado level (see Mallon 1995; Thomson and LaFrance 1999). The active pole of this liberalism (according to Inclán) would not be the state associated with a monetary economy led by the exportation of primary products and importation of manufactured and cultural goods (the paradigm that the porfiriato would sponsor and enforce) but local peasant and rancher culture.

The charro-smuggler could very well be, as Inclán himself proposes at the beginning of the novel, a "national type par excellence" (3). However, the word "national" has a different meaning here than "nation-state." This national type (or proto-national type, e.g., the Valley) comes into existence by avoiding any national-statist interpellation, as shown in the fact that the only representative of "Mexico" (as nation-state) is Bulldog, the former bandit who was made chief of the Resguardo, the nemesis of the Brothers of the Leaf and the symbol of all that is flawed. Inclán subordinates the state to the previous existence (but not in the romantic-mythical sense) of a vibrant cultural community (unlike in Sarmiento's writings, where the state implied the cancellation of the rural community). This community does not exhaust its meaning in nationalism (as is the case with Altamirano's Martín Sánchez Chagollan), and it is not relegated to the past under the form of *Volk* (as with Távora's Cabelleira). Américo Paredes was certainly brilliant when proposing in 1960 that Inclán should be read within a tradition of literature that was not co-extensive with the rubric "Mexican literature," understood as a lettered nationalist artifact. Paredes places Inclán within the series of "cowboy writers" that thrived until the twentieth century on both sides of the U.S.-Mexico border. This displacement takes Inclán's novel away from its place as a rudimentary monument and repositions it in a more contemporary tradition, closer to the narcocorrido than to the romantic novel.

Thus, the Mexican customs and manners of which the novel's subtitle speaks are not representative of the ideology of the decent gentlemen (*hombres de bien*) from the Republic, the Empire, or the porfiriato.[6] The condition of possibility for this dis-identification is that the cultural capital that Inclán brings to the fore and that Astucia represents appeals, on the one hand, to a particular version of the popular (the rancher's culture) and, on the other hand, to nineteenth-century mass culture (the newspaper serial novel). Inclán's relationship with ranching culture has been thoroughly researched and explained (see Porras Cruz 1976). His relationship with mass culture has not. As mentioned, the politics of the gang is expressed in the motto "Todos para uno, uno para todos." This motto is a notorious borrowing from *Les Trois mousquetaires* (1844), by Alexandre Dumas père (1802–1870). Mexican ranchers' borrowing of political programs from French best-sellers is something—translated to our contemporary references—like writing a

Latin American political utopian novel whose ideologue was Morpheus, Neo's Virgil in the film *The Matrix* (1999), another story of obstinate outlaws.[7] Today, we witness this without much of a wince and may even gasp in awe at this most postmodern attitude. But this was not the case in 1865 in Mexico. In any case, what is crucial is that through this double heterodox inspiration, Inclán breaks away from the closure imposed by nationalists à la Altamirano, which defined the national from the vantage point of high culture, incorporating, in a highly restrictive fashion, selected elements of popular culture.

There are two operations that allow Inclán to put this alternative conceptual universe together. First, he rethinks the meaning of the Mexican War for Independence (1810–1821). Secondly, in Astucia's body he collapses the distinction between state and civil society. The debate around the independence war was crucial during the first postcolonial century in order to define the imagined community "Mexico." Conservatives and royalists maintained that the "true" independence war was the one of Iturbide's *Armada Trigarante*, and they considered the Grito de Dolores of September 16 to be a well-meaning, misguided effort that ended in an all-out barbaric rebellion against property and civilization. This interpretation (heralded, most illustriously, by Lucas Alamán in *Historia de Méjico desde los primeros movimientos que prepararon su independencia en el año de 1808, hasta la época presente*) clashed head-on with the Liberal one, which saluted Hidalgo, Guerrero, and Morelos as the true emancipators and founding fathers (Hale 1968). Inclán, who subscribed to the second interpretation, "invented a tradition" that was embodied in the father metaphor because *Astucia*, like *El periquillo sarniento* and *O Cabelleira*, revolves around the prestige of the paternal principle.[8] The charros were a brotherhood (the Brothers of the Leaf). Unlike the bandits in *El periquillo sarniento*, who lacked fathers and were not an association but a horde, the Brothers of the Leaf were heirs and replicas of another brotherhood, that of the emancipators. They are all sons or nephews of veterans of the wars of the 1810s, who fought the wars together.[9] For Inclán, the popular independence war, far from being a fratricidal one—as it was considered by the conservatives—sets the scene for the constitution of the national family as a community that establishes itself beyond and against the state's gaze. This community snatches one of the main reservoirs of memory and symbolic capital from the state and uses it to establish an exclusive relationship. Inclán dissociates the legacy of Hidalgo, Morelos, and Allende from the dubious trajectory of the postcolonial state and links it to its "origins": the rural insurgency that operates outside the law and whose subject is not the "people," as in the populist interpellation, but the multitude (Hardt and Negri 2004). The smugglers are then the true heirs of the legacy of insurrection against a Mexico that—under the metaphor of the tobacco monopoly and the Resguardo—has become or has always been a criminal band. (Bulldog, the Resguardo chief, is a former nonsocial bandit who joined the outfit in order to obtain sanctuary from his former accomplices, whom he had betrayed [Inclán 1865, 158].)[10]

After the annihilation of the band, Astucia is captured by the Resguardo. His initial deposition, however, is far from an admission of guilt and defeat. It is a performance where Astucia challenges the state about the very meaning and validity of the law and reverses the presumption of guilt. Astucia identifies the battle in which his gang was stamped out with a highway robbery by bushwhackers (the Resguardo officials) whose victims were honest traders (the Brothers of the Leaf). Astucia appropriates the trope of otherness that the state was wielding (banditry as a way to de-legitimize subjects) and uses it against the state. He declares,

> Things were very simple. We had, as did Jesus Christ, a traitor disciple, a Judas who sold us. . . . The robbers who held us up were many and even though we fought as men who defend their business and their lives, eventually we were overpowered.
>
> [The police official answers:] But the fact is that you were carrying goods that are expressly prohibited by law to trade freely. In short, as smugglers you have been caught red-handed and punished by the Resguardo and a public force that aided them, according to the memorandums from the Chairman, and the report by the chief of the expedition.
>
> [Astucia replies:] Those reports can say whatever they want, but the facts speak for themselves. I stand by my statement that we were robbed by bandits and robbers. (413)

If Astucia does not plead guilty, he does not plead innocent either. Both options would constitute an implicit acknowledgment of the legitimacy of the process and the trial itself. Astucia is intent on interdicting the very origin of the authority that questions him as well as the value judgments emanating from this authority.[11] He opposes this authority with the full force of the oral law of the smugglers. Furthermore, he establishes an explicit and strong link between that oral law and a tradition of anticolonial resistance that dates back to the opening acts of the Spanish Conquest:

> The crime of contraband that I am being accused of, I deny it; the affirmation that we were caught red-handed is a calumny, because that expression applies to bandits and robbers when they are caught in possession of their booty. We were carrying our loads bought with our own money. The tobacco leaf that we trade was sold to us by their owners, who cultivated them with the sweat of their brows on their property. And, when it comes to the fact that there are laws that ban the free trade of a regulated commodity, I believe that the laws that the Spanish government imposed upon us when we were under their domination should not be in use any longer, . . . because after all these years of war and all the blood shed by good Mexicans that were able to shrug off the yoke, and achieve our independence, it would be plain wrong to try to enforce the same laws that despotism imposed upon us, laws that tied the hands of the sons of the land, hindering their progress . . . and even worse is to use them to whip us with the same whip, when we are told by our representatives that we are free, that our nation is a republic, that everybody is a citizen, that there are no tyrants any longer, and plenty of other things in plain contradiction with reality. (413)

The paternal legacy (the endowment of the insurgent values) that Astucia proudly displays as the foundation of oral law creates a common memory. Before or alongside the memory of their own feats, the charros share the memory of the feats of their elders. This double memory cements their shared sense of community and their practice. It is not only that the charros have a memory (that the novel sets in opposition to constitutive state amnesia); they are also themselves the memory of the insurgency because their smuggling is a reenactment of the rebellious epic of their predecessors. Thus, the Brotherhood of the Leaf is a sort of imagined community formed according to different principles than those of the nation-state. Imagined communities, according to Benedict Anderson, are a product of print capitalism, in which the circulation of books and periodicals as commodities makes the awareness of the simultaneous existence of a community possible (under the form of the ideational community of readers) in empty and homogeneous time. By contrast, the memory of the Brothers of the Leaf circulates in a completely oral medium in the successive tales of each of the charros, which occupy the bulk of the first part of the novel.[12]

The oral reputation as a privileged form of the rural public sphere is the place where the alternative law of the charros "lives." Because of this, Astucia is very careful to protect his reputation, and he uses a complex system of substitutes, pseudonyms, and secrets in order to determine which of his actions will be a part of his public identity. This reputation is the veritable axis on which the military organization of the charros rests: as the Resguardo becomes painfully aware time and again, the Brotherhood is inexpugnable because of its superior knowledge and domination of the terrain. But this dominion is a byproduct of the solidarity between the social bandit and the community, which assumes the form of a network of informants, couriers, lookouts, suppliers, and contributors whose bonds with the gang are solidified by economic incentives and above all by cultural affinities (this distinction between the cultural and the economic is relevant for us, but for them this was not entirely the case).[13]

The focus of Astucia's reputation is his body. Bandit narratives, in general, share in the premodern conception of the body as visible manifestation of sovereignty (see Foucault 1975). In this case, the body is a manifestation of oral law's sovereignty vis-à-vis the state law, visible in the body of the statesman (Bulldog first, the governor later). This is why Astucia and his charros are stronger and more handsome than their enemies. This is also why they always attract women (as was the case with Zarco and Manuela; in nineteenth-century novels sentimental options are mediations for political ones). The collusion between paternal law (which carries the legacy of pro-independence insurgency) and insurgent body (which mediates the relationship between that law and the community) takes place in the transition between the first and the second part of the novel. After the battle in which the gang is eliminated almost to the last man (Inclán 1865, 405), Astucia, whose body is riddled with more than thirty machete and spear wounds, is pronounced dead. However, he comes back to life after three days. (The Christian motif—here linked to the motif of apparent death [*Scheintod*]—is present in the novel more than once.) This happens thanks to the devoted care of peasants and villagers who form a collective identity—a precursor of what developed in El Valle—in the uprising in which they defend the body from the Resguardo's unquenchable thirst for revenge (408). (This is a classic motif of bandit narratives. The corpse of the English robber Dick Turpin, for example, was also saved by the crowd in order to prevent royal surgeons from dissecting it [Seal 1996, 64].) The scars from machetes and spears on Astucia's body are the writing of the state on the bandit's body, in which the weapon penetrating the flesh is an allegory of power (see Teskey 1996, 137–38). It is a material excess (Astucia's enemies keep poking at him with his weapons even though they are sure he is dead [Inclán 1865, 406]) but not a symbolic one. Thus, when Astucia becomes chief of public security of the Valley, those same scars, far from being a badge of infamy, become a mark of honor in the writing of insurgency from which memory springs. Astucia invents a story according to which those wounds were suffered while fighting with Vicente Guerrero against the royalists. In this same story, he was a kind of adoptive son of the hero (454). If we keep in mind that tobacco smuggling is linked, for the Brothers of the Leaf, to the memory of the independence wars, Astucia's yarn is only a half lie. It is false at the superficial level of the facts (Astucia never actually met Guerrero, let alone fought alongside him) but not at the deeper level of symbolism, where the nation-state is equated with colonial oppression. Cascabel, the new chief of the Resguardo, threatens Astucia:

> "Mister" Astucia, because you are a showoff and rebellious type, I have the intention of teaching you a harsh lesson and of not ceasing to persecute you, until I see you hanging from the *palo de la Loba*, where captain Cuitlacoche was hanged.
> . . .
> [Astucia replies:] If in the *palo de la Loba* the *gachupines* hanged captain Cuitlacoche because he was a valiant fighter who defended the independence of his fatherland, right there I will order my men to give you an ass-whipping with stinging nettles, to punish the fact that your elders belonged to Iturbide's empire. (334)

The same motto ("all for one and one for all") that was the unifying principle of the charros' war machine also ensures the solidarity between Astucia as sovereign by popular acclamation (the "one") and the group of notables that supports him (the "all"). His own body, wound-honored, and his name "Colonel Astucia" (again, supposedly given by Guerrero) make race and class differences disappear (at least as a source of conflict) within the "all." They ensure the homogeneity of the social body and the coherence (even lack of differentiation) between civil society and state, principles that for Inclán should have triumphed in the independence wars.

"With cunning and wisdom one can take advantage of any situation" (*Con astucia y reflexión se aprovecha la ocasión*) is the other slogan that ruled the gang. (Predictably, it is a piece of advice that Astucia's father gave to his son with his departing blessing.) In the Valley this regulates relations with the authorities at the state level, relations that range from dissimulation to open hostility. While the brotherhood's principles dictate that nothing may be stolen in the Valley, it is legitimate for Astucia to steal as much as possible from Michoacán (something that he does repeatedly). Just like in the case of nation-states, there is a moral principle of solidarity within the group and a political principle of violence directed toward those exterior to the group (e.g., Michoacán or the nonsocial bandits). This double standard of politics is based upon a stark sense of group survival, the same mechanism at work in the Río Frío band in *El periquillo sarniento*. The (essential) difference is one of perspective: Fernández de Lizardi considered the law of the bandits a non-law, a translucent disguise for the monstrous chaos lurking behind apparent material success and moral solidarity. For Inclán, the law of the bandits is the "original" law, a law in connection with justice, emanating from the con-stituent power (Negri 1999) of the insurgent multitude, before the consti-tuted power (the Mexican state) lost contact with its origin and became a husk or a skeleton, one mobilized for perverse purposes.

Thus, the insurgency of the charros becomes a model for order when compared to the cycle of the governors, a cycle that gives a circular image of history under the form of the eternal return of Santa Anna. This is why, from banditry, Astucia becomes the cornerstone of an alternative state, and the mechanism through which that community becomes a reality is the same in any nation-state: to name and isolate an Other outside the law. This mechanism comprises a twofold process: the resistance against Michoacán outside the territory and the persecution of Rotito's brigands within it (443). In fact, just as in *El periquillo sarniento*, hanging bandits along high-ways (462) is part of the classic state's "pedagogy of terror" (Salvatore 2001). Astucia does the same, with good results: the surviving members of Rotito's gang (including Rotito himself) decide not to return to the area, in order not to risk their accomplices' less-than-enviable fate (462). Astucia represents the collusion between alternative statehood and local violence. This becomes visible in the emblem that Astucia chooses: the lasso (*reata floridena*) with which he threatens to hang troublemakers from the nearest tree. This *reata floridena* is not just any rope. It is the charro's rope par excel-lence, the one that is used in the equestrian and cattle ranching exercises where the charros (as the novel shows repeatedly) are insuperable. Its importance to the charro is why this symbol belongs to the theater of law but at the same time is a demonstration of the cultural solidarity that Astucia is intent upon showing with civil society (similar in this respect to the rosista fighting knife). This coherence is so strong that Astucia actually uses this rope only once, at the inaugural scene of his rule (the raid against bandits). As the novel states, "Everything was flourishing; a lot of traffic from the muleteers, tradesmen, cattle ranchers, and the transit was so safe that nobody had a single reason to complain. If somebody lost an article on the road, whoever found it picked it up and hung it on a tree or brush, and there it would stay until the owner came back to retrieve his possession. This was so because the colonel's *reata floridena* instilled fear in everybody, and luckily he never had to use it with anybody, although he often threatened to do so" (464). In this fashion, violence is quite absent from the depicted world, because Astucia's totalitarian monopoly of violence makes actual violence unnecessary. This is the cornerstone of the success of his program and the culmination of this unusual political fable. In it, a violent subject outside the law brings political order into existence in a place where the distinction between community and oral law is so precise that violence disappears. It is a "nation" whose "state" works in such a perfect fashion that the latter can disappear as such, and the monopoly of violence is so perfect and so legitimate that it can be delegated without risk. This occurs when Astucia buys weapons in the United States and personally arms a group of dwellers in each village.[14] This is the legacy of the war of independence, at last enjoyed by its true heirs and put to work, if only for a fleeting moment.

Astucia, mediator of an alternative sovereignty derived from the popular war of independence, is the possibility of what Margo Glantz calls "an insurgent utopia" (see Glantz 1985). If we accept for a moment this felicitous term, this utopia would be commensurable with the nation-state form, because it would adopt its basic attributes. From this perspective, the Valley that Inclán imagines would be a maquette of the ideal state and the social bandit, a kind of president *manqué* who points out by contrast what the sovereign should be and is not. (Utopia always has a strong element of criticism and parody, according to Robert Elliott [1970].) To a certain extent, *Astucia* is indeed that. However, the novel does not consecrate this utopia as the ultimate aim of the transformations of the *independentista* legacy. Rather, it takes Astucia's logic beyond statehood. The novel makes the Valley only a transient embodiment of Astucia's political agenda. Indeed, it opens up the possibility of considering other forms of the political that exceed the modern paradigm centered on the nation-state.

The very concept of Utopia implies the cancellation (through resolution) of all conflicts. As such, it implies the cancellation of history (conflict being the prime mover in history). This does not happen in *Astucia*. The novel does not end with the agreeable prospect of prosperity and harmony in the Valley but with a disgruntled Astucia relinquishing his position and withdrawing to private life (528). This causes the Valley to enter a renewed period of anarchy and civil strife (530). In one sense, this is regression or jumping back (*vuelta atrás*) that throws the Valley once again into history. In this sense, perhaps there never was a utopia.

"All for one and one for all" is the catchphrase that Astucia uses to persuade the notables of the Valley (443). However, this political axiom is not applied in a homogeneous fashion. For the smugglers, the motto expresses the absolute incorporation of individual identity into collective identity, where, as in a mirror, one is all, and vice versa. For example, Astucia is elected chief of the brotherhood in a draw (86) that confirms the complete reciprocal equality and equivalence of all members within the gang (anyone other than Astucia could have been leader). He is not qualitatively better than anyone else but is only a *primo inter pares*. This sets *Astucia* apart from most narratives of noble robbers, in which the captain is qualitatively superior to the rest of the gang members (the main example being, of course, that of Robin Hood).

Moreover, the bulk of the first part of the novel consists of the life stories of each member of the brotherhood: Pepe el Diablo, Tacho Reniego, el Charro Acambareño, Alejo Delgado. It is difficult—even impossible—to distinguish each story from the next, since all reiterate the same macroproposition: once upon a time there was a young rancher at the brink of perdition, rescued by the intervention of a father or father figure, later incorporated into the Brotherhood of the Leaf. In the same fashion, the charros—with the exception of Astucia—are impossible to distinguish from each other. This lack of distinctive features is not a narrative flaw, an imperfect definition of the characters. It is a deliberate emphasis of the fact that the gang itself has a clear-cut identity, not the individuals that form it.

Finally, when Pepe el Diablo and Astucia hug each other and swear eternal friendship with the oath "All for one and one for all," this catchphrase is the afterword to the long tale whereby Pepe has just narrated his entire life.

His previous life is consequently abandoned, tossed away, and he gives up his identity in its entirety to Astucia and the Brothers of the Leaf (136).

In the Valley things happen somewhat differently. The alliance between the "one" and the "all" entails an analytic distinction between Astucia and his followers, in which "all for one" does not imply the birth of a single political body but of two: the "one" (Astucia, the sovereign) and the "all" (the inhabitants of the Valley). The principle of equivalence is replaced in the Valley by a principle of alliance between heterogeneous identities. In this political arrangement, no one can replace Astucia. The people of the Valley will experience this when Astucia deserts them, a desertion they will lament with "tears of blood" (530). Again, this is confirmed in several instances. For example, even though Astucia is the most important personality in the Valley and even though he has a strong public presence (he makes all the important decisions, he concentrates all public powers in his person, and he never fails to appear at public events), nobody knows his true name and therefore his true affiliations. In addition, the Brothers of the Leaf share a common reservoir of legitimacy in the oral law donned by their parents, since they are all descended from fighters of the independence war. In this sense, "all for one and one for all" is less a founding principle than an iterative one. Through the mediation of the paternal epic, the brothers belonged to each other before being born. In the Valley, Astucia does not share that privilege with anyone. The locus of parental law is Don Juan Cabello's tomb, where Astucia "speaks" to his dead father and where he had the inspiration to become chief of security (438). Nobody knows the location of the tomb, thus emphasizing the exclusivity of their relationship with the *independentista* legacy (473).

Finally, during his adventure in the Valley, Astucia keeps his extended family hidden. His very existence is ignored by the Valley inhabitants. To the world, Astucia is a single man with no known lair. Nobody knows where he comes from or even where he spends the night (473). After rescuing/kidnapping Amparo (his bride), he is able to live with her for years without public knowledge. This reticence, which makes the hero a stranger for those he helps, is more than a classic romantic vicissitude. It is a political distinction of the utmost importance. Even though Astucia is the one who ensures the unity of the Valley (462–65), he always reserves a portion (the most important portion) of his identity outside of this alliance. This reserve remains inactive during the second part of the novel (the "insurgent utopia" part), but it comes to the forefront and destroys the so-called utopia at the precise moment in which it seems most secure and established: when state legality and rural legitimacy converge. This happens with the entrance in the narrative of Mariano G. y D., former president of the supreme court and now governor of Michoacán. Like Benito Juárez, Don Mariano takes over the executive branch of government after an illustrious career in the judiciary, where he was interpreter and administrator of the written law. Removed from the blind legalistic bent of his predecessors, Don Mariano decides to visit the Valley in person, worried and intrigued by the contradictory reports about Astucia and the Valley's situation (496). Pleasantly surprised by what he sees and captivated by the human and political qualities that he discovers in Astucia, Don Mariano confirms Astucia's position as colonel and chief of public security (507–508). This meeting and alliance between sovereign and outlaw (turned sovereign) have an unexpected derivation. Astucia and the governor discover that they were father-in-law and son-in-law (Astucia saved Amparo—the governor's daughter—from being burned alive in a fire, and afterward he married her without her family's knowledge—since they thought she was dead). This situation gives the scene a spectral duplicity. On the one hand it is possible to think that the meeting happens under the aegis of state law, now enriched by the legitimacy that Astucia was able to obtain, and that the family subplot is only an emphasis that makes the chain of conciliations between the local and the national ever more solid. This interpretation would make this scene analogous to the one in *El Zarco* when Martín Sánchez Chagollan (the legitimate local violence) and Benito Juárez (the legal national violence) meet and seal a foundational pact in which state and civil society converge in an (imaginary) indissoluble fashion. This interpretation is possible, but it is not correct.

Another interpretation puts us close to what is really happening. The governor and Astucia seal a different kind of alliance—an alliance as a family. They seal their alliance outside the written law, under the aegis of the oral law of the Brothers of the Leaf. The rendezvous between Astucia and the governor, instead of bringing Astucia to the realm of state sovereignty, traps the governor in the lure of a principle of subnational or heteronational affiliation.

This meeting seemed to be laying the foundations of the insurgent utopia (now dispossessed of its most dangerous aspects). It is in fact the beginning of the end. Because of it, Astucia is unfaithful to the principles that he himself established for the Valley: "We will never leave our territory for any political cause, because we do not support any party" (450). He seeks to recruit among his "all" a force to provide armed support to his father-in-law, whose position was at risk (527–37). This contradiction is only superficial. It shows that the true principle that guided his politics was always the family one, and the word "all" in "all for one" had two meanings. On the one hand, the conspicuous one, it included the dwellers of the Valley. On the other hand, the "original all" (526), the extended family of the Brothers of the Leaf, was the hidden axis around which the Valley spun (without the inhabitants suspecting it). If Astucia never wanted to fight in favor of any of the political parties that convulsed the political life of the early republic (Astucia does not acknowledge any political entity to the denomination "party"), he does not do so in favor of a utopia of self-determination (the Valley), but rather he pursues his own patriarchal agenda (the family).

The denouement of the novel is, from this point of view, predictable. Astucia, disappointed at the lack of support from the "all" that remain loyal to the Valley and to the rules Astucia had laid out earlier, gives up his post and "buries" his identity of erstwhile bandit and colonel, becoming again Lorenzo Cabello, civilian (528–29). His father-in-law quits his position as governor, disgusted by political life, and Enrique, Astucia's heir, quits the legal profession, in which he was expected to launch a promising political career. They all retire to Lorenzo's hacienda, and the family finally becomes the only place where the motto "All for one and one for all" seems to be sustainable in the long run.

From a certain point of view, the ending is politically pessimistic, since the national project fails. Unlike the family metaphor studied by Doris Sommer, where the private sphere duplicates itself in the public-national sphere and the family is the imaginary foundation of the nation-state, here the family entails a deliberate withdrawal from the public realm. This is not even a withdrawal to "private life" since this distinction assumes a public sphere shaped by the state. From another point of view, however, the novel opens itself to a completely new dimension. *Astucia* tells a political fable whose teleology is not the nation-state and whose failure does not risk barbarism. Rather, *Astucia* acts as a stage for other modes of politics, where civil society does not converge with the state and where it is precisely the strength and complexity of this civil society, divided in innumerable affiliations without a synthesis, which pose an obstacle to the construction of a nation-state. Putting the political thought of the nineteenth century in touch with the limits of the liberal paradigm, without turning to the barbarism trope or the void of society, is what makes this "minor" piece of nineteenth-century prose a radical contemporary of our most urgent debates.

8 | Zárate

Banditry, Nation, and the Experience of the Limits

Parece como si se quiere saquear la República para abandonarla después. Cada día me convenzo más por lo que veo y oigo en el país, que la hermosa organización de la República la ha convertido en otra Sierra Morena. *No hay más que bandoleros en ella.* ¡¡Esto es un horror!! Y lo peor de todo es, que como un mártir, voy a batirme por la santidad de las leyes.
　　Simón Bolívar, letter to General Urdaneta, 1826

Nuestras guerras civiles no son sino la exteriorización de una morbosidad, el poner por obra, con pretexto más o menos hábil, cierto fondo latente de banditismo.
–¿Un bandolerismo disfrazado, entonces?
Sí, señor; un bandolerismo disfrazado.
　　Rufino Blanco Fombona, *El hombre de hierro,* 1907

El General Rafael Urdaneta, el ilustre guerrero que fue después Presidente de la Gran Colombia, nos ha dejado también una pintura pavorosa del estado en que se hallaban los pueblos en aquellos mismos días: "De aquí para adelante [hacia Caracas], decía desde Trujillo, son tantos los ladrones cuantos habitantes tiene Venezuela."
　　Laureano Vallenilla Lanz, *Cesarismo democrático,* 1919

Eduardo Blanco (1839–1912) appears to be the exact opposite of Luis Inclán. While Inclán's novel abandons the grand narratives of statehood, Blanco devoted some of his best pages to precisely this project. But this disparity is more illusory than real. Blanco survives in contemporary literary history because of two works: *Venezuela heroica* (1881) and *Zárate* (1882). The first work is a series of narratives, more or less independent of each other, that correspond to particular battles of Venezuela's Independence War. It comprises stories animated by an obvious glorifying purpose. The second piece, *Zárate,* was written in the interval between the publication of the first and the second enlarged editions of *Venezuela heroica,* and it is the story of Santos Zárate, a llanero bandit who operated in the Aragua valleys. The narrative tells of his origin, his exploits, his odd dealings with the Delamar family, his repentance, and his untimely death.[1]

Venezuela heroica was the first best-seller in Venezuelan publishing history. Two thousand copies sold in a few weeks, and there were five more

146

printings in two years. These were records that would not be matched until decades later. Because of this success, in 1882 Blanco was elected Individuo Correspondiente de la Real Academia Española (Krispín 1997, 462). *Venezuela heroica* traces its origins to a mythical scene that supposedly was the inspiration for the novel.² This scene gives us *in nuce* all of the novel's ideological coordinates, and by contrast it illustrates the nature and the risks of Blanco's enterprise in writing *Zárate,* so close in time but so different from its predecessor. Told and retold *ad nauseam,* the anecdote runs more or less like this: in 1861 the elderly Páez directs the Guerra Larga with the Conservatives. In light of the unfavorable turn of the campaign, and fearing (like the federal enemies, in fact) that the war would get out of hand and become an uncontainable popular rebellion or an epidemic of banditry, Páez and his Federal counterpart General Falcón decide to meet in the Carabobo plain to study the terms of a possible peace agreement. Blanco attended the meeting as Páez's aide-de-camp. During the interludes of the negotiations, Páez narrated *in situ* the alternatives of the Carabobo battle, one of the most glorious moments of the Independence War: "Over there was Bolívar," "Over there was positioned the British Legion." At a certain point, General Falcón addressed Blanco and, putting his hand on his shoulder, said to him, "Young man, you are listening to the *Iliad* narrated by Achilles himself!"

All the elements of the nationalist thrust of *Venezuela heroica* are there. It is a great national epic (the *Iliad*), which links the llanero spears (occasionally patriotic) to the old Homeric swords.³ It is the state-sponsored totalizing narrative (under the species of the national hero) that symbolically unites a memory and a territory (see Conway 1996, 199). It has a fixed cast of individuals (Bolívar, the British Legion, Páez) who are set up as exclusive characters of that narrative. Finally, it has a conversation among peers (white letrado statesmen) as the sole locus of memory.

Aside from circumstantial political options—Blanco was a Conservative (Silva-Beauregard 1994; Bolet Toro 1998, 2000)—*Venezuela heroica*'s impulse is the same as the one identified with the era of Guzmán Blanco (1870–1888): an emphatic attempt to tie all social circumstances to a single imaginary of the nation-state, the cornerstone of which would be the consecration (sacralization) of Bolívar's memory.⁴

Venezuela heroica was the "gospel of the Fatherland" as Laureano Vallenilla Lanz called it, remembering his childhood reading of the book (quoted in Plaza 1996, 177). *Zárate,* on the other hand, is considered the birth of the

Venezuelan national novel (Barnola 1963, 21), and although it proposes itself as an equally pious (albeit secular) work, it runs risks that the other work does not.[5]

At first glance its cast of characters is, if not identical, at least complementary to that of *Venezuela heroica:* proud veterans of the Independence War, in a spiral that goes from the glorious caudillo to the modest soldier somewhat inclined to indulge in liquor (e.g., Páez, Colonel Gonzalvo, Lieutenant Orellana, Sergeant Camoruco), young army men infused with nationalistic spirit and a reverence for legitimate authority (Horacio Delamar), hacienda owners in the old patriarchal style (Don Carlos Delamar), and letrados or artists (Lastenio Sanfidel). Just like the axis of the aforementioned anecdote is Páez, the axis of the post-independence world in *Zárate* is the sugar producing hacienda that, with diverse fortunes, Don Carlos Delamar owns and runs. The hacienda is a "portion of paradise" in the midst of the devastations of a recent war that did not give quarter.

However, *Zárate* is more than an undivided celebration of a founding father (Páez) or of a particular social synthesis (the large agrarian patrimonial estate). This slippage of meaning happens because of the encroachment of power and prestige of an unlikely guest among this congregation: it is Santos Zárate, the llanero brigand who not only shares an honorable place at Don Carlos's table but who is also inextricably linked to the destiny of the Delamar family and who is actually responsible for its salvation.

Thus, *Zárate* may be read not only as a novel with an exclusive nationalist thrust but also as a text in which the contradictions and impossibilities of the Venezuelan national project in its "Guzmán Blanco" version come to the fore. If in Inclán's work the social bandit trope is unequivocally used as an integral part of a project to vindicate a suppressed political tradition (popular "liberalism" dating back to the 1810s), in Blanco's novel the purpose is more ambiguous. On the one hand Zárate is a conceptual character (a term coined by Deleuze and Guattari) used as part of a conservative critique of the present. This critique is triggered by the perceived decadence of a cherished cultural order through the advent of modernity. Banditry, in this perspective, is a consequence of the meltdown of a cultural order that enthroned the faulty leadership and spurious politics of newcomers such as Sandalio Bustillón (representative of the new Liberal classes on the rise during the Guzmán Blanco era), who was unable to solidify the moral economy of rural Venezuela (something that the conservative *prohombres* such as Don

Carlos Delamar and Páez are born to do).[6] This hierarchy-led cultural order would capture the violence of rebellious subjects such as Santos Zárate and put it to "good" productive uses.

On the other hand, the bandit trope goes beyond Blanco's stated purpose. The bandit functions as a kind of "return of the repressed" in his political unconscious (Jameson 1981), and *Zárate* touches the "blind spot" in the national project in which the standing of conservative founding fathers cannot hinder their complicity with the abject outlaw, since Zárate seems to be essential to their hold on power. At this point the paternalist metaphor (the conservative leader redeeming the rural poor) dissolves, and the positions seem to reverse (the outlaw *qua* outlaw becomes the cornerstone of the patriarchal order). After this contact with the abject, in all its impurity, the novel recoils with horror: it is a horror concealed as resignation before the fate of the souls lost for the national project and the sad destiny of the Apure llanero who could have been Páez's brother-in-arms in the "glorious journeys of Mucurita, La Miel or Las Queseras" (432) but who ended up as an outlaw with a reward of two thousand pesos on his head (422).

The following pages will develop this twofold argument building upon the contributions of Silva-Beauregard (1994), who appropriately reads the novel as a critical allegory of Blanco's present.

During the colonial period, the extended family was the privileged juridical-political-economic identity. The Constituciones sinodales (1687), for example, required judges of the ecclesiastical tribunals to differentiate between "family fathers" and "promiscuous multitudes." "Family fathers" did not mean anyone with the ability to father a child. The term identified a particular sector of society that shared power with the clergy and the secular government. Not all neighbors that headed a Christian family were thus family fathers; instead the term referred to the relatively small group of people who had, in addition to wife and children, real property, servants, and slaves (Pino Iturieta 1988, 45). Don Carlos Delamar is, without a doubt, a family father. The novel takes its first gamble with the metaphor of fatherhood as the axis of the social order, through which the large estate—patrimonial, slave-manned but benevolent and of illusory colonial lineage—is presented as a legitimate and even natural principle of social organization.[7]

The hacienda is the space where all social conflict is annulled. There is no racial conflict because slavery is an institution oriented not toward the exploitation of the workforce (119) but to the sheltering and development of bodies as well as the evangelization and disciplining of souls (the slave quarters are more cloister than prison).[8] There is no economic conflict because the sugar hacienda does not covet land or natural resources, and it opens its pastures and waters to poor peasants (113). There is no political conflict because Don Carlos refuses to choose sides during the war, and he leaves Venezuela for the duration of the conflict (111).

In the natural order of the hacienda, all social practices are redundant because they are geared not toward the transformation of the social milieu but to the perpetuation ad infinitum of the status quo. This is why the feast (of which there are at least three in the novel) and not the ritual of production is the model of social practice in *Zárate*. From the beginning, the characters belong to a social position that the novel equates with a moral position in which everyone, with the exceptions of Santos Zárate and Sandalio Bustillón, is comfortable.

This has two less-than-surprising corollaries. In the world of El Torreón there is no labor and no violence. No one is ever seen working except in chapter XVI in first part of the novel, "Un idilio al través de una reja," and throughout in the various activities of Teresa and Clavellina (e.g., they sew a dress). But in both cases labor is oriented toward conspicuous consumption (the feast) and not toward the production of a commodity.[9] By the same token, the plots of sugarcane that sustain the hacienda's economy are never mentioned except as a refuge or dwelling for evil (e.g., the episode in which Lieutenant Orellana finds Zárate/Oliveros in the cane field [342–43]). On the other hand, the legitimacy of the patriarchal order is so overwhelming that, in the patriarch's vision, any violence (penal violence, or slave disciplining) is unnecessary (119, 130, 162). If labor and violence have disappeared, it is because El Torreón exists in a backwater outside time and history. Because of that, the novel refers repeatedly to the paradisaical condition of the hacienda (182, 184, 187, 189, 289), and the garden and the nearby picturesque landscapes (solely decorative) are the only feature worthy of attention in the entire agrarian production unit.

However, this image of the hacienda as a *locus amoenus* (which would make *Zárate* a late version of *María*) reaches a limit even before the plot unravels it. There is a duplicity that marks the identity of the hacienda, and it is inscribed in its very name. Patrimonialismo as natural order conceives itself outside of history. This lack of temporality, when formulated in political terms, appeals to the medieval/feudal paradigm, where the house is a fortress (*castillo*) and its dwellers *castellanos*.[10] Apparently, the most medieval feature of the hacienda's architecture is the turret (*torreón*) that gives the property its name. However, the turret belongs not to the manor but to the sugar mill (112). Thus, the martial emblem of feudalism (the imposing turret that awes the serfs as a key piece of the theater of law) is transfigured by the poorer reality of peripheral capitalism. The feudal emblem thus belongs not to a timeless feudal order but to the (imperfectly hidden) order of production and history: to a production technique (and a commodity) on its way to becoming obsolete.[11] (Coffee was the commodity on the rise in Venezuela toward the mid-nineteenth century, and it was the main export by the time Blanco wrote his novel [Yarrington 1997].) The conflicts of the novel stem from this displacement, from the image of self-sufficient capitalism (which the agrarian order imagines itself to exemplify), to the reality of declining sugar production. The conflicts are of two different but concurrent natures, and they are embodied in two characters: Bustillón and Zárate.

In the first case, the vicissitudes of capitalism eroded the seemingly invulnerable order of rural patriarchy and thus gave possibility to the aspirations of illegitimate newcomers like Bustillón, a corrupt and power grabbing lawyer. Bustillón embodies a stereotype that will live on in the characters of upstart letrados of more or less import in other works by Blanco (see "Fecha clásica" and "Drama íntimo") as well as novels by Manuel Díaz Rodríguez, Rufino Blanco Fombona, and Rómulo Gallegos. (One noteworthy example, from Gallegos's *Doña Bárbara,* is Mujiquita, who is apparently the district judge but in reality is secretary to the town's political boss.)

Bustillón is a product of nineteenth-century Venezuela, a country where judicial and legislative activities were kept to a minimum. Litigiousness was extremely low since informal mechanisms of conflict resolution such as mediation were firmly entrenched and the judiciary had very little prestige. (The novel provides a superb example of this: Zárate's and Horacio's pardons.) The natural field for professionals educated in the law was political office, which in nineteenth-century Venezuela was linked to the vagaries of caudillo politics (Pérez-Perdomo 1990, 11). There was no autonomous judicial sphere and no opportunities for a career in the judiciary. Bustillón, then, was not necessarily a cynic but rather someone who naturally linked his prosperity to the caudillo in power or became a political boss himself by building a power base. Both practices, not based on the "natural" mechanisms of hierarchy as depicted in El Torreón, are condemned by the novel.

Richer than Don Carlos (412), Bustillón wants to legitimize his position through marriage with the beautiful Aurora, Don Carlos's daughter (411). Capitalism, generalizing the logic of the commodity, entails the rupture of the ideology that supports a simple and discernible origin for values, since in the market value depends on the interaction of contingent forces. Bustillón represents that ruin, since, though lacking in value (understood as lineage or origin), he is a powerful man in the budding state. As Paulette Silva-Beauregard correctly points out, Bustillón is an allegory of the Guzmanato, the dubious credentials of its most eminent men, the even more dubious projects that legitimized the administration, and the forms of modernization that Venezuela was adopting (Silva-Beauregard 1994, 418–21). In particular, he allegorizes the constitution of a powerful bureaucracy adapted to the new rules of the commercial-bureaucratic Venezuela that Guzmán Blanco was building (Lombardi 1982, 187–205). Bustillón's body is the metaphor that the novel uses to indicate his spurious origin (and thus his lack of value). He is, of all the characters in the novel, the one whose corporality is more sharply evidenced: he is fat, bald, old, and sweaty (71).[12]

In the second case, the convulsions of the Independence War had impaired the capacity of the upper echelons of society to sustain their position relative to the forces that had played a decisive role in the conflict. The bandit Zárate is the representative of these new vectors of violence and of their muddled relationship with the old power holders. As an allegory of the present, however, Zárate represents the demise of the old power structure in Guzmán Blanco's Venezuela as well as the reduction in the gravitation of "the material realities of land-based wealth" (Lombardi 1982, 199) in national politics. Being a landowner, Don Carlos commands no political leverage in the area and no influence at the national level. As the character Presentación in Arturo Uslar Petri's *Las lanzas coloradas* (1931) showed, a sugar hacienda could be a formidable power base from which to launch a career as a caudillo (which is the classic paradigm of caudillismo, according to John Lynch [1992]). It is a power base that Don Carlos is unable to mobilize. Zárate is the trope that embodies this migration of power outside the hacienda toward a nomadic principle that enters into alliances with the traditional landowning elite without being inherently attached to it.

Even though Zárate and Bustillón are anomalous in a social order whose apex is El Torreón, they are not anomalous in the same way and they do not have the same type of relationship to this social order. Disguised as José

Oliveros, Zárate enters the scene (he arrives at the hacienda asking for shelter) at the exact time that the epic of *Venezuela heroica* reaches its conclusion. The sun of the revolution is setting as the storm of the civil war appears on the horizon: "In the days previous to the battle of Carabobo [the same battle around which the anecdote that originated *Venezuela heroica* revolves], the sun was setting amid the thick clouds of a rainy afternoon of May, 1821. Don Carlos Delamar was seated, as was his custom, in the gallery of the exterior courtyard of the ancient hacienda manor, when he saw entering the courtyards, through the street made by the aligned lemon trees, and heading slowly to the lodging of the foreman, a shabby traveler riding a sad, emaciated horse, that made evident in its gait the most extreme dejection" (160). This scene is the exact reverse of the *Iliad* that the young Blanco heard with excitement. Páez's story focuses on the epicenter of the battle and its illustrious participants. (We should remember that the battles in the *Iliad* are a sum of individualized encounters, challenges, or random fights between well-defined heroes.) Santos Zárate's entrance (he goes to El Torreón to sack the hacienda and murder its residents) takes us to the margins of the battle, to a space of centrifugal violence, populated by poor peasants who perhaps fought those battles of history but whose violence, in spite of the best letrado illusions, was never limited by the national epic. Indeed, after the end of the war, "[b]ehind the soldier that laid down his weapons, appeared the bandit. From the very beginning of the peace era, numerous gangs of malefactors infested the roads and sought refuge in the forests of some of our provinces. The neighborhoods of the countryside, the forlorn hamlets, the defenseless villages, and even the towns when not protected with regular troops were the frequent theater of robberies and murders, perpetrated with unheard of audacity" (45).

Unlike Dionisio Cisneros, who stubbornly defended the king's cause, Zárate "did not defend his criminal villainies with the transparent shield of politics. He was more candid. During the last years of the Independence War he had practiced the honorable profession of highway robber, stealing with commendable impartiality from both Venezuelans and Spaniards, not allowing the political affiliation of his victims to influence the commission of his crimes" (46–47). Zárate is, then, the emergence of a heterogeneous principle (for the novel: incomprehensible and malign, at least at the beginning) in the foundational scene of the nation. Unlike the royalist enemy, against whom a homogeneous national identity can coalesce, the bandit breaks down the "among us" (*entre nos*) aspect of the totalizing national narrative, because he proves that in the drama of independence there was an impostor. The narrator explains, "When the war of Independence was over, and all our eminent men were engaged in the task of reorganizing the country, just like all our citizens were busy recovering through hard work the material well-being lost by long years of persistent fighting, *Venezuela exhibited a new cancer*, hidden until then by the smoke of combat and by the political mask with which ordinarily the basest passions cover themselves. But lacking the pretext of war, the disguises were unsustainable" (45, emphasis added).

In *Venezuela heroica* the nation is a body that awakens with independence (xvii). In that body Zárate is a cancer (45).[13] What he looks like is unknown, but he is there; it is believed that he is in a certain location when he is really somewhere else (or he is in many other places at the same time [253–64]); when everyone is relieved that he has been eliminated, he resurfaces as a metastasis (68–69). The bandit hunt involves the domination of the body as a metaphor of the state takeover of the territory. But the bandit is not an exterior enemy like the Spaniard, another body and as such with an intelligible form possible to locate (and exterminate). Rather, he is an enemy whose logic is not understandable. The independence epic, as narrated in *Venezuela heroica,* is an epic as long as it assumes the presence and mutual acknowledgment of two adversaries in the same space. This space is at the same time material and symbolic: the disputed battlefield. Zárate is heterogeneous to this paradigm because he never engages his enemy in battle if he can help it. And, like in the Güere forest, the battle is waged in order to exit the battlefield and to escape the siege that the state laid. If Zárate wins, it is not because of his battle skills but because he is able to escape identification (395–400).

Zárate thus seems to be a more threatening menace than the royalists because he challenges not only the enjoyment of property but also the very origin from which the right to own property emanates:

The spite and exasperation of provincial authorities had reached a maximum. Such a daring feat [the series of robberies that Zárate and his gang had just carried out], in addition to the criminal offense that it involved, was stigmatized as an insolent provocation to those in charge of guarding and maintaining public morality, as a bloody mockery to the investiture of magistrates. . . .

Detachments of regular troops went up and down roads. Everywhere bayonets were gleaming, and soldiers swarmed, anxious, each more than the next, to satisfy the just anger of their disrespected superiors. But they did not find anybody upon whom to exert the full force of the law and of their anger. . . .

In spite of the adverse fact that the enemy was nowhere to be found, there was the intention of declaring a state of siege in the province. And, just like if Boves had returned from the dead, and if it were those bloody days that preceded La Victoria y San Mateo, and the even more disastrous defeats of La Puerta, agitation was extreme, and the alarm incessant, and the panic of our rural folk was reaching a climax. (264–65)

Thus *Zárate* begins by contrasting a patriarchal imaginary in which limits are natural and legitimate, to a reality where limits are lacking and where Zárate holds an alternative sovereignty. He not only disputes the control of roads, haciendas, and inns with ineffectual posses (*partidas de campos-volantes*) (46) but also claims absolute dominion of the Güere forest. These dense, sparsely populated woods are the dark counterpart of Carabobo, and they are symbolically linked to a memory of violence and terror that is not the memory claimed by the nation-state:

The Güere forest, like the tragic Breton forests, abounded in fantastic traditions. It was publicly known that on dark November nights gigantic black birds, whose painful squawks imitated moans and heart-wrenching cries, swooped in on the *samanes* of dense foliage close to the road that traverses the forest, and with formidable flapping of their wings fluttered about in the dense shadows. This flapping was heard from long distances, giving the impression of the faraway rumble of a hurricane. These birds were considered to be the lost souls of those murdered while in mortal sin in those places, and there was no lack of people who swore having seen and heard those infernal tricksters, together with witch dances and wandering beheaded bodies.

But, in addition to the supernatural, it was certain that, from remote times, the aforementioned forest had had an atrocious reputation. By the mid-eighteenth century, a renowned highway robber, whose surname was Cúchares, had chosen the forest as his hideout, after quitting the hilly gorge of the Cucharos, close to San Mateo, that still carries the name that they gave to the gang of that obdurate malefactor. . . . But it was only the robbers who committed such atrocities in the forest of Güere. The terrible passions that were stirred in Venezuela during the initial years of the Independence War chose the forest repeatedly as a place to quench the thirst for cruel vengeance. Even in 1816, when Mac-Gregor and Soublette undertook the glorious retreat from Ocumare to Juncal, they found while crossing the forest, still warm and throbbing, the corpses of twenty-nine patriots murdered by Chepito González. (391–92)

The forest conjugates an alternative knowledge, a cultural capital that for the letrado conscience is only evil superstition.[14] The novel, in fact, devotes an entire chapter (entitled "Viejas preocupaciones") to explaining the origin of these superstitions and to categorizing them as if it were an ethnography of local knowledge. In this nationalist ethnography, there are pieces of knowledge that are to be preserved and that are therefore linked to the hacienda as a cultural space. But there are also those that are a danger and that are invalidated by their association with the bandit.

Thus, the forest of Güere is not really a hideout but another realm entirely. When the state finally decides to smash banditry in its very lair, it does not attempt a police operation but a conquest. The army advances upon the land inch by inch, shoulder to shoulder (just like in *O Cabelleira* or in *Os sertões*). This is no military parade but the inaugural violence upon a thus far impenetrable territory that did not belong to the state. Blanco states,

> More than five hundred regular army soldiers and an equal number of state militias, moving from the wee hours of the morning, executed the orders of the military commander and . . . the dreadful forest, so feared, was surrounded by an extensive siege of bayonets that, when they penetrated the forest, reduced the vast circle that they comprised.
>
> *Maybe it was the first time that so large a number of people dared to penetrate* the somber fastnesses of that agglomeration of bulky trees and impenetrable thickets, under whose shadows so many crimes have been committed since remote times. (390, emphasis added)

But this conquest is far from a frontier epic (even if rustic and inglorious). Like classic stories of social bandits, the army can only enter the forest with some chance of success if Zárate has been betrayed. In this case, the traitor is Tanacia (390), the witch that Zárate uses to maintain the fraud of his supernatural knowledge in front of his gang (239–41).[15] What is crucial here is that the collapse of the gang is caused by an internal rift and not by the superior efficacy of the state. This rift occurs because Zárate transgresses an oral law (the unwritten code of maternal love) and not because the state law was able to create a conflict within the gang. Tanacia betrays Zárate when he forces her to make her son's (Cascabel's) betrayal to the gang evident, thus condemning him to death (249–61).

Zárate's anomaly, when contrasted with the imaginary of the nation-state, goes even beyond this. At the beginning of the novel Captain Horacio

Delamar, his veterans, and his friend, the painter Lastenio Sanfidel (a Tulio Arcos or Alberto Soria in *Sangre patricia* and *Ídolos rotos* by Manuel Díaz Rodríguez *avant la lettre*) entered the Aragua Valley commissioned to pursue Zárate. This is a mission that Horacio does not particularly enjoy but that will allow him to visit his uncle Carlos and his cousin Aurora after an absence that lasted for years. Upon reaching La Victoria, they are informed that Zárate has been captured. The prisoner turns out not to be the famous bandit but a minor accomplice. When the mistake is discovered, it is too late because he had already been poisoned (by the real Zárate, in order to prevent his being accused by the captured brigand). However, the possibility of the substitution is what makes the scene significant. Zárate had been a scourge upon the region for years and was already a somber national celebrity (Páez himself commissioned the army detachment under Horacio's command). No one had ever seen him, though; no one knew his face, his race, or his whereabouts at any given time. Because of this, he could have had any face or any race, and he could be truly ubiquitous.

What does this scene tell us? More than life or property, Zárate challenges the disciplinarian grille, the *principium individuationis* upon which a community co-extensive with the nation-state pretends to be founded. Zárate is a mere name, a "floating signifier" (Laclau 1996) that conjugates the fears and imaginary desires of the collectivity.[16] The not-very-fearsome reality of the prisoner is secondary:

> —Here he is, here he is; we have him—the ones stationed by the river yell to exhaustion.
>
> And between the double line of soldiers, riding the back of a donkey, with his hands and legs well tied, the ignoble figure of the prisoner can be seen by the surprised crowd. He was a kind of wild beast: dirty, clothed in rags, pale and trembling, of vile as well as cowardly demeanor, with a wounded and hatless head, the hair sticky because of clotted blood. He did not have any of the features with which his apologists had described him, and they were embarrassed, spited, and surprised. . . .
>
> When the crowd recovered from their initial disappointment, they started to hail the army official that had caught the outlaw, and they exaggerated his immense bravery, his incomparable cunning, and his illustrious victory. . . . [W]hile all eyes were fixed upon the handcuffed brigand, they started to find in the visage and in the countenance of the unfortunate the typical features of ferocity, energy, and temerity. In all truth, these features were not at all apparent, except in the overexcited imagination of those that thought they were witnessing them.

—Jesus Christ!—exclaimed the general store owner—; look at his eyes; they look like two burning embers.

—And the teeth!—added another, a shy one, exhibiting his own teeth—; that guy has eaten human flesh!

—Pay attention to the wrinkle that crosses his forehead, and the protruding jaw bones. These are very meaningful signals—argued the sacristan with his buddy, the veterinarian of the town who put on airs of an experienced anatomist.

—What a head!—exclaimed, while standing by a portal, a bow-legged bondsman who pretended to be a phrenologist—; you can see in that skull all the very developed protuberances related to criminal passions.

—And what can you tell me about the facial features!—yelled the apothecary noisily.

And everybody assented and bowed before all these just and deep observations. (50–52)

Zárate dines with familiarity at Don Carlos Delamar's table and partakes of the conversation *inter pares* that circumscribe the imagined community "Venezuela." Zárate is beyond any possibility of knowledge or comprehension (and not because he is a master of disguise, like Joaquín Murieta in Ireneo Paz's novel). The contradiction between the two statements is only illusory. As an anomalous principle in the social body, Zárate is the absolute exteriority that, in turn, ruins all pretensions of interiority. But, as an alternative principle of violence that ruins the distinction between interior and exterior, it poses another danger: it replaces the principle of violence upon which the interiority was imaginarily founded. In narrative terms, this interiority is formulated thus: Zárate threatens to replace Horacio as the main bearer of (legitimate) violence centered on the state (Páez) through the mediation of the law.[17]

There are two moments when this risk becomes obvious. The first is the celebration of the Virgin of Candelaria, in Turmero. During the bullfight (which, in the Hispanic realm, is the most important celebration of hierarchical society [see Viqueira Albán 1987]) Aurora's handkerchief flies from her hand and falls into the arena. Horacio—Aurora's parent-approved suitor —rushes to the arena to recover the piece, but he ends up at the mercy of the angry bull. An anonymous spectator (Zárate in disguise) enters the fight and kills the bull, saving the young captain for the first time. When everyone tries to congratulate him, he has already disappeared (338–39). Santos saves Horacio a second time when he prevents not only Horacio's death be-

solute lack of affectation or effeminate characteristics) are emphasized (138–40, 195–97), whereas with Bustillón, his voice tells the world that he is pompous, sneaky, and ignorant of correct pronunciation (*seseo*) (72).[20]

Another crucial example of the distinctions between the oral and the written word is the order issued by Páez that stops Horacio's execution just in the nick of time (436). (He had been sentenced as Zárate's accomplice, because Bustillón's artfulness had succeeded in framing Horacio.) But the written order exists and is valid only because of the oral pact between Páez and Zárate.[21] Blanco reserves for Páez and Don Carlos the same symbolic place, where the just voice equals legitimate authority: "Since our forefathers were rustics, they had the good faith, in matters of epithets, to speak plainly and to give everything and everyone their proper names. In this fashion, things and people were called by their real names, without subterfuges, circumlocutions, or hyperbolic exaggerations: a cow was a cow, and a rascal was a rascal. To steal was a mortal sin in politics as in social interactions. The one who committed such an act was called a thief, and as such was regarded and punished" (237). This crystal-clear order of things (based upon a regime of signs without gaps between language and referent) defined a legitimacy that was not synonymous with the written law (whose spurious representative is Bustillón) but that existed before the law did and was superior to it. That legitimacy is what makes possible the alliance between the center and the margin, an alliance through which the nation reconciles with itself: Páez and Don Carlos are the only ones that Zárate respects, and since he is invincible, the oral pact is the only way to recover him for the national project.

In *Zárate* (unlike, for example, *El Zarco*) there is no simulacrum of popular sovereignty. The voice of the agora, the voice of the people in dialogue in the public square, is just noise, superstition that extends bandit rule (235–37), or fabrications, lies, exaggerations, and errors, as in the case of the false Zárate that appeared in Turmero (51–54, 325–28). Both scenes in which the popular voice appears refer to the false Zárate (51–54) and to Don Carlos's family and the soldiers who come to protect Turmero. In other words, the popular voice always appears to be addressed to a position of power and violence that exceeds it. And the popular voice always errs in understanding that position of power (e.g., the detainee was not Zárate, the cloud of dust was not cattle). This is to say: when speaking for themselves as a group, the people are not a political agent; instead, they are inert and almost nonexistent.

But popular orality is not a risk in the novel, since it is, in the last analysis, harmless. It is superstitious or inconsequential, like the insufferable litanies of Romerales. The true risk to the conservative national project is the written word when it is not legitimized by the voice (that is, when it is without value, origin, or interiority). This risk is personified by Sandalio Bustillón, the letrado lawyer who usurps the authority of the voice. Examples of this usurpation are the laws he uses to establish himself as one of the area's power brokers (265), as well as the forged letters, addressed to Zárate, that he attributes to Horacio. (These letters put Horacio on the verge of an infamous execution [388–89].) However, the most radical effect of a letter detached from a legitimate origin is the very fact that Zárate exists. His existence is a symptom not of the decline of the patriarchal order but of the risks of moving away from it. In the pre-history of the novel Bustillón, who is using his position as administrator of justice clumsily or maliciously, is responsible for the unspeakably cruel death of Zárate's mother (84), and Zarate's revenge follows Bustillón to the end. In fact, Zárate is rarely violent except in his unflinching desire to exact revenge from Bustillón (75, 83–108). So the absence of a legitimate oral principle is what, for the first time, introduces illegitimate violence (and not the other way around).

Zárate is never captured. He redeems himself via the oral pact with the sovereign. In the tradition of the noble bandit, the interview with the sovereign entails his incorporation as the strong arm of the ruler (as in the case of Robin Hood of Sherwood, in which Robin becomes archer for Richard the Lion-Hearted). This reconciliation happens in the case of Zárate because Páez acknowledges that the transgression of the written law (his numerous robberies and murders, as well as the illicit association to commit crimes) is secondary when contrasted with fundamental fidelity to the oral code of bravery and loyalty (432–36). The scene of reconciliation is thus exclusively based on a performance, one in which Zárate does not show any sign of repentance.[22] Instead he exhibits a temerity that to a certain extent parallels Don Carlos's valor when he offers shelter and care to Zárate disguised as a suspicious stranger:

[Zárate is astonished by Páez's refusal to grant him a pardon.]
—This means than that you do not pardon [Zárate]?—added the stranger in a begging tone.
—No!

—So there is no salvation possible for him?

—No!

—And he can only expect death?

—Yes!

—Well then, General—this strange defender of the condemned exclaimed with desperation, rising to his feet—, do with [Zárate] as you please, here he is.

— Where?

— Right here, general. I am Santos Zárate! . . .

—All right then—said Páez—, I will grant you a pardon, but with the condition that you become a decent, law abiding citizen. . . .

—Do you promise?—added Páez.

—I promise—mumbled the bandit, gasping for air because of his emotion. (434–35)

Páez pardons Zárate and the latter secures a pardon for Horacio at a critical moment (436). Without waiting to see Horacio's reaction to the good news, the bandit rushes to interrupt the ill-fated forced marriage between Aurora and Bustillón and to eliminate the latter (who dies hanged, just like a bandit [447]). Thus Zárate saved Don Carlos's honor and opened the possibility of marriage for Horacio and Aurora, who finally had made their feelings for each other clear (after numerous misunderstandings) (384).

This is an ending that apparently follows the rules of poetic justice, but not quite. It would have meant irreparable fallout. It would have made the bandit, with his latest murder (Bustillón's hanging), the explicitly acknowledged savior of the patriarchal order (an order that in the novels passes for "Venezuela"). That is, Bustillón's plot, which made Horacio appear as Zárate's accomplice, would have been confirmed in a way that Bustillón would have never suspected.

This alliance/collusion has antecedents. Santos and Horacio are associated in the novel through the common metaphor of Saint Michael, the warrior archangel. At the beginning of the novel, when Horacio and Lastenio appear unexpectedly and their identity has not yet been revealed to the residents of El Torreón, Clavellina notes Horacio's martial demeanor and exclaims, "Jesus! . . . this is the Archangel Saint Michael!" (137). When Zárate is pardoned by Páez, he goes back to El Torreón to avenge Don Carlos. In that moment, the narrator says that Santos is the "devil transformed into an archangel" who carries out divine retribution (446). Saint Michael, most importantly, is the saint whose statue adorns the hacienda's oratory (123), the oratory being the center of social interaction. The one who "becomes" Saint Michael would become bastion and axis of the patriarchal order.

No one is more qualified for this role than Zárate. He has superior cunning (he repeatedly deceives Horacio), superior ability and physical force (he repeatedly saves him), and superior knowledge of the true inner workings of power (he is able to secure a pardon when Lastenio and Monteoscuro failed). If the narrator were to confirm Zárate's superiority, he would have irrevocably confused the places of Horacio and Zárate, to Horacio's disadvantage. The novel would have completely superseded its own nationalist presuppositions and moved toward a very different political dimension, one in which the Güere forest, as a source of knowledge and sovereignty, would have imposed itself on Caracas (and even on Europe).

It is at this point that *Zárate* exhibits the true violence of the national project, the enactment of the consciousness of the fact that the state is built upon: nonstate violence. This is the non plus ultra of nationalistic fiction. Therefore, this consciousness must be repressed, although, as in any process of repression, there is a transaction. In this case, the transaction is the novel itself, which dramatically depicts as repressed what must be repressed (that is, what is not intended to surface). This is the same paradox Benedict Anderson explains when talking about the reassuring fratricide: it is the national memory as the memory of an event that is incessantly remembered as having already been forgotten. Toward the end of the novel, Horacio, who incredibly did not know that he owes his life, fortune, and honor to Zárate, bursts into the place where the bandit had just executed Bustillón. Upon seeing him, he attacks Zárate and without explanation kills him (without Don Carlos, who did know that he owed the honor of his name to Zárate, intervening to stop the fight [453]). Lastenio arrives shortly thereafter and asks,

> —Answer me, gentlemen, who has murdered this man?
> —Your friend—replied the priest.
> —Horacio!—cried out Lastenio, horrified.
> —Yes, indeed—replied Monteoscuro—. But it was in a fair fight.
> —What a horror, what a horror!—murmured the shattered artist—but it is true that Horacio ignored it.
> —Ignored what?—everybody inquired.
> —That he owes his life to that man.
> Don Carlos raised his eyes toward heaven, as if looking for an explanation to

all these unfortunate events [*tantas amarguras*]; and when Lastenio ended his story about the heroic deed of Zárate in order to save the captain's life, the old man, dejected, bowed his head, whispering:

—It was God's justice! (457)

"God's justice" seems to be a pretty inept euphemism for the murder of a man who had been pardoned and redeemed of all his crimes and had redeemed everybody of their own mistakes and ineptitudes. Horacio justified himself through the subterfuge of the "fair duel" (*combate leal*) (456). But he appealed to an oral code of bravery, one that, up to that moment, he had opposed (because it would have entailed justifying Zárate and his logic of revenge to the bitter end, a logic that had been explicitly condemned before).[23] Why then does this appeal to "God's justice," this literal deus ex machina, bring all meditation on and all inquiries into the death of the hero of the novel to a close? (Horacio should have been the hero, but he is hardly heroic.) The reason is simple: Zárate's death (assassination) cleanses the polluted national body. This pollution threatened to bring down the edifice of patrimonial ideology. Thus, this death restores the symbolic borders that made the marriage of Horacio and Aurora, the legitimate "national romance," possible. The murder also interdicts Páez's sovereign decision: Horacio is not killing Zárate, but he is reducing Páez's standing as sovereign outside the law. Zárate's death shows that there cannot be any contact between the state or the state-sponsored community and the bandit's violence. This hides the contingency of political decisions, a hiding that is the desperate recourse upon which all acts of foundation rest.

9 | *Martín Fierro*
Banditry and the Frontiers of the Voice

"If you cannot steal a horse without compunction, you have not been properly
brought up," cried the third. "In the Banda Oriental," said the fourth, "you are not
looked upon as an honest man unless you steal."
      Gauchos of the *blanco* party, in W. H. Hudson's *The Purple Land*, 1885

José Hernández's *Martín Fierro* is the story of a law abiding, hard-
working, family-oriented gaucho wronged and exploited by civil and military authorities. Forcibly and arbitrarily drafted to the Indian frontier in the
south of Buenos Aires province, he was deprived of his family and all of his
earthly possessions. This course of events turned him into an army deserter,
a barroom *malevo,* and an outlaw in the avenger tradition (although, unlike
Zárate, he never sought retribution against the justice of the peace who was
at the origin of all his misfortunes or the army officials who abused and
robbed him during his years as a soldier). He eventually escaped and attempted to live among the pampa Indians, only to find that his life there was
equally miserable. Disenchanted and having lost his bosom friend Cruz
(who saved him from certain death at the hands of a posse), he returned to
"civilization" and was reunited with his children. After Fierro failed to give
blood satisfaction to the relative of a man he killed in a duel during his outlaw days (a challenge that was preceded by the famous *payada* between
Fierro and the challenger, the Moreno), the Fierro family dispersed again.
Before this, Fierro changed his name in an attempt to bury his outlaw identity, which kept catching up with him in ways he no longer wished for since
he had renounced the idea of fighting "for show" (*por fantasía*) (Hernández
1872/1879, 466).

Jorge Luis Borges once wrote about *Martín Fierro* that "[i]n American and
European literary circles I have been questioned many times on the topic of
Argentine literature. I have invariably answered that Argentine literature
(so disdained by those who ignore it) does exist, and consists of at least one
book, . . . *Martín Fierro*" (1953, 562). This position has hardly (if ever) been
challenged. However, it has been reasoned differently since 1872, when *El
gaucho Martín Fierro* was first published in a humble pamphlet by La Pampa
Press. *Martín Fierro* (the single name that now encompasses two separate

165

poems, *El gaucho Martín Fierro* [1872] and *La vuelta de Martín Fierro* [1879], from now on referred to as *La ida* and *La vuelta*, respectively) has spawned an almost infinite number of commentators, imitators, epigones, and editors from the monumental to the popular.[1] *Martín Fierro* has come a long way from the cautious praise it received from Hernández's contemporaries. Aside from the social niceties they expressed, it is clear that they valued *Martín Fierro* only on the controversial criterion of its best-seller status. Hernández has since been compared to all major authors in the Western literary tradition, from Homer to Conrad to Kafka (Martínez-Estrada 1948; Borges 1953). The payada, the impromptu singing style of the gauchos that Hernández turned into a literary convention, has since been linked to the traditions of Greek, Germanic, Provençal, and Spanish oral poetry (Lugones 1916; Rojas 1917–1923). As a political poem, it has been appropriated by the right as well as the left, by conservative elites (Lugones 1905), and by populist nationalists (see Astesano 1963; Solanas 1972–1978), by authoritarian dictatorships (such as the infamous Proceso de Reorganización Nacional [1976–1983]) as well as anarchists (Marín 1933; Ghiraldo 1906). In some cases, the authors of these appropriations have misread crucial parts of the book. One such case is Eduardo Astesano's mediocre *Martín Fierro y la justicia social: primer manifiesto revolucionario del movimiento obrero argentino* (1963). What is significant is that Fierro was not a proletarian. His whole saga is predicated on his failed effort to resist becoming a rural proletarian. But the ideologeme that is actively interpreted is violence, not the clear class positions assumed by the characters. The centrality of *Martín Fierro* in Argentine cultural life is such that it was conceivable for Martínez-Estrada, the best essayist of twentieth-century Argentina, to write an intense interpretive work on *Martín Fierro* and then propose it to be an all-encompassing interpretation of Argentine life itself (see *Muerte y transfiguración del Martín Fierro: ensayo de interpretación de la vida argentina* [1948]). According to Borges, *Martín Fierro* is a book that "can be anything for anybody [*todo para todos*] since it is capable of unending repetitions, versions, perversions" (1949, in Borges 1974, 537).[2]

The history of this gaucho embodied for generations to come the political predicaments of the subject "before the law." Indeed, *Martín Fierro* has a unique place among the literature discussed in this book. It is the only work narrated in the first person, with the bandit telling his own story. The poetic convention is that the poem is the narrative of Fierro's misfortunes, which he sings for other gauchos while strumming his guitar. The gaucho malo as the axis of the narrative does not appear in the *gauchesca* genre before *Martín Fierro*. However, his figure would occupy the genre almost in its entirety from that point on.[3] The trajectory from the "us" in the dialogues and *cielitos* in the early gauchesca to the soliloquy in Hernández's poem and Antonio Lussich's *Los tres gauchos orientales* (1872) is for Ángel Rama the index of the disappearance of the gauchesca as a true political genre (1976, 51).[4] From then on, the gauchesca would position itself in a space of what I would call a "restricted politics."[5] However, the position of the outlaw as narrator and solitary hero of the narrative had a political thrust with huge repercussions since it was intended to overlap with that of the letrado as author in opposition to the state (Hernández was a political outcast when he wrote *La ida*) and in vindication of rural society (he had been a supporter of the last large rural uprising, the López Jordán rebellion in Entre Ríos). For the briefest of moments, there was collusion between letrado and rural outlaw whereby one could serve as a metaphor for the other (Halperín Donghi 1985, 287), and this relationship would not be repeated in Argentine culture.[6] The collusion was possible since both letrado and outlaw were subjects "before the law."

If the origins of the word "gaucho" are still hard to determine, its usage is not. The first recorded appearance of the word in the region was a complaint in 1774 from colonial officials about gauchos or robbers operating in the Banda Oriental (Slatta 1983, 8–9). It is the same period in which Félix de Azara used the terms *gauderio* and *gaucho* as synonyms for criminals and runaway cattle smugglers living in the Banda Oriental (Slatta 1983, 9–10), a meaning that Carrió de la Vandera, in *El lazarillo de ciegos caminantes*, suggested but did not fully develop (1773, 120). A century later, Colonel Sandes (in charge of the campaign against Peñaloza) routinely used the words "gaucho" and "federalist" as synonyms for "rural bandit" (de la Fuente 2000, 166), while the inhabitants of the rural areas used the word "gaucho" to name cattle rustlers or murderers, and the verb *gauchar* came to mean "to steal" (de la Fuente 1998, 272).[7] Even though, as Josefina Ludmer points out, the gauchesca engages in a debate on the meaning of the word gaucho (in which the gaucho constantly oscillates between extremes: patriotic gaucho or outlaw gaucho), this oscillation is only possible as a secondary, polemical moment, since the gaze of the state had already fixed the gaucho in one of those identity positions.

Endemic banditry was, as in all agrarian societies, an everyday reality in the Río de la Plata region. English and American travelers in the area made constant reference to banditry. Francis Bond Head (*Rough Notes Taken during Some Rapid Journeys across the Pampas and among the Andes* [1826]) emphatically states that the countryside was "heavily infested with *salteadores*" (147) and that "in the pampas it is absolutely necessary to carry arms, since there are many *salteadores*, especially in the desolate province of Santa Fe" (40). He backs up this assertion with a number of stories about highway robbers (40, 57, 65, 75). In the appendix to the book, he states that one of the main reasons why it was impossible to establish a mining enterprise there (the main motive for his travel) was "the savage robbery customs of the gauchos" (163). When talking about the nature of the inhabitants of the pampas, Charles Darwin in *The Voyage of the Beagle* mentions prominently that "many robberies are committed" and that "many lives are lost in trifling quarrels," adding that the population actively aids murderers (since they think that it is an offense against the state, not against the community), and that the judiciary and police are completely inefficient (1839, 139–40). William MacCann, writing in *Two Thousand Miles' Ride through the Argentine Provinces* (1853), tells how

> wherever I went, and whomsoever I met, I heard accounts of horses being stolen: one man had six fine cart-horses taken, which, having never been saddled, could be of little use to the thieves, if intended for a journey; another had devoted all his leisure to the training of a pet tropilla [team or drove of horses] for himself, and when his horses were perfectly docile they were stolen; a third, who was on a journey put out a valuable horse to eat a little grass, and though, as a precaution, he tied him to a long rope, in a few minutes the animal disappeared; a fourth (an Irishman) forcibly illustrated the adroitness of horse-stealers by exclaiming, "Sir, they would scoop a horse out of your eye, if you put him there." (64)

MacCann himself participated, involuntarily, in an act of cattle lifting: "My first inquiry was touching [on] the ownership of the beast [the one they were eating]: 'Has she a mark?' 'Yes.' 'Then she belongs to someone; and in plain, honest speech, we have stolen a cow: for which offence, if prosecuted, we are liable to [face] a severe penalty.' Such acts, however, are so common on the frontier, particularly when travelers are benighted, or unable to obtain other food, that the morality of the deed is measured by a very different scale to cattle-lifting in Britain: besides the difference in the value of the animal" (138–39).

Banditry (as a label applied to all poor rural populations) emerged as a defining metaphor in the context of a centuries-long struggle for cattle, horses, hides, and people to work them in the Río de la Plata region from the eighteenth until the end of the nineteenth century.[8] As part of the economic and military needs of an export-oriented economy (intensified during the post-independence international and internecine wars), agrarian elites maintained contradictory demands vis-à-vis the rural population. On the one hand, they imposed a model of globally integrated rural capitalism, with a defined concept of property for land, water, and cattle and a rural popu-lation comprising disciplined rural proletarians. On the other hand, they denied the paysanos what they should have had as a condition of being the rural proletariat: the free selling of labor as a commodity, freedom of move-ment, payment in currency rather than in goods, the right of association, and the right to vote. The elite class thus regulated in a patrimonial manner all aspects of rural life. Sometimes this control meant using "traditional" cultural modes; sometimes it meant resorting to blunt force applied by the state. This sui generis mode of agrarian capitalism collided head-on with ru-ral populations that maintained free access to *orejanos* (cattle born in the wild and hence without an owner) and *cimarrones* (runaway cattle) and a somewhat freer right of transit and change of employer.

As a strategy of intervention in this conflict the landowning elites crimi-nalized the rural population, establishing an almost complete conceptual overlapping between the notions of poor rural inhabitant and bandit (Ro-dríguez-Molas 1968, 36, 66–67), punishing any form of resistance to the rules and needs of the elite (e.g., alcoholism, desertion from forced military service, gaming, homicide) as a crime and mobilizing growing state re-sources for coercion. The legal body that prosecuted vagrants, *bagamundos* (*sic*), cattle rustlers, and brigands exhibited notorious consistency through time. The *Recopilación de leyes de Indias,* as well as the *Nueva recopilación de leyes de indias,* imposed floggings and the galleys for men without known oc-cupation (Gori 1976). Book IV, Title XVIII of the *Recopilación de las Indias,* by Antonio de León Pinelo, is devoted in its entirety to the figure of the *baga-mundo,* an emphasis that continues in the requirement to carry identifica-tion and employment cards (*papeleta*), which the Bourbons instituted in the eighteenth century as part of state officials' growing preoccupation with the floating population of rural zones in the Río de la Plata area (Storni 1997, 344). One of the first legislative acts of the Creole Junta (created in Buenos

Aires in 1810 to rule in the name of Fernando VII) was the "Proclama y Reglamentación de la milicia" (May 29, 1810), the goal of which was to enact a rigorous draft, which included "all the vagrants and men without a known occupation from eighteen to forty years of age" (Rock 1987, 99). These provisions were reiterated and specified by the Decree of March 23, 1812, by Sarratea, Chiclana, and Rivadavia, later by Director Supremo Gervasio Posadas (1814), by Director Supremo Ignacio Álvarez (1815), by Gobernor Rondeau (1818), and even later by Ministro Rivadavia (1823) (Rock 1987, 99; Storni 1997, 320–22). By comparison, the complex disciplinary network that characterized the rosista regime rested upon stern local control of the rural population through the figure of the justice of the peace (a position created in 1821 after the suppression of the cabildos) and the intervention to an unknown degree of the state to a previously unheard of degree in the everyday life of rural populations (Salvatore 1996, 2003). The fall of Rosas and the consolidation of the state witnessed two pieces of legislation that built upon this long tradition: the Ley de Levas (1858) and the Código Rural (1865). The latter (like the Código Rural of Santa Fé province in 1901) "transcribed with almost no modifications archaic provisions enacted more than a century before by governors and viceroys of the Río de la Plata and was applied to a system of production that was becoming more commercial and capitalist" (Rodríguez-Molas 1968, 106).[9]

Martín Fierro was heralded as an expression of the vindication of rural populations against the state. For Hernández, banditry as a historical phenomenon was produced by the state. As such, it was considered by Martínez-Estrada as the anti-*Facundo* (1948, 3:677). Within the context of our particular line of inquiry, *Martín Fierro* stands in stark contrast to Sarmiento's writings. *Martín Fierro* exalts (at least in *La ida*) the legitimacy of violence when grounded in the cultural capital of a subaltern society, while Sarmiento supports the suppression of gaucho society as a precondition for nation-state building (or at least its disarticulation *qua* society whose cornerstone is violence). Banditry is for both authors the defining trait of rural society, but for each of them banditry pertains to a different moment of the historical process. To reiterate, Sarmiento considers banditry the normal condition of rural (non)society; therefore it is the starting point of the conflict that the state has as its mission to suppress (as Sarmiento himself did in La Rioja). The risks of not suppressing banditry are well known: the enthronement of outlawry in the Rosas regime. For Her-

he saw fit / He appeared and on the spot / He drove a bunch of us away / The roughest ran away / and they were able to get away / I did not want to escape / I am a meek person and there was no reason to get away" (114). The last verse poses two different problems: on the one hand, Fierro seems to have no capacity for violence ("I am a meek person" [soy manso]). This is not a personality trait. The entire world of the estancia, as depicted by Fierro, is devoid of violence. Why? "There was no reason" (No había porqué). The landlord was supposed to protect his gauchos, and the "oral law" was not a code of bravery and challenge but of rituals of deference and submission to authority learned at the estancia. Otherwise, there is no way of understanding Fierro's unwillingness to escape or fight or why he (incredibly) marches unescorted to the fort when ordered, carrying with him all his prized possessions (117), or why he endures three years of poor rations, punishments, lack of payment, indebtedness, forced labor for private persons, and the very absurdity of pretending to protect a frontier that was completely porous to Indian invasions, since the soldiers lacked the preparation, firearms, and horses needed to repel them (117–45). "Soy manso" thus meant that there was an accepted (however unequal) status quo in which violence was understood to be at the disposal of the hacienda master. As long as this status quo was valid and in force, no violence was present in the rural order. That is the fatal miscalculation of Fierro: "no había porqué," meaning "the protection of the master should be enough" to secure his being undisturbed.

As Elida Lois noted, the poem is addressed to the elite, either those in power or those making a bid for power (Lois and Núñez 2001, xlv).[11] Fierro's intended audience is clear since the political drama that triggers the narrative bypassed the gaucho entirely. Fierro's reluctance to enter into the patronage network that the justice of the peace crowned at the local level, and to vote according to his desires (115–16), was a huge political mistake, but it was really not Fierro's mistake. It was a symptom of the crumbling rural order in which political affiliations were coextensive with economic ones (and Fierro voted with the landlord). The conflict that eventually produced the bandit was an intra-elite conflict, of which Fierro was the innocent victim, not a class conflict in which Fierro was the rebellious (or reluctant) peasant because, as we saw before, Fierro was a far cry from rebellious.

This fading of the patrimonial alliance that Fierro longed for at the beginning of the poem produces the possibility for the lonely voice of the gaucho on the one hand and, on the other, of the appearance of the gaucho as a gaucho malo—a nomad, a de-territorialized warrior. (As Martínez-Estrada noted, "[T]here are no gauchos with masters of any kind; nobody depends on anybody—except from the Moreno—they are not peons" [1948, 3:717].) It is coextensive with this de-territoralization that oral law emerges, not before. In other words: oral law does not refer to an idyllic pre-state era when gauchos freely roamed the pampas. This era never existed because gauchos were the product of a peculiar form of colonial mestizaje (Rodríguez-Molas 1968).

Oral law as the law of bravery, challenge, and revenge is not the law of the rural community but the code of the outlaw, produced in the conflict with the state. Just as the state produced banditry as the trope with which to outlaw its challengers, the outlaw produces oral law. This radically changes the nature of singing (considering that singing is crucial to the identity of the gaucho). Ludmer mentions that the two tones of the voice are lament and challenge and that the voice of the gaucho is the intonation of these two tones (1988). However, there are no challenges before the becoming-outlaw of Fierro: the scene that the judge interrupted is an impromptu singing but not a challenge (Hernández 1872/1879, 113–14). Also, it is *after* he becomes an outlaw that the pulpería ceases to be a place for community and becomes a place for fighting. Due to the breakdown of the pact across classes, violence became rhizomorphous, and the laws of the challenge did not follow class, party, or cultural lines. Rather, bravery was exclusively a self-sustaining value. This is why Fierro's fights in the pulperías look like drunken rages, although they are more than that. They are the manifestation of a violence for which there is no code outside of the code of the challenge. It is violence without a transcendent meaning (in addition to the identity making effect). This is why Cruz switched sides: oral law as the code of bravery is completely immanent. It has no final cause, no identity outside combat, no community outside the community of the brave.

From this point of view, the flight to the desert makes complete sense. It is the quest for a warrior community that drove Fierro and Cruz to cross to the other side, a place where the segmentarity characteristic of agrarian capitalism was irrelevant. In Fierro's enthusiastic description of life among the Indians, there is no distinction between work, combat, and leisure, between inside and outside, between Christians and pagans, between theft and war (200–202). Life among the Indians would summarize the best of the two worlds that Fierro had experienced so far: a community outside the regulations of agrarian capitalism (the agrarian arcadia), and the nomadic war machine (the outlaw life). With this optimistic, fearful prospect, *La ida* ends.

This experience proves an utter failure, however. Between *La ida* and *La vuelta* the Desert Campaign (Campaña del Desierto) occurred, and it wiped out the Indians of the pampas. In *La vuelta* the disappearance of the frontier had its counterpart in the erection of a symbolic barrier between the gaucho (who now belonged to "this" side in its entirety, although in a clearly subordinated position) and the others, the Indians who were characterized as bandits like Fierro, Cruz, and the rest of the Christians (277–300). In *La vuelta*, the disappearance of the frontier as an organizing signifier of the national imaginary (Argentina as a frontier territory) made the space homogeneous. Thus the segmentations are those determined by the nation-state, without possibilities for escape.[12] This is why in *La vuelta* all the characters meet again, while in *La ida* all disperse without that possibility (just like in *El periquillo sarniento*), and why there are no longer real challenges to state law. (*La vuelta* has a picaresque tone—particularly with respect to the characters of Vizcacha and Picardía—that is completely lacking in *La ida*.)

The disappearance of the frontier establishes an additional demarcation, this time temporal, between a past condemned to disappearance (to which the gaucho formerly known as "Martín Fierro" belongs) and the present. The paysano whose name we do not know belongs to the present since he has renounced oral fame and has entered the homogenizing order of the commodity (selling his labor in the labor market).

Like Perico in *El periquillo sarniento*, Fierro came back from the desert and integrated himself into the order-in-the-making that he had earlier deserted. David Viñas (1994) cleverly pointed out this parallelism. However, there are certain essential differences. Perico did not become a bandit himself, and he did not cross that threshold, which is what it made possible for him to write, since he does not lose his epistemological privilege. Perico reenters society on his way to the top, while Fierro enters as a conforming subaltern. Fierro comes back, and he apparently brings with him certain cultural capital that he shared with his sons and Cruz's. However, unlike Perico's cultural capital (which ensures his position at the top of the family-as-society, and the memory of his deeds) Fierro's cultural capital is one of self-denial. On the one hand, it has no power to promote effective intervention in reality (it is wisdom of accommodation). On the other, far from founding a family and a memory, the return is the act that heralds its definitive disintegration. Fierro's authority (embodied in his advice) is but an illusion.

Supposedly, the advice is the wisdom of the frontier that Fierro hands down to his offspring. But that Other space to which the advice (as accumulated experience) refers no longer exists. Therefore, the spatial difference becomes a cultural (temporal) difference; the heterogeneity becomes evolution. Fierro possesses a wisdom that is useless in the present and becomes folk wisdom (and Fierro becomes a folk hero). As Tulio Halperín Donghi points out, "The model that Hernández prefers for his regenerated hero is not the one offered by the creators of epic poetry. As he declares in 'four words of conversation with the readers' that preface *La vuelta,* it is that of the wise man who, in archaic or exotic civilizations, endows the treasure of philosophical and moral teachings destined to enter the traditional patrimony of nations with the mysterious authority that emanates from his very person" (1985, 311). Thus, if *La ida* clears the path for Eduardo Gutiérrez, Roberto Arlt, the Montoneros of the 1970s, and *Plata quemada* by Ricardo Piglia, *La vuelta* clears the way for *El diario de Gabriel Quiroga* (1910) by Manuel Gálvez, *Don Segundo Sombra* (1926) by Ricardo Güiraldes, as well as *Romances de Río Seco* (1938) by Leopoldo Lugones and *Desierto de piedra* (1925) by Hugo Wast, in which local wisdom is a legitimating memory for the urban, nationalist, and conservative *letrado.*

10 | *Juan Moreira*
The Gaucho Malo as Unpopular Hero

Pero amigo, ya sabemos lo que son novelas . . . y lo que son cuentos. Ustedes, los hombres de pluma, le meten no más, inventando cosas que interesen, y que resulten lindas. Y el gaucho se presta pa'todo. Después que ha servido de juguete a la polesía le toman los leteratos para contar d'el lo que se les ocurre.

Hormiga Negra, *malevo* from San Nicolás, hero of the eponymously titled novel by Eduardo Gutiérrez, interviewed in 1912 for *Caras y caretas*

Ese bárbaro folletín espeluznante [*Juan Moreira*], esa confusión de la leyenda y de la historia nacional en una escritura desenfadada y a la criolla, forman, en lo copioso de la obra, la señal de una época en nuestras letras. Esa literatura gaucha es lo único que hasta hoy puede atraer la curiosidad de Europa: ella es un producto natural, autóctono, y en su salvaje fiereza y poesía va el alma de nuestra tierra.

Rubén Darío, *España Contemporánea,* 1901

Juan Moreira (1879) was the second novel written by Argentine writer Eduardo Gutiérrez (1851–1889). Its story is in many ways compatible with that of *Martín Fierro*. Like Fierro, Juan Moreira is a respected and well-to-do paysano, ensconced in a life of work and progress. He is the owner of some land, some cattle, and a prosperous freight business dedicated to carrying agrarian products to the local train station for transport to Buenos Aires.[1] He lives peacefully at home with his wife, Vicenta, and his son, Juan junior, in Matanzas County (a *partido,* according to Buenos Aires political nomenclature). As in Cruz's case, having a beautiful wife proves to be his undoing. Don Francisco, the *teniente alcalde* of the partido, had conceived a violent passion for Vicenta and, spited by her lack of reciprocity (she decided to marry Moreira, disdaining Don Francisco's overtures), starts to persecute the paysano in the many ways available to a powerful rural official. Moreira endures the harassment silently, knowing all too well that law does not equal justice in rural Buenos Aires. This continues until Moreira is unjustly humiliated. He was demanding repayment of a debt that Sardetti, the Italian general store owner, not only refused to pay but even to acknowledge (the claim was based on a verbal agreement, without any kind of paper trail). Not only does Moreira's grievance remain unresolved but his head is clamped in the stocks and he is physically and verbally abused. Pushed beyond his limits, Moreira kills Sardetti and starts a nomadic life either as a free-wheeling bandit or as an electoral thug, fighting posses in the open as well as occasional challengers in barrooms and pulperías. This outlaw life ends one fateful evening in a brothel in Lobos. Betrayed by Cuerudo, a trusted but resentful ally, Moreira is surrounded by members of the Buenos Aires police force. He fights bravely against his many adversaries (surrender never enters his mind), and he is even able to overwhelm them. But the die was already cast. Moreira, having temporarily shrugged off his pursuers, is about to make a bold escape by climbing the back wall of the brothel, which would have put him within reach of his famed horse and the open horizons of the pampas. But Sergeant Chirino, unbeknown to Moreira, is hiding behind the wall of the well, trying to avoid a showdown with the lethal paysano. When he sees that Moreira is distracted by trying to climb the wall, he finds an opportunity: he stabs Moreira in the back, pinning him to the wall. Moreira tries to keep on fighting (literally to his last breath) but to no avail: his life and his career end there.

If the commonalities between Moreira's and Fierro's stories are apparent, the divergences are no less so. The saga of Fierro ends with his coming back from the desert and a life among Indians to enter into the new agrarian order in his role as father, citizen, and worker. Moreira's struggle ends only with his death at the hands of rural (in)justice. It is no surprise that Moreira was hailed as a radical answer (or at least a radical gesture), in which the gaucho malo vindicates "the popular position of confrontation and violence to the bitter end" (Ludmer 1994, x). Drawing on this contrast between the end of *Martín Fierro* and the end of *Juan Moreira*, Ludmer presents a provocative idea: *Juan Moreira* was the true continuation of *El gaucho Martín Fierro*, the one that prolongs its political edge (1994, xi; 1999, 229). *Juan Moreira* was the uncompromising alternative to the resigned accommodation offered by *La vuelta de Martín Fierro*. While the latter paved the way for Rojas and Lugones, who canonized *Martín Fierro* as the epic poem of the nation and the gaucho as the national icon of the "Argentine race" (Rojas 1917–1923; Lugones 1905, 1916), *Juan Moreira* presents the gaucho malo as the popular "hero of the [resistance] to the modernizing leap" (Ludmer 1994, x).[2]

There are a number of corroborating factors. The summary of Moreira's life with which Gutiérrez opened his novel is one. Here Gutierrez unveiled the proposition that the narrative will try to demonstrate that, in the traditional social bandit vein, "the cause of the immense criminality in our rural areas is the exceptional nature of our authorities" (11). (This notwithstanding, the statement in later novels became more and more of a formulaic overture, thus depleting its force as a political proclamation. Cases in point are the overtures of *El tigre del Quequén, Pastor Luna,* and *Juan sin patria,* among others.) Another corroborating factor is the rather shocking effect that Gutiérrez's *folletines* (serially published novels) had within the lettered city and the aggressive reaction that they generated. (See, for example, the angry comments by Navarro Viola in the *Anuario bibliográfico de la República Argentina* [1880, 1886], the even harsher remarks by García-Merou in "Los dramas policiales" [1881], or the musings on Juan Moreira's psychological profile by José Ingenieros [1910], among others.[3]) This rejection was directed at the author and his works, as well as at the sociological phenomenon the novel spawned: the so-called *"moreirismo."* Vicente Quesada claimed that the "literary influence [of criollismo] was highly pernicious. And, from a sociological point of view, what is even more worthy of blame, it has denaturalized the gaucho type, inflaming the *compadrito,* and has perverted the *acriollados* immigrants. To sum up: it could be said that its exclusive objective has been to flatter the basest passions and to lionize the brigand" (Quesada 1902, 37). José Ingenieros, in *La sicopatología en el arte,* explains that

> Around the year 1900, stimulated by the press and the theater, an epidemic of "moreirismo" ravaged Buenos Aires. From time to time, from the outskirts of the city, some low-life—like "el Melena," "El nuevo Juan Moreira," and others like these—added to his habitual attire certain elements of the old gaucho apparel and decided to violently resist the authorities. Possessing the guitar—which as a general rule he could not play—the neighborhood lout started shuffling around the places where liquor was sold, singing some "traditional" stanzas off key, learned in poor-quality chapbooks, almost always put together by Catalonian or Italian editors. Before the police get them to jail, some crime reporters busied themselves advertising them in the major newspapers, thus creating an environment conducive to crime that it is indispensable so that other predisposed subjects would decide to imitate the "moreirismo." (1903, 352)

This seemed to ensure Moreira's place in Argentine cultural memory as the ultimate icon of popular opposition to the state's violence. Moreira as a signifier articulated to class, cultural, or political struggles traverses a road that goes from popular theater (the wild popularity of the adaptation of *Juan Moreira* by Podestá and Gutiérrez helped found national popular theater) to

Plata quemada (1997), Ricardo Piglia's novel that retells Moreira's story as an allegory of resistance to the realities of late capitalism (with heavy influence from films by Brian de Palma and Quentin Tarantino).[4]

Some knowledge of the post-Gutiérrez *folletines criollistas*, which thrived in the late nineteenth and early twentieth centuries, can help us determine some of the ways in which this memory was selectively constructed. The *folletines criollistas* replicated the novel's plot almost *ad nauseam*, this time in verse form.[5] These versions were published under diverse titles, and the authors used various pseudonyms or published anonymously (Horacio del Bosque, Manuel Cientofante, Félix Hidalgo, "El Gaucho Talerito," S. Rolleri, Alfredo Mario French, Silverio Manco, and Ramón Aguirre are among the authors).[6] Given the shortness of these chapbooks (thirty-two to thirty-six pages in small format), they are brutally condensed versions of the original plot. However, these versions are remarkably consistent in certain respects. None of these versions omits the debt-related death of Sardetti or the bloody retribution against Don Francisco. Even the 1886 theatrical version by Gutiérrez and José J. Podestá and an 1884 circus skit of *Juan Moreira* included these episodes. In fact, the theatrical version opens with the debt-related incident between Sardetti, Moreira, and Don Francisco and Sardetti's death, closely followed by Don Francisco's death. Actually, according to Enrique García-Velloso's contemporary testimony, the scene between Moreira and Sardetti defined the very nature of Argentine theater (its language, its plots, the expectations of its public, the very nature of that public) at the end of the nineteenth century (quoted in Viñas 1973, 69).

This omnipresence seems warranted. With these two deaths (one being that of the purported representative of the market economy and the other being a representative of the state), "Moreira makes the necessary passage required of all heroes of popular justice" (Ludmer 1994, xii). This heroic character is reinforced by the manner of his death: an infamous stab in the back. (This is another scene present in all *folletines criollistas*.) But the omissions are no less significant and consistent than the inclusions. All the versions (at least those I have access to) omit the fact that Moreira worked (twice) as an electoral goon (90–100, 242) and as Alsina's bodyguard (101–104). Also, none of the versions mentioned that "the only man that Moreira loved in this life," Marañón, was a justice of the peace (224) and as such was a representative of the institution that in the gauchesque and criollista imaginary summarized all the evils unleashed upon rural Argentina.[7] Also, no post-Gutiérrez version mentions that Moreira was briefly a successful and respected member of the posses (*partidas*) that he later fought and vilified so vociferously (he even swore to kill as many posse members as possible [166]). The fight with the posse has a place in Argentine culture comparable to that of the showdown on Main Street in American culture: the scene where heroes are born and tried in the fight against oppression and injustice. It is rarely mentioned, however, that Moreira played both sides of this scene, and that he did so comfortably. Unlike Cruz, Moreira had no sudden awakening that made him switch sides to help the valiant but downtrodden gaucho malo. He did not leave the posse for political reasons either, but only because he wanted to prosper economically and marry (thus reinforcing his adaptation to the realities of agrarian capitalism). Moreira's legend as an exemplary social bandit rests then on forgetting his compromises with the state, compromises that go to the core of his identity. Moreira is above all a fighter; secondarily he is a singer; and finally, he is a provider and a spouse. But Moreira as a war machine is an assemblage of man, horse, dog, and dagger. The novel goes well beyond the classic motif of bandit narratives dealing with the superb horse and the flashy weapons of the bandit: in this novel there are extensive and frequent passages about the care that Moreira lavished on his animals and their value in combat. There is even an entire section devoted to the protagonist's dagger. But this assemblage had an equivocal origin: both dagger and horse were presents from Alsina (104), so Moreira's identity as war machine is problematic since the state is at the very center of its constitution. (In Deleuze and Guattari's reflection on the war machine [1980], the war machine is *a posteriori* captured by the state.) Finally, there is another forgotten element in the text: the fact that, before Moreira is betrayed by Cuerudo, he is betrayed by the province of Buenos Aires when his protector Marañón falls from favor (249–50). This large-scale betrayal results in a full-blown persecution of Moreira (249) that eventually catches up with him. Moreira is a victim of the state, but of an internal struggle within the state. It is a struggle that divided the rural population along lines other than those of class and in which the bandit was no longer the sovereign warrior of legend.

This massive omission seems to be essential to the construction of Moreira's memory in Argentine culture, and it has affected literary criticism as well. In this respect, Ludmer's "Los escándalos de Juan Moreira" (1994) was a huge leap forward, since she introduced the notion of the "double politics

to the notion of the "popular" (the notion is in fact a cornerstone of the theoretical work she began in 1988 with *El género gauchesco* (*The Gaucho Genre*).[8] She even makes Moreira's double politics a condition for the existence of the popular hero. I would propose a different version, that of a Moreira whose collusion with the "conservative order" (Botana 1977) prevents his being a "popular hero" but not because he fell short of meeting the demanding standards of the popular hero (which he did). Instead, the narrative points to an essential rift within the popular and to the fact that "popular" as applied to the rural population is a construction ex post facto by readings of the novel. In other words, I would like to rebuke, first, the reading of the character of Moreira as the anchor around which a popular subject is constructed and, second, the reading of Moreira's struggle as representative of the struggles of the entire rural population. Contrary to reconstructing a homogeneous popular subject around Moreira, I would like to highlight the conflicts that place Moreira in opposition to the rural population and reason their effects on the identities that play out in the narrative. The "Moreira as popular hero" reading is possible because it is usually from Moreira's perspective that the conflicts are addressed (following here the narrator's lead, as García-Merou noted early on). I would also read Moreira in reverse (Beverley 1999), from the perspective of the paysanos in the novel who did not fight "as a luxury" (276), from the perspective of those who never benefited from Moreira's shadowy compromises (whose name is Legion), from those who do not share his alliances and hatreds (often formed on a whim), and ultimately, from the perspective of the abject character of the novel, Cuerudo.[9] "La noche de los dones," the superb story that Borges included in *El libro de Arena* (1975, in Borges 1996), heralds this change of perspective and the discovery of the unpopular nature of Moreira. Ostensibly, "La noche de los dones" is a short story about memory. In particular, it is the story of the old man's memories on the night of April 30, 1874, in which he received the "gifts" of knowing love and death. But this is also a story about the construction of social memory and of how Moreira's is constructed upon unavoidable falsifications (several crucial details in his narrative—which has the weight of a witness testimony—contradict the "official" account).[10] Moreira's social memory is also constructed upon a monumental forgetting: the fact that Moreira was not perceived by his peers as a popular hero of resistance but, more modestly, as a "drunken *orillero*," avoided with disgust and feared by women and paysanos alike. Of course, this account does not amount to a rediscovered solid truth. In fact, the old man's memories are (perhaps irretrievably) contaminated by the circus memories of the gaucho.

When examining his career as a thug hired to threaten opposition voters, scholars have always placed emphasis on the relationship between Moreira and his protectors (Alsina first, Marañón and the *mitrismo* later) and how Moreira established alliances based on the common recognition of the code of bravery and honor. The locus of this common ground is the voice (e.g., it is the way that Alsina spoke to Moreira that won the gaucho over to his cause [102]). The symbols of this alliance are the dagger and the horse that Alsina presented to Moreira as a gift. This collusion between social bandit and sovereign, as we saw in the case of *Zárate*, is commonplace in bandit narratives and may serve different purposes according to the occasion. (In *Juan Moreira*, it legitimized certain party identities akin to Gutiérrez.) But there is another way to look at this. We can look at this collusion as the moment in which Moreira became an oppressor of the rural poor, whose voting and citizen rights he violently (and self-righteously) violated.[11] When Moreira was working as part of the electoral machinery of the *mitristas*, he did not strive to win the minds and hearts of the paysanos but to terrorize them into submission and compliance; these are hardly the ways of a popular hero. After one of his boastful displays of bravery, for example, "the paysanos were so subdued that they declared . . . that they had decided not to vote in the election, since they did not want to be at odds with Juan Moreira [since] a stab by him could not be undone" (245). Predictably, "[e]lection day came and it was won by a landslide [*esta fue canónica*] because there was no paysano who dared to vote against Don Juan Moreira" (245). Note the "don" embedded in the indirect speech (the narrator is loosely rendering the talk of the paysanos). For them, Moreira, in this position, was far from "one of their own."

Following Ludmer's reasoning, it is possible to say that *Juan Moreira* is a "return" to Hernández's *La ida*. It is a return indeed, but to a completely different place than that postulated by Ludmer. It is a return not to the flight to the desert, understood as a radical gesture, but to the opening scene of the drama where Fierro falls prey to the draft because the judge was persecuting him since he failed to vote according to the judge's wishes. ("I knew the Judge had a down on me, / For I'm no politician; / On voting day I had stayed away, / And somebody since had heard him say / That those that didn't vote for him / Were helping the opposition" [269].) His entire life unravels from this point on. We could very well imagine that Moreira was one of the merciless goons who drafted the peaceful Fierro out of the pulpería where he was singing. Or if we let our imagination go in another direction, Fierro was one of the fearful paysanos driven like cattle to the voting places of Moreira's faction, intimidated by the violence of the elite electoral machine.

Fierro, pursued by the posses looking for the barroom murderer and deserter, decides to cross the frontier with Cruz into Indian territories, looking for a surrogate community in which to live and maybe to prosper.[12] Toward the middle of the novel, Moreira, also with the police in hot pursuit, goes to live among the Indians (170–80). But there is a major difference: Moreira is looking for a hideout at the margins of society; he is not looking for a community. The Indians among whom Moreira lives are subject to the cacique Coliqueo, and they were no longer fierce, fearsome warriors. They were "friendly Indians" (Indios amigos) who directly depended on the military chief of the frontier and who lived from the rations and salaries that the state irregularly gave them. They no longer organized raids (malones) but rather hunting expeditions (boleadas) with the consent of the military authority so as to exchange their hunting prizes for liquor at local general stores (170). Even though the Indian huts (tolderías) were made of foul-smelling mare hides and the Indians were lazy gamblers and heavy drinkers, they did not oppose civilization (like the hellish Indian village in La vuelta), since the tolderías were, for all practical purposes, no different than the urban slums. The tolderías were a degraded space, most certainly, but the threat they represented was internal to the space of the nation-state: it was the threat of "crime" and "vice" (more in an end-of-the-century fashion) and not that of "barbarism."

Fierro failed to blend into the Indian community, but this was because the Indians themselves chose not to accept him (276–78). Moreira never has the goal of blending into the Indian community, and he does not wish to coexist peacefully with it. Instead, he seeks to exploit and deceive the Indians, as shown when he wins money in rigged gambling sessions. He actually has to leave the tolderías because of a gambling dispute (180), unlike Fierro, who had to leave because he fought and killed an Indian defending a captive from unspeakable abuse and torture. In this episode, Moreira is less of a bandit than a pícaro, not different from the much-vilified general store owners (pulperos) who cheated the Indians of their hunting treasures by some measure of cheap alcohol. Moreira, therefore, is no different than Sardetti: he justifies the robbery because he was only robbing Indians (one can imagine that Sardetti justified his own abuses because he was just robbing gauchos), and he boasts about this adventure in pulperías to general delight (197). We could argue that Indians are no measure for community making in the case of a Creole who fought against them for a long time (169). This may be true. But from this point on Moreira becomes a professional cheater; he cheats his "fellow gauchos" out of their money and always gets away with it because of the sheer fear of his dagger (234). The one man who dared denounce his cheating, Rico Romero, ends up dead (235).

Moreira does not seem to be that well liked among paysanos either. It is true that the novel records many instances in which Moreira is praised, consoled, and even, in some cases, cheered while entering a general store (119). Moreira is even surrounded by flattery and deference. But flattery and deference are hardly a measure for affection in the rural world, where deference does not equal friendship, let alone an alliance (Scott 1985; Guha 1983). Flattery and deference belong to the "public transcript," and as such they are performances. In this case they are the performances of the weak in front of the powerful (Scott 1990). These performances do not mean real appreciation but an acute perception of a situation of unequal power on the part of the subaltern. The "hidden transcript" is accessible in this case only by what the weak do not do or do not say, and there are many things that they do not do or say. Among the paysanos, after many years as an outlaw and "popular hero," Moreira has only two allies: Julián (who is captured at the brothel the same day that Moreira dies) and his brother Inocencio (who ends up as a member of the police force [258]). The paysanos are mostly spectators to Moreira's exploits; they never actively help him and they never wish to join his emancipatory crusade against the posses.[13]

When Moreira leaves Matanzas because he has killed Sardetti, there is no community to help Vicenta (something unthinkable in the case of a "real" literary social bandit, whose community takes pride in the steadfastness of its support, which is precisely what would make him a social bandit). The many folks who are supposedly Moreira's friends (who ate his beef and drank his liquor at his wedding party [17]) fail to help Vicenta in any way, letting her almost starve to death (157). Not only do they not lend her a helping hand but they allow her to believe that Moreira is dead, which means that they were not even paying her an occasional visit to save face in front of Moreira. And this was not even the deserted world of *Martín Fierro,* where this could have been credible. *Juan Moreira*'s world was a populated one, with neighbors and cities and means of communication. Moreira's community actively failed to act. Even his bosom friend, the compadre Giménez, saw in Vicenta's situation an opportunity not to exercise mythical rural solidarity but to snatch Vicenta from Moreira (157). Finally, when Moreira dies, no one visits his grave, which is guarded by the faithful dog Cacique (Moreira's loyal pet and companion), except for Julián (294–97). Giménez and Moreira's friends were clearly traitors, but "traitor" may only be a trope for the incomprehensible (as in the case of Silvio Astier, the hero of Arlt's *El juguete rabioso,* who was also an avid reader of bandit stories). If we are so eager to understand Moreira's motives and to argue that he kills because his identity is pinned to an oral code of retribution, why not try to determine the motives of Giménez and the others? The narrator never does that, but we can guess. We can imagine that, for Giménez, Moreira was not a hero of popular violence. Like the gauchos of Borges's poem "Los gauchos," who may never have heard the word "gaucho" or who may have heard it only as an insult, Giménez would have had no idea of what "popular violence" meant, and he would have been outraged to hear that Moreira was the hero of that violence. For him, Moreira was at best a bully and a showoff (his attire and countenance were closer to that of the contemporary gangsta-rapper than to the ascetic gaucho of the *Martín Fierro*) and at worst an enemy to be feared, but never a hero. (Giménez was not condemned by the community for taking advantage of Moreira's predicament, and this lack of punishment or even censure is decisive in evaluating where his sympathies lay.) The many challengers that Moreira faced (and defeated) always insisted on this: that Moreira was a bully and that they resented Moreira's arrogance and patronizing style (one challenge occurred because someone rejected Moreira's invitation to drink [122]). But we fail to heed their voices, as if the only challenge worth listening to was Moreira's. This makes sense if we consider him the axis that directs and gives meaning to all violence "from below" and if we consider the gaucho voice a harmonious chorus attuned to Moreira's voice. It does not make sense, however, if we consider the world of popular violence a rhizome and a discordance of competing voices.

To reiterate, the voice of the paysano is barely recorded. There is a case, though, that gives us a glimpse into a world of muffled resentment and wounded honor (Moreira seemed to think that his was the only honor worth defending). When Moreira is hiding out at the ranch of Santiago (Julián's brother) in Cañuelas, a friendly paysano approaches the ranch to let Moreira know that the local posse, reinforced by the posse from Navarro, is going to look for him there. Without thanking the paysano for the advice, Moreira answers, "If you are a friend of the captain, tell him that all posses put together are not enough to catch me, and if he doubts what I am saying, let me know when they are all gathered and ready, so that he sees that with all of them I am just getting started" (141). Moreira, who was very appreciative when it came to favors from rich people, seemed to be disdainful toward poor folk and treats the man like an errand boy, not an ally. The paysano is offended by his attitude: "I am not a snitch—replied the paysano somewhat resentfully—and if I have come to give you advance notice it is because I am a friend of Don Santiago, and because I have an appreciation for you because of what you have done" (141).

This lack of capacity or interest in establishing alliances among the rural poor is not exceptional. In the case of Cuerudo it proves fatal. Cuerudo offers Moreira his friendship, convinced that he would be unable to defeat him in an open fight. Moreira, instead, treats him as a servant (274). Predictably, this triggers resentment that quickly becomes betrayal. Cuerudo is the one who informs the police that Moreira would be at La Estrella, the brothel in Lobos where Moreira's career is brought to an abrupt end (276).

Cuerudo is the Judas of the novel (267), while Moreira's death has a Christ-like resonance. But as Borges taught us in "Tres versiones de Judas," Judas was quite a complex character, and the drama of the Passion may be read in more ways than one. Cuerudo is in fact Moreira's secret mirror, since he is as much of a traitor as Moreira, and since (just like Moreira) he is able and willing to enter into alliances with the state and its representatives in order to defeat his enemies. He possesses martial prowess and bravery, and he also fights the posses as a luxury, just to prove his bravery (270). He is even a superb singer, just like Moreira (although he has a more festive style). Cuerudo then is not Moreira's Judas but Moreira's truth. Cuerudo is the living proof that Moreira is not a popular hero because there is no popular in the novel, only a complex network of nontotalizing subject positions, of passions, of resentments, of fragile and fugitive alliances that do not coalesce into an all-encompassing identity, into an all-encompassing conflict (such as the state versus the popular). There is no popular because the space of the novel is the space of the equivocal passions of the multitude.

This diffuse network of elements is the reason for Moreira's pervasive melancholy (124, 130, 166, 260). Alejandra Laera (2004) suggests that Moreira's melancholy is pathological (suggesting a hint of naturalism in Gutiérrez's writing [325]). I would propose instead that it is the result of the loss of totality in Moreira. Moreira longed and mourned, sang and cried for some lost past. This past was not (as in *Martín Fierro*) an arcadia or his former life with Vicenta which, in spite of his claims and public outcries, he did not seem too eager to resume (Marañón offered him the opportunity to do so, and he refused with very weak excuses [109]). His longed-for past included serving in the national guard and fighting the war against the Indians. This prehistory of the novel, abundantly referred to, but never actually narrated, is what made Moreira what he was. This is a crucial difference from *Martín Fierro:* while Fierro was a peaceful paysano, Moreira was not. He enjoyed participating in raids against the Indians, and there he won a reputation (he was called "el guapo") that he would act out only during his outlaw years. In the national guard, Moreira found a community (albeit one that cut across class lines) and a self-evident, self-sustaining hierarchy. The lost harmony, the "destiny" against which Moreira sourly complains, is the state's "betrayal" of this mode of community, which ends along with the Indian wars and the constitution of a professional army. Moreira longed not for a popular community but for a warrior community, one in which he could have become a glory of the fatherland. (One should not forget that Moreira "came to life carved in bronze" [5]; he possessed the necessary qualities to become a state hero.) He longed not for a moment before the state but for the epic of the state. (The only two of his challengers whom he deeply respected were Navarro, a veteran from the "heroic campaign of Paraguay, where every soldier was a hero [200], and Varela, a policeman [291] and hence a state representative.) This is the reason for Moreira's melancholy, and it is the true void within him. Moreira is a defeated gaucho even when he seems to be sovereign because he is not equal to history (as warrior epic) any longer. The last gestures of defiance, like his knife duels (which he despises), are not an apotheosis but only another form of defeat (his sadness and disgust after each of them are proof of his defeat).

From an elite perspective, Moreira's melancholy in *Juan Moreira* is mirrored in the ennui of Andrés in *Sin rumbo* (1885), by Eugenio Cambaceres (1843–1889). Both Gutiérrez and Cambaceres reflect on a post-Indian, post–civil war Argentina, the disappearance of the frontier, and the stabilization of a political order. In both novels, the loss of the multiclass alliance embedded in the wars (Andrés's father used to go to the wars joined by his faithful gauchos, gauchos whose daughters Andrés rapes) meant the loss of a destiny, a loss that would be fatal for both characters. (Andrés committed suicide after his last attempt at redemption—fatherhood—failed, and Moreira committed "suicide by police," as Gutiérrez clearly suggests [277].) In a world without direction, Moreira's nomadic life replicates Andrés's moral wanderings.

Between the two, there was a true hero of the resistance against the modernizing leap: the gaucho Contreras in *Sin rumbo.* Like most true fighters, he is only a shadow in flight. Contreras reflects the true destiny of his class: forced proletarianization in the enterprises of the agrarian oligarchy (he is a worker in Andrés's wool producing establishment). Unlike Moreira, who is always looking for a compromise with the powerful, Contreras hates Andrés (see the opening scene of *Sin rumbo,* in which Contreras, unable to withstand Andrés's abuse, makes an attempt against his life, only to find that the dagger of the gaucho is no match for the landowner's revolver). Unlike Moreira (who as an outlaw lived by mysterious, never mentioned means since he did not have a regular income), Contreras has to swallow his pride and return to work for his enemy (all the while resenting his economic and cultural submission, and again making an attempt on his master's life). And unlike Moreira, he deals a fatal blow to his enemy: he sets fire to the warehouse where the entire wool production was stored, thus precipitating Andrés's end. His disappearance in the dark at the end of *Sin rumbo* is the exact opposite of the title character's disappearance into the horizon in Ricardo Güiraldes's *Don Segundo Sombra* (1926). They are both fading shadows, and they both go, but Contreras goes with a last gesture of defiance and rebellion (his shadow is the shadow projected by the fire of a struggle).[14] Sombra on the other hand is "more an idea than a man" (his disappearing shadow is the shadow projected by the setting sun [Güiraldes 1926, 314]). In a world without direction, Contreras seems to be the one who knows where to go and what to do. History had condemned him equally, but his secretive figure has the fearsome stealth of the shadow, the destructive power of fire, and a true heroic dimension, unlike Moreira, who will find in Leopoldo Lugones a reinvented warrior community (*La guerra gaucha*) and his posthumous raison d'être.

11 | *Alma gaucha*
The Gaucho Outlaw and the Leviathan

Moreira as the paramount embodiment of the gaucho malo was either saluted as the ultimate icon of resistance to the modernizing leap or derided as the quintessence of the worst tendencies in Río de la Plata society. These tendencies have been collectively termed moreirismo. The sociological studies of José María Ramos Mejía (*Las multitudes argentinas* [1899] and *Rosas y su tiempo* [1907]), Carlos Octavio Bunge (*Nuestra América* [1903]), Juan Agustín García (*La ciudad indiana* [1900]), and José Ingenieros (*La sicopatología en el arte* [1903]) have all pointed out, from different perspectives, that the lionizing of the outlaw as cultural hero is key to understanding the distortions of the social and political process in Argentina (Buchbinder 1998; Svampa 1998; Salessi 1996). Bunge considers Juan Moreira, Juan Cuello, and Pastor Luna, "the popular Argentine bandit-heroes," as privileged examples of certain character flaws (*taras*) peculiar to Argentine racial and cultural heritage, such as arrogance, laziness, and melancholy—all of which turn into fatalism and a lack of respect for the law (161). The promotion of these character flaws (*taras*) in poetry, dramas, and novels amounted to a major social risk since they "ignited the regressive instincts in the popular soul" (Sánchez 1941, 621).

The assault against moreirismo led some intellectuals to enthusiastically endorse the legacy of resignation and integration in *La vuelta*.[1] Florencio Sánchez (1875–1910), the foremost playwright of the period, was a preeminent figure in the cultural effort to depose moreirismo from its central place in Argentine culture (Viñas 1996). Sánchez, writing in 1916 an essay published in his 1941 collection *Teatro completo,* understood moreirismo as "villainy and crime, from the point of view of the ideas, and bad taste, from the point of view of form" (1941, 622). Hence his plays depict the sometimes painful but inevitable transition toward a modern Argentina, in which moreirismo is not an option of resistance. In his most important plays on rural life (*M'hijo el dotor, La gringa,* and *Barranca abajo*) old gauchos (Olegario, Cantalicio, and Zoilo) have a central role. They represent (and are) the memory of another time when a man was only as good as his dagger and when gaucho culture was the law of the land (at least in nostalgic terms). But the

190

old gauchos are also witnesses who are painfully aware of the fact that times had changed. Cantalicio and Zoilo are indeed wronged men. Like Moreira, Fierro, or Cruz, they were insulted through an attack on the honor of their household and their standing as proprietors and respected members of the community (*vecino*). They were dispossessed of their earthly belongings, either through an injustice that was protected by the law (as in the case of Zoilo) or through the shift in market forces (agriculture displacing cattle raising and better cattle breeds replacing Creole cattle, as in the case of Cantalicio). These old gauchos make feeble attempts to recover this past in which the rules of a challenge (*duelo*) were still in place, but the contrast could not be more telling. In the case of Cantalicio, what began as a Fierro-like barroom challenge against the gringo(s) who dispossessed him of his land and his community standing ends very differently. Cantalicio breaks into tears and becomes an object of compassion for those whom he had challenged. Furthermore, if in *Martín Fierro* or *Juan Moreira* the state (through its representatives) was one of the contenders in the conflict, in Sánchez's plays the state is *above* the interests and conflicts of the individual. The state is depicted as the true realization of either the moral ideals of the community or the blind (and, for some, crushing) forces of historical change. (Cantalicio and Zoilo are dispossessed through court challenges, but the identity of the judges is never known and the justice of the ruling is never really questioned.) The fact that the old oral law has been phased out is emphasized in *M'hijo el dotor* by the fact that the offender is Julio, Olegario's own son. This is why the resolution always entails the defeat of the old gaucho and the erasure (or token conservation) of the memory of the past: Olegario dies, Cantalicio becomes Victoria's father-in-law (Victoria is the gringa who married his son and who loves him in a patronizing fashion), and Zoilo commits suicide (not before surrendering his knife, the symbol of his rebellious identity, to Aniceto).

In his lecture "El teatro nacional" Sánchez considered the transition that he depicted not only an inevitable effect of modernization in Argentina but also a qualitative leap within the cultural field that would leave behind (and below) the Moreira-Sardetti scene as the cornerstone of national theater. Among the founders of this new, regenerated theater, to whom Río de la Plata culture must offer thanks "for the death of Moreira, of Cuello, and of Hormiga Negra," Sánchez mentions Martiniano Leguizamón (1858–1935) and his "very likable *Calandria*" (Sánchez 1941, 622). Indeed, *La vuelta* as "disciplined gauchesca" (*gauchesca domesticada*) (Rama 1976, 147–53) is echoed in the saga of the *matrero* Servando Cardoso (a.k.a. Calandria) in the drama by the same name (1896). *Calandria*—based on the life of a historical matrero whom Leguizamón actually met—takes place in Entre Ríos between 1870 and 1879 (similar in this respect to *Martín Fierro* and *Juan Moreira*). Calandria was, like Hernández, a *jordanista* and therefore a staunch federalist; like Fierro, he was an army deserter and like Moreira, he was a matrero with fluid relations with the law. With better luck than Fierro and Moreira, though, Calandria was able to reposition himself and benefit from all the reconciliations that the new order had to offer (this happened only in Leguizamón's fictional account: the historical Calandria was killed by the police).[2] While trying to cross the border to Uruguay with Lucía, the girlfriend with whom he had eloped, they are caught by Saldaña, the captain in charge of the division that Calandria deserted. Saldaña did not take Calandria into custody. Rather, he offers him the position of tenant (*puestero*) in an estancia where Saldaña was about to take a position as foreman. The owner of the estancia is a politician who rose from caudillo to senator and later to minister, a position from which he was able to fully pardon Calandria (the landowner's trajectory parallels Calandria's: from insurgent to integral part of the new agrarian order). Just like in the rural Mexican utopia presented in *El periquillo sarniento* (San Agustín de las Cuevas), the Brazilian one in *O matuto* (the Bujary sugar mill), or the Venezuelan one in *Zárate* (the hacienda El Torreón), in *Calandria* all the members of the rural world achieved a reconciliation in the symbolic and economic space of the large property, each one in a different position within a hierarchy: one as landowner, one as foreman, and one as colonist. Furthermore, just like in *La vuelta* (but without the crepuscular feeling of melancholy and defeat that permeates the same scene in *La vuelta*), *Calandria* ends with the hero renouncing the oral communal law symbolized in the name:

> Silvestre: Hail to Calandria!
> Calandria: No;
> That bird has already died
> In the cage of these arms (*To Lucía*)
> But my friends, there has been born
> The hard-working paysano! (Leguizamón 1896, 59)

However, not all rewritings of the conflict enacted by Fierro will embrace this happy and consensual resolution where the past is abandoned without loss and the future is embraced without fear. Anarchist writers found in the gaucho malo the possibility of translating into Argentine social conditions a line of thought that exalted the bandit as "the genuine and sole revolutionary, a revolutionary without fine phrases, without learned rhetoric, irreconcilable, indefatigable and indomitable, a popular and social revolutionary, non-political and independent of any State" (Mikhail Bakunin quoted in Hobsbawm [1969] 2000, 120). *Alma gaucha,* Alberto Ghiraldo's drama, rewrote the gauchesca tradition in the new conditions brought about by the opening of a new century.

Alma gaucha is the story of the misfortunes of the paysano Cruz at the hands of a state that repeatedly wronged him. (The onomastic identity with Fierro's companion is not at all a coincidence, of course.) But in Cruz's story the classic scene of bandit narratives (a state representative exceeding or abusing his position) is secondary relative to the founding act of the drama: the forced conscription that sends Cruz to an army post in Buenos Aires. Cruz has thus been unsuccessful in avoiding conscription (Ghiraldo 1906, 20). Ludmer has pointed out that the gauchesca has to be read as a genre that engages the law in a conflictive fashion, challenging its meaning, its application, and the conditions of its utterance. This sheds light (at least in a preliminary fashion) on the meaning of *Alma gaucha,* a play that is a contemporary of Law 4031 of 1901, which established obligatory military service in Argentina. This is the main thrust of the drama: to highlight the fact that a perfectly legal act, carried out according to all the niceties that go with the rule of law, amounts to a crime (137) (unlike the draft in *Martín Fierro* or the imprisonment in *Juan Moreira,* which were abuses by individual officials with grievances against the heroes of the narratives). There are no excesses, no blind spots, and no ambiguities. It is the correct enforcement of the provision of the law that amounts to a crime.[3]

This initial violence by the state, the act of forceful appropriation of the body of the gaucho, is not directly depicted in the play, and Cruz refers to it only briefly (23). While in *Martín Fierro* the draft is the opening act of the narrative, in *Alma gaucha* it had already happened. This having-already happened has to do with the fact that in the drama, there is no real outside-of-the-state law. But Cruz does not renounce his haughty sense of independence despite being condemned to menial jobs around the army post and despite having had numerous blow-ups with the lieutenant who singled him out because of his reluctance to enroll. The last of these incidents ends with

Cruz in the infirmary. Cruz, unable to withstand further abuse, challenges the lieutenant to fight. The latter, instead of following the "rules of engagement" of the gaucho challenge, grabs a gun and shoots Cruz in the arm (34–35). While Cruz is recovering from his wound, the lieutenant pretends to give him the opportunity to desert the post to avoid compromising inquiries on the incident, but he does so only to frame Cruz as a deserter (36–57). Cruz is captured and sent to the military penitentiary of San Juan in the Isla de los Estados (Tierra del Fuego), the inhospitable southern tip of Argentina. There, he joins a prisoners' rebellion focused on escape. The rebellion/escape fails miserably, mainly because of conflicts among the escapees themselves, who did not seem to be able to abandon the authoritarian habits of which they were victims (61–115). Cruz kills one of the leaders of the breakout attempt who was blatantly abusing (even murdering) his fellow escapees, and when recaptured Cruz is judged by a military tribunal, for both the murder and the rebellion. In spite of the best efforts of his defender, an anarchist lawyer, he is sentenced to death and summarily executed (121–59). He bravely dies in front of a firing squad, unrepentant and still questioning the law that delivered such a stern sentence (158–59).

Alma gaucha is unique in that it draws from both *La ida* and *La vuelta*, which, as Ludmer has noted, are at the origin of alternative (even opposed) traditions in Argentine culture. From *La ida* it borrows the memory of rural insurgency pertaining to the gaucho malo as the cornerstone of Cruz's identity. Cruz was the son of an outlaw who followed Fierro's original lesson about the frontier, the one that says for a gaucho malo "all the lands are equally good" (Hernández 1872, 201). Cruz discusses with other soldiers why the lieutenant has such animosity toward him:

> First soldier: When it comes to Cruz, the thing is that they have ill will toward him [*le tienen idea*] because he did not want to enroll, or he forgot to do it, I do not know. . . .
>
> Cruz: It was not an oversight, my friend. It was a decision. I have no reason to deny it.
>
> Second soldier: I like your attitude. Would you like to explain yourself? Tell us.
>
> Cruz: It is a long story, and comes from my father, who fought with the Indians.
>
> First soldier: Against the Indians, you are trying to say.
>
> Cruz: I do not make such gross mistakes, my friend. He fought alongside them, against the army, you know? A runaway gaucho [*gaucho alzado*] with com-

plete justification, he was persecuted by the justice officials and then he headed toward the frontier.

First soldier: Is your father alive, my friend?

Cruz: He is alive and he knows a lot of things. More than all of us put together. (Ghiraldo 1906, 20–21)

Two things stand out in this fragment. First, the father of this Cruz succeeded where Fierro and *Martín Fierro's* Cruz failed. This senior Cruz lived amicably among the Indians and fought and plundered alongside them. Cruz senior returned to civilization, but his return was not a defeat, a symptom of the gaucho's inability to articulate a truly insurgent community (as happened in *La vuelta,* where Fierro and Cruz were flatly rejected by the Indians and lived a marginal existence). Therefore, Cruz's return did not mean renouncing the wisdom of the frontier. Second, Cruz senior was still alive, and his legacy (the "many things that he knows") was vindicated by his son as relevant to the present, a defining force in his own identity (unlike the wisdom of the aging Olegario of *M'hijo el dotor* whose son Julio denies him any knowledge valid in this day and age, a denial that eventually killed his father). Like Inclán's Astucia, Cruz the son of *Alma gaucha* lived and died by the law of the father, and this law is a legacy of uncompromising outlaw violence, opposed to the biopolitical violence of the state (the army post in this drama has less to do with military instruction and more to do with the formation of disciplined bodies).[4] It is this law of the father that prevents him from enduring the daily humiliations that the lieutenant imposes on him. In *Martín Fierro,* Picardía, the son of that epic's Cruz, is proud of his father's outlaw reputation, but more as a matter of show than anything else. Picardía's illustrious ancestry did not prevent him from living a picaresque life based on accommodation and petty advantages (Hernández 1879, 392–433). Picardía (who also endured a period of military service) distorts the law of the father into the badge of infamy of Creole politics (*política criolla*) masterfully depicted in Roberto Payró's *Las divertidas aventuras del nieto de Juan Moreira* (1910).

But *Alma gaucha* inhabits the space of *La vuelta:* it is a space in which the frontier has disappeared and forced incorporation into the order of agrarian capitalism is the only option. To coin a formula that I consider apt: *Alma gaucha* enacts the gesture of *La ida* in the world of *La vuelta.* The world of *Alma gaucha* takes the closure of *La vuelta* to a claustrophobic extreme. In

Gutiérrez's novel, Juan Moreira dies because he is incapable of crossing a limit: the wall that separates the brothel from the open range, where he would have stood a chance. Moreira dies, but within the imaginary geography of the novel there still was—at least as a chimera or as an illusion, as a hope for the future or as a memory of the immediate past—the pampas, the infinite desert beyond the law, or the cacique Coliqueo's toldos, the space on the fringes of the law, where an alternative was still possible. Even these last chimeras are deflated in *Alma gaucha*. The territory is striated without rest; hence there is no exterior from disciplinary *dispositifs*. The army post is no longer a prison for forced labor as in *Martín Fierro* (a prison that allowed for many transactions outside the gaze of the state) but a place of continuous surveillance oriented toward the production of disciplined bodies, as the parody of the sweeping technique at the beginning of the play shows (Ghiraldo 1906, 9). As one of the soldiers mentions, "Here you learn everything all over again. And everything has to be done in three steps" (10).

I mentioned that the interval between *La ida* and *La vuelta* is the interval between the suppression of the frontier and the consolidation of a homogeneous space where the arm of the state reaches (ideally) throughout the entire territory under its nominal sovereignty. *Alma gaucha* is a step in this direction. The land is not only a geographic area striated by the state but it is also literally a military post, a prison, a disciplinary institution, or a courtroom. The drama begins and ends with the sound of the bugle, the "voice" of the state, thus establishing the limits of the representation, and nothing ever happens outside the state realm. Even during the rebellion, the escapees are unable to leave the island, which is a prison in itself. The Isla de los Estados is a completely depopulated land, without any barriers, properties, or roads. But deserted no longer equals "the desert" (as in *Facundo* or *Martín Fierro*, where it was a place for depraved or exalted alternative forms of socialization). Indeed, the Isla de los Estados is the reverse of the pampas, because it has no gravity as a frontier (it is close to a border with Chile, but far from a frontier) and it belongs to the state in a way that is not apparent. Even when the state is not visible (in *Martín Fierro* and *Juan Moreira*, the reach of the state was the reach of the state's armed officials), it is not visible because the entire space to be represented is the state (the entire island is the prison). This is why the prisoners' rebellion was doomed from the beginning: in *Alma gaucha*, there is no longer space for "popular" sovereignty. The mutineers, once they escape the penitentiary proper (which was rather easy to do), are incapable of preserving bonds of communal solidarity that would help them work toward their common project because they are already subjects of the state (and therefore bound to replicate the ways of the hierarchy even if that implies killing each other).

The legacy of the outlaw exists, but it is embodied in a solitary man who is unable to form an alternative community by himself (Cruz is therefore close to Moreira in this respect). However, *Alma gaucha* does not herald resignation in the face of the inevitable. Instead, it favors a new articulation of the outlaw legacy: in this case an articulation between rural insurgency and anarchist intellectuals. This alliance assumed two forms: the first is the dialogue among paysanos gathered around the fire, enjoying some *maté* together and talking about current events. This is the classic scene of *gauchipolítica* sociability, as depicted in the gauchesca from Hidalgo to Lussich. However, in *Alma gaucha,* the oral is only a mediation of the written word, because the gauchos read the anarchist press (37–38), which takes the place of patriotic dialogue as the centerpiece of the gaucho public sphere.

The second form of the alliance is the defense that the attorney attempts on Cruz's behalf. However, this alliance fails. It was doomed to fail, since it was unable (maybe even unwilling) to redraw the rules of the political game and since the conditions of the alliance were the implicit acceptance of the legitimacy of the state. Unlike the proud Astucia, who did not plead innocent to the charge of tobacco smuggling but flatly denied the right of his captors to judge him, the defense strategy does not interdict the right of the court, or of Cruz, or the definition of crime maintained by the military judges. When pressed on the subject, the lawyer explicitly says that it would have been "an unforgivable audacity on my part to make a eulogy of crime . . . in front of a War Tribunal" (123). Unlike Astucia, who denies the authority of the state official to try him, the lawyer pertained to the state law, and thus he limited himself to proving the innocence of the defendant in the terms defined by the state's law. Even if the tribunal had acquitted Cruz, he would have been defeated, since what was crucial to his identity (the law of the father) would have been phased out. Therefore, his execution was really redundant (and his fatalism acquires another meaning: it is not the stereotypical fatalism of the Latin American peasant but a clear awareness of the exhaustion of political options, an exhaustion that is indifferent to the vagaries of the trial).

Ghiraldo poses a problem that he does not resolve: how to invent in a context of undisputed state domination forms of political challenge that are able to effectively address new conditions while remaining true to the memory of the old peasant insurgency. Cruz fails, but his son may have the answer, which is why he urges Alma, who wants to die with him, to live in order to save his son and his memory as well as that of his own father.

Cruz, like Moreira, dies against a wall, having failed to cross a limit (in Cruz's case, there is a nonexistent limit: the extinguished frontier). Both are defeated bodies that give up their souls in a last gesture of resistance. For Moreira, that gesture is still an insult, a threat, an attack:

> I am not dead yet! I am not dead, you sons of bitches [*maulas*]!—he yelled, and brandishing the dagger he charged against the group that was attacking him. . . .
> Here, *maulas!*—he continued—. Here I am!—and he flourished the dagger with a powerful movement that stopped the advance of the group intent upon finishing him off in his tracks. . . .
> [Moreira] tried to charge again, but up from his gorge came blood that completely soaked the front of his shirt, making him fall to his knees, utterly debilitated by the massive loss of blood. (290–91)

Cruz's last gesture is no longer an attack. It is only an attempt to make use of his voice, thus contradicting the law that condemned him to death. Cruz's last words are precisely, "[T]he Law, the Law" (*¡La ley! ¡La ley!* [159]), an odd mixture of resignation and defiance, of clinging to his outlaw identity to the very last. It is still a political gesture, even an extreme gesture, consistent with the legacy of the bandit. As Gordon Teskey reminds us, the voice is what differentiates bodies from meat, and a differentiated voice (a voice that is not yet suppressed by violence or appropriated as part of a chorus by the sovereign) is the ultimate political gesture. But this political gesture remains empty of content, since "the law" could be either the law that condemned him or the law of the father, and this point of undecidability makes Cruz's utterance ready for appropriation.

12 | *Los bandidos de Río Frío*
Banditry, the Criminal State, and the Critique
of Porfirian Illusions

> No todos pueden robar de igual modo. Unos roban militarmente, quiero decir,
> en el campo y exponiendo el pellejo, y otros roban cortesanamente, esto es, en las
> ciudades, pasando bien y sin exponerse a perder la vida; pero esto no todos lo
> consiguen, aunque los más lo desean.
>
> Aguilita, bandit chief in Río Frío, in *El periquillo sarniento*

Alphonse Dubois de Saligny, a French representative in Mexico in the mid-nineteenth century, pointed out that banditry, far from being a fleeting challenge to the rule of law, was "the only [Mexican] institution that can be taken seriously and that functions with perfect regularity" (quoted in Vanderwood 1992, 3). His clever depiction of a world upside down was not without an agenda. He was a convinced interventionist, and he was among those who orchestrated the fateful imperial adventure of Maximilian. For Dubois de Saligny, the semiotic catastrophe of postcolonial Mexico as embodied in the trope of banditry-as-institution (which was also powerful in Julio Guerrero's writings) justified the intervention and the empire supported by Napoleon III, his field marshals, and his troops. He considered this conquest the only possibility of nation-state building in Mexico (in the same way that for Guerrero, banditry justified Díaz's authoritarian rule).

Imperial thinkers do not have to be terribly original (witness the continuous use of similar tropes in cases such as contemporary Afghanistan or Chechnya). But, when they are consistent with their own logic, they go well beyond imperialist bad faith. This is why one can approach Dubois de Saligny's affirmation, which contemporary travel literature corroborates, and interpret it to mean the opposite of what he originally intended.[1] Dubois de Saligny reveals the hidden, impossible truth of every institution: its incessant truth of catastrophe. If banditry can be a model institution, the only institution worth this name, it is because all institutions share their violent origins, their problematic legitimacy, and their entirely contingent nature with banditry. State institutions are founded upon the negation of the precariousness or nonexistence of the limit that separates them from their (imaginary) opposite, and this precariousness comes back to haunt the letrado imagination. The dilemma of the impossibility of deciding between law enforcement and law breaking is always there, even when it is forcefully suppressed (as in Altamirano's *El Zarco* or Sarmiento's *Facundo*), superseded (as in Guerrero's *La génesis del crimen en México*), mobilized for hegemonic purposes (as in Távora's *O Cabelleira*), or problematically acknowledged (as in Blanco's *Zárate*).

The uncomfortable theoretical consequences of Dubois de Saligny's *esprit* can be read as the driving force behind the almost eight hundred pages of densely packed text that make up *Los bandidos de Río Frío* (1891), the monumental novel by Manuel Payno (1810–1894). Viewing the novel from this perspective allows us to read it in a different fashion and not as a large, totalizing, *costumbrista* or premuralist canvas of nineteenth-century society or a premonition of the *folletinesco* character of post-revolutionary Mexico (Monsiváis 1997). From this perspective, almost every aspect of the novel has been subjected to analysis, and this line of analysis has produced useful contributions, from studies on the gastronomy present in the novel (Díaz-Ruiz 2001) and the depiction of popular culture to the depictions of the Indians and the language used in the novel.

Payno's use of the bandit trope in *Los bandidos de Río Frío* is a means of engaging in a radical (albeit subtle) critique of both porfirian modernity as well as the presuppositions that ideologically consolidated the porfirian nation-state in the making. From this perspective, I read Payno's novel as a genealogy of Mexican modernity. (Glantz advanced in this direction when she put forward the notion of the novel as a "utopia of theft" [*utopía del robo*] [Glantz 2003].) Recall that Fernández de Lizardi was able to exorcise a double risk in his narrative: that of the bandits of Río Frío becoming a "republic" organized from below, thus challenging the principles espoused by the letrado elite, and that of the letrado himself permanently losing his epistemological privilege by becoming a bandit. Payno not only faces these risks but also takes them to an extreme since the story he tells is precisely the story of the collapse of the distinction between state and criminal organization. But Payno's investigation is not directed (as was Fernández de Lizardi's) by class or cultural anxieties. Payno's tale does not reflect the anxiety about rising insurgency and the possibility that it might overthrow an entire political and cultural order. In Payno, the criminalization of the state happens "from above." It belongs to the inherent dynamic of the state itself. In this respect,

Evaristo had endured personal insult, but he cannot take an insult to his work. The scene ends in a bloody fight, and Evaristo barely escapes jail time (63–68). But the fight has a deeper meaning: for Evaristo it marks his realization that in Santa Anna's Mexico, value and price were permanently divorced, that no matter how hard he works, how accomplished his products, there would always be a complete lack of prospects for him. From this point on, he enters into a steady moral decline, which, through murder and banditry (261), ends with him on the gallows (724). This is the classic scene of initiation into banditry in which an injustice initiates the outlaw's career. The difference is that it is translated into a conflict embedded in the logic of the market, and Evaristo receives (and learns) a harsh lesson. Capitalism is denuded of its illusion of a mutually beneficial and voluntary exchange of commodities and presents itself as a mechanism oriented by violence to the forceful dispossession of the other. Banditry is Evaristo's sui generis adaptation to the truth that the fight with Don Carloto and the failure to sell the case revealed to him. This experience also causes him to break away from any possibility of community (besides the bandit gang). A sufficient example is that immediately after the episode with Don Carloto, he begins his unfaithfulness to Casilda, his common-law wife, whom he eventually abandons for Tules (72), whom he later kills in a drunken rage (94).

The second character is Juan Robreño. He is the classic avenger. Juan Robreño's story brings to light the immanent relationship between the premodern order, its class and race distinctions, and violence. Juan was an officer in the army and the son of the administrator of the Hacienda de San Diego, close to Durango. The hacienda was the ancestral estate of the "wealthy, noble and powerful Don Diego Melchor y Baltasar de Todos los Santos, knight of the Gran Cruz de la Orden de Calatrava, marquis of las Planas, and count of San Diego del Sauz" (25–26). After becoming a widower, the count, a stern and merciless character, moves with his daughter Mariana from Mexico City to the hacienda. There, the inevitable happens: Mariana and Juan, on vacation at the hacienda, immediately fall victim to a star-crossed passion (31). When the count finds out about the relationship, which deeply offends his ingrained sense of caste pride, he immediately exiles Juan from his lands and confines his daughter to her Mexico City mansion (where she bears the product of this forbidden love in the form of a child [40]). After enduring life on the military frontier for a while, Juan deserts (41) and eventually turns to banditry and extortion in the Tierra

Caliente under the orders of Relumbrón (543), while nursing the fire of vengeance that burns inside his soul (542).

Evaristo, who is the son of a working class family, turns to banditry when he becomes painfully aware that the early postcolonial Mexican version of capitalism (namely, *agiotismo,* the using of fraudulent state contracts as the means to secure rent) offered him little if any prospects. (It is mentioned in the novel that only an *agiotista* would have the means to buy Evaristo's sewing case [62], but in fact, a member of that parasitic bourgeoisie would rather buy a European, machine-made sewing case [63].) Juan, son of the rural middle class, turns to banditry when he becomes aware, in an equally painful fashion, that premodern caste prejudices meant much more in post-independence Mexico than the idea of abstract citizenship and equality before the law (34). (The count could have had Juan killed just for aspiring to marry above his class, without fear of prosecution, but he chose not to do so as a token of consideration to Juan's father, an old and faithful employee [33].)

Evaristo and Robreño represent a measurable challenge to the state. This is the challenge of banditry as disorder or disruption (disruption of travel, of agrarian activities, of economic development) that aggressively threatens the state, but from the outside. This threat, however, changed its sign when it appeared rearticulated by the third of the bandit characters: Relumbrón (or "Flash," thus nicknamed because of his ostentatious attire and lifestyle). His character is based on the historical figure of Colonel Yáñez, military aide of presidents Bravo and Santa Anna, who used his proximity to power to build an impressive criminal network. He was eventually unmasked, and after a long and tortuous judicial process he was condemned and put to death (Castro and Alvarado 1987). This collusion between throne and hideout, center and periphery, is undoubtedly reminiscent of certain peripeteia of popular novels (hence Monsiváis's meditation on the *folletinesco* nature of postcolonial Mexico). But Payno goes well beyond the mere *cause célèbre.*

The story of Relumbrón is a meditation on the anomalous form of Mexican modernity during the porfiriato. Relumbrón is a different type of bandit, one closer to Dick Cheney than to Pancho Villa. He takes to extremes the logic that governs the peculiar form of Mexican modernity by linking state institutionality, a predatory version of a market economy, premodern prejudices, and violence. It is thus impossible to differentiate robbery from government and violence. Even though his power rests on coercion, this coercion becomes imperceptible just as it does in successful nation-states. In this respect, Relumbrón seems to be closer to Astucia, but there are essential differences.

Relumbrón puts together an extensive network of robbery (urban theft and rural banditry), a rigged gambling operation, a protection racket, an extortion system, and a profitable large-scale money counterfeiting scheme (512). These enterprises span several states and are supported by an efficient system of information (with servants operating as moles in all well-to-do households in Mexico [600]) and of manufacturing (in order to secure highly lucrative non-bid government contracts). As the novel tirelessly points out, Relumbrón's network functioned with more regularity and efficiency than any institution of the Mexican state.

Payno's fictional meditation escapes the simple opposition between state monopoly of violence and nonstate violence. He does not make the bandit the nemesis of the state making process (as does Altamirano) or an alternative to the state making process (negative in the work of Fernández de Lizardi, positive in that of Inclán). Payno presents an almost absolute collusion between state and bandit gang. In *Los bandidos de Río Frío,* the state does not face its others: the state *becomes* its other (or, from a different perspective, the state becomes what it is). Alienated from the ideology that legitimizes it (its foundation in the law), the cannibalization of the state by the bandit gang shows the fragility of the distinction between nation-state (the very form of interiority in modern social synthesis) and its other (crime). Banditry is not the exterior that has to be exorcised when all aspects of social life are traversed by it and when the counterpoint for comparison disappears. This counterpoint would be, when it comes to banditry considered as chaos, "order and progress"—the code words around which the mythology of the porfirian nation-state was constituted. Order and progress are what bandits bring to Mexico, because in *Los bandidos de Río Frío* banditry does not resist modernity (as in the Hobsbawmian version of banditry). Banditry is a raw, savage form of modernity, which takes some of its more emblematic aspirations to the limit (the limit of the absurd and of decomposition). This is accomplished in several ways.

First, the bandit state exerts an effective territorial sovereignty. Río Frío was the epicenter of banditry in central Mexico during the first half of the nineteenth century due to its topography and the fact that it was crossed by the main highway of the time, one that linked the capital city and the port of

Veracruz. Close to the capital, Río Frío was nevertheless a frontier in the classic sense of the term. It was outside state control, unincorporated into the tax system, uncontrolled except by sporadic military interventions (like the Pyrrhic victory of Captain Baninelli [96]). Relumbrón, as the leader of a gigantic bandit organization, is responsible for transforming this frontier into a territory under the continuous and homogeneous sovereignty of his organization. The form that his incorporation takes may seem heterodox. Instead of suppressing the bandits, he recruits Evaristo—the bandit chief, as well as a ranking officer of the Rurales—and makes him his subordinate (507), in charge of pursuing bandits. Thus, the gang becomes a platoon. Everything remains the same in Río Frío: passengers are still regularly dispossessed of their money, but highway robbery is replaced by (in)voluntary contributions to support the constabulary (372). Surprisingly enough (or maybe not so much), the historical record provides us with a literal version of this collusion. Traveling toward Xalapa, Brantz Mayer, secretary of the U.S. legation in 1841–1842, was accosted by an evil-looking (though lavishly equipped) group of riders. His official escort (also evil-looking, but very poorly equipped) assured him that there was nothing to worry about, because it was only a local detachment put in place to improve security for the travelers. However, Mayer was not fooled: "I questioned, and still doubt the truth of this story, as I never saw a more uncouth, or better mounted, armed and equipped set of men. Their pistols, sabres and carbines were of the best order, and their horses stanch and fleet; but they may have composed a band of old well-known robbers, pensioned off by the Government as a guard; and willing to take regular pay from the authorities, and gratuities from travelers, as less dangerous and uncertain booty with constant risk of life" (Mayer 1844, 20). By turning bandits into bandit hunters, Relumbrón accomplished two crucial tasks: he territorially bound Río Frío to Mexico (with "Mexico" now meaning his office as the hub of the entire operation) and he vindicated his role as the sole revenue collecting agency, thus fitting perfectly into Margaret Levi's definition of "predatory rule" (1988).

By becoming the privileged law enforcer and the sole collector of revenue in the area, the bandit also becomes the sole agent of violence, which is the second way that banditry's savage modernity achieves its extreme aspirations. In the santanista republic, before what can be justifiably called the Relumbrón era, revolts sprang up everywhere (35, 409), relations between states and the national government were always on the brink of war (408), and the control of the center over the peripheries was a fiction. From the capital, Relumbrón accomplishes a criminal centralization through the control that his lieutenants exert upon several states: Juan Robreño in Tierra Caliente, José Gordillo in Sombrerete, Evaristo in Chalco, Cecilio Rascón in Río Frío, the Tuerto Cirilo in the capital (574–75). No one robs without Relumbrón's permission, and there are no uprisings without his instigation.

A third factor is that the bandit state is an effective revenue collecting machine. That criminal monopoly of violence (or as Relumbrón preferred, "the monopoly of robbery" [507]) solved, incredibly, the classic Latin American obstacle to state consolidation: the impossibility of making the bourgeoisie pay taxes (Centeno 2002, 6, 133–37). In addition to the contributions required for ground transit and collected by Evaristo, Juan Robreño, using threats that never needed to become realities, accomplishes the difficult task of making the sugar haciendas pay him a regular tax, a sort of property tax (620). Hacendados paid regularly and even gratefully, since the protection racket ensured the peace in a formerly restless agrarian landscape. So not only does the threat of violence not become a reality, but it disappears from perception to be replaced by hegemony (647).

The bandit state imposed an unheard of level of order and institutional regularity upon Mexican society, and thus, it allowed for the international recognition of Mexico among the concert of nations. Before Relumbrón, traditional banditry (e.g., Evaristo acting by himself) made the threat of foreign intervention all too real. Even such a small matter as the murder of Tules made ripples throughout the world, to the point of making the bonds of Mexican debt plunge (333). The attack against an English subject (the wife of the administrator of the silver mines) unleashes international pressures. Today the episode is hard to believe, but this was not so in the nineteenth century and the "War of the Pastries" proves that abundantly:

On the contrary:
The organization that Relumbrón gave to the affairs [his criminal affairs, which by their scale had become public affairs] rapidly yielded benefits to the city and the highways. Coaches made round-trips with complete regularity and without the slightest inconvenience. Hilario [Evaristo's lieutenant in Río Frío] had acquired a degree of politeness such that he and his men seemed to have just graduated from a French school. If passengers gave them [the bandits] money, they received it with signs of appreciation. If they did not give them anything, they always bid adieu by taking their hats off and retiring to their post in an orderly

fashion. The official courier of the English envoy made his monthly trip with utmost swiftness, and he always found on his way mounted people who helped him to change horses and who joined him for two or three leagues. When Don Rafael Veraza thought that there may be danger, or he was in need of help climbing a steep road or avoiding the muddy spots in the highway where he could not gallop, he only had to blow his whistle, and from the woods came people on foot or on horses ready to give aid, guide him through byways, and take him to safety. The English ambassador was delighted by this, and he wrote very favorable reports about Mexico to the Foreign Office. In the city, frequent robberies in streets and houses had ceased completely. Families lived in complete safety in Tacubaya, San Ángel, and San Agustín de las Cuevas. Mixcoac, once upon a time a center for thieves, looked now like a Capuchin abbey, such was the silence and quiet of the place. Don Pedro Martín de Olañeta and the rest of the judges just sat there twiddling their thumbs since there was very little to do, and they only busied themselves with bar fights. (599)

Thus, the bandit state preempted the regular administration of justice; no crimes were committed, so the judiciary was superfluous. This is so because Relumbrón exerts a total, panoptic surveillance of the Mexican population, through a well-oiled intelligence service in place in each of the wealthy houses in Mexico, employing maids, cooks, and ironing women, hired through recommendations that Relumbrón controls. He becomes what the novel calls an alert eye (*ojo vigilante*) that is contrasted with both the state's complete lack of capacity to exert a minimal degree of control over its "own" population and with the president's blindness, since he is unable to see that his rule is a farce and that his power has been stolen from under his feet.

But the bandit-state is not a barbarous anomaly (like the rosista bandit-state in Sarmiento), since it is not a caudillo-like structure. Instead it is run by a "modern" bureaucracy, one that is impersonal and rational. Banditry is what Relumbrón calls "method, science, a perfect order . . . without violence or abuses" (509). Thus, robbery transformed into the principle of social organization is not a metaphor of disorder, a decomposition, or uncontrolled transformation of paradigms (as it is, for example, in Baroque literature). Robbery in the novel is the very embodiment of order, even of Christian morality. When faced with the doubts expressed by the silversmith who is his accomplice (and who is later revealed to be his father) and when reminded of the likelihood that he will spend eternity in hell, Relumbrón objects:

> In the first place, we are not talking here about murdering, mauling, or abusing anyone. We do not want to take bread from the poor, either. To the contrary, in my plan it is crucial that everything be done with method and order. And you can see that in this there is almost no sin, and even if there is, it cannot amount to more than a venial one. When it comes to the money of the rich, it is a matter of controversy if stealing is a mortal sin or a meritorious action. The Bible, which I have read almost in its entirety, says that the rich have an obligation to give to the poor, and the truth is that they do not give them even a sip of water. (514)

This perfect order accomplishes what the santanista state could not accomplish: the incorporation of vast sectors of the population that had previously been marginalized into the bandit network. By doing this, Relumbrón achieves a perfect synchronicity of the community, as opposed to the deep heterogeneity that divided Mexico (456). In his novel Payno depicts sectors of the population of Mexico City and the Quencio Valley who live in situations of extreme marginality. These individuals are the usual victims of state (in)justice. In most cases, they lack health care and the most basic infrastructure. Relumbrón showed a clear disposition to integrate these sectors of the population into an administrative totality (thus heralding the twentieth-century welfare state). In addition, Relumbrón controlled all state contracts for military uniforms and various materials, and of course he gave the contracts to his own enterprises. This is the classic agiotista way. In these corporate enterprises, however, Relumbrón employed a huge number of women, and he paid them much higher wages than what was usual in Mexico for similar work. In return for this largess, these women provided information about the households with which they had contact throughout Mexico City. Through the women's wages, the bandit state incorporated ever widening sectors of the population into the modern monetary economy, while abhorring the company stores (tiendas de raya), a classic porfirista institution.

Payno, however, is not proposing a new order, some "robber utopia" (as in Astucia) in which Relumbrón would be elevated to the condition of founding father of the new state that would finally fulfill the many broken promises of Republican Mexico. We should not forget that Relumbrón is a "conceptual person," a critical instrument that functions as a reductio ad absurdum of the modern state's presuppositions. Thus, Relumbrón's bandit-state is at the origin of its own demise, as a sort of index of the demise that —according to Payno—threatens the porfirian state itself.

Payno is capable of catching a glimpse of the identity that lies between nation-state and bandit gang, one that pre-dates revenue extracting and discipline enforcing institutions. He is also able to pinpoint their crucial difference. According to the novel, this difference is a cultural one. Any institutional synthesis, whether a state or something else, but particularly a state, must base its operation upon a transcendent principle that ensures its internal coherence (what Laclau [1996] called the "grounding of the political"): in modern states the principle is an emancipatory one, and it is called "the nation." In the case of the Brothers of the Leaf in *Astucia*, this principle was the *independentista* legacy oriented toward the common good of the smugglers and their families. In contrast, the organization that Relumbrón consolidates does not hold sacred any principle other than profit. Unchecked profit for its own sake (493), the dazzling spectacle of gain and loss—exemplified in Relumbrón's compulsive gambling (460) and his complete inability to balance a budget (459)—are the mainstays of his worldview. As the novel states, "Up, up, money and more money: how it is acquired doesn't matter" (495).

Relumbrón does not regard himself as a criminal. He is not one, in fact, but not because he does not appropriate the property of others by means of force or deceit. He is not a robber because neither within the story nor in the individual is there an exterior to robbery, a transcendent instance (law) different from the complex of money as the foundation of value and private violence as a means of acquisition that would serve as a backdrop against which his actions could be considered robbery. Says Relumbrón, "Listen to my private beliefs, since I think it is time that I share them with you. Half of all the inhabitants of the world have been born to steal from the other half. And that other half that has been robbed, when they realize it and ponder it, start devoting themselves to stealing from the half that previously stole from them and snatches not only what had been robbed, but what they owned legally. This is the struggle for life" (507). This universalizing of robbery as the primary instinct of humankind is what Payno called the "monomania of robbery" (532), the transformation of possessive individualism into the sole principle of identity. That is why, in the novel, robbery can equal a regular commercial transaction and not the rupture of the commercial order. (This is indeed something that decades later Frederic Lane would suspect when putting forward the idea of robbery as the image of all economic activity, an activity in which the state enjoys a monopoly [1979].)

Don Manuel Escandón is the one who advances this idea in the novel. Having suffered a holdup at the hands of Evaristo's gangs (who were still learning the ropes of their trade), he records the loss as capital, since it was a debt that thieves acquired with him. It was a debt in all likelihood impossible to collect, Escandón hurries to add, but not essentially different from others (278).

Relumbrón denies state law as the origin of value. "What right has the state to claim a monopoly on the minting of money[?]" he argues (547). Money was the value that Relumbrón postulated as the one that was superior and exclusive. Nevertheless, Relumbrón's value system was internally contradictory, since he himself put the value of money into question by his large-scale counterfeiting of silver coins. Then, he was not supplanting the state's axiological origin with any other origin; he was just ruining any consolidated attribution of origin. The very name Relumbrón (meaning glitter or flash) pointed toward this secondary character, this lack of "real" value and his nature as being an image without an original. Thus, the bandit-state cannot be a nation-state (or more precisely, it is a failed nation-state) because it does not create an alternative universe of symbols or alternative affiliations upon which it could find a principle of regularity, permanence, and loyalty over time. That is why, with the same speed that it forms itself and rises to absolute dominance, it falls apart. And this does not happen through any external pressure. It is not that the president suddenly becomes effective or that conventional honesty makes a comeback. The bandit-state falls apart because money cannot consolidate anything by itself. Relumbrón's execution at the end of the novel is thus redundant. He had already experienced the limitations of his attempts. In fact, he is executed because of his only act of "old school" banditry: a robbery followed by a murder in the home of Count Sauz. This hit was Relumbrón's last-ditch effort to replenish his exhausted coffers. But there can also be another meaning to this robbery: by breaking into an ancestral treasury of gold and silver coins, Relumbrón was attempting to rebuild his wealth and dominance on a different basis by trying to ground his dominance in a value that was not subjected to the vagaries of market exchange.[2] His empire had crumbled to the ground long before that because his invisible hand had been unable to keep coherent an organization based upon the monomania of theft.

In this sense, Relumbrón's bandit empire is a critique of the market economy taken to its logical extreme, to its naked, untenable truth of unfounded violence and arbitrary value. It implies, in the high moment of nineteenth-century nationalism, a laying bare of the ideology of the nation as a conceptual scaffold of savage peripheral capitalism. This fable of the bandit-state is thus an allegory of the porfirista present, where its rising and its cannibalization of the santanista equals the rising of the porfirian state from mid-century chaos. But in Payno's novel, it does not arise as "order and progress" but as another name for chaos. The bandit gang is an image of the limits of the modernizing project and of its secret (or not-so-secret) truth.

Part III

The Triumph of the Nation State

The Bandit as Devious Brother
and as Suppressed Origin

13 | *Os sertões*

Original Banditry and the Crimes of Nations

No ano noventa e sete
O exército brasileiro
Achou-se comandado
Pelo general guerreiro
De nome Artur Oscar
Contra um chefe cangaceiro

Ergueu-se contra a República
O bandido mais cruel
Iludindo um grande povo
Com a doutrina infiel
Seu nome era Antônio
Vicente Mendes Maciel.

> João Melchiades Ferreira da Silva,
> "A Guerra de Canudos," 1897

Os sertões: campanha de Canudos (1902), by the Brazilian writer Euclides da Cunha, is, among other things, the account of four successive campaigns, one more formidable than the next, launched between 1896 and 1897 against the town of Canudos. This "bandit cave" (as the commander in chief of the fourth expedition described the town [371]) lay deep in the Bahian sertão and was defended with awe inspiring tenacity and success by jagunços ("glorified bandits," in the words of army and press releases [423]) guided by the millenarian leader Antônio Conselheiro. These campaigns finally succeeded in defeating the jagunços, at the cost of thousands upon thousands of lives on both sides, including that of Conselheiro himself. *Os sertões* is also an attempt to reveal the reasons for and conditions behind the millenarian movement that looked for refuge in a forbidding, isolated landscape. It also sought to unmask those behind the protracted holocaust (carried out with the aid of European weaponry) that literally swept the movement off the face of the earth.

Os sertões, this "Bible of Brazilian nationhood" (Joaquim Nabuco's pronouncement) not only ranks among the most important works of Brazilian literature but also is endowed with a unique dynamism since its canonical status is unequivocally vindicated by such dissimilar institutions as the Aca-

215

demia Brasileira das Letras and the Movimento dos Trabalhadores Rurais Sem Terra (Landless Workers Movement) (Abreu 1998). Both before and after the publication of *Os sertões*, Canudos (a name shared by the town, by the millenarian movement that erected it, and by the campaigns that crushed it) has been subjected to countless interpretations, with positions ranging from glorification to bitter denouncement.[1] Da Cunha stands apart because he does not avoid addressing Canudos's paradoxical character vis-à-vis the Brazilian narrative of nationhood (1902, 453). In *Os sertões* Canudos is presented, in an unapologetic fashion, both as a foundational epic and a catastrophe. The campaign is hailed as the martial forge of the nation, where a community is formed when soldiers from the most distant corners of the nation converge upon Canudos, their Republican ardor ignited by a "formidable desire for revenge" (249), which was triggered by the defeat of the third expedition. These men cease to be mere soldiers and become the embodiment of the nation: "the cataclysm of war shook loose all the superficial layers of nationality, thus exposing the deeper elements of these resigned and stoic Titans" (432). This community also has a civic dimension, which is displayed when Bahia resonates and reacts as a single soul, rushing to the aid of the wounded soldiers of the fourth expedition as they return from the front (431). Bahia becomes a home for maimed and exhausted soldiers, and because of its nurturing role it also becomes a home for the nation; all of Brazil makes the ultimate sacrifice of sending their sons to the old capital to engage in the decisive fight that would rescue the fourth expedition from its dire straits. This gathering of forces in Bahia equals for da Cunha a return of the wandering sons of Brazil to the cradle of the nation (440).

The same bloody campaign that seems to be reduced to the birth pains of a nation points to the fact that Brazil was, above all, a geographical fiction (453), one in which there was "an absolute and radical disparity" (453) between the coast and the backlands. While marching toward Canudos, soldiers were far from engaging in a crusade to recover the innermost sanctuary of the nation. They were "engaging in a foreign war" aimed at conquering a "foreign land" (453).

As Laclau reminds us, however, "the principle of contradiction does not apply to society" (1996, 6), and it applies even less to writing. So, this contradiction is carried even further by da Cunha. Moving away from the privilege accorded to the army as the place where citizens were born out of a holocaust, da Cunha goes so far as to affirm that the jagunço was the bedrock, the essence of Brazilian nationhood (*o cerne da nacionalidade*) (1902, 170, 504, as well as 1939, 561–62). From this point of view, the right of the army to crush Canudos was highly questionable, so the statements that open and close the narrative are not surprising: Canudos was "in the integral sense of the word, a crime" (1902, 100), and "[t]he trouble is that we do not have today a Maudsley for acts of madness and crimes on the part of the nations" (515). But da Cunha's position with respect to this crime is far from comfortable. He was embedded in the fourth expedition as a correspondent for a newspaper and was thus at the scene of the crime, as an ally, partner, and guest of the criminals. But the jagunço, the victim of the crime, is also a criminal (that is why the state mobilizes its armed forces to suppress him). At the same time, the jagunço is hailed as the foundation of Brazilian nationhood (therefore, endowing his murderer with an identity). This inextricability (that reproduces the inextricable character of Canudos) makes *Os sertões* an excellent point of entry into the problems addressed by the last chapter of this book.

Previously, this book examined two opposite roles that banditry played vis-à-vis letrado national projects. Chapter 2 examined banditry as the trope that delegitimized rural insurgency and cast it as the irreconcilable Other of the national project (as in *El periquillo sarniento*). Its elimination was therefore considered crucial to the conciliation of the various centrifugal forces tearing at the nation (as in *El Zarco*). Consequently, there were no shared spaces between letrados and bandits (although this stark separation was always at risk and eventually failed). Chapter 3 analyzed cases where banditry was a trope mobilized to criticize these national projects, either exalting the bandit legacy of rural insurrection as an alternative to the nation-state (as in *Astucia*), showing the similarities between banditry and the state (as in *Los bandidos de Río Frío*) or depicting various alliances between bandits and letrados as alternative paths to modernity and/or statehood (as in *Zárate*).

There is yet another way of conceiving the collusion and the conflict between bandits and letrados. In the works of Euclides da Cunha, Leopoldo Lugones, Mariano Azuela, Laureano Vallenilla Lanz, and Rómulo Gallegos, outlaw violence is exalted as the origin (acknowledged or denied) of the nation (and the present state of affairs of the nation, either the Brazilian republic, the Mexican revolutionary state, the Argentine oligarchic state, or Venezuelan agrarian capitalism). But the logic of this attribution is peculiar, since it places rural insurgency at the core of the nation while at the same time it distances it as a past event (and the condition of this past character is, in most cases, the suppression of rural insurgency by those now hailing it). Thus, outlaw insurgency is an origin, but this origin is not present in the present as such. Outlaw violence is exalted only as a memory and a legitimizing symbol, and therefore it is cancelled as a real historical force. This cancellation imposes a symbolic continuity at the same time that any real continuity is impeded, any real link severed. The transition from outlaw violence to state violence does not proceed as the homogenous development of an identity but is made possible by a split that separates the state (as constituted power) from outlaw violence (as constituent power). This is the paradox of nationhood, in which the state (considered as the locus, or the embodiment and guardian of the nation) pays eternal homage to those it had to suppress to become what it is. This is what Benedict Anderson called the "reassuring fratricide," in which nations imagine their genealogies through a careful administration of memory and forgetting and in which certain (violent) events essential in their historical narrative are reconstructed by superimposing a national dimension unknown to the real participants of the events. In various ways this "past" insists upon the present, and banditry continues to haunt the letrado imagination, not as a ghost of the past but as a force continually operating in the present and even defining it.

Os sertões was pivotal in the "invention" of the northeast as a cluster of representations of a racial, economic, and cultural nature and in the creation of the image of a dual Brazil (something that Nina Rodrigues fell short of) based on a so-called "vision from the coast" (visão do litoral) that would last, in some fundamental aspects, to the present (Levine 1992, 41). The northeastern backlands were cast as a region of inferiority and backwardness, a region that naturally spawned outbursts of violence and fanaticism like the paroxysms that came forth from Canudos. This causal link between the physical and climatic makeup of the sertão, its demographic and ethnic features and the rebellion of Canudos, is abundantly argued in Os sertões (as reflected in its tripartite structure: "A Terra," "O Homen," and "A Luta"), and it appeals to contemporary positivistic references (Costa Lima 1997; Amory 1999). But Os sertões also highlights the fact that Canudos is marked from the very beginning by a conflict with the state, and it would not have existed without that conflict.

Antônio Conselheiro was a wandering *beato* in a plurisecular northeasterner tradition. His apostolate was confined to the preaching of a strict but rather orthodox morality and to reconstructing churches and cemeteries often in ruins due to the chronic shortages of money and church personnel (Levine 1995). He was mostly rejected by the backlands clergy, but the Church's argument against Conselheiro was framed "in terms of legitimate authority instead of the question of his orthodoxy or heterodoxy" (Johnson 2005). His persecution by the state police in 1893 (which was motivated by mistrust within the Church and among the local elites) caused pilgrims to retire toward the interior of Bahia (da Cunha 1902, 227) and the foundation of what would become the "mud Troy of the jagunços" (*a Troya de taipa dos jagunços*) (171). Therefore, Canudos is less a product of the sertão than that of the interaction between sertão and coastal elites.

Indeed, without the harassment and the later campaigns that dispersed the ashes of the movement to the wind, we would know nothing of Antônio Conselheiro. He would be one more among the many nineteenth-century *conselheiros* and *beatos* of northeastern popular religiosity (Levine 1995, 125). He would be a footnote to the story of Padre Cícero, the successful founder of the utopian community of Joazeiro (Della Cava, 1970). We would only have traces of this elusive passion, lost in the intricacies of the caatinga, which historians would reconstruct with some difficulty from correspondence between *coronéis* and members of the Catholic Church. Antônio Conselheiro would have a quaint but harmless legacy: dozens of rural churches and cemeteries rebuilt in the sertão. Instead, he and Canudos are the historical figure and the event most studied in Brazilian history. The destruction of this attempt at forming an alternative social organization not regulated by racial or class dynamics is the condition of possibility of its memory: in the national imaginary, violence immortalizes its other. It immortalizes nonstate violence. It is this deep entanglement that makes not only these two events (the construction of Canudos and the hurricane of violence that swept over it) rather predictable but also events that are nowadays united—and denied as conflict—in the neutral geographical denomination "Canudos." Canudos was a reassuring fratricide, and as such it is the cornerstone of the Brazilian national imaginary and the indelible mark of its modernity.

In *Os sertões* the most compelling predicate of Canudos (and of the world from which Canudos sprang) is that of excess (112). Excess is understood as a lack of balance (*desequilíbrio*). This defining feature of the sertão (198)—seen in its population (99, 176–77), the religious expressions of this population (197–99), Conselheiro (212), and Canudos (243)—has a double genealogy. It was inherited from the early days of colonization, which took place at a time of complete moral disorder in Portugal (197), disorder that was preserved intact in the sertão and was deepened and enhanced by the particular characteristics of the backlands climate (143).

This lack of balance is evident everywhere, particularly in the form of violent oscillations, and it is one of the organizing tropes of da Cunha's text. The land is marked by the "extreme violence" of contrasts (111), constant and dramatic "cruel oscillations" of freezing cold and burning heat (111, 119), flood and drought (111, 116), whirlwinds and still, heavy air (119–20), a nature "barbarously sterile and marvelously exuberant" that "finds pleasure in the play of antithesis" (135, 183). This logic of excess is one of internal contradiction: torrential rains do not nurture the land but have a "corrosive acidity" (113), rivers flow away from the sea toward higher rather than lower ground (116), some rivers do not discharge into the sea at all (116), landscapes are the opposite of what they look like (116–17), and sunlight gives the scorched desert the appearance of a glacial landscape (131).

As a locus for extremes, the sertão is also a void, the metaphor that both opens and closes the narrative. This void is specified at many levels, beginning with the sertão as a dry sea (113) with dried-up lakes or empty riverbeds (112, 113). But it is also a void on the map: "Our best maps, conveying scant information, show here an expressive blank, a hiatus, labeled *Terra Ignota*, a mere scrawl indicating a problematic river or an idealized mountain range" (107, also 346). It is a void in the narratives of scientists and travelers (118) and a void in historical studies (199), an undecipherable enigma (346), a "mutilated page in the number of our traditions" (346). "Inaccessible and unknown" (107), the sertão remained lost and forgotten after the initial explorations (173–75). But this void is populated by forces out of control: torrential floods (113), heat that makes stones explode, blinding light (113), tremendous erosion (112–13), plants that grow even greener and healthier in the middle of a drought (such as the cacti and the *juazeiro* [128–29]), or plants that grow from bare rocks, such as the *cabeças de frade* (130).

Human beings, on the other hand, are a "perfect moral translation of the physical factors operating in the land" (183).[2] Therefore, the same oscillation between extreme forces is to be expected. In fact, climate seems to have "engraved in the organization of the sertanejo its extraordinary roughness" (196). The sertanejo is a Hercules-Quasimodo marked by stark contrasts between ugliness and beauty (179), strength and weakness (180), passivity and violent outbursts (181), tiredness and tirelessness (183), defeat and victory (183), "extreme cruelty and maximum devotion" (200, with an example on 254), "perverted by fanaticism or transfigured by religious faith" (200). All of these contrasts are succinctly contained in one term that gives us the nature of the sertão and, by inclusion, of Canudos as a social arrangement: "disciplined banditry" (*banditismo disciplinado*) (254).

The presentation of Conselheiro as the pinnacle of a natural social process is indeed surrounded and defined by banditry. To begin with, da Cunha depicts the sertões as classic bandit country: "the backlands are a refuge for the criminal. Whoever goes along these trails and, by the side of the road, sees a cross standing above the grave of the assassin's victim does not pause to investigate the crime but lifts his hat and passes on" (486). Conselheiro's own biography is framed by the feud that cut short the lives of many an ancestor (208). In terms of religious fanaticism, Conselheiro was preceded by the Serenos, millenarian companies of penitents and flagellants who quickly declined into banditry and plunder (202–203), a life that was particularly suitable for Conselheiro's first followers (214).

But it is Canudos, center and axis of the sertão (Bernucci 2002) and depicted as an "enormous bandit's den" (da Cunha 1902, 486), that draws our attention, particularly because this bandit den was a city and it was the second most populated city of Bahia (Levine 1995). Ángel Rama famously pointed out that the Latin American city, from the remodeling of Tenochtitlan in 1521 to the inauguration of Brasilia in 1960, had been a child of human intelligence (*un parto de la inteligencia*) ruled by an ordering rationality (1984, 1). As such, it is opposed to and cancels the formless reality of the Latin American rural landscape in two ways. First, its material order duplicates the social hierarchy, thus inscribing and naturalizing this hierarchy in a regime of visibility. In this order, it is crucial that there be both a material center (the city center, where power and the signs of power reside) as well as a symbolic center (the sovereign), which is the final reason of this order. This analogy between city and social hierarchy makes the city a readily legible text. As in Sarmiento's case, the scandal of Rosas's rule (as well its epistemological uniqueness) was that not only was the city unable to give form to formless rural violence, but in an inconceivable reversion of rule, rural violence was directing the forms of city rule and life. This was the "vacuum in Rosas's rule" to which Sarmiento referred. In the case of Canudos, the situation was even more extreme. Canudos did not oppose the chaos of outlaw rural violence nor was it overpowered by it. It was created by it. This is why it was a "monstrous *Urbs*" (da Cunha 1902, 227), a veritable nightmare of reason, and the inversion of all the vectors of intelligibility in Latin American letrado reason. It was not a city erected as a gesture of affirmation of letrado-state authority; rather it was erected as its denial, as a refuge for people persecuted by justice (310). This is why it is "a sinister *civitas* of mistake" (227), a familiar but at the same time strange landscape, since its houses are a "gross parody of the ancient Roman abode" (228). It is also a parody because Canudos's spatial disposition faithfully reflects its social order, that is to say, the utter lack of any intelligible social order, thus making it a labyrinth (371) of houses and passages, which duplicates in mud the labyrinths of the caatinga. As da Cunha puts it,

> As this colossal *tapera* took shape, it appeared to reflect in its physical characteristics, as if by a stereographic process, the moral attributes of the social strata which had found refuge there. It was the objectification of a tremendous insanity. A living document whose implications were not to be evaded, a piece of direct *corpus delicti* evidence on the aberrations of a populace. . . .
>
> There was no such thing as streets to be made out. Merely a hopeless maze [*dédalo desesperador*] of extremely narrow alleyways barely separating the rows of chaotically jumbled, chance-built hovels, facing every corner of the compass and with roofs pointing in all directions, as if they had all been tossed together in one night by a horde of madmen. (227–28)

In order to accomplish its civilizing mission, the Latin American city was to be the denial of the space upon which it was built: the wild pampas, the pagan temple and the altar of human sacrifices, the heathen city. As Rama points out (in other terms), the city is de-territorialized when its links to its surroundings are severed and it is re-territorialized in the Empire first, in world market and culture later. Then its relationship to its hinterland is reestablished, not as one of belonging but one of domination. Canudos does not cancel the land from which it came, but it is an accomplished and faithful product of the land. The metaphor for this link is mud, the building material for all houses, which makes them almost indistinguishable from the land itself (da Cunha 1902, 229, 469).

Also, Canudos is a scandal because it does not deny sertanejo banditry (251) but springs forth from it and takes it into another dimension. Even though it represents the end of wandering for Conselheiro's followers (and life in a city is the opposite of nomadism), at its core it conserves a nomadic imprint, an air of the warriors' headquarters (229). This air of restlessness remains since the jagunço, one of the most "somber characters" of Brazilian history and, according to da Cunha, a regional variation of the cangaceiro (255) and inheritor of some features of the bandeirante (253), is by definition a nomad (252). Before the founding of the city, Canudos was an abandoned hacienda used as a refuge by bandits (226), and this character endures in its present incarnation as the city of the chosen people. But it is not only an enlarged refuge for bandits (233, 235), the "sinister heroes of the dagger" who became Conselheiro's best disciples (235) and who, in a complete inversion of the concept of crime, were in charge of policing the city (236). Canudos produces bandits, since sertanejos arriving at Canudos become jagunços in the claustrophobic atmosphere of the city: "The simple sertanejo, upon setting foot in the place, became another being, a stern and fearless fanatic. He absorbed the collective psychosis and even ended up adopting the name which up to then had been reserved for rowdies at the fair, bullies on election day, and the pillagers of the cities—the name of jagunço" (233). This is the exact opposite of the imaginary of the Latin American city, in which the rural bandit, when arriving in the city, becomes a citizen. Such was the famous transformation of Facundo from gaucho malo to statesman in *Facundo*, a transformation that he paid for with his life, or the redemption in *Doña Bárbara* of the Luzardos in Caracas, when Santos and his mother fled Altamira's unbridled violence. This becoming-bandit is a fearsome instance of homogenization that, given the fact that nature and society respond to the same principles of evolution, reproduces the caatinga. Another proffered example of this homogenization is where the vegetation, exposed to violent changes in the weather, seems to gradually conflate into a single species of plant (125–26).

If the imaginary of the nation-state implies the (ideal) homogeneity of all inhabitants under the all-encompassing rubric of citizenship, which entails equality before the law, Canudos achieves a barbarian equality in which the becoming-jagunço represents the monstrous state of mestizaje, "the perfect fusion of the three races" (487, 512). Canudos is a furnace (233), a diabolic version of the melting pot (the innocuous metaphor for happy *mestiçagem*).

This furnace melts the sertanejos into "a uniform and homogeneous community, an unconscious brute mass, which, without organs and without specialized functions, continued to grow rather than evolve, through the mechanical juxtaposition of successive layers" (233). This lack of differentiation, as an alternative principle of social constitution, is furthered by the fact that, just like in the case of the Río Frío bandits in *El periquillo sarniento*, in Canudos there is no private property (234), men enjoy women in common (235), and there is no differentiation of roles and functions (233), civil status, social standing, or even age or beauty (240). This is not a community but a monster, a "human polyp" (233), which is a reduplication of the monstrous nature of Conselheiro (213). Not only does the city not subdue rural banditry, but it is the center and the origin of banditry. From Canudos, "turbulent bands would set out to roam the countryside. . . . For an extended radius around Canudos, estates were laid waste, villages plundered, cities taken by storm!" (236).

At the beginning the war places two clearly differentiated sides in opposition. The army is the violent principle of state-making; it is sent from the city to conquer the territory, as if for the very first time (453). The army clings to the symbols of statehood and modernity: the uniforms that the caatinga rips mercilessly (268), its woefully inadequate plans, formations, and strategies (280, 352–57), and its cumbersome weaponry (335, 357). The jagunços do not defend their land; they are the land. Land and jagunço in *Os sertões* fight alongside each other, and the caatinga acquires human features (266, 425), even to the point of resembling a military formation (267) that fights in close combat with the army (268, 425). The jagunço is shown as literally emerging from the land (as in the Greek myth) as a sort of fantastic apparition (269, 286, 413), attacking in rhythmic waves as if it were a natural force (394). And the ultimate defeat of the jagunço implies a return to the earth (288, 489). As da Cunha puts it, Marshal Machado de Bittencourt won the war when he realized that the enemy to be defeated was not the jagunço but the desert (444).

Canudos is impossible to defeat not only because of the bravery and tenacity of the jagunços but also (and mainly) because it is illegible, refractory to the logic and the letrado protocols of interpretation (278–79, 423) to the point that even assessing the number of enemies is impossible. The army does not know if the fighting jagunços are two hundred or two thousand in number at any given point (382). An essential part of the war lies in the inversion of signs: in Canudos the attackers are the ones besieged and forced to remain in a conquered position (393, 420), victories are disastrous and fearsome (263, 415), defeats are advantageous while advances are less risky than retreats (282), and superior manpower and firepower are fatal weaknesses (393, 438). The confusing nature of the war replicates the confusing nature of Canudos. Canudos is new, but it was born old and in ruins (227).[3] It is weak, but it is therefore powerful and resilient (cannons are impotent, since cannonballs puncture the mud walls without exploding and without collapsing them [392]). It is open on all sides but inaccessible (327, 415), opposing the enemy not with towers and walls but with "thousands and thousands of entries" (415).

The jagunço gang actively and successfully resisted the army siege. This resistance plunged the army (and the nation) into a catastrophe but not the catastrophe of defeat. It was instead the catastrophe of pollution. In fact, Canudos pollutes the war. The war did not only happen in Canudos. The war became Canudos, and it became one of its manifestations or its attributes since it ended up entirely subjected to its logic. Canudos is then the logic of barbarism, which is predicated on the land (135, 425), the jagunços (455), Conselheiro (514), and, later on, the war (420, 455, 506) and the army (429, 483). Canudos is more than just refractory. Less than a besieged city, Canudos is a maelstrom, an abyss (*voragem*) (113, 479), a trap (*mundéu*) that attracts the army to besiege it (327, 369, 391, 393, 419) and to devour it (503) with its many digestive tubes (326).

Canudos devours the army. The devouring metaphor names the huge death toll suffered by the army (abundantly referred to throughout the narrative). It also names a more ominous thing. As in many monster narratives, the monster hunter (the army) is possessed by the monster (Conselheiro, the jagunços [213, 434]) and becomes a monster himself (Cohen 1996). In *Os sertões*, this is the story of how the entanglement between the army and the jagunços meant the becoming-jagunço of the army (428). The war against the jagunços launches first the army and then the entire nation on a time traveling journey toward the past, toward cannibalism (294), and toward the original banditry (*banditismo original*) (278) whereby the hidden origin of the army (and indeed of all armies) reappears when the army reverts to the condition and status of a horde.

The Europeanized national army, whose function was not only to defeat the "disciplined banditry of the jagunços" (151) on the field but also to uphold statehood as a principle, has to dissolve itself in the sertão (192), be-come a multitude to actually win the war (134–38, 222), cease being a disci-plining machine, and become a nomadic war machine. It has to become its enemy to defeat it, which implies, paradoxically, the eventual (and invisible) triumph of the jagunços, regardless of their empirical defeat.

This transformation occurs in phases. It begins with the third expedition and is focused in particular on the commander in chief, Moreira César. In da Cunha's portrait of him he comprises the same constellation of predicates as the jagunços: he lacks psychological balance (desequilibrado) (301), has a body that belies his true strength (300), and exhibits a monstrous personal-ity since it is a mixture of contrasting characteristics (301). He is equidis-tant from the criminal and the hero (300) and is a mixture of the knight and the bandit (301).

The fourth expedition, locked in a fatal stalemate, presents for da Cunha "the perfect resemblance of an agglomeration of outlaws [forajidos]" (389), just like the wounded soldiers returning from the front (428). The expedi-tion was in utter disorder, without an advance party or a rearguard, without formations or distinctions among units (390), and without a supply line, thus forcing soldiers to become jagunços in order to find food (395). The campaign transformed the officers into "town-fair bullies" who cast aside the symbols of rank and "engaged in knife fights" (490), since they had be-come medieval fighters, equal in their Republican fanaticism to the mil-lenarian fanaticism of the jagunços (417). The army headquarters was made by rebuilding a seized portion of Canudos. But instead of being a shining ex-ample of the virtues of civilization and a beacon of instrumental reason and administrative order, the headquarters would have appeared to anybody who entered just "another suspicious town of the backlands" since it was im-possible to distinguish soldiers from jagunços (468). (Da Cunha, when nar-rating the final stages of the siege, imagines the possibility of the jagunços abandoning their positions and inadvertently mixing with the soldiers, so indistinguishable had both sides become.)

Thus, Europe and its military techniques are impotent, and it becomes increasingly evident that a Brazilian war has to abandon the "superior tech-nical organization" that characterizes modern war and revert to "original banditry" (278). Thus, in the foundational epic the suppression of the mon-sters becomes "monstrous and absurd" itself (278), the nation reverts to a horde, and the sertão invades the city. The wounded soldiers of the army, who had become bandits themselves (429–30, 434), expanded the destruction of the war and brought the reflux of the campaign to the streets of Bahia (430). Even Rio de Janeiro's Ouvidor Street (the showcase of Brazilian modernity and Europeanized taste, abundantly featured in Machado de Assis novels) was the equivalent of a corner of the caatingas. Da Cunha writes that "[b]ackland lawlessness was precipitously making its entrance into history; and the Canudos revolt [was] by no means confined to a corner of Bahia[;] it was spreading to the capitals of the seaboard. The man of the backlands, that rude, leather-clad figure, had partners in crime who were, possibly, even more dangerous" (346).

"The end," the penultimate section of the book, has a disquieting ambiguity when read from this point of view. It is the end of the war, certainly. But da Cunha's beginning of the section points to another end. It is the end of war as the West knew it: "From day to day the struggle had been losing its military character, and it ended by degenerating completely. The last remnants of a meaningless formality were now abandoned: deliberations on the part of the commanding officers, troop maneuvers, distribution of forces, even bugle calls; and finally, the hierarchy of rank itself was practically extinguished in an army without uniforms [and] which no longer knew any distinction" (512; see also 495).

The war is won because of the impassiveness and organizing qualities of the secretary of state for affairs of war (*secretário de estado dos negócios da guerra*), Marshal Carlos Machado de Bittencourt, who finally managed to give the state the upper hand by putting together a long overdue supply line, which ultimately kept the war effort alive (441–42). But this measure comes too late, in a way, since the army winning the war through the superb planning of the minister now is no different than the jagunços fighting with Comblains and Mannlinchers: it is still a multitude (321). Therefore, "civilization" had already been defeated, and it had become a tool of barbarism. The campaign was no longer the extreme enforcement of the law: it was an action of sheer revenge (485–86). The steady stream of troops and supplies that allowed for the winning of the war does not hide the fact that they were feeding a gaping void, the void of Canudos into which the army had been sucked. "Canudos was appropriately enough surrounded by a girdle of mountains. It was a parenthesis, a hiatus. It was a vacuum. It did not exist. Once having crossed that chain of mountains, no one sinned anymore" (444), and the wholesale slaughter of prisoners was thus beyond the law and beyond the reach of history. The nation is founded upon this abyss, upon the vortex of Canudos. The essence (*cerne*) of nationhood is thus empty, and the nation subdues the sertão when the entire nation becomes the sertão and outlaw violence reigns sovereign. This is a disaster, but it is not a disaster that happens to the nation, as in the debacle of the French army in the Franco-Prussian War as narrated by Zola in *La Débâcle* (a novel that has been linked to *Os sertões*). It is the disaster of nationhood, a disaster that, precisely because it is overwhelming and all-encompassing, is completely invisible. As in the Blanchotian disaster, it is one "that ruins everything, leaving everything just like it was" (Blanchot 1983, 9).

14 | *La guerra gaucha*

Bandit and Founding Father in the Epic of the Nation-State

El gaucho va a ocupar la escena, a llenarla con sus pasiones primitivas, sus odios
y sus amores, sus celos obstinados, sus aventuras de leyenda; pero el gaucho que
sólo vive ya en la historia, el engendro maduro de los desiertos y el tipo altivo y
errante de un tiempo de transición y transformación étnica.
    Alberto Acevedo Díaz, *Ismael,* 1888

Al hombre valiente lo sufría hasta ladrón.
Era la primera virtud.
    Patriot Landlord, in *La guerra gaucha,* by Leopoldo Lugones, 1905

Que nuestra tierra quiera salvarnos del olvido
Por estos cuatro siglos que en ella hemos vivido
    Leopoldo Lugones, "Dedicatoria a los antepasados (1500–1900),"
    in *Romances de Río Seco,* 1938

The use of gaucho violence as a trope for conflicts within national culture reached a turning point around the centennial of Argentina's 1810 Revolution. Like the colonial baroque feast, the pomp of the centennial was at
the same time a dazzling performance celebrating the power of a state at its
peak and the testimony of a not-so-hidden anxiety. The legendary splendor
of the centennial marked the zenith of the Argentine "export-led growth
model" (Bulmer-Thomas 1994) and the finest moment of the commercial
and landowning class that animated and enforced the model during the previous century (Salas 1996). However, the very success of the model created
formidable challenges to it.

Poor peasants and workers from the Mediterranean Basin and Central
and Eastern Europe concentrated in huge numbers in a few cities once their
hopes for landownership were defrauded. This brought about the rise of the
"social question" (*la cuestión social*). The social question implied a variety of
challenges. Among them were political challenges to elite domination from
the rise of syndicalism of various orientations, particularly socialist and anarchist, as well as of new parties and organizations that did not respond to
the forms sanctioned by the conservative order, to mutual aid societies and
terrorist cells. There were also cultural challenges, such as the appearance of

229

new venues of cultural production that ignored, competed with, or super-seded the sanctioned spaces of the lettered city, and demographic challenges like the accelerated transformation of the social landscape, which occurred to a degree and in a way that was not predicted. Even linguistic challenges appeared, such as the real or imagined threat of losing Spanish as the na-tional language, which prompted aggressive legislation to control, at the federal level, the enforcement of a Spanish-only policy in classrooms nation-wide.

The rise of the middle class posed another kind of political challenge that could not be (and was not) ignored. In 1890 the middle class made a thun-derous entrance onto the political scene with the revolution headed by the Unión Cívica that brought the Juárez Celman administration to an end. Af-terward there was a perceived need (both within and outside the ruling elite) to reform the political system, particularly the electoral system. Doing so would entail a redefinition of the meaning of the vote and of citizenship, obtaining political rights against a model of restricted democracy that only ensured civil rights, and redrawing the relations between state and society (Botana 1977; Botana and Gallo 1997, 114–22; Halperín Donghi 1999, 21–55). This reform was initiated in earnest during Julio Argentino Roca's sec-ond term as president (1898–1904), and it continued and deepened during the presidencies of José Figueroa Alcorta (1904–1910) and his appointed successor, Roque Sáenz Peña (1910–1914), with the law that would carry the name of the latter, making male suffrage secret, obligatory, and univer-sal. In 1916 this change would initiate, with the election of Hipólito Iri-goyen as president, a new political cycle in Argentine history (Botana 1977; Botana and Gallo 1997, 87–98).

Finally, on the foreign front, the imminence of the Great War and the revolutions that were rattling the West (the 1910 centennial and the Mexi-can Revolution, which began in the wake of the Mexican centennial of its war for independence, were strictly contemporary) heralded what was per-ceived to be the end of an era. This implied a reexamination by the ruling elite of its place and relevance in Argentine society (something that was a given since the fall of Rosas) and a search for new ways to legitimate its his-torical performance as well as its continued importance in contemporary Argentina (Jitrik 1960, 18; Viñas 1973; Viñas 1996).

The group of self-labeled "Creole founders"—a euphemism for the land-owning elite and its intellectuals (Svampa 1994, 87)—thus attempted a vindication of the provinces vis-à-vis cosmopolitan Buenos Aires by tapping into the cultural capital of criollismo. This implied a complete inversion of certain tropes, such as that of society as a body. For Sarmiento, European immigration was going to transfuse healthy new blood into a national body bled white by civil wars and contaminated by its Hispanic heritage (Sarmiento 1845, 1883). Toward the end of the century, this metaphor was turned on its head: immigrants were now the ones carrying physical and social diseases, from "sexual deviations" to "dissolving ideologies," in their blood. This change can be traced to early naturalistic fiction (Eugenio Cambaceres's *En la sangre* [1885] or Antonio Argerich's *¿Inocentes o culpables?* [1884]) and to the social sciences (José María Ramos Mejía's *Las multitudes argentinas*) as well as to political discourse (see Onega 1969; Salessi 1996; Nouzeilles 2000).[1] The aforementioned elite strategy also implied an inversion of the geographical and social referents of the civilization versus barbarism dichotomy (which remained, however, a distinct framework for understanding social reality). Now, a new brand of barbarism (that of low-class, ethnically inferior, radical immigrants) inhabited the cities, whereas rural culture (the former locus of barbarism) was considered Argentine classical heritage. *Mis montañas* (1893), by Joaquín V. González (1863–1923)—a major player on the political scene at the time—is a good example of literature written with an eye toward the invention/vindication of a rural precapitalist tradition or at least (as in *Martín Fierro*) of a benevolent patrimonial capitalism. Additionally, the author attempted a double dissociation from his native province (La Rioja) and this province's most immediate association in the national imaginary with caudillismo (thirty years before, rebellion-ridden La Rioja had been considered by Sarmiento and Mitre to be a "bandit hideout"). According to Maristella Svampa, "Once rid of the old image of the caudillo . . . the Interior provinces could be thought of as the natural repository of tradition, the place where Argentine identity could find its most arcane sources" (1994, 90).

In concert with this shift, there was a rewriting of the entire Argentine history, reaching an (imaginary) conciliation between liberal projects and caudillismo. If caudillismo had been considered a disruptive phenomenon of the historical journey that ran from independence to modernity (with Rosas being seen as a remnant of or a throwback to colonial times), then toward the turn of the century liberalism and caudillismo appeared as manifestations of a single evolutionary principle.[2]

All this repositioning would coalesce to dramatically revise the place that gaucho violence occupies in the narratives of nationhood, as well as the place of the ruling class vis-à-vis that violence. To accomplish this task, the elite found its most brilliant representative in Leopoldo Lugones, who would carry out this task in two outstanding prose pieces: *La guerra gaucha* (1905) and *El payador* (1916). *La guerra gaucha,* which Roberto Giusti in 1912 called "an epic at the same time admirable and impossible to read" (quoted in Ghiano 1955, 108) is a collection of short stories, each one devoted to an episode of the protracted guerrilla warfare waged by the gauchos and led by the caudillo Martín Miguel de Güemes. This warfare was carried on in the Salta and Jujuy provinces in northernmost Argentina against the Alto Perú royalists (1814–1818) after Belgrano's defeats in Vilcapugio and Ayohuma put patriots on the defensive. *El payador* is a long essay on *Martín Fierro* (based on a series of lectures delivered in 1913). The thesis put forward in the essay is that *Martín Fierro* is an epic poem (akin to *The Iliad, The Aeneid, El Cid,* or *La Chanson de Roland*). Concurrently, *El payador* argues for the posthumous vindication of the gaucho, not as the hypostasis of barbarism but, to the contrary, as the "hero and civilizer of the Pampa," the "only one who could contain the advances of [Indian] barbarism with success" (Lugones 1916, 49–54).

La guerra gaucha and *El payador* address different aspects of the same ideological complex since they address gaucho violence in its role in two different (but complementary) conflict scenarios: the independence wars (*La guerra gaucha*) and the war against the Indians (*El payador*). Thus, war was for Lugones the cultural forge of the nation as in Manuel Gálvez's *El diario de Gabriel Quiroga.* Each work addressed two different moments of gaucho violence vis-à-vis the temporality of the nation-state: the constitution of gaucho violence as patriotic violence (*La guerra gaucha*) and the culmination and disappearance of gaucho violence in the dialectics of nation-state foundation (*El payador*). This dialectics is neutral since for Lugones the nation-state was not a political principle, the product of historical forces or historical decisions, but the embodiment of cosmic law, the ultimate avatar of the evolution of matter into spirit (hence nationalism as the most perfect doctrine that frees humankind from materialism and egoism).

As the title of each work indicates, gaucho identity comprises two complementary predicates: fighter and singer. There are various ways in which violence and voice are expropriated to be put to the service of the state. In a line of thought that competed (and eventually defeated) moreirismo, Lu- gones exalted gaucho outlaw violence as unequivocally patriotic and epic. He even equated it to that of the Homeric heroes of *The Iliad* as the origin of their respective national cultures. However, Lugones denied gaucho vio- lence any autonomy, a feature that, as Lugones himself acknowledges, was crucial to the Homeric heroes beginning with Achilles, whose rebellion and refusal to fight alongside the Greek army was the raison d'être of *The Iliad* (Lugones 1915). Gaucho violence is not considered a simple and self- conscious origin for the nation (which is precisely the risk embedded in moreirismo—the exaltation of the gaucho bandit as a nomadic war ma- chine). For Lugones, the gaucho malo has to be represented as already co- opted by the elite and therefore denied and transcended by its incorporation by the state as a synthetic moment. This is what allowed the Argentine oli- garchy to claim exclusive rights to this violence and what made this vio- lence, as it appears in *La guerra gaucha,* invisible. *La guerra gaucha* seems far removed from the gauchesca. However, Lugones appropriates one of the crucial gestures of the gauchesca: the use of the gaucho voice and the gaucho body to serve a state-centered letrado political agenda. Lugones made *Martín Fierro* the Argentine version of *The Iliad.* He could have very well composed his own *Illiad* (humbleness never ran strong in Lugones's person- ality). But a strict equivalent of *The Iliad* would not have been useful in 1900s Argentina, since *The Iliad* narrates the war of an aristocracy solidly in its place (Lugones 1915, 18). This could not be (and was not) the case in *La guerra gaucha* because the Argentine aristocracy was an embattled one in both political and cultural terms. Therefore, it was important to make the war the scene of a multiclass alliance that would serve as a legitimating scene for that aristocracy. *La guerra gaucha* indeed enacts a cultural alliance between classes (it is important that this alliance is in the past, of course), and the cornerstone of this alliance is the transcultural code of valor as the signifier that forges the national identity. (Unlike *Alma gaucha,* where the distance between gaucho and army is at a maximum, in *La guerra gaucha* the collusion between gaucho and soldier happens through the transcultural code of valor.)

Lugones presents the voice of the gauchos (who sing, challenge, and tell stories), but it is a voice inhabited by another voice: a state-oriented version of the modernist lexicon. The voice in the gauchesca is described in terms of an alliance between "a heard voice and a written word" (Ludmer 1988,

132).[3] In the work of Lugones, the alliance between the vanished gauchos and their killers (the elite) has a spectral quality. The voice in Lugones's gauchos is a transparent conduct for the written word, a fiction of orality closer to the declamatory tone of his *Odas seculares* than to Hidalgo's *Diálogos patrióticos*, whose reductio ad absurdum populates the pages of *La guerra gaucha* (e.g., the dialogues around the campfire). This is possible because the voice of the gaucho no longer matters in itself. Unlike the cycle that runs from Hidalgo to Hernández, where the alliances outside the lettered city were still real (Hernández and the jordanistas from Entre Ríos, for example), *La guerra gaucha* and *El payador* are inscribed within the circle of exclusive sovereignty of the lettered city. The gaucho voice did not enter per se in any scheme of conflict; instead, it entered as an instrument. There were other voices to fight against, voices that presented new challenges, because they were voices that, unlike the gaucho ones, which were easily reducible to a past condemned to oblivion, were full of future, of experimentation and novelty: the *lunfardo*, the *cocoliche*, and the *ítalo-criollo*.

The radical expropriation of the gaucho voice makes all its political tones disappear. It transforms the agora (the gaucho campfire of the patriotic dialogues) into a chorus (Teskey 1996) in which the gaucho voices are mere reflections of a single voice: the voice of the sovereign, who, in fact, never speaks for itself (see the last story of *La guerra gaucha*, "Güemes," which is the silent contemplation of a silent figure).

The story "Sorpresa" provides a concise example of this entire process. It is the story of a blind old gaucho who had traveled with the patriotic guerrillas as a sort of "organic intellectual" of the montonera; he is called the "priest" of the group (Lugones 1905, 54). The blind man sang "village songs, the romance of some famous bandit, with octasyllables entangled in the strumming like birds in tree branches, a small light twinkling in the water of his eyes. At night, when everybody was warming themselves by the fire, and the blind man spun a yarn . . . each man recognized in him the features of a father" (53). The old man is the memory of a tradition of peasant violence that is older and that goes beyond the national epic: banditry and Indian uprisings are his repertoire (he sings *Ollantay*, passed down to him from the times of the Tupac Amaru insurrection, as well as ballads celebrating the exploits of famous brigands). But the short story is precisely the scene of the erasure of that memory and its replacement by another "memory." The old man, at the commanding officer's instigation, replaces his old songs with the "new sound" of the national anthem played on his ruinous violin (53). The official is a frenchified youngster. (This mixing of letrado and soldier is crucial to the self-perception of Lugones, as he explains in *El ejército de la Ilíada*.) The young officer has as his models for war Joachim Murat and the French Napoleonic army (the very embodiment of the state building army). He had listened to the anthem before, but the blind man's rendition has a special quality, "as if from the races in ruins a plurisecular hope would come to life again, coming forth from his mouth in musical form" (53). The erasure of the pre-nationalist memory of insurgency is the precondition of the occupation of the voice by the state, but the scene of erasure is hidden, since it is presented as the voice of the Indians now legitimating the Creole epic. It is crucial that the replacement of memory happen through the intercession of an official who is also a poet.

The gaucho now has only a simulacrum of voice: the trivial folk songs (*vidalitas*) were replaced by the neoclassical voice of Vicente López y Planes (author of the lyrics of the national anthem). The blind gaucho is equated with Mariquita Sánchez de Thompson (Argentine writer and socialite, the first person—as legend goes—to ever sing the anthem in her drawing room) and the military bands of the centennial. The gaucho is no longer *gauchipolítico,* a political and cultural force that has to be taken into consideration, but instead, as Lugones points out when referring to another character in the story, he is "the fool of the fatherland" (*Tontito de la Patria*) (1905, 177). And it is not by chance that one of the characters is an idiot: the gauchos are furious patriots but in an elemental fashion through their participation in the vision of the caudillo. Not surprisingly, all the gauchos that witnessed the performance of the anthem are to die in a royalist ambush. The prose is telling: "Already without hope, they justified themselves with their death . . . from the primeval woods, their cry of hope told the mortals how the nations arose. . . . A beggar and ten ragged insurgents with their grave crawling up their legs . . . hairy as animals, sung celebrating their own holocaust, somber announcers of a dawn that they would not see" (57). This attribution of a neoclassical character to the voice of the gaucho is not an arbitrary interpretative gesture. For Lugones, the gaucho poet is strictly classical, a descendant of the Greek aedas and Provençal troubadours (1916, 89), and the gaucho system of retribution and oral reputation can be equated with the Homeric hero quest for vengeance and fame in *The Iliad* (1915, 19). Thus, the national project is symbolically linked to the larger Western tradition.[4]

La guerra gaucha shares with works such as *Mis montañas* the exaltation of the landscape and the customs of the interior provinces as depositories of an uncorrupted national tradition, a tradition that the elites claimed as their own against the "plebes from overseas," in Lugones's words. Unlike González, however, Lugones does not present an idyllic or pastoral version of the provinces. Disguised by a style in which the exquisiteness, achievements, and failures of modernism are taken to an extreme (J. L. Borges 1974; Ghiano 1967, 14), violence in *La guerra gaucha* is strikingly explicit and vicious, something that is rarely (if ever) noted. This is even more remarkable since the violence is not stylized, as in the undoubtedly gory but highly choreographed and entirely predictable knife fights in Eduardo Gutiérrez's novels, which are more of an opportunity to exhibit skill than a life-and-death situation. On the other hand, Lugones never deceived the reader about the moral qualities of his anonymous heroes. The gauchos that fight the war are deserters, fugitives, cattle rustlers, matreros, criminals, murderers, and highway robbers (1905, 30–31, 34, 72, 75, 79, 83, 86, 109). His gauchos are called a gang (*gavillas, pandillas*) (31, 43), and when captured, they are executed as such (32, 199). The patriotic insurgency was even called the montonera, Sarmiento's ultimate badge of infamy.

In *La guerra gaucha* there is an element of class struggle, one in which the gauchos "hated the King as an annoying and arrogant master [*patrón*], under the figure of his officials and his taxes, [the fatherland] being more persuasive to them not as a political principle but as an instinct for freedom defined by the hardship endured. Famines, hatred for the white skin so susceptible because of its being contaminated; longing for the Indian, the roughness of nakedness" (1905, 41–42). But there is much, much more than that. The subject of the war is a chaotic mixture of races, ages, classes, and conditions that has no immediately intelligible meaning: the dumb, the blind, the cripple, the old, children, and women. The multitude partakes of the fury of the insurgency with all its unleashed energy. This is what terrified the Spaniards: the guerrilla as a proliferation of singularities that, as Bartolomé Mitre points out in *Historia de Belgrano,* acknowledges "neither center nor caudillo" (1857, 142). But the book is not a celebration of the multitude as constituent power. It is instead the scene of the transformation of formless rural violence into a national army, even if in virtual form. It is rural violence with a direction. In fact, the book does not even strike the reader as violent.

Let us consider an example. "Vivac" is the story of a gaucho, either black or mulatto (*moreno*), who, without any scruples, feeds his dog the body parts of Spaniards killed in battle. He laughs at the horror of his commanding officer before the spectacle of the dog eating a human arm that he has just pulled from his baggage: "—what the hell, my second lieutenant! You have to make do with whatever you have! [*A falta'e pan güenas son tortas*]!" (Lugones 1905, 189). This episode reminds us of some other infamous depictions of racial Others in nineteenth-century Argentine literature: the black females that ferociously fight with dogs and each other for scraps of animal entrails or a piece of lard and the slaughterhouse folks who are callously indifferent to the gruesome decapitation of a child, both in *El matadero* (Echeverría 1871, 100–101), or the Indian in *La vuelta de Martín Fierro* who tied the wrists of his female prisoner with the intestines of her own freshly gutted son (Hernández 1879). Surprisingly enough, the cynicism of the mulatto did not equal barbarism for Lugones. Why not? The reason is simple: the excessive violence of the black man was solidly anchored in a hierarchy crowned by the founding father (*prócer*) Güemes. The violence of the black is no longer his own but that of Güemes, and then it became macabre local color or patriotic epic. Güemes gave meaning to the violence of the mulatto, making barbarism illusory: even with his cruelty and cynicism the mulatto is "forging the nation." But this generosity on the part of Lugones is not without cost. In order for gaucho violence to be divested of its persistent association with barbarism, it also had to be divested of all class or race content and be solidly grounded. Thus the risk of *La guerra gaucha* is the risk embodied in Rosas or Conselheiro: that of running an uncharted, uncontrolled course and creating a monster, a fearsome and incomprehensible challenge.

Throughout the book, there are plenty of references to the fact that the land itself is the enemy of the royalists (Lugones 1905, 42, 111–13, 176, 177). This pathetic fallacy in which the storm cries "Long live the Fatherland" ("*Viva la patria*") is more than a late romantic digression, since it accomplishes a vital purpose. It grounds (and hides) the political through the signifier of the land. The northernmost provinces are rather deserted and depopulated in Lugones's rendering. But this vacuum, this desert could not be farther off than Sarmiento's desert: this is a desert created as an epic (such as Belgrano's policy of scorched earth when retreating in front of the advancing Spanish army). The landscape is empty only to allow the nation to shine with undivided grandeur (the sun of May that ends the narrative). For Lugones, the fact that the land is the ultimate locus of the nation and that it is itself fighting the war served the purpose of collapsing the immemorial (the nation) into the historical (the state), thus preventing politics from appearing on the scene. In this sense, hierarchy is not a relationship of power but the form of a cosmic mediation. The founding father is not a leader but the embodiment of the will of the land.[5]

The appearance of this embodiment happens at the end of *La guerra gaucha* (the section "Güemes"), where all the micropolitical and local acts of violence, as depicted in each short story, were reappropriated in the majuscule metaphor of the body of Güemes. (And this happened just in time: "Güemes" is preceded by a story that epitomizes the risk of gaucho violence: a private vengeance that assumed the paradigmatic form of "barbarism"— the slaughter of a letrado [217].) "Güemes" is mainly the description of what a Spaniard of the retreating La Serna army sees from his spyglass. In particular, it is a morose description of the visage and body of Güemes. This is the moment of closure that shows us that the war is not a "gaucho war" at all but a war of the statesman who transmits to his subordinates the overpowering passion that animates him. Patriotism is the name of this passion (all other passions are illusory), and it is presented in *La guerra gaucha* as an exclusive attribute of a single subject: Güemes. If Conselheiro was "at the same time the passive and active element in the tumult" (205), this ambiguity is not at all present in Güemes. He is unequivocally the active element in the equation of peasant insurgency.

Throughout the book we see the gauchos die and suffer and kill. We see their bodies maimed and mutilated:

> In the villages hairy mutilated bodies wandered around like beggars and horrifying figures out of a nightmare. There was one that expelled fire from his entrails punctured by a bayonet. Another one, with gangrene up to his waist—his eyes ferocious with fever as two glasses of burning alcohol; another one that due to his many ulcers went crazy of impotence, already smelling like a corpse, with a shot in his hip teeming with maggots; another one, bearded, the head bent over his chest permanently, his neck broken by a two-handed sword blow; another one who philosophically chewed on his coca leaves, while with a straw the healing woman sucked on the pus of a spear wound. And there was the more atrocious one whose entire face was excavated by a single hole: lips, nose, eyes torn out by a bomb shell. And he was still alive! (220)

But the horror of war is literally invisible. The maimed bodies are not bodies at all: they are only prolongations, emanations of the body of the caudillo, appendixes or blurred replicas of Güemes: "All, old, child, female and Indian mirrored him [Güemes], each of them representing a piece of him. And each sour moment melted within his heart; and each act of heroism crawled into his heart in the form of sublime flames; and from him his ideas emanated under the form of riders toward all the points of the horizon, until they faced death and under her spell they fell among lightning bolts" (284). "In the villages, in the woods, from the beggar to the old woman, from the warrior to the little child, from the animal to the inanimate object, an equal fit of bravery, as if bravery were being transmitted to them by the inspiration of the caudillo. And all because of his love, all that tactic of platoons [*partidas*] scattered in thousands of leagues, but influenced by the slightest movement of his finger following his orders as if by instinct, like the horse the will of the rider" (283).

This is why the narrative is anonymous (the characters do not reappear from one story to the next, and frequently they are not even identified), not because it was a "popular," collective epic but because for Lugones the entire war had only one protagonist: the caudillo. The body of the caudillo is a body, but it has an essential difference from the gaucho body, unlike Rosas's body, which is only *primo inter pares*. Rosas, the gaucho whose horsemanship was celebrated ironically, is merely one among many gauchos. Güemes is a different kind of body. He is a body with a soul. It is not his personal soul, but the fatherland as a soul—Lugones believed the nation to be a living, immaterial entity (1916, 21). Because of this, Güemes never had to be present as a character in *La guerra gaucha*. There were references to him, however, first as a signature in the letter (1905, 105), then as a distant image in a lens (217). But he is not present as an acting, individual body because he is present as the overarching, acting principle of the entire narrative.

In this fashion, gaucho violence does not work as a metaphor of conflict within the nation (as in the previous cases) but rather as a figure of (false) synthesis within the nation. The body of the founding father endows meaning to violence like the gaucho horse, whose mad frenzy takes on a martial meaning under the will of the rider, as Lugones explained (283). Up to that moment, the gaucho malo trope was a divisive metaphor that enacted the conflict between two co-present contenders in the field of the social. The path of rural violence in Argentina ended up affirming an identity that, at the beginning, Sarmiento vehemently denied: the identity of caudillo and nation-state, of gaucho and the sun of May (the one emblazoned on the national flag). Thus concludes *La guerra gaucha:* "The royalist spyglass, distracted for a moment, focused for the last time on the red cassock. The solar gold melted in a layer of splendor. Epaulettes and hat sparkled in myriad atoms of light. The light gleamed even more. The chief's horse moved a little, and then, in the exact place that a moment ago his head occupied, the May Sun [*el Sol de Mayo*] shone in full force" (292).

15 | *Los de abajo*

The Feast, the Bandit Gang, the Bola
(Revolution and Its Metaphors)

Just to be square, I'll have to report Juan Sanchez' remark:
"Is there war in the United States now?" he asked.
"No," I said untruthfully.
"No war at all?" He meditated for a moment. "How do you pass the time, then[?]"
     John Reed, *Insurgent Mexico*, 1914

La lógica del soldado es la lógica del absurdo.
     Luis Cervantes, journalist, in *Los de abajo*, 1915

The tense relationship between unleashed rural violence as constituent power and the state's capture apparatus can be traced in a work that was almost a contemporary of *La guerra gaucha* and *El payador* (although written in conditions that could not be more diverse): Mariano Azuela's *Los de abajo* (1915/1916). Twentieth-century Mexico has indeed been "in the shadow of the Revolution," as Héctor Aguilar Camín and Lorenzo Meyer aptly put it (1994). Until just recently, there was almost no conflict or cultural manifestation that was not positioned in a space where the Revolution and its legacy (either lionized or vilified) occupied the center. The Chiapas conflict of the 1990s is a good example of this. Both contenders—the revolutionary state and the Ejército Zapatista de Liberación Nacional (EZLN)—claimed a legitimacy that stemmed, in both cases, from their establishing a relationship more or less exclusive with the Revolution. This claim to a heritage is a discursive phenomenon, if one wishes to call it so, an "invention of tradition," but it was most operative in the way that the adversaries handled the conflict after the initial armed confrontations.[1]

The formative character of the revolutionary experience obeyed several causes. One of them was the way the revolutionary state propitiated a "narrative of the Revolution" as a vast interpretation of the recent past and the imminent future. This narrative was put together in a piecemeal fashion, in novels, but also in public celebrations, paintings, murals, monuments, history books, and speeches. It crafted the Revolution as a unified event "present before itself" from the beginning. This narrative was staged by a cast of

241

internally coherent subjects: "the People," "the Reaction," and "the Fatherland." That reification of a series of events under the all-encompassing rubric of "Revolution" (Knight 1994, 27) made it the culmination of a multi-secular process of emancipation. This process could be the Mexican "Great Liberal Tradition" (independence, reform, revolution), or it could be traced to a vaguely defined pre-Hispanic tradition.[2] This process made the Revolution the foundational event for the state that presented itself as springing forth from it, that based its legitimacy in it, and at the same time transcended it, transforming revolutionary violence into institutional consensus. Revolutionary rural violence was the "myth of origin" of the state, but at the same time it was what the state had to deny as present. The expression "institutionalized revolution" is not, from this point of view, a contradiction but the product of a dialectic in which the state presents itself as the *Aufhebung* or sublation.

As we can see, this is the same operation that Lugones implemented. The essential difference is one of context: Lugones posthumously vindicated a violence that had long been suppressed. The rural violence that the revolutionary state was trying to co-opt was still dangerously close in time and space: this narrative was started in the 1910s, in the midst of the civil war. It acquired coherence and force during the 1920s and achieved a more or less stable form during the 1930s after the virtual cessation of large-scale fighting with the defeat of the *cristeros* and the 1929 formation of the Partido Nacional Revolucionario (eventually PRI), which ensured a procedure for presidential succession more or less free of conflict.[3] The narrative of the Revolution had diverse manifestations: monuments (e.g., the monument to the Revolution), public spectacles and annual commemorations (the annual parade to celebrate the Revolution), historical works and fine arts (the justly celebrated experience of muralism), and literary ones (the literature of the Revolution).

In recent years there were numerous attempts at dislodging this concept of the Revolution as a unitary, overarching event, and reconstructing the complexity of the heterogeneous conflicts that made up what we call today the Mexican Revolution. Among these efforts we can count the works of Alan Knight (1986, 1994), Gilbert Joseph et al. (1994), Héctor Aguilar Camín and Lorenzo Meyer (1994), and Jeffrey Rubin (1997), among others. Their work guides my analysis of Azuela's *Los de abajo*, the most important work in the genre of the novel of the Revolution.[4]

Los de abajo is a bandit narrative. It was written without a national inspiration; its purpose was not that of a revolutionary epic, since that epic did not yet exist. It was transformed, however, into a narrative on the origins of the revolutionary state, a "national epic" (Menton 1988). This process, in which the state "appropriates" an artistic form, parallels the process in which "the post-1915 'revolution from above' was built on the ruins of a prior (1910–1915) 'revolution from below' that the Carrancistas were ultimately able to contain and co-opt" (Knight 1986, 2:497). *Los de abajo* features the transformation of revolutionary "sound and fury" in the potent but disciplined voice of civil celebration, and the bandit, lord of the sierra, is the peasant that silently parades in the state commemoration, under the paternal gaze of the political boss.[5] Banditry is the metaphor for legitimate (but blind) political violence. The death of the bandit at the hands of the imminent state (Demetrio is murdered by carrancista machine guns [Azuela 1915/1916, 138–40]) suggests the *real* disappearance of popular violence and its replacement as mandate and symbol in a mythical time that legitimated the national state. Thus, the disparate conflicts that the novel narrates become a single reassuring fratricide.[6] In a second move, banditry becomes a metaphor of excess for the state capture apparatus and its modes of symbolizing experience.

The history of Demetrio Macías and his gang has all the features of social banditry. Demetrio—a type halfway between the Hobsbawmian "avenger" and the *haiduk* or guerrilla-bandit (Archer 1982)—was a peasant forced to "take to the sierra" because of a fight with Don Mónico, a local political boss (Azuela 1915/1916, 41). This grievance was further aggravated by the desecration of both his home and the honor of his wife by the soldiers assigned to his pursuit (4–7). Demetrio's gang is not formed around an articulated or explicit program but around the impulse to avenge particular affronts (Hobsbawm [1969] 1981, 42). The gang is held together less by long-term common vindications than by links of parentage or solidarity (Azuela 1915/1916, 8–9). Each individual joined the band for different reasons, and these reasons fail to supply the unity (either of consciousness or praxis) that would be expected in a revolutionary group. The local conflict was intersected by the national one, but it is not assimilated by it. Don Mónico's bad faith made Demetrio a *maderista*, which originally he was not (41). The ambition and manipulative style of Luis Cervantes (a journalist who joined Demetrio's gang as "secretary") made Demetrio a *villista*, which he was not

and never completely became. In both cases, the national political definitions are adventitious to the inner logic of the gang (43). This is true even
in the case of the relationship between Demetrio and the villista caudillo
Natera, which was not cemented in a common cause but in personal loyalty
and mutual advantage (122). Furthermore, the illegality sanctioned by the
state is confronted with the legitimacy that Demetrio and his band enjoyed
as the condition for the strength of the gang (15). When that precarious legitimacy is shattered, the faith of the gang is sealed, either because of treason or because of a lack of material and strategic sustenance provided by
the peasant community (126). Finally, in *Los de abajo* the signifier "bandit"
is used by everyone as a means to strip the adversary of political clout: bandits (*bandidos, ladrones, latrofacciosos, comevacas*) are always the others (5,
11, 20, 27).

Throughout the years *Los de abajo* has accumulated superlative qualifiers:
"epic of Mexicanness" (Menton 1988), "masterpiece of the novel of the Mexican Revolution" (Mansour 1988), and a revolutionary novel and a revolution in the novelistic genre (Paul Arranz 1999). Until the Latin American
Boom, it was considered "the novel of America," the narrative counterpart
to *Ariel* (1900) by José Enrique Rodó (Ruffinelli 1996b, 242). In 1950,
Azuela received proof of the state's validation par excellence: the National
Prize of Literature, from the hands of President Miguel Alemán. Azuela
would die two years later, which would provide an additional opportunity
for his canonization. The funeral was majestic, attended by almost all secre-
taries of state and authorities of the PRI. Azuela's body was buried in the
Rotonda de los Hombres Ilustres, a special place in the Dolores Cemetery
where the state places the most distinguished figures in its cultural history
(Ruffinelli 1996b, 251).

Los de abajo was made into an item of learning and indoctrination, with
editions of the novel ordered by state governments to be freely distributed
to peasants and workers (Azuela 1960, 1077). Demetrio, a local bandit
chieftain who became a revolutionary because of equivocal compromises,
was now the literary icon of the Mexican hero. Throughout this transformation from bandit to epic hero (a metaphor for the entire national community), which operates via the reception of the novel in the context of the institutionalization of the Revolution, we can reconstruct an episode in the
history of an unresolved antagonism. This is the antagonism between the
mode in which the revolutionary state interpreted the conflict that *Los de*

abajo describes, and a mode that I will call "nomadic," which exceeds and decomposes those operations, yielding a *plus* of meaning that cannot be appropriated by the nation-state identity paradigm.

The gang, in this approach, will not be considered an *Ur*-form of the popular subject, a subject without language or consciousness that a posteriori would be provided by the state, but as what Deleuze and Guattari call a "nomadic war machine" or what the novel called "*la bola*." Demetrio and his band were not a pre-political and transitional phenomenon that would obtain meaning from something it was not (a social class). Rather, in the revolutionary sound and fury we can glimpse a fully political mode of intervention. This mode of the political resists the ways of territorialization, the constitution of identities and practices characteristic of the ideology of the state. This resistance aims at a new mode of thinking about the Revolution, outside the frame of intelligibility of the narratives of the nation-state. Whereas Lugones was able to invoke the ghosts of the past—the victims of the murders committed by his own class—and make them speak on his class's own behalf in such a way as not to leave any residue of their previous, threatening incarnation, this is not the case in *Los de abajo*. Demetrio and his gang are also transformed into a vision of a superseded past, but they still carry enough passion, enough force, to give us a glimpse into another world, one that is hostile to the letrado world.

To address the novel through a digression, consider one of Diego Rivera's murals. It offers an example of a way of conceiving the war that *Los de abajo* simultaneously repeats and breaks away from. It operates as a sort of maquette of the state functioning as a capture apparatus and of the irreducibility of the fluxes that escape from that apparatus. *La quema de los Judas* is Diego Rivera's mural in the Patio de Fiestas of the Secretaría de Educación Pública. It was painted between 1924 and 1926 (simultaneously with the "rediscovering" of *Los de abajo* by Mexican literary criticism) upon José Vasconcelos's request during Álvaro Obregón's presidency. *La quema de los Judas* is an urban festivity with a carnivalesque meaning. It originally consisted of the burning of effigies of Judas the day before Easter as part of a ritual of cleansing and renewal. In time, the effigies of Judas were replaced by those of unpopular political personalities.

In an exemplary fashion, the mural illustrates the ways that constituent power is transformed into the "people" and the *bola* into the "Mexican Revolution." In the mural, the commotion of the social and the modes of signifying the social, and of whose meaning little or nothing is known, become a link in the multisecular history of the emancipation of the popular subject as well as a link in the reencounter of the popular subject with itself. The space represented in the mural is structured around a stark opposition between "above" and "below" (the same opposition that at first glance structures *Los de abajo*). This opposition is constituted by a line (a line of clouds caused by explosions—the effigies are filled with explosives). This line divides that which is above from that below without rest or intermediate space. Above, grotesque figures are hanging from a wire, and there are three easily identifiable characters: a priest, a military man, and a capitalist (the three of them Creole, with the appropriate apparel for their respective professions). Below, barely emerging from a cloud, there is an indigenous or mestizo multitude that lumps together peasants in traditional garb, proletarians, and urban poor. The background of the mural is urban in appearance.

La quema de los Judas is not only a mural about popular celebrations or entertainments in Mexico. It also must be read as a national allegory. The space depicted in the mural should be understood as a scene whose true space is that of the nation, and the act of burning as a metaphor for revolutionary war, with the line that divides the top from the bottom acting as an active interpretation of the meaning and the subjects that fight this war. The war (the mass of clouds), which separates the subjects of the scene, gives "those from below" (from now on *los de abajo,* as in Azuela's title) their collective identity and endows them with their exclusive passion: to destroy "the ones from above [*los de arriba*]." *Los de abajo*—unlike *los de arriba*—have only a collective identity: their faces are barely visible, they are all alike, they lack individual expression. All the bodies of *los de abajo* are stooping, crouching, ducking from *los de arriba,* or attacking them: throwing rocks or looking for rocks to throw. No one has a position that is not in relation to the clouds and to *los de arriba.* No one in the mural ignores what is happening, and no one fails to acknowledge the line and the meaning of the line. The line between the above and the below, the space that delimits, is totalizing; it does not allow for any residue in meaning. (This is what Laclau called the holistic and dichotomic dimensions of emancipation [1996, 1].)

The war is not represented as a separate object or event but only as shapeless clouds. However, these clouds are what make the representation possible because they divide and organize the scene and they assign subject positions in the physical/axiological space of the mural. The clouds, grouped toward the middle, rescue the scene from chaos and establish an all-too-simple segmentation in the space of the national without internal distinctions. Therefore, war territorializes *los de abajo* as "people" (as a collective, undifferentiated unit) in the national space. If the clouds were to be uniformly distributed throughout the entire mural, this would mean multiple scenes of conflict. Thus, the simple and totalizing assignation of a "popular subject position" would be impossible (Laclau and Mouffe 1985, 131).[7] The war would be fragmented into the innumerable struggles of the multitude, and with that, the above/below distinction, essential to the representation of the social, would be gone, as would the possibility of state interpellation.

The division in the mural can be thought of in even more radical terms: the clouds (the war) divide the human (*los de abajo*) from the inhuman (*los de arriba*, the effigies). In the mural there are no women. We could imagine that there are no homosexuals. Also, all regional, cultural, and ethnic differences are obliterated, with the goal of forming a single national/popular subject as the subject of that war. Inversely, the revolutionary war is specified as the only mission of that subject. This would be a first dimension of meaning. But also, war is a popular celebration, and this is a second territorialization, in which time is introduced as a significant factor. From this point of view, war is not disruptive, but—quite to the contrary—it is imaginarily inscribed in an immemorial mechanism of repetition; it is inscribed in the traditions of the popular subject.

War as popular celebration implies a reversal of the identity process. It does not create the popular subject as an effect, but it is presented as an attribute of a pre-existent popular subject, completely constituted before the war (what Laclau called the pre-existent dimension of emancipation [1996, 1]). The contingent character of all identity is forgotten and becomes necessary, ahistorical. In war, the mural seems to indicate, the people become themselves, they find themselves, they discover what they have always been. War, from this viewpoint, does not create or destroy: it puts things back in place. War establishes a division in the social but does so as a means of bringing consciousness to identities and subject positions that pre-existed war.

Here we arrive at a third dimension of meaning: the mural offers a representation of a conflict as if it were immediate and unequivocally national. But the ultimate conditions of visibility of the mural are the conditions that the revolutionary state offers: the wall of the state institution (in this case, the secretariat of education, where the mural is painted). Through the mediation of the state (and only through it) the people accede to self-awareness. We could say, then, that this is a statist representation of war, in which the state finds its legitimacy, narrates the history of its "origins," and constitutes the subjects of this war (the people, the reaction) in its ultimate and univocal relationship with the said state. Thus, the mural is only credible (and intelligible) within a certain narrative of the revolution, viewed from the perspective of the revolutionary state.[8] This narrative makes the state the *Aufhebung* (sublation, sublimation) of the revolutionary war, of the warrior hubris in favor of the rational sphere of legal and ethical duty embodied in the state.

The mural is then a narrative about revolutionary insurgency, but (as in *Os sertões* and *La guerra gaucha*) it can also be thought of as a narrative of counterinsurgency (Guha 1988).[9] The becoming-visible of the war implies, as a condition of possibility, that it was transformed in prehistory by the state, something that the state simultaneously appropriates and relegates to the past, assigning it an exceptional and transitional character. Since it is a revolutionary war, the conflict that the mural cancels (and acknowledges by doing that) is the conflict between the multitude, the "constituent power" and "the constituted power" (constitutional, legislative, and so forth), in which the latter presents itself as the final cause and only channel of representation of the constituent power. This is not by chance: between the war, of which the mural is an accomplished metaphor, and the mural itself mediates the Constitution of 1917, a creature of triumphant carrancismo. The mural is then a vision of the war from the point of view of the constitution. But the procedure is rather unique. The constitution interprets the war, transforming it into a "popular" war (a war that has the constitution itself as its final cause). The procedure of inversion transforms war into a mediation. If the war has a meaning—or if it can be represented—it is because it is at the origin of the state, but it is an origin that is conceived as fully preserved in what has originated from it.

Los de abajo seems to be trapped in the same space of visibility conferred by the constitution as a juridical act. More precisely the constitution mediates between the first two editions of the novel (1915 and 1916) and its "rediscovery" in 1924 (for the history of this rediscovery, see Monterde 1973; Englekirk 1975; Ruffinelli 1996b). This rediscovering was not by chance, not an act of literary justice, not even the reflection of a change in taste. It corresponded to a moment of suture and symbolic erasure of differences. The rediscovery belongs less to the history of literature than to the history of the Mexican state and its mechanisms for the constitution of hegemony. It is significant that the rediscovery of Azuela, the publication of *La raza cósmica* by Vasconcelos, the massive plan for basic education, the constitution of a workers' movement akin to a government, the building of a powerful new bureaucracy, the formation of a party that would hegemonize the state, and the emergence of muralism are all contemporary phenomena.

A philological example will clarify how this process of suture and symbolic erasure of differences operates: in the early editions of *Los de abajo* there is the following subtitle: "Vignettes and Scenes of the Current Revolution" (*Cuadros y escenas de la revolución actual*) (Ruffinelli 1996b, 3).[10] In the *Obras completas* (1958), the subtitle already was "Novel of the Mexican Revolution" (*Novela de la Revolución Mexicana*). This slight modification can be read as evidence of a triple movement of totalization and suture. The first movement is from the "scene" (i.e., the aesthetic-ideological procedure that, because of its very fragmentary form, resists spatial, temporal, or psychological totalization) to the novel, understood as the modern mode par excellence of totalizing the social experience. The second movement is from the "current Revolution" (i.e., the disruption of the pacts, the maddening of the signs, the advent of that beyond representation) to the Mexican Revolution (the restitution of that experience to a multisecular narrative of emancipation). This idea is even more explicit in a later text by Azuela, *Precursores* (that is, "precursors of the Revolution"). The book is divided into three sections that tell the story of three bandits: Andrés López Martínez ("el Amito"), Manuel Lozada, and Antonio Rojas. In each case, Azuela identifies a component in bandit insurgency that takes him close to the later "ideals" of the Revolution (land distribution, peasant vindication, etc.). The third movement is, complementarily, from El Paso—where the novel was first published while Azuela was in exile—to Mexico City, and from the *folletín* to book form. This is the parabola of the novel and the novelist to the heart of the institutionalized revolution.

In the early edition's "cuadros y escenas," the space of Demetrio and his men is a space outside—and opposed to—their imaginary inscription under the sovereignty of the nation-state. In the later "novela de la Revolución Mexicana," what is implied is that the space of the battle did not become a territory of the Mexican state due to the specific victory of one of the sides in the battle, a historically situated process, but that it was always already fully inscribed as a territory of the Mexican nation-state. The transition from "cuadros y escenas" to "novela de la Revolución Mexicana" implies the necessary forgetting in the constitution of the nation. This is the forgetting of the irreducible character of the opponents and the reinterpretation of the conflict as a conflict between brothers, "always already Mexicans." It is not by chance that at the same time that *Los de abajo* is rediscovered, Obregón coins the expression "the revolutionary family," a term that President Plutarco Elías Calles would impose during the maximato, thus projecting toward the past the conciliation violently achieved in the present (T. Benjamin 2000, 69). Nor is it coincidental that the term Revolution (capitalized) is enshrined. A symbol of this is the transfer of the remains of Madero, Villa, Carranza, and Obregón (bitter enemies in life) to the Monument to the Revolution, as if to a family funeral monument.[11] The novel itself provides a decisive moment for this reappropriation of the novel to the symbolic repertoire of the nation-state in the death of Demetrio Macías in the heat of battle:

> The smoke of the guns hangs thick in the air. Locusts chant their mysterious, imperturbable song. Doves coo lyrically in the crannies of the rocks. The cows graze placidly.
>
> The sierra is clad in gala colors. Over its inaccessible peaks the opalescent fog settles like a snowy veil on the forehead of a bride.
>
> At the foot of a hollow, sumptuous and huge as the portico of an old cathedral, Demetrio Macías, his eyes leveled in an eternal glance, continues to point the barrel of his gun. (Azuela 1915/1916, 140)

It may seem strange to mention the nuptials (the morning of Demetrio's death was a true "heavenly morning" [*mañana de nupcias*, literally "a morning for nuptials" (138)]), the statuesque, the cathedral quality, the bucolic nature of the scene since in fact this was a fierce and deadly battle. In *El Zarco* the consecratory scene of the new state and its coupling, the new civil virtues, is also a "*mañana de nupcias*" with the marriage of Pilar and Nicolás. This marriage also carried with it the elimination of the bandit.[12] This is the point at which Demetrio becomes a symbol. The sierra becomes the city (the very center of the city, the cathedral). A civil and religious ceremony is about to happen: the elevation of Demetrio, his consecration. This consecration has a civic meaning (the glory) but also a religious meaning (the martyrdom). Demetrio becomes the symbol of the frustrated or achieved Revolution, of the dead revolutionaries and their epic hubris that the revolutionary state claims as its own heritage. If we read the last pages of the novel, we can notice how the ending implies the transition to another time ("The eyes intently fixed forever") that is not the time of actions but of myths. With this elevation of Demetrio, Azuela ceases to be a collector of erratic "scenes" and becomes a writer identical to history. He becomes, as Lugones became, the one who can "speak on behalf of the dead" and say "what they 'really' meant and 'really' wanted since they themselves 'did not understand'" (Anderson 1983, 198). Azuela becomes the one whose duty it is to remind each Mexican of the series of tragedies that form the family history.

The signifier *los de abajo* seems from this perspective to become reversible, related to a contingent position only in an ongoing conflict. The words of the title appear just once in the novel, in the first action of Demetrio's gang. Here "los de abajo" are the federales, the huertistas: "—[Shoot] to those below . . . to those below [*A los de abajo . . . a los de abajo*]—shouted Demetrio, aiming his rifle toward the crystalline current of the river" (12). The novel ends with the death of Demetrio and his men in an ambush by the Carranza troops (the *carranclanes*), at the very same spot where the ambush of the federales took place and where Demetrio's career as a bandit began (138). Now, *los de abajo* are Demetrio's gang (139). This reversibility seems to unite the contenders under the common rubric of the popular, the "barefoot *Iliad*" of which Carlos Fuentes spoke (1998), in which the differences between Trojans and Achaeans are secondary vis-à-vis their common bravery. Thus, the decomposition of segmentarities (federales, villistas, and carrancistas are or could all be *los de abajo*) is reappropriated, "overcodified" by the state with the goal of subordinating it to the major signifier of Mexicanness. The meaning of the conflict is reinterpreted as a conflict among Mexicans, one that is only possible among Mexicans, thus making it a privileged feature of Mexicanness. The conflict, the real rent in the social fabric, is resignified as a symbolic suture in the same way that Benedict Anderson spoke of the reassuring effect of fratricide. This is a way to interpret the fact that *Los de abajo* is at the same time a bandit novel and a foundational novel: it turns Demetrio and his gang into a moment of the popular subject, unconscious of itself and intimately contradictory. These contradictions are synthesized and transcended in the revolutionary state where violence becomes reason.

But this is not all. In *Los de abajo* there is something more, something that the previous determinations cannot name. More specifically, throughout the novel there are several instances in which Demetrio refuses to name the meaning of the war:

> [Luis Cervantes]—All I have tried to do is to make myself understood about this point. I wish I could convince you that I am a true coreligionist [*correligionario*].
> . . .
> —Cor . . . what? —inquired Demetrio, turning an ear toward Cervantes.
> —Coreligionist, sir, that is to say, I pursue the same ideals and I defend the same cause that you do.
> Demetrio smiled wryly:
> —And tell me, what cause are we fighting for?
> Luis Cervantes, completely at a loss, did not know what to reply. (19)

Luis Cervantes later asks Demetrio,

> —Look, General; if as it seems this bola is going to continue, if the Revolution keeps on, we have enough money already to go and live abroad in grand style—.
> Demetrio shook his head in dissent. —You would not do that? But, why would we remain? Which cause would we be defending now?
> —I cannot explain it, *curro;* but I feel it is not something a man would do. (95)

Demetrio's wife later asks him,

> —Why do you keep on fighting, Demetrio?
> Demetrio frowned deeply. Absent-mindedly, he picked up a stone and he threw it to the bottom of a gorge. He stared pensively toward the abyss, and he replied:
> —Look at that pebble? how it is unable to stop. . . . (137)[13]

There are two different ways to conceive this resistance to naming. One would be that this resistance functions as lack of class consciousness, as testimony to Demetrio and his gang's inability to articulate the grievances that threw them into lawlessness and rebellion as a program and praxis. Even though Demetrio is involved in struggles that we would not hesitate to call fully political (from the letrado viewpoint)—such as the struggle against huertismo—Demetrio would remain fundamentally pre-political. Interpreted in such a fashion, this excess or void continues having the revolutionary state as its center, as the focus of its exigencies, of its rationality. Those excluded from the Revolution would be "the people," and the bandit-revolutionary would be something like the dark side of the popular subject. According to this interpretation, we would remain trapped in the space of representation laid by the state, and the mode of the unsaid would be the mode of the "potential," of that which could have been but was not. *Los de abajo* has been read (and continues to be read) in this fashion, and this has been the way the novel of the Mexican Revolution developed—as an endless catalog of the shortcomings of the Revolution.

The other way of thinking about this excess is to conceive of it as being "beyond" the state, a beyond that is fully constituted ("fully" in the equivocal sense in which Gayatri Chakravorty Spivak speaks of the subaltern consciousness as full consciousness [1988]). It is heterogeneous to the meaning of war that the state promotes and to the form of thinking that the state form determines.

Let us return to the scene between Demetrio and Cervantes. Demetrio's silence, his malicious or clumsy question ("And tell me, what cause are we fighting for?"), is not the establishment of a law, of an interior space of sovereignty or determined loyalties. (We must remember that toward the end of the novel, his gang consists mostly of former federales and that there were no procedures for entering or leaving the gang.) Demetrio's question is the sheer act of interrupting a major language (as Deleuze and Guattari defined it [1975]), that is, Cervantes's language, which comes from the letter, the center, and modernity. To think of this interruption in terms of the bola (95), the war machine, is what allows us to escape from the prejudices that make Demetrio synonymous with barbarism, hubris, or lack of a true political project.

Resistance to naming the meaning of the war (the lack of an efficient cause different from war itself) is the specifically political dimension of *Los de abajo* (the dimension that *Los de abajo* at the same time shows and closes). This is so because the resistance in naming points to a different register of the political. It points to a nomadic form of politics that exceeds the signs of the nation and its forms of sovereignty. This politics does not imply "citizen" or "people," since it operates through fixed political identities. It does not imply turning Demetrio and his gang into "representatives." Making Demetrio a representative would be the first step in making him an Achilles, thus removing him from his class and race markers (these markers are not that important to Demetrio himself, but the way he detaches himself from these markers is not the same way the state would detach him from them). No-madic politics also does not imply making Demetrio and his band reducible by state mechanisms of representation, nor does it refer (exclusively) to the fact that Demetrio and his gang move about incessantly. It refers more to the fact that their politics cannot be grounded to fixed points in the manner of state-centered politics. The same happens in Rafael F. Muñoz's novel *Se llevaron el cañón para Bachimba* (1931), which also uses a spatial metaphor. Alvarito, who joined Pascual Orozco's Colorados, lays out a division of the social realm that, even though it is very clear, is completely enigmatic:

> At that precise moment the human landscape was divided in front of my eyes, by the red ribbon that fit like a crown on the top of my hat: inside, the Reds [*colorados*]; outside, all the rest. What did we Reds want? How had the revolution been betrayed? Why were those outside the circle, who until yesterday were friends of our chiefs, now against us? I did not know the answer and I did not care to know. I was a Red and that was all.
> — Go Reds! [¡*Arriba los colorados!*]
> Go where? What for? [¿*Arriba de dónde?¿Arriba de quién?*] It did not matter: triumph meant to go somewhere. (Muñoz 1931a, 789–90)

The nomadic politics of the bandit gang never appeals to "Mexico" as the final cause of the war. In fact, the novel produces the word "Mexico" only twice, and the contexts in both cases are most telling. The first use of the term is an erroneous reference to a fact that did not happen: the death of Félix Díaz (Azuela 1915/1916, 41). The second use appears in a letter that the chief of the *federales* imagines writing to General Blanquet, feigning a victory over an enormous force of Constitutionalists:

> A rebel army, five hundred strong, commanded by . . . attacked this town, which I am charged to defend. With such speed as the gravity of the situation called for, I fortified my post in the town. The battle lasted two hours. Despite the enemy's superiority in men and equipment, I was able to defeat and rout them. Their casualties were twenty killed and a far greater number of wounded, judging from the trails of blood they left behind as they retreated. I am pleased to say there were no casualties on our side. I have the honor of congratulating Your Excellency upon this new victory of the Federal army ¡Viva the general Don Victoriano Huerta! ¡Viva Mexico! (55–56)

In *Los de abajo,* "¡Viva Mexico!" is the greeting of assassins (the captain participated in the reactionary rebellion called the Decena Trágica, an immediate antecedent to Madero's assassination [54]). "¡Viva Mexico!" is only sustained from an ironic distance, the enactment of the false legitimacy of the false state epic.

Demetrio's war is not inscribed in the order of means and goals. Rather, it is a mode of being. The disappearance of the distinction between means and ends is implicit in the word that the novel uses to define the entire process: the bola (95, 121). The bola names the war, but it also names the subjects of that war: the multitude. (Ruffinelli, in the notes to the critical edition of *Los de abajo,* defines the bola as the "crowd, the disorderly multitude" but also as "a popular uprising" [1996a, 148]). The bola is the nomadic war machine, the gang as individuation that comprises the assemblages that constitute it: men, horses, weapons, knowledge, space, the modes of the gang's relationship to the economic means at its disposal, to the women who are raped and the women who are snatched, to other gangs and the loose men that are incorporated into the gang. The bola is the protagonist (not the topic) of *Los de abajo.* That is, the bola is *los de abajo,* of course, but not as the full subjectivity in the modern sense, exerting that subjectivity in the narrative (this is not the tragic and sad story of Demetrio, from his optimistic beginnings to his sad end), but in their relationship to the movements of deterritorialization that traverse them. In the novel these movements go beyond the coordinates we are accustomed to thinking about in novels: characters (and their psychology and their transformations in time), actions (and their reciprocal links, their causal relationships, and their ethics), landscape (and its ethical, aesthetic, or economic connotation). The "bola," the war machine, assembles all these as a new sui generis individuation that forces us to think about them in a different fashion. As Deleuze puts it, "What we are interested in, you see, are modes of individuation beyond those of things, persons or subjects: the individuation, say, of a time of day, of a region, a climate, a river or a wind, of an event. And maybe it's a mistake to believe in the existence of things, persons, or subjects. The title *A Thousand Plateaus* refers to these *individuations that don't individuate persons or things*" (Deleuze 1990, 26). This is evidenced in the way we perceive the logic (transformed into a lack of logic) of Demetrio and his gang. War, when it is not thought of from the state's vantage point (or to be less vague, from a consciousness akin to that of the letrado project of Solís, Cervantes, and even Valderrama, who sympathizes with the Revolution), is always characterized with entropic metaphors for catastrophes that ruin representation. Captain Solís confesses, "You would ask me why I follow the revolution? The revolution is a hurricane, and the man who is sucked into it ceases to be a man and is a pitiful dry leaf blown away by the wind" (Azuela 1915/1916, 62). Valderrama states, "Villa? Obregón? Carranza? . . . X . . . Y . . . Z. . . . What do I care about them? I love the Revolution as I would love the volcano that erupts! I love the volcano because it is a volcano, and the Revolution because it is a Revolution! But the stones left above or below after the cataclysm, what do I care about them?" (128). Just like in the mural, the clouds reappear as metaphors for the insurrection. But, in a very significant fashion, they no longer organize the space of representation; quite to the contrary, they confound it: "Cervantes's smile was so scornful, that Solís, annoyed, calmly took a seat on a boulder. . . . He smiled and his gaze wandered following the spirals of smoke of rifles and the dust clouds of houses felled by cannon fire. And he thought that he had discovered a symbol for the Revolution in those clouds of dust and smoke that climbed skyward in a fraternal embrace, and that afterward, dissolved into nothingness" (72).

The subjects of the bola, when they are not thought of as citizens in arms or inhabitants becoming citizens in the forge of war are always depicted through animal metaphors: mosquitoes (120), bees (120), deer (70), ants (125), and dogs (126). They are always gregarious or multitudinous animals.[14] This is quite the opposite of the epic whose preferred metaphor is the solitary individuated and heroic animal, such as the lion or the eagle (which in the novel is only quoted in a sarcastic fashion when referring to Villa as the "Aztec Eagle" [66]). But this idea of the rebellion as catastrophe or as a return to a "state of nature," animalism, or barbarism is the classic mode in which peasant rebellion against the state is interpreted and where what is omitted (what has to be omitted) is the specific political dimension of the process.

For the state, war is another function, subordinated and coordinated with others: on the one hand there is war (that happens on the front), and on the other there is the extraction of resources from the land (the rearguard). There is a division and taxation of resources, as well as the production of diverse goods to sustain the war effort, the distribution of those resources to the front (according to the dynamics between center and periphery), and the formation of military cadres in state educational institutions.

All of the aforementioned functions are, in the case of the bandit gang, inherent to the movement of the bola. They are never put in relation to an exterior state. Thus, weapons are obtained by capturing the federales' weapons (see the chapter of *Los de abajo* that is entitled "Entre las malezas de la sierra"), and resources are obtained through plunder. The incorporation of new ranks and promotion among those ranks happen only according to the diverse fortunes of the bola. The bola breaks the segmented nature of the state apart, thus giving way to a smooth space without fragmentation. This allows us to understand the nature of Demetrio's roving, setting the speed of the gang (as sheer nomadism) against the movement (with a direction) of armies. The concept of the bola allows us to differentiate the nomadic nature of the gang from aimless wandering that was defeated from the beginning. Azuela writes, "The joy and pride of the gang lie precisely in the unexpected. And it is because of this that the soldiers sing, laugh, and chatter enthusiastically [*locamente*]. The spirit of the old nomadic tribes stirs in their souls. Knowing where they are going or whence they came does not matter. It is essential to march, always march, never to stop; to be the lords of the valleys, of the plains, of the sierras, as far as the eye can see" (138).

By examining the distinction between closed space and smooth space (385) in relation to the battle as the unit of war, we can see that the battle in its state version is thought of in its constant and essential relationship to a center—a city, a productive hub, a river, an oil rig—that has to be protected. The battle is included within an order of closed space that is not inherent to it but that is determined beforehand. The battle conceived from the state has a forward line and a backward line, an advance and a retreat, a victory and a defeat. Even though Demetrio's band participates in battles, these battles are not essential to their mode of constitution. (The decisive battles —where the fortunes of villismo decline decisively—are not depicted in the novel, and the gang does not participate in them [128].) The bola includes battles against state armies, but it also includes plunder, rape, rest, and vengeance among the same (lack of) priorities. The band is nomadic by nature, unlike the armies that are sedentary and that move toward the battle. The relationship with space in both cases is inverse: in the case of the band, "it is the trajectory that has all the consistency" (Deleuze and Guattari 1980, 384), while in the case of armies, it is the journey that has to be overcome to reach the destination. (This is why during the nineteenth century the guerrilla war of resources was always so successful: space is an enemy for armies since it implies a disintegration of its essentially compact nature.)

Victory and defeat are relevant terms to somebody like Luis Cervantes, who thinks about war in its relation to a center that must be occupied (Mexico City) and as a means to secure some advantages. To the contrary, victory and defeat are somehow irrelevant to the gang, who after the defeat in Zacatecas was "returning just as joyfully as it marched toward combat several days ago, pillaging every town, every hacienda, every village, and even the most poverty-stricken hut that it found along its way" (63). This absence of distinction does not make the insurrection mere chaos or a purely negative or barbaric instance. This brings to mind the destruction and selling of the house library after the taking of Zacatecas or the famous episode of the typewriter, which the gang carried around after the failure of its assault on Zacatecas:

> —Who wants to trade me this gadget?—cried one, all red and tired of carrying his spoil [*avance*]. It was a brand-new typewriter that attracted everybody's greed with its shining nickel.
>
> The Oliver changed owners five times that very same morning. It started out costing ten pesos, losing one or two pesos each time it changed hands. Truth be told, it was too heavy, and nobody could carry it for more than half an hour.
>
> —I'll give you a *peseta* for it—offered the Codorniz.
>
> —Deal—answered the owner, giving it to him immediately, fearing that the Codorniz would have second thoughts.
>
> The Codorniz, for a quarter, had the immense pleasure of grabbing it and smashing it noisily against the rocks. (63–64)

The joyful destruction of the typewriter can be conceived negatively as an act of barbarism (the reversal of a political act) or as a fully (albeit also negative) political act. Of course, this is a politics directed specifically against the rules of the polis: the desecration, inversion, and destruction of the order of signs of the lettered city. The typewriter carries two evident connotations: modernity and legality. The episode, also, is not unheard of in the history of the Mexican Revolution or, for that matter, in the history of any peasant rebellion. Knight tells us that, after the occupation of a district or a significant town or city, it was routine to burn the local archives, to destroy all traces of the letrado legal order. Closer to our own time period, one of the first acts of the zapatistas during their rebellion in Chiapas was to destroy the land registries archived in public offices when they entered San Cristóbal de las Casas on January 1, 1994 (Hayden 2002, 207).

This hatred of the written word and its manifestations has a clear political component: the letter as possibility of ownership record, the guarantee of legality that it provides for the dispossession of the peasantry (incapable in many instances of presenting a regular deed since most often occupation was ancestral). The typewriter is the condition of possibility of a registry of lineages, taxes, and offenses. (Think of this: peasants had contact with typewriters only in state offices, where we can imagine comfort was not their lot and where usually only trouble and hardship could be expected. Typewriters were an instrument of the hated political boss, so the destruction of it was much like the burning of the Judases.) Its destruction is an act against citizenship but one entirely motivated by and coherent with the logic that governs the bola. It is one that opens up to other forms of sociability, to other forms of citizenship.

The bola breaks down the segmentations overcodified by the state in terms of class, race, and gender. This allows us to stop thinking of the social space in the novel as defined wholly and exclusively in terms of class distinctions between above and below; we can then reencounter the diverse flight lines and a "heterogeneity immanent to the popular subject" (to use, in a somewhat modified form, John Beverley's apt expression [1999]). An example of this would be the different roles of Camila and Demetrio's wife (outside the band) on the one hand, and Pintada, who does belong to the gang and whose definition of femininity is unheard of (and is, for "us," predictably grotesque). Furthermore, these different examples point to the disappearance of the distinction between public space and private space, between free time and work, between robbery and war. Also, the lack of racial distinction within the band is conspicuous. (Indians, mestizos, and whites live without an apparent racial hierarchy, and what is more important, race is never a topic of conversation. The only clear distinction throughout the novel is that between urbanites [*curros*] and rural folk, which is to say between the bola and the letrados.) This lack of distinction should not be confused with mestizaje, although later readings of the novel have addressed the topic in these terms. Also, it is important to note the destruction of class distinctions without consequent access to a "classless society" or a "warrior democracy": the distinctions between the interior and exterior (horses enter into houses and barrooms); of marital status (brides are bought, given as presents, exchanged for goods); and of hierarchies (army ranks are gained in a random fashion, invented, or simulated) all disappear.

At the very core of the novel (81) there is a feast in which it is unclear if the gang is celebrating Demetrio's promotion to general or if it is promoting him to general (since the promotion mechanisms within the gang are completely erratic). This feast happens in the bourgeois drawing room that had become either a military headquarters or a bandit den. This space can be accurately characterized as a world upside down, a deliberate inversion and destruction of all the signs that ensured the letrado/bourgeois order. The room's drapes are used for saddles, the books as fuel in bonfires, the room as a stable, Dante's *Comedy* is now a repertoire of "naked broads" (*viejas encueradas*), Pintada dresses up in the best clothes of the lady of the house, the beautiful bride Cervantes bought ends up spending the night with the güero Margarito. From the letrado perspective this is the ultimate image of barbarism. It is the ultimate image of the destruction of the signs of civilization by the blind forces of the rural world. But this destruction is far from blind. As Guha reminds us, "such radical subversion, this *real* turning of things upside down, which is only another name for rebellion, constitutes a semiotic break: it violates that basic code by which the relations of dominance and subordination are historically governed in any particular society" (1983, 36).[15]

The bola can also provide a metaphor of the novel as such and of the place of a confluence between Azuela and his demon Demetrio. *Los de abajo* was written beyond the imperatives of a national cause during the random events of the war. The novel was, like Demetrio, intersected by the cause. But it remains fundamentally antagonistic to that order of the mythology of the revolutionary state. In this fashion, the novel is a battlefield between two diverse forces. On the one hand there is a capture apparatus that reduces all the dimensions of meaning in the work from a defined statist purpose consonant with a revolutionary macronarrative and the constitution of a popular whole, compliments of the revolutionary state. On the other hand, there is a nomadic force that resists and breaks down the state paradigm, thus vindicating the political subjects within the work and their practices that were alien to the nation-state paradigm. From this conflict, the force and shortcomings of the revolutionary narrative find enduring energy.

Cesarismo democrático

Banditry and the Necessary Gendarme
(The Shadow of the Caudillo I)

—Nada sin la guerra se crea. En la naturaleza, una guerra perpetua es la perpetua creadora. La guerra forma pueblos, constituye naciones, hace la unidad y grandeza de las razas. . . . Como hermanas gemelas, de su pródigo vientre nacen la gloria del capitán y la gloria del artista: el laurel tinto en sangre y la obra de arte vestida de candidez impoluta.
   Tulio Arcos in *Sangre patricia,* by Manuel Díaz Rodríguez, 1902

—¡Tenemos jefe!
   Pajarote, a llanero from Altamira, in *Doña Bárbara,* by Rómulo Gallegos, 1929

—De la guerra salen los verdaderos amos.
   Presentación Campos, *Las lanzas coloradas,* by Arturo Uslar Pietri, 1931

In Blanco's novel *Zárate,* the co-optation by the sovereign (Páez) of nonstate violence (Zárate) was the condition of possibility of the effective and incessant domination of the state over populations and territory. The oral pact by which Zárate acknowledges a personal power superior to his own makes possible the state as "abstract machine of sovereignty" (Deleuze's term). It also facilitates the reduction of the Güere forest—the seat of an alternative rationality that the novel calls "superstition" and "crime" just like in the ethnography practiced in *Doña Bárbara* in which El Miedo receives the same epithets—to the political and economic rationality of the state. The pact also shows both Páez and Zárate's shared belonging to an outlaw tradition of violence. The pact, read against the grain, highlighted the fact that the origin of the state is completely spurious, and it implied the foreclosure of any self-sustaining narrative on the nation-state. This is the pact that the letrado elite (Horacio Delamar) cannot conceive or accept if brought to light. (Zárate would be accepted as a bandit, not as a submissive and respectful llanero in the patriarchal manor.) In *Zárate,* the murder that nobody really laments represented the symbolic erasure that makes state mythology possible. The depiction of the erasure (that by definition should be excluded from visibility) is the critical dimension that Blanco's novel achieved.

261

Laureano Vallenilla Lanz would follow a different and riskier path. Instead of suppressing the collusion between statesman and outlaw (and allowing it to reenter as always-already-forgotten), he would reason the historical necessity of linking the sovereign outlaw to the foundation of the national state. He did this in the context of justifying the Venezuelan *gomato,* or rule of Juan Vicente Gómez, for both exceptional and typical reasons, in the convoluted history of Venezuela's path toward the twentieth century.

Manuel Caballero has pointed out that Venezuela has not been able to exorcise Gómez's ghost from national history (1993, 355). Gómez was part of Cipriano Castro's inner circle during the latter's rule (1898–1908), and he ruled by himself or through appointees from 1908 until his death in 1935. He was a turning point in Venezuelan history. An Andean caudillo who reached power partially supported by the old caudillo order (Urbaneja 1988, 53), Gómez brought the caudillo cycle to a close: he suppressed its last manifestations and established the economic, military, and infrastructural conditions that would make caudillismo impossible in the future (at least, in the traditional regional-rural form) (Ziems 1988). A country man with an almost caricature-like quality (although that of a somber and cruel caricature) and possessing a network of supporters that was by far the largest landowning clique in Venezuela, he inaugurated the new urban Venezuela that would succeed him. Of a well-defined personal style, he is the father of the Venezuelan state; before him it was a fiction. This state was one of acceptable administrative qualities, except when confronted with the interests of Gómez and his circle (Urbaneja 1988, 57). The gomato seems to have been deeply rooted in the political tradition of nineteenth-century nonstate violence (a tradition that exasperated Tulio Arcos in *Idolos rotos* and *Sangre patricia* by Manuel Díaz Rodríguez) but that at the same time was committed to enforcing (from a position of force and privilege) the transition toward the twentieth century. This unique character, a sign of the heterogeneous character of Venezuelan modernity itself (Coronil 1997) is what makes Gómez and what he represented an urgent object of reflection for Laureano Vallenilla Lanz, one of the organic intellectuals of the regime.

The idea of the collusion between bandit and sovereign as the specifically Venezuelan mode of democracy, and not as the denial of democracy, is the core argument in *Cesarismo democrático* (1919), the major work of Laureano Vallenilla Lanz (1870–1936). While in Sarmiento's work caudillismo is the form of political organization that remains fundamentally linked to its out-law origin, in Vallenilla Lanz's, caudillismo, even though it springs forth from banditry, is the only form of political organization that can limit it and accomplish the qualitative leap to full statehood, leaving banditry behind. Both Sarmiento and Vallenilla Lanz write in the context of authoritarian regimes whose state policy had banditry as its driving force. However, while in the Argentine case rosismo was an epistemological scandal and an incomprehensible monstrosity, in the Venezuelan one Vallenilla Lanz considers Gómez the embodiment of the unique form of statehood that naturally emerged from Venezuela's physical and social makeup. For Vallenilla Lanz the gomato is a form of statehood that is at the same time positive (as opposed to ideal) and legitimate.

Vallenilla Lanz, a positivist by upbringing and by conviction, was the official intellectual of the gomato (he was the director of *El nuevo diario* and the National Archives and was a diplomat in Paris), and the Kant of *gomecismo*. (With this expression, we subscribe with all seriousness to Roberto Schwarz's humorous affirmation that in Brazilian political thinking there was no Kant to elevate clientelism to the status of valid political principle even though it in fact regulated Brazilian political and social life [Schwarz 1973].)[1] Breaking away from the secular tradition of liberal thinking (which occasionally exalted dictatorships, but only as "states of exception"), and doing so quite differently than otherwise brilliant intellectuals salaried by caudillos (the most significant, and somehow pathetic case being the Italian Pedro de Angelis, who also coined the expression "*sistema americano*"), Vallenilla Lanz defended Gómez's authoritarian rule. He did so because he was sincerely convinced of its validity, morality (leaving aside the dubious morality of Páez, Castro, or Gómez, who grew rich while in office, something that Vallenilla Lanz did not hide), and above all its historical necessity as an "American system."

While Sarmiento refers with sarcasm to Rosas's own belief that his rule typified the American system (*sistema americano*), Vallenilla Lanz (who vindicated Rosas's historical mission) devoted a lengthy portion of *Cesarismo democrático* to laying the theoretical foundations of Gómez's rule (although he never mentions Gómez by name) and identifying it as a particularly American mode of rule. Unlike Sarmiento, who considered Rosas a throwback to the colony, Vallenilla Lanz links his authoritarian version of democracy to Bolívar's writings and political life, to the point of making his democratic Caesar a product and an enforcer of what he calls the "Bolivarian Law" (Ley Boliviana) (Vallenilla Lanz 1919, 113). Vallenilla Lanz suggests that Gómez is a disciple of Bolívar since he does not believe the president to be blinded by the deceptive glitter of constitutionalism and because he conceives a form of government fit for the Venezuelan people (113).

Together with the *científicos* who supported and oriented porfirian rule in Mexico, Vallenilla Lanz was among the few significant Latin American intellectuals who supported the legitimacy of authoritarian rule as a necessary rung on an evolutionary ladder and as a prelude to and not the ruin of or deviation from formal democracy.[2] Vallenilla Lanz linked authoritarian caudillismo to what he considered racial democracy in Venezuela, in contrast to the corporative domination and racial hierarchy that existed in Latin America countries that officially abided by the niceties of formal democracy (e.g., Colombia).[3] His reputation as the panegyrist of a dictatorship damaged his reputation as a writer (in addition to marginalizing him both personally and intellectually after 1935), and it usurped all the debates surrounding the thesis expounded in *Cesarismo democrático*. In spite of this, contemporary historiography recuperates the originality and relevance of his approach.

The thesis in *Cesarismo democrático* is simple: Gómez is the last in a century-old tradition of caudillos who spring forth from the "organic constitution" of the Venezuelan social body—the "Democratic Caesars" who transformed outlaw rural violence into a principle of political organization.[4] The caudillo is the one who, having been nurtured by the gang as its only possible hierarchical expression, eventually controls and then suppresses banditry as Venezuela's political expression.[5] The first caudillo in Venezuelan history was José Tomás Boves, who made plunder not only a mode of politics but even a government program disguised under a royalist banner. However, the first democratic Caesar was José Antonio Páez, who used plunder as a way of making war but was also able (through the beneficial influence that Bolívar exerted upon him) to become a statesman. Thus, contradicting the principles of liberal constitutionalism (the "artificial constitution" against which Vallenilla Lanz sets the "organic constitution"), his theory of political organization intends to be "positive." The core of his argument focuses on the pillar of liberal historiography: the war of independence as an international, planned, coherent war, directed by a Creole elite that is unanimously patriotic and conscious of its historical destiny. This premise in Liberal historiography assumes a general will that supports (and is supported by) contractualism. Constitutionalism follows from this premise as the paramount principle of social organization. For romantic historiography (e.g., *Venezuela heroica*), war completely destroyed the colonial past and from its ruins a new society emerged, one that ideally corresponded to the principles sanctioned by the constitution. The nation as subject of war did not acknowledge the dividing lines of race or class, and it was centered on the elite hero as the conscience and leader of the nation. Given this dithyrambic idea of war, the subsequent historical process could have been understood only as a "fall" into division and decadence.

Vallenilla Lanz is the first to put forth the interpretation of the independence war as a civil war in which the overwhelming majority of the combatants were Venezuelans. Furthermore, for Vallenilla Lanz the dispute was not centered on the issue of allegiance to the king but on the balance of power between classes and races in Venezuela:

> That war, to which we owe the invaluable good of being able to call ourselves citizens of a nation and not colonists, can be placed in the same category as any of our frequent killings [*matazones*]; of which, by the way, we have no reason to be ashamed either. We should not be ashamed of our slaughters because revolutions, as social phenomena, fall under the domain of psychological determinism in which the human will has only a small role. Furthermore war (and it would be easy to prove this) has been here, as in all countries in all periods, one of the most powerful factors of progressive evolution for humankind. . . .
>
> And why would it be a badge of infamy for Venezuela that the executioners led by Boves, Yáñez, Morales, and Calzada were Venezuelans? No, sirs! Equally French were the executed as the executioners of the Revolution and nobody questions the fact that that orgy of blood "sowed in the ground the seeds of civilization." . . .
>
> In all that long period of most cruel war, I do not see anything but a struggle among brethren, an internal war, and a civil conflict. Even though I look intently for it, I cannot find the international character that legend has tried to give it. (Vallenilla Lanz 1919, 19, 20, 21)

In the debates that followed the first presentation of this thesis in 1911 in the form of a lecture, Samuel Niño, a well-known historian in the liberal tradition, asked if it were true, as Vallenilla Lanz affirmed, that the independence war was a slaughter (*matazón*) among others and not a unanimous epic, then "why temples, why statues, why national holidays, why cemeteries, and history and celebrations?"[6] Niño is less concerned by the truth of what Vallenilla Lanz proposes than by the disintegrating effect of that truth in an imagined community formed around a "will for truth" (to use Nietzsche's term) that in the nineteenth century mounted a formidable historiographic effort to "forget" the dark pacts with bandits, runaway slaves, and llanero plunderers or to attribute them to the monster of Venezuelan history: Boves. The thesis of the civil war effectively deconstructs that will for truth, deeming it to have been modeled on the "*need* to fulfill [the] desire for plenitude and authority" (Spivak 1997, xix), which is to say, an origin uncontaminated by the abjection of the Other (the bandit). This deconstruction becomes the key to Vallenilla Lanz's new interpretation of caudillismo.[7]

For Vallenilla Lanz colonial society was based on two main segmentations: a vertical one according to race and class distinctions and a horizontal one according to the fiercely maintained regional autonomy of urban oligarchies. Vallenilla Lanz proved through massive archival research that the independence war was not fought between Venezuelan insurgents and loyal Spaniards but the white Creole landowners and urban elites (*mantuanos*) versus poor whites, blacks, and castes in a society that—following the Hindu model—Vallenilla Lanz defines as a "caste society." The independence war represented a rebellion of the rural areas and castes against cities and landowners. It was not the breakdown of an old society and the birth ex nihilo of a new society but another avatar in a multisecular conflict in which the mantuano elite did not have the most illustrious part. (Vallenilla Lanz fiercely criticizes this elite, showing how ingrained class and race prejudices directed their political behavior right up to the opening salvos of the independence war, in which the notions of equality and fraternity were suddenly discovered through the reading of Rousseau.) The war was not the shaking off of the colonial yoke but rather the crisis of legitimacy of a social order based upon class and race distinctions. This challenge was not posed by the elite but *against* it (something that Blanco—one of the mainstays of the romantic myth of independence—tried to forget: in *Zárate* the hurricane of the war passed, and the racial and class order of the sugar plantation remained intact). The only change pertains to the superstructure—the republican faith of the landowners replaced the royalist loyalty of yore:

> Whites had been always the masters, the proprietors, the dominant ones, privileged by laws and by customs. . . . Naturally, the hatred of the popular classes was unleashed against this caste, against their lives and their interests. White, well-to-do, and patriot were one and the same for the soldiers of Boves and Yáñez.

White, well-to-do, and *godo* [popular and pejorative denomination for Spaniards or royalists] were for the same Bedouins "all of those who had something to lose" when Morillo, forced to reinstate the Ancient Regime and enforce upon the Venezuelan troops the same strict discipline of the Peninsular army, was deserted by them. These Bedouins augmented the ranks of the patriot army and thus continued their extermination work. (87)

The civil war destroyed the colonial state, but it also destroyed mantuano domination. The colonial state was replaced by a "warrior state that was at the same time the condition and the product of the war effort" (96). As in Azuela's bola, "the warrior state situates plunder [*saqueo*] as the base of its finances [*base de su hacienda*] as well as provisioning, troop recruitment, rewards, and political retaliations. Any attempt at organization that did not conform to the principles of the warrior state was a contradiction or, as in the First Republic, the Constitution of Rosario de Cúcuta, or the laws passed by Congress, an utter irrelevance" (96). The reversion of power to rural areas and the fallout of racial hierarchies left the "criminal *montonera*" (21) as the only principle of social organization able to fill the void:

> Anyone with an independent spirit who reads the history of Venezuela finds out that, even after independence was secured, the conservation of society could not at all be entrusted to laws, but to the most prestigious and fearsome caudillos, just like in the military encampments. "In the warrior state, the army is mobilized society, and society is the army at rest." . . .
>
> [It was] nothing more logical than the fact that Páez, Bermúdez, [and] Monagas were the gendarmes capable of containing the semibarbaric montoneras and the imperium of their personal authority by force, always willing and able, under any pretense, to repeat the invasions and horrendous crimes that in 1814 destroyed, according to Bolívar's eloquent phrase, "three centuries of culture, of enlightenment, of industry" (94).

The caudillo springs forth from the gang. He is (in social terms) equal to his subordinates, hence the inherently democratic value that Vallenilla Lanz assigns to Boves and Páez. But the caudillo—unlike the gang—is an active principle of social evolution (Plaza 1996, 195). He springs forth from the gang as its chieftain, but he can exceed its logic (Boves did not do this, but Páez did) and become a statesman. This is the denial of the gang. This is also what transforms the bandit gang, the criminal montonera, into a political body:

Luckily for the infant fatherland, General Páez came to be a true statesman. This is a concept that those who still think that the science of government is learned in books, and who do not take into account the positive teachings of History, would find strange. One is born a sovereign as another is born a poet. When one reads the biography of Páez with an independent spirit; when one remembers his humble origins, his complete lack of formal education, the kind of war that he had to wage and in which he stood out more as the chief of a nomadic tribe, as the leader of a desert caravan than as an army commander in the rigid meaning of the term; when one takes all this into consideration, his performance as the head of the regular government of the country amid that endemic disorder, that dreadful anarchy brought about by the war . . . he is worthy of the most enthusiastic of eulogies. It would seem like a unique occurrence if History would not put us in front of similar facts once and again. (103)

Immediately afterward Vallenilla Lanz uses an analogy that could not be more telling:

When the sons of Tancred of Hauteville invaded southern Italy, as true highway robbers, and Robert Guiscar, the bravest and boldest of them all, conducted himself "as a true robber" according to what the *Amatus Chronicle,* quoted by Demolins, says, "[I]t is admirable how when they definitively established their domination, they became administrators and true rulers, making industry come back from its ashes, developing culture and protecting property. They reconstituted social hierarchies, and substituted, eventually, order for anarchy." "Those rough warriors—Lenomart adds—which at the beginning did not blush at the fact of acting like bandits, which were completely illiterate, were later sponsors of progress and enlightenment worthy of admiration." (103)

Lugones's caudillo (Martín Miguel de Güemes), just like Vallenilla Lanz's, commands what are essentially associations of outlaws, transforming that military leadership into a form of state-making and into a form of sovereignty that does not contradict the nation-state but makes it possible. Some differences are noteworthy, however. In addition to the fact that Lugones erases the racial topic completely, Lugones's version of caudillismo is much more hierarchical. Güemes leads bandits, without being a bandit himself, thus mediating between the Sun of May (the metaphor for the elite-led revolution) and peasant insurgency, in which the active end of the equation is the Sun of May. It is by participation (in the platonic sense) of the bandits in Güemes's will, as emanations of his ideal body, that they become warriors of the fatherland. Indeed, in *La guerra gaucha* Lugones makes a statement that Vallenilla Lanz poignantly attacks: that the montoneras had a highly developed sense of nationhood and that the caudillo was the one who infused that sense.

For Vallenilla Lanz the movement is the opposite. It is not the state that endows peasant insurgency with meaning, but it is peasant war that destroys the state's meaning of war. In the same movement, peasant war transforms and recreates the state. This is why the llaneros' change in loyalties (something that in *La guerra gaucha* would be inconceivable) is secondary to Vallenilla Lanz's deeper argument: the change in loyalties did not imply a real transformation in the "psychological organism" of the llaneros, who were by definition alien to any sense of elite-defined nationhood.[8] When switching sides, all they did was change leaders: in the "dark bottom" of their mentality and their affections, the majordomo Páez was the true heir of the *taita* Boves.

Making caudillismo a historically valid form of social organization, born out of the criminal gang as the political *Ur*-form of the Venezuelan state, Vallenilla Lanz turns the axiology of liberal historiography and the entire interpretation of the nineteenth century upside down. The "Venezuelan question" was then incorrectly addressed by so-called "crisis narratives" (such as those developed by Manuel Díaz Rodríguez, Manuel Vicente Romerogarcía, José Rafael Pocaterra, or Rufino Blanco-Fombona, among many others), since the roadblock to Venezuelan development was not caudillismo but the fact that politicians were not able to live up to its challenges, lost as they were in the hall of mirrors of constitutionalism. This is why Páez is deserted by the llaneros and why this desertion is one of the origins of the Guerra Larga (89–105).

Banditry gives rise to caudillismo, which is both its highest achievement and its denial. In banditry Vallenilla Lanz found Latin America's most unique political feature (106) and a measure of the tragedy of so many statesmen who fought throughout their lives—many with sincerity and integrity—between the illusion of the lettered city and the realities of rural violence. Maybe the most important of all was Bolívar, who in the twilight of his career wrote, "I am tired of exerting this abominable discretional power, at the same time that I am deeply convinced that only a cunning despotism can rule America. We are far from the beautiful times of Athens or Rome and we should not establish comparison between ourselves and anything that is European" (quoted in Vallenilla Lanz 1919, 145).

17 | Doña Bárbara
Banditry and the Illusions of Modernity
(The Shadow of the Caudillo II)

El origen más impuro es el de nuestro ser: todo lo que nos ha precedido
está envuelto con el negro manto del crimen.
> Simón Bolívar to Santander, 1826

A generalized crime soon becomes a right.
> Gabriel Tarde

Rómulo Gallegos's novel *Doña Bárbara* is the last landmark in our journey, and so we can approach it as the depiction of the (necessarily failed) closure of a historical and literary cycle. Even though the novel was published
in 1929 (well into the twentieth century in strict chronological terms), its
inclusion in this corpus obeys reasons pertaining to literary history and to
political history, as well as to considerations strictly related to the intent
and content of the novel. Its literary techniques and perspective are closer
to the nineteenth century than to the twentieth (Martin 1989, 56–57). Actually, the work "gathers together and assimilates Latin American literary
experience from the time of Sarmiento to the time of the Mexican Revolution" (Martin 1989, 64). In historical terms, *Doña Bárbara* belongs to a transitional period in Venezuelan history. During the 1920s, the factors that
had dominated nineteenth-century Venezuela, such as caudillismo and regionalism, the dubious reach or even existence of a central state, and the
weight of agrarian wealth in the national economy, were being phased out
due to the emergence of the oil economy.[1] This new resource dramatically
transformed the social landscape; oil revenue made possible the development of the material and institutional infrastructure that would give the
Venezuelan state more than a virtual existence. It also gave rise to an urban
middle class that challenged the old caudillo order, an order embodied in the
rule of the aging (but still firmly in command) Gómez.[2] In some respects,
Venezuela entered the twentieth century with the death of Gómez in 1935,
just like Argentina entered the century with the end of Conservative rule in
1916, or Mexico with the Revolution. Because of this, *Doña Bárbara* is a
novel that stands at the dividing line between two centuries. In fact, this

270

liminal position is explicitly stated in the novel. As is well known, *Doña Bárbara* seems to herald the closing of a historical cycle marked by unbridled violence, premodern social arrangements, and radical heterogeneity in which the existence of two societies living side by side (Caracas and the backlands) made the very idea of "Venezuela" a political fiction. By contrast, the novel glimpses the dawn of a new order defined by the rule of law—a nation whose cultural (and therefore social) cohesion has as its cornerstone a national intellectual with a well-defined mission (vis-à-vis challenges from both subaltern classes and foreign powers) and an economic system that is able to harmonize the homogenizing needs of modern capitalism with a respect for the uniqueness of the Venezuelan experience (one of the classic features of populism, at least as an ideal).

Doña Bárbara is the story of Santos Luzardo, a Caracas letrado returning after many years to the Altamira hacienda, his ancestral homestead in the Arauca Valley. He had no longing at all for his childhood home. He and his mother had fled the hacienda after his father killed Santos's brother over political and family disputes (Gallegos 1929, 134–35), and he intended to sell the land sooner rather than later and return to Caracas to resume his life as an urbanite (138). In any case, the hacienda was collapsing due to mismanagement (the fate of the absentee landlord) and the rapaciousness of Doña Bárbara, owner of the adjacent hacienda, El Miedo, formerly known as La Barquereña, who had been robbing Altamira of both land and cattle in order to expand her own property (138). After a short while at Altamira, Santos Luzardo discovered that it was not going to be easy to dispose of the land of his elders. After all, he was also a llanero, and he discovered that he belonged to the land as much as the land belonged to him (174). He decided to remain in Altamira and make things right, putting the hacienda back in business, using the know-how of a modern letrado turned businessman. He was a lawyer, and as such he intended to challenge Doña Bárbara's abuses not with violence but with the sole force of the law (231, 261).

The body of the novel narrates the ensuing struggle between Santos Luzardo and Doña Bárbara over limits and predominance in the Arauca Valley. However, both contenders undergo unexpected transformations. Santos starts to shed his city skin, becoming more and more at ease with the violent ways of the llano. Doña Bárbara ceases to be the insatiable man-eater and falls in love with Santos Luzardo. She is unaware that her own daughter Marisela is also in love with Santos. Marisela is the daughter of Santos's cousin Lorenzo Barquero, a former hero of Santos and now an irrecoverable drunkard with whom Marisela lives on a tiny patch of land between El Miedo and Altamira. Confronted with the reality of her love being impossible and secretly confessing defeat by the superior willpower of Santos and Marisela's youth, Doña Bárbara disappears in the infinite jungles of the south, whence she originally came (464). With Lorenzo's death and Doña Bárbara's disappearance, Marisela becomes the legal owner of El Miedo. As owner, she marries Santos Luzardo, and with this marriage Altamira (now including El Miedo) is restored to its former splendor.

One of the reasons for the national and international success of *Doña Bárbara* (as well as for its later critical and political demise) was the neatness of the oppositions it sets up between the two camps and that play out the central conflict of the novel (beginning with the transparent names of the feuding haciendas, as well as of the main characters). This opposition comprises an all-too-legible national allegory. According to this allegory, the conflict between Santos Luzardo and Doña Bárbara is a rewriting of the secular struggle between civilization and barbarism (and its associated signifiers: urban versus rural, white versus mestizo, reason versus superstition, progress versus tradition, rule of law versus outlaw violence, male versus female, rationality versus passion and sexuality, and so forth). *Doña Bárbara* was thus read as a revision of Sarmiento's paradigm, one that has been adapted to conform to the new circumstances of the early twentieth century. The fact that this was a narrative that spoke to an authoritarian power and was written by an intellectual faced with the option of exile (like Sarmiento) made the parallelism with Sarmiento even more credible.

This is how the novel has been read for many years. And, as Carlos Alonso showed in detail, this is a path that any reading of the novel has to traverse, since strong indications on the part of the narrator that the novel has to be read in an allegorical fashion are embedded in the novel itself, allegory being "a narrative technique employed to construct the events depicted in the novel" (Alonso 1990, 120, 122). In recent decades, however, there have been several significant attempts to bring to the fore the complexities and paradoxes of the allegorical interpretation, both in its formal as well as its ideological aspects. Besides Alonso, Roberto González Echevarría (1985), Doris Sommer (1991), and Nelson Osorio (1995) opened new dimensions in the reading of the novel through their own criticism of the rigid version of the national allegory previously espoused by literary criticism.

Both González Echevarría and Alonso conduct a deliberate misreading of the novel (Alonso 1990, 134–35). González Echevarría, in Borgesian fashion, reads *Doña Bárbara* from the perspective of Gabriel García Márquez's "Los funerales de la Mamá Grande" (1967) and Severo Sarduy's *Cobra* (1972), "in order to expose some of the mechanisms that make *Doña Bárbara* a modern novel" (1985, 46). He relegates to the background any social/political interpretation, which is usually paramount in readings of regionalist fiction. González Echevarría still reads the novel as an allegory, but the content of the allegory is radically revised since he reads it as an allegory about writing itself (but one that is fraught with contradictions and is ultimately open-ended). González Echevarría's argument is nuanced and illuminating. Reduced to its minimum expression, it reads like this: the conflict between Santos Luzardo and Doña Bárbara is the conflict between a wish to "fix meaning in writing" (Santos is obsessed with the interpretation of the letter of the law, property titles, and the determination of boundaries, limits, rights, and obligations) and an impulse toward "permanent dissemination," the breaking of boundaries and nullification of differences (49), an impulse embodied in Doña Bárbara. According to González Echevarría, "Doña Bárbara, illegitimate, possessing supernatural powers, endowed with a disseminating and contradictory erotic power, an androgynous being . . . who is sacrificed in the novel, is an archetypal figuration of the *pharmakos* in whom the powers of writing are invested" (56). This contrast between opposing principles presupposes, from the point of view of the narrator, a hierarchy in which Doña Bárbara, as representative of the aforementioned disseminating principle, must be suppressed in order for writing (as a legitimate relationship between a signifier and signified) to be born. But in truly deconstructive fashion, González Echevarría shows how this metaphysical opposition is deconstructed by the novel itself. Altamira was founded by Evaristo Luzardo, "El Cunavichero," who appropriated the land by violence, not by right. Therefore, "violence and rewriting replace the mirage of a clear beginning, a legitimate principle" (49). *Doña Bárbara* read under this light is an allegory of writing that presents both its conditions of possibility and its limit and ruin.

Alonso follows a different but ultimately compatible path. He shows how the simple allegorical scheme (Santos Luzardo/civilization versus Doña Bárbara/barbarism) is complicated by the fact that the allegorical force is dispersed throughout the novel and is not necessarily focused on or reduced to the main characters. In the first place, the allegorical nature is not confined to the main characters. There are a number of other elements (the bull, the crocodile, Luzardo's and Doña Bárbara's men, the mare, and so forth) that also have to be read allegorically. For Alonso this poses two kinds of problems. First, there are now three levels of meaning in the novel instead of the two levels of "classic" allegory. For example, when Santos's llaneros kill the "*espanto del Bramador*," a famed and fearsome crocodile, it is implied that the crocodile refers to Doña Bárbara. What was formerly explicit content (Doña Bárbara as a metaphor for barbarism) now becomes latent content (with the crocodile now being the explicit content). This proliferation of levels introduces the risk of the reader no longer being able to distinguish between levels (an essential protocol for the correct reading of any allegory) or to clearly define where the allegorical dissemination stopped. Also, if anything in the novel seems to have an allegorical content, the novel runs the risk of overflowing (and ruining) the allegory as a closed system of signification due to the impossibility of unequivocally establishing the repertoire of signifying parts.

Alonso reads *Doña Bárbara* as an attempt to fix through interpretation this constant slippage of meaning (1990, 125). In fact, the novel is replete with interpretive performances of the law, of signs, of apparitions, of omens. The subjects of these interpretive performances constitute the entire cast of characters: Doña Bárbara herself (Gallegos 1929, 362), Santos (259–61), Míster Danger (241), the llaneros of El Miedo (276–77), and the llaneros from Altamira (181, 305). This slippage of meaning that the novel tries to stem is due to the fact that allegory in the novel does not function as it is supposed to; the excess of meaning contradicts the view that allegory comprises discrete, accountable elements. Alonso debunks the idea that *Doña Bárbara* is the monologic epic of the national letrado as cornerstone of the national project, and he thus allows us to read into the novel a struggle between cultural anxieties and disciplinary impulses.

Osorio, using another critical approach, returns to a "social" interpretation of the novel while trying to refute its purported Manichaeism. Instead of reading the novel as an allegory of writing (as González Echevarría does) or a failed allegory (like Alonso does), Osorio reads it as what we may call a dynamic allegory, in which the relationship between the terms within the allegory changes throughout the narration. In fact, he puts forward two divergent theses. In the first one, there would be an evolution from barbarism to civilization, metaphorized in the education of Marisela, the daughter who finally accedes to the pleasures and responsibilities of civilization. In the second theme, the relation is not one of evolution but rather of dialectic: "[T]he opposed terms of 'barbarism' and 'civilization' . . . should not be understood here as an irreducible antinomy, but as thesis and antithesis within a dialectic contradiction. The synthesis, to speak in Hegelian fashion, would be the cancellation and preservation of both, a new world that would unite the *reality* of the plains with the *ideals* of civilization" (Osorio 1995, 1570–71). This, of course, would be the new Venezuelan national culture. This synthetic drive would advance the ideology of transculturation put forward decades later by Rama within a developmentalist format.

The active element in this dialectic is Santos Luzardo as ethnographer/cultural arbiter and as one who differentiates "superstition" (relegated to barbarism proper) from "llanero culture" (the exalted bedrock of Venezuelan national culture). The latter comprises some llanero practices and views (e.g., the integration of the plain, the rodeo, branding, the crossing of the rivers, the fierce loyalty, etc.) but not others (cattle smuggling, nomadism, animism, etc.). It also comprises specific types of llanero personalities (Antonio being the prime example). The signifying matrix of this dialectic would be the marriage toward the end of the novel between Santos Luzardo and Marisela, Doña Bárbara's daughter, which operates as a populist symbolic suture between partners of very unequal power. Thus, "the fiction of elite control" needs a fictional grounding, namely "falling in love and getting married to the object of control" (Sommer 1991, 288). In these two cases the emphasis is on the fact that literature and/or letrado practices are the driving force behind the project of national consolidation, and in this respect the novel, as representative of a "new form of bourgeois ideology," is a "founding document" of twentieth-century letrado-led populism (Beverley 1987, 107–8).

My reading of *Doña Bárbara* follows González Echevarría's and Alonso's leads by using the tools of deconstructive analysis to address the topic of allegory in the novel. But instead of doing so by "changing the subject" and putting the topics of civilization and barbarism in second place behind a reflection on literature, I would like to deconstruct the national allegory in its own terms, reading *Doña Bárbara* as a (critical) reflection on violence and the relationship between violence and the agrarian order. Banditry will be the signifier that serves as the critical tool in my reading. It is my contention that barbarism (as a predicate of Doña Bárbara) cannot be properly understood without a consideration of banditry. Banditry is at the origin of barbarism, and it deeply informs its logic. In some respects, we could say that barbarism is (as in Sarmiento) the name for banditry when elevated to a principle of agrarian (dis)organization.

Bandits (who in the Orinoco doubled as river pirates) are the protagonists at the primal scene (to use Sigmund Freud's term) of barbarism, in which Barbarita undergoes the transformation from an innocent mestiza orphan who aspires to reach civilization to the "harmful one" (*la dañera*) and the "man-eater" (see the chapter of *Doña Bárbara* entitled "La devoradora de hombres"). Barbarita was an innocent teenage cook aboard a ship that traded in suspicious goods. It was on the ship that she met Asdrúbal, a wanderer from the city who was also employed as a cook. She immediately fell in love with the sensitive and well-educated man who taught her to read and write. Barbarita hopes to leave the ship with him and thus avoid being sold by the captain of the ship to a cruel jungle baron as another member of his harem. Asdrúbal is indeed her best hope for realizing her dream of a better, more civilized life. As for Asdrúbal, he intends to settle in a city and start working in a position more suitable to his capabilities. But fate intervenes: Asdrúbal is killed, and in a mutiny the crew of the pirate ship gang-rapes Barbarita (Gallegos 1929, 141–46).

After this scene Barbarita ceases to be the victim of bandits and becomes "a terrible woman, a captain of a gang of bandits, in charge of murdering whoever dares to oppose her wishes" (122). Banditry is thus what prevented the "natural" evolution from noble savage (which Barbarita was) to civilized woman. Banditry is what sets in motion the mechanism of revenge against males and greed that defines Doña Bárbara. Banditry is the original trauma that constitutes the scene for the face-off between civilization and barbarism.

But banditry is more than this. It is also the material foundation and the operational mode of the entire rural order in the Arauca basin, where cattle ranching and cattle rustling (*cachilapear*) tend to be confused with each other (233). El Miedo is "a safe sanctuary for any criminal [*facineroso*] who happens to arrive in Arauca" (204). Among those criminals there are the Mondragones, "three brothers, originally from the plains of Barinas. Because of their bravery and their many crimes [*fechorías*] they were nicknamed Onza, Tigre, and León. On the run because of crimes committed in the plains of that state, they passed into the state of Apure, and after marauding and rustling cattle for a while, they entered into the service of Doña

Bárbara" (204). The Mondragones are the spearheads in Doña Bárbara's strategy for territorial expansion. They lived on the boundary between El Miedo and Altamira, and they were the ones in charge of gradually and incessantly moving the landmarks that served to tell where one property ended and the other began (204). Melquíades complements the strategy of territorial expansion with highly skilled and specialized cattle rustling (usually cattle and horses from Altamira). When needed, he also renders his services as hired assassin (369). Melquíades's efforts at cattle rustling were aided by Don Balbino Paiba. He was Altamira's foreman during Santos's absentee period, and in collusion with Doña Bárbara he ran Altamira into the ground. He rustled cattle for Doña Bárbara (and for himself on the side) when he became Doña Bárbara's lover and the foreman of El Miedo. Paiba was a former highway robber, responsible for holding up and killing Carmelito in order to rob him of the load of heron feathers belonging to Santos Luzardo, thus precipitating the crisis that draws the conflict between Altamira and El Miedo to a resolution. The resolution occurs with Paiba's execution by Doña Bárbara's henchmen as a love present to Santos Luzardo (murders are the only "presents" that Doña Bárbara knows how to give) and then her ultimate disappearance.

Legal support for this scheme of large-scale banditry is provided by ño Pernalete, the town political boss and the only representative of the state in the novel. He too was a former bandit, responsible for the death of Carmelito's family. (They were landowners before ño Pernalete and his gang killed most of them and condemned the rest to poverty [271–72].) El Miedo and ño Pernalete work in perfect harmony, and the Law of the Llano (*Ley del Llano*), the sole legal framework that regulates relationships among landowners, was made (and enforced) according to Doña Bárbara's interests (258).

The ranks of El Miedo are made up solely of bandits under the stern rule of Doña Bárbara (a hiring practice that seems to have been common for llano landowners [Izard 1983, 17]). And the economic logic of the hacienda is not one of development of the productive forces of the land but one of ever increasing plunder. Doña Bárbara accumulates money in great quantities, but she never transforms it into capital. It instantly "disappears from circulation" (Gallegos 1929, 152) and is buried in some secret locale. The gold-filled gourds are a metaphor for the condition of money under Doña Bárbara's care: it is not capital but robber bounty (we should remember here, of course, the mythical buried pirate treasure). In this respect, the distance from Altamira could not be more telling, since Santos applies all of his financial gains to the capitalization of the hacienda. The most telling case is the plan to use the money from the sale of the heron feathers to fence Altamira with barbed wire: a fitting metaphor of money buried into production, and land transformed into capital.

Doña Bárbara is described throughout the novel as a sphinx (like Rosas) and a monster (like Conselheiro) because of her heterogeneous nature. El Miedo, the creature of Doña Bárbara, is no less heterogeneous, since the hacienda conflates a rapacious sense of land ownership with the nomadism inherent in banditry, hence Doña Bárbara's famous and purposely contradictory statement when her ambition for more territory was mentioned: "she would answer mockingly: —But I am not half as greedy as I am depicted. I am just satisfied with a bit of land, enough so that I can always be at the center of my property, regardless of where I might be" (translated in Alonso 1990, 132).

Santos Luzardo and Altamira seem to be opposed point by point to these attributes, since respect for the rule of law is what Santos strives to enforce, defining by it his relationship with the land (the novel is a long dispute over boundaries), with cattle (defining which cattle belong to whom), with men (his subordinates and allies as well as his competitors and enemies), with the market and with the state (his relationship with ño Pernalete), and above all, with violence (refusing to take matters into his own hands). The law as the signifier that distinguishes between forms of violence (legal violence as opposed to outlaw violence) is the defining mark upon which the allegory of civilization versus barbarism rests. No other marker divides the fields of contention so neatly, since class, race, gender, and rural/urban are signifiers that cut across this duality.

The problem is that the herald of civilization and enterprise in the llano is *defined* by the world of outlaw violence that Santos Luzardo explicitly repudiates. His entire "civilizing" effort is framed (both at its origin and at its destination) by banditry. If Doña Bárbara's wealth has a spurious origin (she seduced Lorenzo Barquero and then snatched the hacienda from under his feet [Gallegos 1929, 148–51]), the origin of Santos Luzardo's fortune is not much different. The Luzardo dynasty, whose last urbanite descendant is Santos, was founded through the use of violence. The first Luzardo was Don Evaristo Luzardo, "El Cunavichero," a nomadic llanero "who went around barefoot and using *guarrasí"* (131) and who took possession of the land with the same methods as the "bandit captain" (*capitana de una pandilla de bandoleros*), Doña Bárbara (122). When Luzardo goes to San Fernando to study the legal status of his lands in order to establish arguments to counter Doña Bárbara's de facto appropriations, he is forced to acknowledge that "after a meticulous analysis of the rulings in favor of the woman, he could prove that everything—bribe, embezzlement, open violence—had been remarkably easy for the boss of the Arauca. But he also discovered that all the abuses that had been committed against his property were possible because his rights to Altamira suffered from the flaws that the acquisitions made by men of prey always have, and his remote elder, Don Evaristo, El Cunavichero, was one of these men" (138). "The man of prey [Don Evaristo] despoiled the aboriginal settlers of their just domain [*aquella propiedad de derecho natural*], and when they tried to defend it, he exterminated them with fire and sword" (141). El Cunavichero is the equal of Doña Bárbara, in particular if we remember that violence against women and violence against land are equated in the novel. Doña Bárbara, in addition to having been raped, seems to have been the daughter of a rape: with regard to her, the novel mentions the violence of the "white adventurer on the dark sensuality of the Indian women" as well as his violence on the "virgin lands" (141).

Even though he speaks differently, Luzardo is keenly aware of this violence. When he accepts the spurious sentences of the judges as a "decided matter," Luzardo is implicitly accepting that he was not the victim of an injustice, since he cannot trace his property titles to a "just" origin from which the actual state of affairs would be a departure. Before the injustice of the fraudulent ruling of the judges, there was another injustice: the illegal appropriation of the land by the Luzardos. To consider the ruling a decided matter (*cosa juzgada*) is to acknowledge and erase the original violence of which the present corruption is only a derivation.

This view could be refuted by saying that Santos Luzardo's mission is to erase this legacy of violence from his identity. And this is reasonable from a subjective point of view. However, his identity as a "civilized bourgeois" is essentially linked to his class position (otherwise, he would be an equal to the well-meaning but innocuous Mujiquita, a former fellow student of Santos Luzardo now under the aegis of ño Pernalete: it is Luzardo's class position that allows him to be brave, unlike Mujiquita, who has to be a coward, since he needs the money ño Pernalete pays him). This class position, based on his right to his land, is as legitimate (or as illegitimate) as Doña Bárbara's since the titles to his land are based upon original violence. This original sin that goes to the very core of his class position can be forgotten (and Luzardo does just this as soon as he is aware of it), but it cannot be erased since it operates in a continuous fashion throughout the narrative.

This dynamic between forgetting and legitimation is implicitly acknowledged in the fact that Santos Luzardo upheld a law that he knew was illegitimate, since it was "polluted" by violence in each of its instances. *Doña Bárbara* is understood as a plea in favor of modernization, where modernization equals the rule of law. Time and again, Santos Luzardo shocks (and disappoints) his laborers when he fails to take action against Doña Bárbara's attempts against his property (robbery, arson, etc.). However, the Law of the Llano, the framework through which Luzardo tries to make good his land rights, is also called the Law of Doña Bárbara since it was tailored to fit her needs (263). Therefore, there is no real opposition between law and barbarism, since the law was born to enforce the "rights" of barbarism and banditry, and the right to dispossess others of land and cattle. There has to be a forgetting of the violent origin of any law, of any right, in order to argue for its enforcement, for its validity.

In the novel, the transition from nature to capital (culture) is the fencing of property with barbed wire. This particular property was the unmovable segment of land that was reflected in a land registry (according to state-enforced property rights), and fencing it would terminate the endless conflicts over its boundaries. The barbed wire would allow for an improvement of cattle breeds (*cruza de razas*) as well as an improvement in the quality of pastures. It would also do away with wild cattle (*ganado cimarrón*) and with a llanero culture based on the ranching of cimarrón cattle. Antonio Sandoval is leery of the project of fencing Altamira: "In spite of that, Luzardo kept thinking of the need to establish the custom of fencing. With it, civilization in the plains would begin. The fence would represent the triumph of rights against the all-powerful action of sheer might; it would represent the necessary limitation of man before principles" (233). But this symbol of civilization, of human self-restraint, is built upon a crime. Santos Luzardo plans to fund the fence that would definitively separate Altamira from El Miedo through the sale of heron feathers. The feathers, on their way to market under Carmelito's care, are stolen by Balbino Paiba without Doña Bárbara's knowledge. When she finds out, she tries to give Santos the ultimate proof that she is a new person, capable of good deeds. Consequently, she orders that Paiba be killed. Additionally, even though she knows the truth, she blames Paiba for the murder of Melquíades (Luzardo thought that he was personally responsible). At first, Luzardo is keenly (and painfully) aware of the consequences—in moral and legal terms—of his action, since it makes him an equal to any member of Doña Bárbara's gang, with a bloody oral reputation for bribery and ruthlessness (427). But, when the murder of Melquíades is covered up by Doña Bárbara herself and when Santos discovers that it was not he but his bodyguard who killed Melquíades (the bodyguard ambushed Melquíades from a tree, the very definition of the treacherous, cowardly murder), Luzardo decides to "forget" this crime, which was the basis of his triumph, just as the Delamars decided to charge "God's justice" with Santos Zárate's death.

The herald of civilization and the staunch defender of the rule of law as abstract concept, Santos does not hesitate to approve of this double crime and even to confess the scope of his cynicism: "In spite of the gravity of the situation, Santos could not help smiling: Pajarote's [Melquíades murderer] god, like the friend in ño Pernalete's story, had no scruples in twisting the law to suit his own purposes [*no le producían escrúpulos los puntos sobre las haches*]" (454).

The divide between civilization and barbarism is not the relationship between violence, property, and law, as Santos Luzardo likes to think in order to legitimize his position. He (and his family) as well as Doña Bárbara accumulated property through outlaw violence, and they held on to their properties in identical fashion by conniving with the same illegitimate authority (ño Pernalete) and by accepting the validity of the same spurious laws. Perhaps the only difference is that while Doña Bárbara rises to the challenge that her own actions pose and acknowledges that she is the intellectual author of her actions, Luzardo kills through his men and pretends that he is not responsible for those deaths (again we see the figure of Destiny as a thin veil of bad faith, as in *Zárate*).

Once Doña Bárbara and Míster Danger are eliminated and once all the land in the area belonged to Altamira, the barbed wire—as Danger acknowledged—seemed to be unnecessary since there were no neighboring properties to delimit the estate. But this is not the case. The purported symbol of respect for the law and the rights of others in a community whose cornerstone is the morality of the market becomes what it has always been: the symbol of monopolistic capitalism. Fenced Altamira continues to be the perpetual act of El Cunavichero's violence. It is violence against the rights of the llaneros, for whom ancestrally the land was undivided and freely traversable and cattle were free for the taking. Now, the violence among equals (landowners) disappears, but it is only the dawn of a new era of violence, one of class violence in which the status of the llaneros will be further depressed. (If during the feud between owners their alliance was necessary and sought out, this is no longer the case. They are no longer allies, just proletarians.)

Even though at the end Santos Luzardo defeats Doña Bárbara (in fact, Doña Bárbara retreats from the struggle that she could easily have won either by killing Luzardo and/or Marisela or having them killed), ño Pernalete remains the political boss of the area. What is more important, his wisdom is entirely validated by the denouement of the novel. Ño Pernalete's legal wisdom is summarized in the metaphor that he uses for the justice of the plains, *"poner los puntos sobre las haches"* (to dot the h's), alluding to the way the conflicts are resolved outside the law. Furthermore, the Law of the Llano remains firmly in its place. Why? Or more decisively, *Cui bono?* Santos Luzardo, obviously, is the one who benefits from the law. The dream of agrarian capitalism is still a dream tainted by violence. Ño Pernalete has always been a bandit who violated the law, but he is also the law enforcer of the area. The difference is that he is a bandit who does not threaten Luzardo, a bandit with whom "civilization" can live.

The way Santos and Doña Bárbara conduct their respective amorous relationships (we should not forget that, in typical nineteenth-century style, this political fable is cast as a romantic one, too) is, according to the narrator, one of the points where the differences between the two are clearest. However, the difference is not that decisive. Both Luzardo and Doña Bárbara are linked to the land through a possession that it is both sexual and economic. It is sexual first and economic only later. Doña Bárbara becomes the mistress of La Barquereña by seducing, completely draining, and ultimately overpowering the well-meaning, weak-willed Lorenzo Barquero. (The episode is impressive because Bárbara was a peasant girl with no means or power except her sexuality, and she was in a pitched battle for dominance with a young and educated landlord. Bárbara even warns Lorenzo of her intentions. The novel deems that a crime, although it is not that different from the career of other illustrious literary social climbers, such as Julien Sorel in *Le Rouge et le noir.*) Santos Luzardo is an adult landlord who has lived in Europe. He seduces Marisela, an illiterate girl barely out of puberty, who had never been in a city and almost never in a house, who has an alcoholic father incapable of protecting her from the lascivious advances of Míster Danger, and who has been neglected and even abused by her mother. The novel does not suggest that Santos is, in fact, taking advantage of a situation whereby it was very easy for him to seduce the naive girl and convince her that he was her knight in shining armor. Aside from Santos's sincerity, the real outcome of the romance is that Santos will legally become the owner of both Altamira and La Barquereña (the latter will disappear). The novel considers this a redemption. However, of the two situations where the sexual metaphor is cast as a metaphor for class alliances or struggles, the one in which Doña Bárbara offers her sexual appeal in a bid for dominance has better moral qualities: she was not taking advantage of a far weaker prey, as Santos was. The stakes were higher, and the choices for the opponent were certain. Marisela's education seems to replicate (and symbolically fulfill) Asdrúbal's education of Doña Bárbara, which was brutally cut short by the murder of the former and the gang rape of the latter. But there is a decisive difference: the relationship between Barbarita and Asdrúbal was one of equals (the only difference being knowledge). The relationship between Santos and Marisela is riddled with inequalities (class, race, and culture). Therefore, the idea that this is a return to a pre-violence stage proves again to be a myth.

In the final analysis, the allegory in *Doña Bárbara* is untenable because barbarism is the soul of civilization just as banditry is the soul of the rule of law, and no gesture of historical closure is able to leave that behind. Barbarism is not something lost in the remote past and superseded in the present; it is obscurely living in the present since it is the basis of present relationships. Civilization is instead a surface effect (and with this we return to *Os sertões,* in which Machado de Bittencourt's administrative prowess did not hide the fact that he was efficiently supplying the materials for a holocaust). Maybe it would be better to speak of barbarism in *Doña Bárbara* as a signifier with a double meaning. Barbarism refers to the original violence in the constitution of the agrarian order. This barbarism is unmovable because it goes to the core of that agrarian order once we take into account that it was responsible for the transformation of nature into capital. But barbarism also refers to a particular mode of being in agrarian capitalism. Barbarism is long-lasting feuds between capitalists, such as the one that divided the

Luzardos and the Barqueros (see the chapter entitled "El descendiente de El Cunavichero"). Barbarism is the accumulation of money when that currency does not become capital ready for investment: the coins (*morocotas*) that Doña Bárbara buries in some secret location (152), contrasted with the money from the sale of the heron feathers that allows for the purchase of the barbed wire that the llano does not produce. The quintessential nonproductive bandit treasure in literature is, of course, that of "Ali Baba and the Forty Thieves" (*Arabian Nights*). After the murder of the forty thieves, Ali Baba puts the treasure to good use, to rise "to high degree and dignities" (Burton 1897, supplemental volumes, 4:402). Significantly, Ali Baba never reflects upon the fact that the treasure is tainted with blood and violence (his killing of the bandits, and the killings performed by the bandits themselves) and that his respectability has an utterly spurious origin. Strikingly, neither does Luzardo in *Doña Bárbara*.

Feathers and barbed wire, exports and imports to and from the city mean a more solid integration into the national market. In this respect, the relationship between civilization and barbarism must be specified according to which barbarism we are talking about. This last meaning of barbarism can be dismissed when a superior form of capitalism triumphs and a national bourgeoisie takes over, superseding internecine struggles of the past. But the original gesture of the violent appropriation of nature remains active, and from this perspective civilization is only a derivative concept, a barbarism that does not speak its name. Civilization versus barbarism is then an opposition between two models (or two variations within the same model) of agrarian capitalism in which banditry is the common matrix to account for its origin and dominance. The image that ends the novel is a fitting (although unrealistic) representation of this: the llano, undivided as far as the eye can see. But this is no longer the virgin plain; the lack of limits bespeaks the limitless expansion of landed property, peaceful through the elimination of banditry, and the transformation of the llanero into a submissive cowhand of the new capitalist enterprise, which is led by the well-meaning but stern and enlightened national bourgeoisie. Maybe because of this, because Gómez knew that the novel ambiguously exalted what he represented and because he was never the rough peasant that he pretended to be, he liked the novel very much. After all, Gómez, like Doña Bárbara, only wanted "a bit of land, enough so he could always be at the center of his property, regardless of where he might be."

Conclusions
Representational Strategies and Paradigms

Three Representational Strategies

This book has provided a map of the conflict arenas where the bandit trope came to play a role (or, to use a different and perhaps more precise metaphor, this book has provided a map of the conflict arenas that the bandit trope came to embody). This study has endeavored to isolate three major ways that letrado elites depicted rural insurgency as banditry. I deemed the first strategy "Bandit as Other." In this mobilization of the trope, the bandit is a radical other, the sum of all fears of the lettered elite. As such, he has to be destroyed (what I called the "theater of law" as part of an "allegory of legitimation") for the national project to advance in any meaningful way. I called the second strategy "Bandit as Instrument of Critique." In this case, banditry is mobilized by a letrado agenda, but not as the despised and feared Other of the national project. In this case, banditry is more of a mediation through which the letrado engages in an intra-elite polemics with alternative political positions. The uses vary accordingly, and while this book does not pretend to have exhausted the possibilities, it did try to present a representative sample of possibilities from traditionalist conservative paternalism (as in Blanco), regionalism (Távora), "populism" (Hernández), to liberalism (Payno) and anarchism (Ghiraldo). The last strategy was dubbed "The Bandit as Devious Brother and as Suppressed Origin." In this case, the bandit, according to each particular need, is incorporated into the narrative of the origins of the nation-state as the origin of the violence of the nation state: he was the foot soldier in the independence wars (Lugones, Vallenilla Lanz), he was a revolutionary (Azuela), or a frontiersman (Gallegos). Ultimately, he was suppressed through the sublation of that violence in the "superior" realm of the nation-state, where bandit violence becomes the rule of law.

As this book sought to prove, all three of these strategies are riddled with internal contradictions. As radical other, as critical device, as legitimating device, the letrado depiction of banditry always intended to deactivate difference, to cancel banditry as the refractory core of Latin American reality. But this project always failed: time and again difference reappears, thus making all attempts at suture a failure. This dynamic between an attempt at suture and the reopening of meaning is responsible for the continuous dynamism of the bandit trope in Latin American cultural history.

A Representational Paradigm

A series of recurrent motifs appeared in the bandit narratives analyzed in this volume. These motifs are not unique to Latin American bandit narratives but appear also in Western narratives of outlaws from the Robin Hood ballads all the way to the *A-Team* television series (1983–1987) and the motion picture *The Matrix* (1999). Hobsbawm has cataloged a number of them, and it seems that their remarkable uniformity in time and space was the initial stimulus for his book *Bandits* ([1969] 1981, 9).[1] The motifs are as follows: (1) the social bandit starts his career because of an injustice against him. He is persecuted by authorities because of an act that, according to the norms of the peasant community, is not criminal (e.g., avenging an act against his honor). The inaugural act of the saga of the social bandit is then a crime, but one of which he himself is a victim; (2) the social bandit's mission is to right wrongs (*desfacer entuertos*). These may be the wrongs committed against him (vengeance) or against others (reparations); (3) he steals from the rich and is prodigal with the poor; (4) after his career is over, he can reenter his original community as a respected and authoritative member; (5) he does not kill except when it is just or necessary; (6) he is admired and helped by "his" people, whose material and cultural universe he shares; (7) he cannot be captured or killed, except when he is betrayed by a friend or a female; (8) he is invisible; (9) he is invulnerable; (10) he may have supernatural powers; (11) he is a staunch enemy of the local authority (justice of the peace, sheriff, political boss) that victimizes the community but not necessarily of the highest authority: the king, the caudillo, the president (Hobsbawm [1969] 1981, 42–56).[2] Some of these motifs are relevant to the Latin American case, while some of them are not. Some of them carry definite ideological weight. Some of them do not. However, I would like to provide here a specific representational paradigm (Hall 1997, 232–63) for the characterization of banditry that encompasses but far exceeds the repertoire of motifs enumerated by Hobsbawm.

The portrayal of banditry in the nineteenth century conjures up a number of orientalist motifs. Without giving in entirely to the concept of "internal colonialism" put forth by dependency theory, I believe it is important to note that the Latin American lettered city built an image of rural society (in particular of pastoral ones, the focus of my examination) using the same order of tropes that the intellectuals from the European metropolis used to construct the "Orient" as the object and prey of colonial adventures.[3] Time and again, we find comparisons between Latin American plains and Asian ones. Bandits are not rural rebels with specific ties to their cultural environment; they are Tatars, Bedouins, Huns, Arabs, or Mongols.[4] The rural societies of which bandits are a totalizing trope are not societies embedded in history. Like the oriental ones, they seem to be without history or to be only history (in a stasis outside time, politics, and progress). In the context of this study, these are two ways to assert the same thing: that rural societies do not belong to the present historical circumstance ideally characterized by "progress," and furthermore, they are not an object of knowledge by themselves but only a link in the previously established chain of remissions and analogies that ensures the fixation of their identity by "hooking them up" into a pre-existing paradigm. Sarmiento does this, for example, when comparing Artigas's montoneras with Asian nomadic tribes (Sarmiento 1845, 68).[5] Some intellectuals even tried to ground these analogies in science. The Argentine José María Ramos Mejía, in his masterpiece *Las multitudes argentinas* (1899), makes an attempt at a "comparative anthropology" by equating the rural populations of the Argentine pampas and the Litoral (present-day Santa Fé, Entre Ríos, and Corrientes provinces) with the rural populations of "ancient" Asia (200).

Between orientalism *proper* (the construction of Asia as the Orient that Edward Said famously studied) and the vernacular orientalism that we are proposing here, we can think of the mediation of the European travelers who in the nineteenth century also resorted to the analogy between rural Latin America and the Orient.[6]

Banditry is not considered a social phenomenon but a natural event. In bandit narratives, brigandage is metaphorized by what Guha calls "entropic metaphors" (1988, 46): swarms of wasps, packs of dogs or wolves, herds, ants, floods, earthquakes, erupting volcanoes, storms, clouds, or wildfires. By making banditry a catastrophe, a plague, a natural prodigy, the conflict that banditry enacts migrates from where it belongs (the political and economic order of social relations) into "natural history." Therefore, it makes conflict as such disappear. An eruption is not a conflict but an event, even an "act of

God." Naturalizing banditry as something that "grows" or "springs up" eliminates its agents as humans. It naturalizes the social order against which the rebellion is posed while suppressing the political dimension of peasant resistance that the bandit represents. More importantly, it hides the dimension of violence that the state repression of banditry entails (uprooting a weed is not violence: it is a procedure). This is a movement complementary to orientalism, in which difference is fixated and reduced when taken away from history, thus denying its political (contingent) character and the power relations that sustain it.

Bandits are monsters or wild beasts. Again, this point dovetails with the previous ones. The idea of the criminal as a monster vomited by nature is not new in the West (see Foucault 1975, 90). Caco, the mythological cattle rustler that Dante Alighieri (1265–1321) locates in the eighth circle of his *Inferno* (c. 1319), is perhaps the most illustrious of the bandits turned wild beast or monster. Caco was a shepherd (a common occupation for bandits), but Dante made him a centaur. (In this he may have had an antecedent in another illustrious bandit narrative, Apuleius's *Metamorphoses,* in which bandits are also compared to centaurs [see 1989, 197].) In the Latin American case, where the festive take on the bandit theme of Quevedo's *jácaras* is rare, the monstrosity of the bandit has little to do with his grotesqueness or ugliness (in many cases—such as the characters Jesuíno Brilhante, Juan Moreira, or Zarco—the bandit is depicted as extremely handsome, even as a deceptive model of masculinity). The bandit's monstrosity also has little to do with his cruelty or the character of his passions. This does not mean however, that the bandit is never depicted as ugly or grotesque (especially since he may be a mixture of human and nonhuman characteristics). But the key factor lies elsewhere. Monstrosity is the "maddening" of signs, orders, and distinctions that the "world upside down" of peasant insurgency presents (Guha 1983). It has to do with the bandit's flight from the state's *principium individuationis* (decisively linked to race during the nineteenth century). A single example will suffice: Zárate is indeed considered a monster or a wild beast (especially a tiger, a wolf, or a fox) not because of any excess or physical deformity (quite to the contrary, he was rather pleasant-looking), but because his race is impossible to determine. He terrorized the Tuy valleys, yet no one had ever seen him. The bandit is before or beyond humanity because, as in the case of Sarmiento, he rejects the order of determinations upon which the social rests. For the state, "subject" equals "subject of the law," and there is no conceivable exterior to this bi-univocal determination: the exterior is the inhuman.

At the end of the nineteenth century, this tropical order was entangled in the positivist repertoire of the criminal as an atavistic throwback to prehistoric times (as in the cases of Nina Rodrigues and Julio Guerrero).

In nationalist bandit narratives, banditry belongs before or outside time. In the cases that I examined, banditry brings to bear a particular relationship with the nation-state temporality that for nineteenth-century intellectuals was *temporality itself* vis-à-vis the stasis of barbarism, which lives outside time.[7] The synchrony (or painfully experienced lack thereof) between the time of the new nations and the time of Western progress is one of the axial topics of political thought in the Latin American nineteenth century: the trope of barbarism is one of the forms that this reflection assumes, with the bandit barbarian as a living anachronism.[8]

A particular imagination of time informs bandit narratives. Even those narratives that "sympathize" with the bandit (e.g., *Martín Fierro* or *Juan Moreira*) relegate the bandit to the past as a form of myth or folk residual sociability or to the future as a precursor or forerunner ("He came an age too late; / Or shall we say an age too soon?" ponders Wordsworth in the superb poem "Rob Roy's Grave" [1803–1807]). In the scene of the foundation of the state, the bandit dies or disappears at the hands of a character who represents modernity or statehood. Even under the form of the "noble robber" or "noble avenger" (e.g., Martín Fierro) the bandit is always expelled to an exterior or toward the past without communication with the present. The death of the bandit is imagined as an epochal turning point that inaugurates a new time. His survival, on the other hand (as in the case of *Zárate*), would imply either that the state accepts him as something that exists beyond its apparatus of capture or that the state is unable to obliterate him. In this last case, the monopoly of violence is a fiction and the state remains trapped in the time of banditry. This was the case for *Os sertões*, in which the impossibility of defeating the jagunços using the preferred European tactics made the army implode into "banditismo original."

Bandit narratives are male narratives that function as the reverse of the national romance. In all of the cases I examined throughout this book, banditry is a male phenomenon. This is not a matter of choice: bandit narratives are over-whelmingly male narratives that take place in a homosocial space (Phillips 1987, 184; Seal makes the same assertion for the Anglophone world [1996, 2]).[9] This does not mean that females are absent from such narratives but that they are denied agency: females are depicted as extensions of male identity and as such, they are either victims, pawns in all-male conflicts, or traitors to their male counterparts (in some cases, they are all three).

This assertion has a corollary: in foundational romances, love is an inte-grative metaphor whereby the offspring of the couple upon which the narra-tive focuses represents the continuation and consolidation of the national project into the future. In the case of bandit narratives, the romantic rela-tionship within the rural community is destroyed, and the son is usually lost. A state official (e.g., a military official, judge, or political boss) or a ha-cendado often rapes, kidnaps, or disgraces a female (sister, wife, or mother of a peasant or rancher) and provokes the transformation of peaceful peas-ant into fierce bandit.[10] This sequence of events cancels the possibility that the rural romance would become a national one and it would bequeath the bandit's cultural capital (e.g., nonstate legitimate violence) to the future of the nation. Bandit narratives are, just like romances, foundational alle-gories. However, the condition for the foundation is that the bandit dies without offspring, so that the future is not "contaminated" by him. That is to say, nonstate violence does not contaminate the future by laying claims to legitimacy.

Bandit narratives have a core scene: the bandit feast, which functions simultane-ously as a presentation and/or negation of rural/peasant cultural capital. As Guha indicates, when a peasant rises up against master or state, he does so in violation of time-honored, elite-enforced cultural codes. These codes de-fine his existence as a disadvantaged member of the rural community. In this context, "to rebel was indeed to destroy many of those familiar signs which he had learned to read and manipulate in order to extract a meaning out of the harsh world around him and to live with it" (Guha 1988, 45). Peasant rebelliousness, in addition to being a struggle for ownership or con-trol of resources, is "a world turned upside down" (in the Bajtinian sense of the word); it is not mere chaos but a political performance that parallels and challenges (though perhaps in a more ephemeral fashion) those elite per-formances of domination. Thus, peasant rebellion is reactive as much as affirmative. These peasant performances are not provident because they do not have an economic meaning (such as burning down a crop or feasting on the master's reserves) but a symbolic one: an egalitarian performance of re-covering one's own body, ridding oneself of the yoke of elite dominance. An-ton Blok, following E. P. Thompson, calls these expressions the "counter the-ater of the poor" (Blok 1998, 99). (In *El luto humano*, José Revueltas talks of an "empowering denial" implied in the wholesale revolutionary destruction of crops.)

To reiterate, bandit narratives are a theater of law. This theater, however, contains within itself a representation (and a cancellation) of the coun-tertheater of the poor. For instance, the nationalistic novel depicts the ban-dit feast that takes place in an alternative social space (the pulpería), a space snatched from high society (the hacienda ballroom), or a desecrated or de-filed space of high sociability (the church altar).[11] The representation of such spaces becomes a travesty or a transgression of the conventions of the let-tered order. This feast, of course, is for the intellectual the very image of chaos, barbarism, and degradation. Thus, bandit narratives are a presenta-tion of the countertheater of the poor as a key component of the peasantry's cultural capital. At the same time, however, these narratives deny it, regard-ing it as mere chaos and exiling the peasantry's cultural capital from culture.

Banditry suggests a specific relationship to territoriality that the elite bandit nar-rative cancels. Banditry implies a principle of territorial sovereignty opposite to and competing with that of the state (it is by nature asymmetrical to that of the state, as Guha correctly points out). Because of this, famous bandits have been nicknamed according to state positions: "El Rey de los Campos de Cuba," "O Rei do Sertão," "O Gobernador do Sertão." Some bandits, such as Lampião in Brazil, even issued passports or collected taxes from travelers, who carried the papers and paid the taxes in order to secure transit through bandit territory or to avoid being victims of vandalism.[12] Jean Ampère in *Promenade en Amérique* (1855) wrote that passengers traveling from the fed-eral district of Mexico decided to carry only a small amount of money due to the certainty that they were going to be robbed. This practice among travel-ers caused a crisis in the whole highway robbing system, but it proved to be a passing one. Shortly thereafter, a proclamation appeared on many walls in Mexico City, and in it a certain "Bandit General" threatened stern reprisals unless travelers started carrying sizable amounts of money on their trips.

From then on, a fee system was established whereby passengers were able to buy a safe conduct pass that, shown upon request, prevented them from being held up (López Cámara 1967, 234).

Facundo and *Os sertões*, two of the works that more decisively examined the relationships between banditry and state formation, are reflections on territoriality, not (or not only) in the romantic meaning of "landscape" but also as a locus that defies all attempts to represent it with conventional European methods. In this sense, bandit narratives are the opposite of *María* (1867), the exemplary novel by the Colombian writer Jorge Isaacs (1837–1895). *María* is the closest that Latin American literature would ever come to an English country house novel, in which rural society is represented through class lenses as a community of landowners and in which the peasantry is either landscape or folklore (Williams 1973). In bandit narratives, this romantic paradigm fails, and the backland is not a reservoir of gentle traditions but rather the stage of brutal battles for power and wealth. Bandit narratives enact a double gesture: they simultaneously summon and erase these struggles from national memories.

Bandit narratives imply a fundamental uncertainty of identity. This is a literary motif that may come from European literature, from Robin Hood, Rob Roy, or the border bandits in *The Monk*. It is invested with a political-cultural meaning in the Latin American case, however. There is always a strong possibility of an inversion of the two sides of the law, because banditry represents the fragile moment before the birth of the law, what Carl Schmitt called the "exception" that links the bandit as outlaw and the sovereign as outlaw. (Since the sovereign is the one who makes the decision about the exception, he is at the same time within and outside the law.) The bandit is thus a creature that belongs to two eras at the same time and that has the uncanny ability to move between them with incredible ease. Facundo Quiroga, in the case of Argentina, could have been a hero of the wars of independence or a founder of nations, but he ended up an outlaw (Sarmiento 1845). Páez was a "Bedouin chief," but he was also the father of the Venezuelan nation (Vallenilla Lanz 1919). The cangaceiro Cabeleira was a "great spirit who could have been one of the nation's glories if his boldness and his steadfastness had served noble causes before spurious interests and cruel necessities" (Távora 1876, 71). This shows the fluidity of the limits between law enforcement and law breaking, a cause of much contention and anxiety for elites. This anxiety is at the origin of most bandit narratives. (It is also a common literary motif—many times based on historical records, such as in the case of *Carmen*, by Prosper Mérimée.)

Although further discussions and more examples could probably be added to these pages, I am confident that they have made a contribution to a field of study that was always acknowledged yet had received scant critical attention. Ultimately, this book should shed some light on the anxious yet patronizing and fear-ridden relations between the lettered city and its others.

Notes

Introduction

1. "Lettered city" (*ciudad letrada*) was a term coined by Ángel Rama. It is a particularly useful hybrid that names, among other things, the cluster of institutions that depend upon the ownership or administration of the technology of the written word as a basis for their political power (e.g., the state; educational, artistic, or commercial entities; financial corporations; or the judicial system). It also names the cluster of individuals who obtain a differentiated social identity from their belonging to the aforementioned institutions: state officials, lawyers, notaries, priests, physicians, writers, journalists. The term also refers to the ideology and rituals that sustain this dominance, in particular the ideology that sustains the dominance of literature (in a wide sense that includes fiction, oratory, poetry, and political journalism) as a dominant practice within society.

The notion is critical to understanding the relationship between lettered practices and the state in Latin America, where writing was a "tightly regulated activity, through which the individual manifested his or her belonging to a body politic" (González Echevarría 1985, 44). It allows us to define a characteristic mode of formation and reproduction of the elite that crosses (without ignoring) class, race, and gender distinctions. This concept is also key to explaining the patterns of transformation and continuity of certain cultural paradigms from the colonial period to the present.

2. My approach to the monster as a cultural artifact is indebted to *Monster Theory*, by Jeffrey Cohen (1996).

3. I refer to Prieto's *El discurso criollista en la formación de la Argentina moderna* (1988); Ludmer's *El cuerpo del delito* (1999); and Gerassi-Navarro's *Pirate Novels* (1999). Other works have addressed the topic of the representation of banditry in literature. Among them are Cecilia Cartwright's dissertation, "The Cangaceiro as a Fictional Character in the Novels of Franklin Távora, Rodolfo Teófilo, and José Lins do Rêgo" (1973), and Giorgio Marotti's *Santi e banditti nel romanzo brasiliano* (1988). These are detailed and useful works of literary criticism, but they stand apart from the line of cultural criticism I am pursuing. Of course, some of the works that I analyze have a rich and complex critical tradition that will be taken into account in each respective analysis.

Of all these works, Gerassi-Navarro's *Pirate Novels* is probably the most similar to my own project. Like my own, *Pirate Novels* studies how outlaws as fictional characters became "metaphor[s] for the brutal struggles of the collective imaginings of a

nation" in nineteenth-century Spanish (or Latin) American literature (Gerassi-
Navarro 1999, 188). Banditry and piracy have been repeatedly linked and even identified by some of the foremost specialists in the field as related forms of nonstate violence (Shaw 1984, 7; Billingsley 1988; Tilly 1975b; Tilly 1985; Thomson 1994). In
American jurisprudence of the nineteenth century, both banditry and piracy were
considered crimes against humankind (Prassel 1993, 24). As characters in literary
works, bandits are called pirates and vice versa since they practice nonstate forms of
violence and thus claim a space of sovereignty. Thomas Gallant (1999) collapses both
forms of nonstate violence in the single denomination of military entrepreneur, and
he thus equates bandit's and pirate's roles in the global expansion of capitalism and
the formation of nation-states. In some languages (Greek, for example) pirates and
bandits are subsumed under a common denomination, and the oldest extant novel
of Western culture (*Callirhoe*, by Chariton) addresses them in an undifferentiated
fashion. I do not adhere entirely to that line of thought, since sea pirates and bandits
function in the text of Latin American culture in different ways. From colonial times,
the pirate serves the Hispanic empire as a metaphor for the Other (the Protestant
empires or the French). This Other is usually associated with another state (such as
England, France, or the Dutch republic). The bandit, however, defies the state from
within the state's territory, lacks any affiliation to another state, and moves outside
statehood in the modern sense (Thomson 1994). This distinction in the nature of pirate versus bandit as depicted in literature (and thus giving rise to two divergent paradigms of representation) distinguishes my work from Gerassi-Navarro's.

This distinction blurs in the case of river pirates. However, they seldom appear in
Latin American literature. The best known of those that do are the river pirates in *La
casa verde* (1965) by Mario Vargas Llosa and the Orinoco River pirates that gang-
raped Barbarita in Rómulo Gallegos's *Doña Bárbara* (1929). The trauma of this rape
transformed a formerly quiescent woman into Doña Bárbara, the fearsome "capitana
de una pandilla de bandoleros" of the Arauca Valley (Gallegos 1929, 122). With some
important exceptions, such as the Mexican Santanón, who robbed both on land and
on water, Latin America lacked groups of the importance of the outlaws of Cave-in-
Rock of the Ohio and Mississippi Rivers (see Vanderwood 1992, xx; Rothert 1996).

4. To say that the state labeled rebels as bandits is a generalization, an anthropo-
morphism, and ultimately an erroneous statement. In using this phrase, I am following the practices of a number of institutions, and these practices are not always coherent. However, due to the scope of the project at hand, I cannot dispose of the
concept. Therefore, I would like to follow Alan Knight's precaution: "My own worka-
day belief is that the utility of such concepts becomes apparent only as—and to the
extent that—they provide the machinery for making sense of concrete examples"
(1994, 25).

5. This split is a constitutional feature of all tropes of otherness, according to Stuart Hall (1997, 229).

6. I use the expression "bandit trope" following Laclau and Mouffe's idea that "synonymy, metonymy, [and] metaphor are not forms of thought that add a second sense to a primary, constitutive literality of social relations; instead, they are part of the primary terrain itself in which the social is constituted" (1985, 110). As such, social identities are constituted as tropes, something that Stuart Hall also perceived when he talked of "race as a signifier" in his 1997 film/video, *Race: The Floating Signifier*.

7. I take the term "popular illegalities" from Foucault's *Discipline and Punish* but use it in a somewhat different fashion than he does. For me the phrase means the wide repertoire of practices originally beyond the state's reach that the nation-state has to suppress or put under its control: hunting, transit, assembly, trade rights, land use customs, private retribution in the face of offenses, private resolution of feuds, and even routine appropriation of property (such as the Potosí's *kajcha* or the Ecuadorean *chugchi*). It is important to note that my adoption of the term does not imply an uncritical endorsement of the notion of the "people" as an analytical tool.

8. The Gabriel García Márquez novel *Cien años de soledad* (1967) presents a reductio ad absurdum of this process of labeling. When the workers of the unnamed banana company (a fictional version of the United Fruit Company) go on strike, the government predictably sides with the company, issues a decree whereby the strikers are declared a gang of thieves (*cuadrilla de malhechores*), and authorizes the army to kill them on the spot (the usual treatment reserved for bandits). The massacre at Macondo's train station (a rewriting of the 1928 historical massacre of the Estación de Ciénaga) ensues (422ff.). The strikers were obviously not bandits; they were not even peasants but rural proletarians and railroad workers. However, any attempt against private property, any affirmation of a right in the face of the state and capital, is deemed an illegal act and acted upon as such.

9. As ¡*Vámonos con Pancho Villa!* accurately shows, this change in their social status (from liberators to bandits) also triggers changes in their behavior: Villa becomes more paranoid, violent, and rapacious. This shift, in turn, further confirms their social standing as bloodthirsty bandits. Criminologists have called this dialectic between labeling and behavior triggered by labeling, in which labeling becomes a kind of self-fulfilling prophecy, "secondary deviance" (Johnson 2000, 167).

10. For a complete list of and discussion about these rules, see Foucault 1975, 94–101; for an analysis of the labeling concept, see Lamnek 1977).

11. Scott's distinction points to the ways in which elite and subaltern sectors in any given society interact and conceive key components of their social experience according to the context in which they are placed. The same rural status quo, for example, would be described by a peasant in rather different terms if the conversation is with another peasant (i.e., hidden transcript) or with a landlord or village boss (i.e., public transcript). Conversely, the realities of village economy are discussed differently among landowners or prominent villagers than between landowners and peasants. Popular bandit narratives generally belong to the public sphere, but they voice

concerns and desires that can be openly expressed as such only among the believers (hidden transcript). In this case, bandit narratives are a venue for the expression of political grievances that otherwise would be met with retribution by the elite.

12. Malverde is well known in Los Angeles and Chicago as well as in Culiacán—just like the narcotics that are cultivated in or transported through Sinaloa. As for Heraclio Bernal, Wald even ventures the hypothesis that he was the historical model upon which the figure of Jesús Malverde was based (2001).

13. For an ample account of the literary versions of Joaquín Murieta see Leal 1999 and Thornton 2003. For a consideration of Murieta within the tradition of Hispanic resistance in the United States see Stavans 1995, 1996.

14. "Humanos Mexicanos"—one of the most popular themes of the album *Mucho Barato* (1996), which gave instant celebrity to the Mexican hip-hop group *Control Machete*—is a celebration of Pancho Villa and popular insurgency against the United States and its immigration policy. This celebration comes long after the image of Villa had been expropriated for exclusive use in PRI mythology.

15. A little-known predecessor of Hobsbawm was Constancio Bernaldo de Quiros. In his book *El bandolerismo en España y México* (1959) he highlighted three of the features pertaining to banditry that Hobsbawm (who knew and quoted his work) would express in a more programmatic fashion: (1) the relationship between banditry and agrarian social conditions, (2) the "social" character of banditry, and (3) its importance as a cultural phenomenon. An even more important predecessor of Hobsbawm (although this point has never been noted, at least to my knowledge) is Jorge Amado. His novel *Seara vermelha* (1948), fashioned after the then-mandatory prescriptions of socialist realism, features the story of Lucas Arvoredo (a fictional version of Lampião), as well as that of the Beato Estevão (in turn a fictional version of Antônio Conselheiro). Amado unequivocally presents them as "primitive," "prepolitical" rebels who legitimately resist the advances of capitalism and the state but lack class consciousness, and therefore they resist (and fail) using their premodern cultural capital.

16. To my knowledge, there is no sound approach to Latin American banditry from a criminological perspective. Dretha Phillips (1987) attempts to tackle the issue, but her article is inconclusive. She accurately shows how most criminological theories are either redundant or inappropriate when addressing Latin American banditry, but she fails to provide an approach of her own. In this volume, I resort time and again to the term "labeling." This usage is not to be construed as an undivided allegiance to the labeling approach. However, I think that it is the most constructive way to address the topic since the labeling approach focuses on the social and cultural conflict implied in the process of defining banditry from the state's perspective (which is key in Hobsbawm's definition). In addition, the labeling approach avoids the hierarchy implicit in the idea of "subculture" (something that revisionists inadvertently adopt) since it would link banditry to peasant culture, thus not regard-

ing it as a degraded or anomalous version of mainstream culture. Labeling theory allows us to see how banditry is a key moment in the political conflict that creates the contingent divide between "culture" and "subculture."

17. In the literature of Spain's golden age (e.g., *El peregrino en su patria* [1604] by Lope de Vega or *Los cigarrales de Toledo* [1623] by Tirso de Molina), there is a distinction between the *bandolero*, which, like Hobsbawm's *haiduk*, was endowed with certain political clout and often led by nobles seeking redress for grievances, and the *salteador*, the free-wheeling highway robber looking for profit.

18. In the field of Latin American studies, Richard Slatta's *Gauchos and the Vanishing Frontier* (1983) and his remarkable edited volume *Bandidos: The Varieties of Latin American Banditry* (1987) should be mentioned. Vanderwood's classic volume *Disorder and Progress: Bandits, Police, and Mexican Development* (2nd ed. 1992) should also be mentioned, as should Linda Lewin's article, "The Oligarchical Limitations of Social Banditry in Brazil: The Case of the 'Good' Thief Antônio Silvino" (1979), and Peter Singelmann's article, "Political Structure and Social Banditry in Northeast Brazil" (1975).

19. In *Domination and the Arts of Resistance* (1990) Scott replaces the value-laden term "pre-political" with the term "infra-politics," in which "infra" does not stand for "being inferior to" but rather as "having a hidden or half-hidden existence in adverse contexts."

20. This is one of the ways in which Pier Paolo Portinaro understands the sometimes uneasy equilibrium in the relationship between state and society. He proposes an apt formula: "the state is at the same time the subject of high politics and the neutralizer of low politics" (1999, 35).

21. I am indebted to Adela Gutiérrez for most of the information pertaining to Isidro Velázquez.

22. Thompson puts forth the notion of "theater of law" in his study of the Blacks, a notorious band of poachers composed of peasants and yeomen engaged in a struggle for hunting and transit rights against a sector of the English nobility during the eighteenth century. The dispute was of an economic nature. The nobles wanted to impede the common exploitation of game, wood, and fruit, all of which were essential to the survival and viability of peasantry as a class. However, a fascinating feature of the conflict was that it did not have a strictly economic dimension. Thompson reconstructs what he calls "the counter theater of the poor." This countertheater of the poor was based upon anonymous letters, vandalism, and poaching that had only defiance (not gain or nutrition) as its goal: "The plebs asserted their presence by a theater of threat and sedition. . . . [T]hey were part of the counter theater of the poor. They were intended to chill the spine of gentry and magistrates and mayors, recall them to their duties, enforce from them charity in times of death" (1974, 400). Against the peasantry's both real and symbolic challenge, the nobility erected a carefully devised dramatic style whose purpose was to symbolically reinforce its domi-

nance. Executions, pomp and circumstance, exhibitions of might, and buildings were all part of a conscientious theater of law.

Anton Blok, in his illuminating examination of the cultural aspects of banditry in the Lower Meuse Valley and its repression, reactivates the notion. He states, "Confronted with massive and sustained forms of subversion, members of the ruling class, loosely tied together in a regional network of kinship and marriage, restored their domination through the theater of the law, drowning the voices of insubordination in the process. In this assertion of cultural hegemony, the courtroom, the place of detention, the street and the place of execution provided the setting for the emphasis on and the distinction between the integral body, on the one hand, and the violated, dishonored, and decaying body, on the other—a distinction that served the restoration magically as *pars pro toto*" (1998, 105).

23. For some, the very expression "modern state" is a pleonasm, because no previous political synthesis can be properly called "state." For a good summary of this debate, see Portinaro 1999, 29–33. On one side of the debate stands Brunner, for whom the state is synonymous with nation-state (and modernity), while others, such as Anthony Giddens and Heinrich Mitteis, acknowledge the existence of different models of states (or as Mitteis prefers, "states-in-becoming") since the Middle Ages (Portinaro 1999, 29).

24. Examples outside Latin America or the Hispanic world are no less telling. As Nathan Brown explains in the case of nineteenth-century Egypt, "The definition of banditry as a national problem was an integral part of state building in Egypt. . . . Banditry as a national problem was invented as a political weapon by Egypt's rulers as a part of the process of creating a stronger, centralized state apparatus and as an effort to keep that apparatus out of British hands" (1990, 259–60). When Britain occupied Egypt in 1882, "the 'Commissions on Brigandage' constituted an attempt by the Egyptian government to retain a measure of control over state building, to ensure that Egyptians would still control law enforcement and local administration even as the British occupied the country" (271). In a move unforeseen by the "inventors" of Egyptian banditry as a national issue, the British used precisely the "bandit problem" as a reason to fully intervene in all aspects of the administration (277).

25. Barrington Moore, in *Social Origins of Dictatorship and Democracy*, maintains that European feudalism was basically organized gangsterism guided by plunder as a goal, which became a posteriori a model of social organization (1966, 214). This is a statement that Salustiano Moreta (1978) confirms in the case of Spanish feudalism, while Gilles Deleuze and Felix Guattari in *A Thousand Plateaus* conceive pillaging bands (bandits or pirates) as a model for all organizations, from prehistoric nomadic bands to postmodern multinational corporations (1980, 367).

26. "Order" and "chaos" are not inherent qualities or facts but political perspectives on them. "Chaos" at the national level can mean "order" and even prosperity at the local level. Florencia Mallon provides a compelling example in the Mexican con-

text. The Reform Wars (1857–1861) and the subsequent war against the French intervention and empire (1861–1867) were unique "political opportunities" (McAdam, McCarthy, and Zald 1996) that indigenous and mestizo communities of the Puebla sierra took in order to create a "popular" form of liberalism. The elite had to negotiate with this "popular liberalism" in order to obtain essential military support. "Chaos" for these communities meant the possibility of articulating their own political project and carving a niche in regional politics. "Order," on the other hand, meant for them the beginning of the end since pacification allowed for increased state encroachment and the decline of their military importance, which meant the end of their relative autonomy and bargaining capabilities. The same case could be presented in Tomochic, where a state of perpetual warfare against the Apaches meant for the military colonies of Chihuahua a sizable degree of autonomy that disappeared as soon as the Apache threat was over.

27. In the Anglo tradition, there was a legal framework for this type of exceptional state dating back to medieval times. One example is the adaptation of the New South Wales Felons Apprehension Act that the Victorian parliament passed in order to pursue Ned Kelly (an Australian bushranger of the late 1870s). Under the provisions of the act, "those proclaimed as outlaws could be shot on sight by anyone at all. Anyone suspected of harboring or aiding outlaws could be arrested and presumed guilty on the unsupported allegation of another person" (Seal 1996, 152).

28. Aijaz Ahmad's criticism of Jameson's rhetoric of Otherness may be the most famous of all. It can be summarized as (1) the epistemological and political incongruence of a theoretical construct such as "third world literature"; (2) the lack of theoretical value in a "world theory"; (3) the impossibility of sustaining the idea that conceives the third world/first world relationship in exclusive terms of otherness; (4) the inadmissible homogenization of the cultural and economic specificity that the very notion of "third world" implies; (5) the erroneous idea that the "third world" is massively dominated by a single ideology (nationalism) by its corresponding cultural form (national allegory); (6) the lack of acknowledgment that in the so-called "first world" a large proportion of the fiction written—especially that written by minorities—could be ascribed to the "national allegory" model (which would invalidate the idea of national allegory as an aesthetic mode pertaining to the "third world," or the distinction between first and third world altogether); and (7) the simplistic mode by which Jameson outlines the dialectic that links the social and the literary.

Chapter 1 | *El periquillo sarniento*

1. The metaphor upon which the novel rests (the sovereign-as-father) had a long colonial lineage. It is part of the larger trope of the kingdom as family, where the "Mother Church" completed the parental couple (Taylor 1996). For the topic of genealogy in Lizardi's work see Stolley 1994.

2. See Spell 1971; Goic 1982; Rama 1984; Benítez-Rojo 1996; Moraña 1997a; Vogeley 2001.

3. For the *arrastraderito* as a political metaphor, a cornerstone of Fernández de Lizardi's critique of the colonial lettered city, see Dabove 1999.

4. Unlike the literary concoction of the bandit gang as a highly organized and stable armed group with a deep sense of identity (mirroring "straight" institutions or groups), historical gangs were usually composed in a haphazard fashion, and prison relations ran high among recruitment mechanisms. Most bands were extremely loose knit and constantly changing. As contemporary Acordada officials tell us, they were more like events than organizations (Taylor 1982, 46–47). For a similar assertion in the Chilean and Argentine cases, see Pinto Rodríguez 1991 and Fradkin 2005, respectively.

5. For an examination of labeling in the context of peasant insurgency in nineteenth-century Mexico (when rebellion is labeled as banditry), see Vanderwood 1992.

6. For the complex relationship that Lizardi had with censorship and the Church, see Spell 1971.

7. This idea of banditry as passage can be further proved in *El periquillo sarniento*. To begin with, access to the bandit hideout implies the descent into a "deep gorge" (5:31). Also, at a certain point in the narrative, Perico realizes that the gang is doomed and that he should try to quit this most compromising company. He cannot, though, because he ignores the way back to the highway and to Mexico. Even though Mexico City and the Río Frío hideout are close in "literal" spatial terms, Perico states that between them lies a "haunted labyrinth" that he cannot traverse (5:40). The measurable literal distance is then turned into the symbolic infinite distance of the labyrinth, a motif of passage par excellence (Eliade 1960).

8. This image does not lack motivation. Beyond the royalist image of the bloodthirsty marauder or the nationalist image of the ideal-driven guerrilla fighter, Eric Van Young has pointed out that rural insurgency in many cases had an isolationist character and a goal of developing community-based "mini-utopias" (Van Young 2001). Archer points out how, by the mid-1810s (exactly when *El periquillo sarniento* was published), the war had reached a stalemate and "Royalist soldiers entering insurgent territories were surprised to discover peaceful farming operations and a tranquil rural life enjoying pre-Revolutionary calm" (1982, 84–86).

9. Jefferson Rea Spell, in the classic Porrúa edition of *El periquillo sarniento*, provides a different version of this sonnet. However, the variations do not change the basic idea of the scene: the idea that Januario's corpse has to be read (or listened to) because it conveys a message. For a comparison among all early editions of the novel, see Spell 1963.

10. That this is an "ethnography" of a bandit society, and not one of the practice of robbery itself, is proven by the fact that there is no robbery depicted in the

episode, except for the attempted one that destroys the band. The inner workings of bandit society are what concern (in both senses of the word) the narrator.

Chapter 2 | *Facundo*

1. See, for example, a very similar scene (reference to Salvatore Rosa and all) in the story of the painter that is told in *The Italian Banditti*, by Washington Irving (included in *Tales of a Traveller*).

2. See the scene of the deciphering of Sarmiento's departing message: "On ne tue point les idées" (Sarmiento 1845, 4).

3. For later articulations of the civilization/barbarism paradigm in Argentine political culture up to the present, see Svampa 1994. For a history of the reception of *Facundo* as a cornerstone of Argentine culture, see Sorensen Goodrich 1996.

4. Sarmiento revisited banditry throughout his entire career. In his later works, such as the reports that, as president (1869–1874), he delivered to Congress, banditry was merely a problem of rural security that a thriving state was able to face with increasing effectiveness and resources. Sarmiento equates the progress in the repression of cattle rustlers and highway robbers to the increase in customs revenue, army reforms, the expansion of the railroads, and the resolution of the Paraguayan War. In his travel narratives, banditry is an opportunity to indulge in some local color (fear of bandits and tales of bandits would dispel the boredom of a stagecoach trip) or to condemn the backward culture of Spain (see the letter to Lastarria dated November 1846 in *Viajes por Europa, Africa y América* [1909]). Banditry could also be a metaphor for lost opportunities in the project of civilizing the region or social decline under the Federation (see *Recuerdos de provincia* [1850]). In Sarmiento's writings it could also be the symptom of a turbulent political situation, such as the one in Chile or Peru during the 1870s (see his doctrinal and journalistic articles), or even a metaphor for the "language wars" that accompanied the civil war, in which federalists devoid of political ideology ransacked Unitarist political capital.

5. In the journal *El grito de los pueblos* (1839), we can repeatedly see the image of Rosas stabbing the *Patria*, allegorized in the classic image of a woman (Moro 1974). This motif will persist in *Amalia* (1851), by José Mármol, as well as in *El matadero* (1839–1840, published 1871), by Esteban Echeverría, in some exile dramas (*Rosas*, by Pedro Echagüe) as well as post-Rosas narrative (e.g., the cycle of novels on Rosas by Eduardo Gutiérrez, or *Los misterios del Plata* [1846] by Juana Manso) and drama (*La divisa punzó: drama histórico en cuatro actos* [1923], by Paul Groussac).

6. Sarmiento clearly perceives that excess, vis-à-vis pre-existent representation paradigms, cannot be adequately depicted through a European lens. This is why he mentions that the most cunning politicians of France "have not been able to understand anything of what their eyes have seen, when hurriedly glancing over the American power that challenged that great nation. . . . South America in general, and the Argentine Republic among them, lacks a Tocqueville who[,] armed with the knowl-

edge of social theories, like the scientific traveler of barometers, octants and compasses, would come to penetrate the depths of our political life, as in a huge field as of yet neither explored nor described by science" (1845, 9).

7. Sarmiento—without a hint of irony—speaks of the elections that put Rosas in office, this time giving him the Suma del Poder Público (1835): "There never was a more popular government, one more desired or supported by opinion. The Unitarists, who had had nothing to do with the entire affair, received him, at least with indifference; the Federalists 'lomos negros' with scorn, but without opposition, the law-abiding peaceful citizens expected him as a blessing. . . . [U]nder such happy auspices, the elections, or rather ratifications began in all parishes, and the polls were unanimous, except for three votes that opposed the delegation of the *Suma del Poder público*. Is it possible to imagine how, in a province with four hundred thousand inhabitants, as the Gaceta tells, there were only three votes contrary to the Government? Could it be the case that dissidents did not vote? Not at all! There is no record of any citizen not going to cast his vote[;] even sick people got out of bed to go give his agreement, fearful that their names be recorded in some black registry" (1845, 204).

8. For the lineage of the euphemism "people," meaning the elite, see Guerra 2003.

9. Caudillismo would leave a deep imprint on Argentine culture. Indeed, the debate over the gaucho bandit (*gaucho malo*) and the caudillo as the natural political derivation of gaucho lawlessness was at the origin of Argentine sociology, historiography, and criminology. Vicente Fidel López (*Historia de la República Argentina, 1883–1893*) insists on the fact that caudillos should be considered out-and-out criminals (Buchbinder 1998, 36–37). C. O. Bunge even labels the entire period between 1820 and 1861 as the "era of banditry" (*tiempos del vandalaje*) (1913, 241). The "era of brigandage," he assures us, left its mark on national politics (*política criolla*) and is the reason for the difficulties of the nation-state. Similar condemnations of the *política criolla* that link rural banditry and statehood can be read in Roberto Payrós's novel *Las divertidas aventuras del nieto de Juan Moreira* (1910) and Florencio Sánchez's essay "El caudillaje criminal en Sudamérica" (1903).

10. Nominally under the authority of the Spanish Crown, the area beyond the Río Negro was sparsely populated and imperfectly controlled. Claimed also by the administrators of the missions, it was prey to marauders from Rio Grande do Sul, and it was, above all, the place where nomadic Indians (*charrúas* and *minuanes*) lived (Chumbita 2000, 59).

11. Contrary to these postulates, Ricardo Salvatore (2003) and Jorge Myers (1995) for the Argentine case and María Inés de Torres (2000) for the Uruguayan case show how Rosas and Artigas based their hegemony upon the active and clever use of the written and the printed word.

12. This perception of Rosas as the founder of a state—even if an anomalous one, according to Sarmiento's standards—contradicts the later classical liberal perception

of the period between 1820 to 1852 as alternatively "Anarchy"/"Tyranny," a dark interregnum between "Independence" and "National Organization" (Salvatore 2003).

13. Taking this single action is just a sample of the entire modus operandi of the Federation, he concludes: "Rosas's system consists of making the Republic into a huge sack whose opening he has in his hands." This image is truly classic. The engravings in anti-Rosas publications printed in Montevideo (such as *Muera Rosas!* or *El grito de los pueblos*) promote this motif. In these engravings, Rosas and his cousins, the Anchorenas, appear as robbers receiving citizens' contributions in either a sack or a safe (see Moro 1974).

14. For a study of Sarmiento's "invention of the desert" as a physical expression of a post-revolutionary political and institutional vacuum, see Botana 1994 and González Echevarría 1990, 114. Recent studies on the nineteenth century have accomplished a threefold reformulation of the idea of the pampas: (1) they destroy the image of the pampas as a "desert" (Garavaglia 1999); (2) they refute the traditional image of the poor rural population as mostly comprising vagrant gauchos always on the brink of outlawry (Garavaglia 1999) and the no less pervasive image of rural Buenos Aires as divided between dispossessed gauchos and powerful ranchers (*estancieros*) (Gelman 1998); and (3) they disavow the prejudice of the montoneras as composed mostly of seminomadic shepherds (de la Fuente 2000). To the contrary, there is growing evidence that peasants made up a significant portion (even the majority) of rural folk and of the montoneras. Therefore, the notion of the "desert" as a void and its population as anomic has to be understood as a construction with clear ideological purposes.

15. For Rousseau, the impossibility of isolated individuals providing for their primary needs is the very origin of society: "As soon as a man's needs exceed his faculties and the objects of his desire expand and multiply, he must either remain eternally unhappy or seek a new form of being from which he can draw the resources he no longer finds in himself. . . . Since man cannot engender new forces but merely unite and direct existing ones, he has no other means of self-preservation except to form, by aggregation, a sum of forces. . . . This is the fundamental problem which is solved by the institution of the State" (Rousseau, *The Geneva Manuscript*). In "What Is the Third State?" Sieyès indicates that for the nation to survive and prosper it needs private activity and public services (Rousseau and Sieyès quoted in Dabhour and Ishay 1997, 35). This is the "invisible hand" of the market that, since Adam Smith's succinct description, has been hailed as the most efficient community building mechanism by nineteenth-century liberals, since, as Montesquieu stated in *De l'Esprit des lois*, commerce was "the profession of equals" and the great maker of democracies.

16. The Banda Oriental in Sarmiento's later work (*Conflictos y armonías*, 1885) is the most striking example of this process in which banditry is rampant and encompasses entire modes of sociability. In this text, cattle gave origin to an entire "civi-

lization" based on leather, which was used as the primary material for everything from riding gear to housing. This lack of demand for products other than those that the land could produce is the material condition for barbarism.

17. Sarmiento made the municipality the core of the political arrangement, as he argued in *Conflictos y armonías* (1885).

18. As the episode of the tiger in the beginning of Facundo's biography shows, violence begets identity: it is Facundo's killing of the tiger that gives him the surname El Tigre de los Llanos. This surname will follow him throughout his entire political career (see an extensive examination of this episode in González Echevarría 1990, 120–25).

19. Thus, Rosas's role as a gaucho invalidates his leadership. On the other hand, federales used this condition as the cornerstone of his reputation and to construct an image of republican simplicity through him. See, for example, Luis Pérez's *Biografía de Rosas* (1830).

20. "Under all circumstances War is to be regarded not as an independent thing, but as a political instrument" (Clausewitz 1832, 121).

21. I do not agree with Scavino's approach to the topic. However, he must be credited with being one of the first (at least, to my knowledge) to address *Facundo*'s paradigm of civilization/barbarism with regard to different ways of waging war.

Chapter 3 | El Chacho Peñaloza

1. For the ideological value that Sarmiento gave to dress, one example will suffice. He recounts in *Campaña en el ejército grande* that "[a]s it happened, I was the only officer in the Argentine army that during the campaign sported a uniform strictly modeled after European fashion. Saddle, stirrups, shiny sword, levita all buttoned up, gloves, French quepi, paltó instead of poncho, my entire person was a protest against the gaucho spirit, what at the beginning was an opportunity for some jokes on me. . . . This, that may look like a trifle, was part of my campaign plan against Rosas and the caudillos, followed to the letter, discussed with Mitre and Paunero, and willing to see it triumph if I remain in the army. As long as the clothing of the Argentine soldier does not change, there will be caudillos. As long as the chiripá exists, there will not be citizens" (1852, 169). For an in-depth examination of the topic of dress and nation formation in nineteenth-century Argentina, see Hallstead 2005.

2. This is why, when Chacho rises up against the national government in 1863, in what would be his last fight, Sarmiento responds with an address to the people of San Juan: "Fellow citizens: Peñalosa [sic] has shed his mask. From the estancia of Guaja, aided by half a dozen unknown barbarians who have made their political apprenticeship at highway crossroads, he intends to rebuild the Republic based on his own blueprint, under the model of the llanos" (1867, 337). And in a proclamation to the people of La Rioja he stated, "The expeditions conducted by these vandals have been severely punished everywhere and now the criminals return to seek refuge in

La Rioja, in order to escape just retribution. Fellow citizens of La Rioja: Peñalosa, you know it well, is too stupid, corrupt, and ignorant for any people or political faction to lend him support. He could be a bandit, but never the leader of a party" (1867, 345).

3. This rejection of Sarmiento's memory, summarized in the Olta assassination, was one of the few points of accord between the extreme right and the extreme left in the 1960s. Both sides claimed to be heirs of Peñaloza's legacy of popular insurgency. In both cases, the montonera endowed each political wing with their symbols and names (the right wing group was called "Tacuara," while the left-wing one was called "Montoneros").

4. De la Fuente tells a different version of this story (2000, 12).

5. The dire poverty of La Rioja made the payment and the maintenance of a legislative body in session nearly impossible for a significant portion of the year. Also, the lack of lawyers or other competent professionals made it impossible to have a fully functioning judicial body or a significant police force (de la Fuente 2000). To appreciate the differences between Buenos Aires and La Rioja a single example may suffice: the 1859 Buenos Aires budget was 187 times the budget of La Rioja—and La Rioja ran a budget deficit that amounted to almost half its allocations, which almost doubles the difference (de la Fuente 2000, 17–18).

6. For the chronic dependence of nineteenth-century Latin American states on import-export duties and the consequences of that dependence when it comes to the process of nation-state formation, see Centeno 2002, 135–37.

7. Also, just like in the classic stories of social bandits, Chacho is captured and executed only because he was betrayed. The Judas in this case is Vera—Chacho's relative—who goes to his hideout to offer him the guarantees that the government was willing to grant if Chacho surrendered. In La muerte de un héroe, Vera's role as a traitor is unequivocal. The historical record, notwithstanding, is more ambiguous when it comes to the role of Vera in the events leading to Chacho's death. Vera's depositions blame Major Irrazábal entirely (Torres-Molina 1997, 256).

8. In La Rioja in 1858, "the two provincial agencies of public order [the Department of Police and the Barracks of the Garrison] had a force of twenty-eight at their disposal. Their meager allotment allowed for the upkeep of three horses between the two agencies" (de la Fuente 2000, 19).

9. In El Chacho, Sarmiento expresses the same concept: "The laws of war between two nations favor the people when they deny the authority of the established government, but this is not without conditions. These people have to be represented by regular (even revolutionary) governments, defended by standing armies, and shown political goals, such as desire for independence, the overthrow of tyranny, etc. When the uprising does not assume this form, the act can be qualified as riot, mutiny, sedition, etc." (1867, 389).

Chapter 4 | *O Cabelleira*

1. In the nineteenth century, the designation *sertão* included all backlands of sparse population where premodern patterns of social organization prevailed (Gomes de Almeida 1981, 47). In a similar fashion, the term "desert" was used in Argentina to describe some of the most fertile lands on the planet. In Brazilian literature, for example, all rural areas were called sertão. This practice notwithstanding, in these pages sertão refers exclusively to the arid backlands of the Brazilian northeast.

2. *O Cabelleira* freely embellishes a cursory mention of this cangaceiro that appeared in book X, chap. III of *Memórias históricas da província de Pernambuco* (1844), by José Bernardo Fernández Gama, as well as in some pieces of popular poetry.

3. The other two are *O matuto* (1878) and *Lourenço* (1881). These two later novels (which can be read as a single narrative) tell the story of the so-called "War of the Mascates" (1710–1711), a military, political, and economic conflict between the landowners (*senhores de engenho*) from Pernambuco against the commercial class (*mascates*), mainly comprising Portuguese citizens who were the commercial and financial leaders among Recife's bourgeoisie (Cabral de Mello 1995). In the 1903 Garnier edition of Távora's *Um casamento no arrabalde* (originally from 1869), the title page mentions this novel as the fourth book of the Literature of the North, but I consider this notation to be a commercial gimmick more than anything else, since the book was written and published before the program was fully formulated (even though the novel contains early expressions of the need for a Brazilian cultural turnaround vis-à-vis its relationship with European culture).

4. Távora's novels take place in Pernambuco. By this token, the North would be coextensive with the later geopolitical category of the northeast. However, at that time, the north also included areas from Maranhão to the Amazonas. The "northeast" is an invention of the late nineteenth century.

5. For *patrimonialismo* in nineteenth-century Brazil within the network of clientelism that defined political relations, see Graham 1990.

6. Only secondarily did the patricians or the mascates, and even more secondarily, some women, intervene. However, the image that Távora puts forth of this violence cannot be separated from the class positions that this conflict reinforces or questions vis-à-vis the traditional sugar mill.

7. Lourenço's modus operandi eerily replicates that of Valentão-da-Timbaúba (see Távora 1878, 18 and 22). Actually, Francisco, the muleteer who captures Lourenço, thought that Lourenço, moving like a shadow between the muleteer's animals in order to steal from the load, was Valentão-da-Timbaúba's ghost (22).

8. Távora's account the War of the Mascates ends in an anticlimactic fashion. The noblemen, persecuted by representatives of the Crown (allied with the Portuguese business leaders who dominated the sugar trade in Pernambuco and with the religious orders that dominated colonial finances) took to the woods, bandit-style, on

the orders of the intransigent nobleman Eça de Falcão. His plan was to declare Pernambuco independent from Brazil—the only way to liberate the noblemen from this insufferable oppression (which, in the novel is nothing more than the oppression of a triumphant market, the same one that oppressed the descendants of the colonial nobles). When the runaway aristocrats decide in an assembly (there are matutos present, but only as assistants, without voice or vote) to fight for independence, the news of the king's pardon reaches them. They immediately decide to remain loyal to the king as a clear demonstration of what was important to them: their own preeminence in the political order, not independence.

9. Throughout Távora's novels, there are numerous references to how "those who have never left the Court" would be unable to conceive or understand by themselves the world his novels are depicting. Thus, the role of the northern intellectual as "cultural translator" is crucial.

10. As Aguiar determined in his informative book on Távora, the latter was rather successful in this endeavor. *O Cabelleira* was favorably received by the northern critical establishment and even inspired a musical composition honoring the author and the novel's character (Aguiar 1997, 240–42).

11. It is in this context (partially detached from biographical explanations) that we should understand the virulence of the polemic with Alencar (another northerner who did not write specifically northern literature) that brought Távora onto the national literary scene. Távora conducted a bitter campaign in newspaper articles that would later be collected in *Cartas a Cincinnato* (1872). The campaign (shot through with professional jealousy, political disagreements, and advertising opportunism [see Aguiar 1997]) is conducted at several levels. It has a stylistic level (Távora questions the metaphors, the style, and the general taste in Alencar's literature) and a referential level (Alencar's knowledge of his material: the plains of Rio Grande do Sul, the sertão, and rural customs). In fact, what Távora indicts is Alencar's place as mediator between an archive and an audience. Távora claims this place exclusively for himself, trying to snatch it away from the most eminent writer on the Brazilian cultural scene.

12. The *coiteiro* is an ally of a given bandit. The coiteiro provides the cangaceiro with shelter, ammunition, provisions, and, in the case of well-placed cangaceiros, political clout. In return, the bandit protects the interests of the coiteiro, should the need arise.

13. This symbiosis between bandit and land is a common characteristic of bandit narratives. It is omnipresent, for example, in all accounts pertaining to the Lampião cycle (see Chandler 1988). In *O Índio Afonso*, Afonso's knowledge of the river allows him more than once to escape parties in hot pursuit of him. This ability to elude capture transforms him, for the narrator, into a sort of supernatural being, essentially a "river spirit."

14. The analogy between banditry and epidemics also appears in Altamirano's *El*

Zarco, applied to the case of the Plateados (1901, 104). For a superb examination of the trope of peasant insurgency as epidemic see Guha 1983, chap. 6.

Chapter 5 | *El Zarco*

1. This topic has been extensively researched. See Grudzinska 1982; Covo 1982; Cruz 1993–1994; Escalante 1997; Monsiváis 1999; Sol 2000.

2. Altamirano began the novel in 1874 and worked on it intermittently thereafter. The first thirteen chapters were read in public and in private sessions in the Liceo Hidalgo during 1886. The manuscript was then sold to the Spanish editor Santiago Ballescá. By the time of Altamirano's death in 1893, the novel had not yet been printed. The first edition appeared in Barcelona in 1901, after a series of incidents that put the manuscript at serious risk of being lost (Sol 2000, 29).

3. The phenomenon of banditry spawned by army deserters and veterans is almost universal. In the Latin American context, examples include violence in Mexico (Vanderwood 1992) and Argentina (Fradkin 2005; Chumbita 2000) in the aftermath of the Independence war as well as the civil wars.

4. By an odd twist of fate, the Atlihuayán ironworks—the place where the proletarian Nicolás made his fortune and forged an identity that would eventually make him Altamirano's model for the new Mexican (male) citizen—would ironically occupy a crucial role in the zapatista rebellion decades later. With the 1915 carrancista triumph, the Morelos insurgents were separated from their sources of arms (especially the crucial ones in the north). To ameliorate this situation, the Atlihuayán ironworks was used by Zapata as a munitions factory (Womack 1968, 247).

5. El Zarco is a fictional character, unlike several others who appear or are mentioned in the novel, such as Benito Juárez, Martín Sánchez Chagollan, Salomé Plasencia, or Marcelino Cobos. Díaz de Ovando suggests that the character could be a "compilation" of several historical bandits, among them the aforementioned Salomé Plasencia and a "Zarco" who was shot in the Alameda of Cuernavaca toward the mid-nineteenth century (Díaz de Ovando 1954; Monsiváis 1999, 18; Vanderwood 1992, 8).

6. Altamirano wrote two laudatory essays on *María:* "La literatura Mexicana de 1870" (1871), and "*María,* novela americana de Jorge Isaacs" (1881). In them he salutes the novel as a counternarrative of European accounts of America (Alejandro de Humboldt, for example, appears time and again in Altamirano's writings, always as a negative horizon) and as the first attempt to depict the American landscape without European prejudices (in opposition to the historical novel in vogue at the time).

7. Upon closer inspection, Yautepec presents an original and picturesque aspect. It is a half oriental, half American town. It is oriental because the trees that make the orchards "are orange and lemon-trees, large, luxuriant, always bearing fruit. . . . It is true that this Oriental ensemble is modified in part by the mixture with other American plants, because the banana trees used to show their slim trunks and their wide

leaves, and the magueys and other *zapotáceas* raise their towering treetops over copses" (Altamirano 1901, 97–98).

8. At the time Altamirano was writing, significant sectors of the Yautepec rural population were still living under the system of communal property. With the inauguration of the Mexico-Veracruz railroad (1873), freight prices in central Mexico dropped dramatically. This change allowed sugar producers to import heavy machinery to boost production, and it created additional need for land for sugarcane cultivation. This agrarian compression translated into growing conflicts between hacendados and peasants and farmers, with hacendados usually having the upper hand, in spite of tenacious resistance. Not by chance, Yautepec was a zapatista headquarters during the Revolution (Womack 1970, 15, 45–51, 227–32).

9. Sexual promiscuity among bandits is, again, a frequent motif in gothic novels. See, for example, *The Monk*, by Matthew Lewis.

10. From another point of view, Nicolás's counterpart would be Luis, the peasant leader in *Esclavos*, a drama written by Carlos Barrera in 1915. Luis is a mechanic in a Morelos sugar mill, a skilled worker just like Nicolás. But, unlike Nicolás, who is an *individual* (Nicolás appears detached from his background, since the paramount identity affiliation that Altamirano highlights as legitimate is citizen), Luis is an organizer and organic intellectual of the rural proletariat, guiding it from premodern abjection to revolution. Luis's class politics is opposed to robbery as politics (e.g., he disapproves of the plunder of the company store, the most infamous institution of the Latin American rural landscape).

11. Nicolás seems to be particularly well equipped for this role. The novel invents an Indian legacy for Nicolás, whose most salient attribute is his "haughty integrity." The Indian legacy is then not linguistic, cultural, or economic: it is a vague ethics of sobriety and self-control, which is to say, the parts of the "Indian identity" that can be easily integrated into a subaltern position in a capitalist agrarian order.

12. As Cruz (1993–1994) points out, Manuela embodies the "fallen woman" myth. The idyllic garden of her family is the place where the scene of temptation occurs. This temptation has a symbol in the serpent-like bracelets that Zarco presents to her (156). (Later, when Manuela disappears, her mother fears that a serpent might have bitten her [189].) The fact that the temptation is in the form of jewelry summarizes the moral and economic aspects of Manuela's temptation. Manuela buries the jewelry (her treasure) at the foot of an oleander. A European, poisonous shrub, the oleander symbolizes the wrong path onto which European culture (and Manuela reads European literature) can lead females when not under the supervision of a letrado, that is, a male guide.

13. For bandit participation in the Three Years' War, see Vanderwood 1992, 37.

14. *Los plateados de tierra caliente* (1891), by Pablo Robles (a.k.a. Peroblillos), a novel contemporaneous with *El Zarco*, is also set in Yautepec and also features Martín Sánchez Chagollan and his bitter struggle against the Plateados. It is a love

story with a tragic end. The agrarian reality depicted is completely different, though. Unlike Altamirano's Yautepec, which is a cluster of small plots, Robles's Yautepec is dominated by the large estate, and the romance cuts across classes (the disputed female is the hacendado's daughter), not races. Also, the connections between the political establishment and banditry (mentioned but never detailed in *El Zarco*) are here more apparent: Marcos Reza, political boss of Jonacatepec, acted in accord with the bandits, and the novel's central conflict is between him and Sánchez Chagollan and ends with Marcos before a firing squad.

15. For details on vigilante organizations in rural Mexico during this period, see Vanderwood 1992, 31. As he points out, the distinction between them and bandits was tenuous at best.

16. After coming to power in 1855, liberals had acknowledged the irrelevance of the former ideological cleavage between centralism and federalism. According to one scholar, "Now that the government was a liberal one, it was advisable to strengthen it, especially since the proximity of the American border weakened the hold of central Mexico on the states to the north, making a further dismemberment of the country possible in the future. Liberals, therefore, became just as centralist as their conservative rivals, although they continued to pay lip service to the federalism with which liberalism had been identified for so many years. A telling manifestation of this change of doctrinal outlook is that, while the 1824 Constitution was the 'Federal Constitution of the United Mexican States,' the 1857 one was the 'Political Constitution of the Mexican Republic'" (Bazant 1991, 35). The alliance between Juárez and Sánchez Chagollan cancels the division of the national territory (at the beginning of the novel, travel between Yautepec and México was impossible) through mutual acknowledgment.

Chapter 6 | Criminology

1. Following an established custom, I use "criminology" as the shorthand expression to name what during the time were considered different disciplines, such as criminal anthropology, abnormal psychiatry, criminal sociology, penology, and so forth.

2. For an account of the ways Latin America was changing toward the end of the mid-nineteenth century, see Halperín Donghi 1967. For the ways in which this affected the letrado institution, see Rama 1984 and Ramos 1989.

3. For the concept of degeneration in Brazilian social sciences, see D. Borges 1993.

4. For an examination of the group's ideology, see Buffington 2000.

5. On porfirian policies and procedures for dealing with crime, see Rohlfes 1983; Buffington 2000; Picatto 2001.

6. See Montesquieu 1748, books 14–18; and Rousseau 1762, book III, chap. VIII, "That Every Form of Government Is Not Fit for Every Country."

7. European criminology was divided between the Italian school (emphasizing heredity in the etiology of crime) and the French school (emphasizing environment). Mexican practitioners tended to inhabit a happy medium, refusing to commit fully to either of the two currents (see Buffington 2000 for particular expressions of this noncommittal attitude).

Chapter 7 | Astucia

1. For a detailed examination of the novel's structure, see Sol 2001a. For an analysis of tobacco smuggling in the context of the diverse forms of banditry in Michoacán during the period portrayed by the novel, see Solares Robles 1999.

2. Smuggling began to be widespread in Mexico during colonial times. It acquired particular force during the eighteenth century, when the Bourbons established different monopolies and taxes on key commodities (gold, silver, and alcohol, among several others) as part of their attempt to "re-conquer" America and increase revenues to finance wars in the colonial metropolis, as in Spain (Vanderwood 1992, 17; Burns 1972). Tobacco smuggling, in particular, was a direct consequence of the state monopoly established in 1764. The monopoly restricted tobacco cultivation to specific areas, regulated prices paid by state-run tobacco processing factories, and issued retail licenses. The monopoly administrators controlled the Resguardo, which was in turn in charge of fighting tobacco smuggling (Deans-Smith 1992, 15). Toward the end of the eighteenth century, the tobacco monopoly was among the three largest industries in Mexico, the others being silver and textiles. The war for independence and the economic and fiscal conditions of the first postcolonial decades had devastating effects on the enterprise. However, in spite of the liberal republican orthodoxy that supported the suppression of monopolies and government stores, the tobacco monopoly survived because even its declining revenues were indispensable. In 1856, as various changes were instituted in preparation for the 1857 Constitution, the tobacco monopoly was eliminated (Deans-Smith 1992, xviii–xxi).

3. Astucia usurped the security post through the shrewd use of letrado institutions: he stole official paper (with a letterhead) from the governor's office and used it to forge his commission.

4. According to Vanderwood, "No common cause existed in provincial Mexico, unless it was a mutual determination to keep central authority at bay" (1992, 28).

5. For an analysis of the language in Astucia, see Sol 2001b.

6. The expression hombres de bien, like the more charged gente decente or the more neutral padre de familia, were moralistic circumlocutions that named an identity complex (white, male, letrado, proprietor, urban, of European sympathies) and defined the criteria of elite belonging.

7. Astucia suffers the same limitations in the definition of the "all" as Les Trois mousquetaires. Furiously egalitarian among themselves, the musketeers and the charros exclude women from the core of their society. In both novels, women who

exceed their conventionally defined role are marked as abject. Also, both musketeers and charros maintain a strict class differentiation: the pages are one case, and the muleteers are a second case. The latter are present throughout the narratives but are little more than domestic animals (Astucia calls his aides, in an endearing fashion, "my dogs"). In both cases, these male warrior societies act in contexts of power vacuums (king and president and governor are equally irrelevant), and the real power is in the hands of an illegitimate agent (Richelieu in the one and the Resguardo in the other).

8. *Astucia,* in fact, does not begin with the story of Astucia himself but with that of his father, Don Juan Cabello, "in his youth one of the most resolved insurgents of the many that rebelled in the Quencio Valley, fighting under the orders of the Rayones, licenciate don Ignacio and general don Ramón, always giving a thousand proofs of his valor. Like most of the good patriots of his time, he sacrificed his blooming youth, his blood and well-being to the cause of independence, retiring to private life in 1822 to again seek sustenance in rural endeavors" (Inclán 1865, 5). With minimal changes, this could be a summary of Lorenzo's life: rebelling against an arbitrary regime (the tobacco monopoly first, insensitive centralism later) and eventually retiring to private life in the bosom of his community.

9. When Lencho and his father go to Tacho's wedding party, Don Juan frolics a little in the outdoors, exercising his tired and illustrious old bones. He says, "You know what, son? I was craving outside exercise a little bit, to shake the valley's dust, and to warm myself under the sun of the *tierra fría.* I am content, I have forgotten my melancholy. I feel like a different person, who has no aches. And if it were not for my wrinkled hands and white beard, I would believe that I was going to meet my friends and fellows just like during the insurgency" (250).

10. This is more than a literary emphasis. As Vanderwood has proved, the initial core of the Rurales, the spearhead and flagship of the repression of banditry in nineteenth-century Mexico, consisted of former bandits. This shift toward the other side of the law was not an obstacle for their being, in many cases, part-time bandits. This compelled Vanderwood to coin the expression "Rural-bandit" for these subjects who played both sides of the law.

11. See Foucault 1975 for an account of several scenes of subjects before the law in which similar counterpoints can be traced.

12. Inclán was a letrado, but a peculiar one, since he was a publisher of popular literature. (Paredes [1960] even suggests that he may have been the first Mexican publisher of corridos.) Because of his occupation, Inclán's idea of literature was mixed with the notion of market. But his intervention in the market was different than Lizardi's, for whom the letrado intervenes in the market to enact a standard, to claim a place from which to impose or preach his morals. For Lizardi, the letrado should not submit to market forces but should educate the buying public. In Inclán, by contrast, "public" means "buying public" and not "public opinion."

13. A similar network was in place for the Kelly gang in Australia, which defeated the most concentrated efforts of the government.

14. When giving away the weapons, Astucia addresses the villagers: "From this moment on you are my soldiers, faithful upholders of your respective authorities, and the Public Security force in charge of reestablishing peace and order to the area. We do not have headquarters, spells of duty, or services of any kind that would cause any inconvenience to our regular business and affairs. As soon as anyone suffers any kind of criminal offense, just climb to the roof of his house and shoot any rogue that wants to take advantage of his possessions. Look for each other among neighbors, villages, haciendas, and ranches" (449).

Chapter 8 | *Zárate*

1. The first edition of *Zárate* (1881) was printed in Caracas by the Imprenta Sanz. The second (1883), also in Caracas, was produced by the Imprenta Bolívar. Silva-Beauregard (1994), Krispín (1997), and Bolet Toro (2000) suggest that the history of Zárate loosely replicates that of Dionisio Cisneros, whom the novel mentions as a contemporary of Zárate (46). The assertion is credible but somewhat dubious. Aside from the (relative) geographical coincidence (Zárate operated in Aragua, Cisneros in the Tuy) and chronological simultaneity (the immediate aftermath of the patriot's victory), there are no major confluences between the careers of both bandits. The only important point in common between the two biographies is that both met with Páez. However, in the case of Cisneros, the rendezvous was exactly the opposite of Zárate's case. Santos appears unexpectedly in Páez's headquarters in Valencia in order to ask Horacio Delamar's pardon, showing temerity that earns his own pardon as well. Quite to the contrary, Páez, joined by a selected group, visits Cisneros in his own hideout (the rebel had refused to abandon it) to seal the definitive peace between the two godfathers (*compadres*) (Palacios Herrera 1989, 221).

2. Blanco told the story to his assistant Santiago Key Ayala, and he interpolated it in *Eduardo Blanco y la génesis de Venezuela heroica* (1920, 60).

3. The analogy between the Independence War and either *The Iliad* or the Persian Wars runs throughout *Venezuela heroica,* with the Thermopylae episode being a particular focus. Ribas, hero of the battle of La Victoria in February 1814, is compared to Leonidas, king of Sparta.

4. For an excellent characterization of the cultural climate of the Guzmán Blanco era, see Silva-Beauregard 1994. For a historical summary of Guzmán Blanco's rule, see Morón 1964, 174–82, as well as Lombardi 1982, 157–211. The effort to glorify the memory of Bolívar began with primary school education; school systems expanded after the passage of a law in 1873 mandating free, mandatory schooling. The relevant historiographical works on Bolívar include *Historia de Venezuela para niños* (1883), by Socorro González Guinan, and *Catecismo de historia de Venezuela* (1885), by Antonia Esteller. At about the same time that *Venezuela heroica* was published

there appeared *Memorias,* by General O'Leary (1800–1854), a book "ordered by the government of Venezuela and sponsored by its president, general Guzmán Blanco" (according to the title page) between 1879 and 1888 and printed on the presses of the *Gaceta oficial.*

5. This statement is originally from Pedro Pablo Barnola (1963), author of the only volume devoted to the novel, which elicited a modest polemic in Venezuelan literary criticism. The first Venezuelan novel *stricto sensu* is *Los mártires* (1842) by Fermín Toro, but since its subject is non-Venezuelan (the setting is English) it was excluded from the list of "national novels." Beyond the problematic relevance of this criterion, it is safe to affirm the crucial (though not inaugural) character of *Zárate* in the Venezuelan cultural landscape.

6. *Prohombre* refers to a truly outstanding man, one prominent in civil society or the political arena because of his civic virtues. Guzmán Blanco was not able to defeat the caudillista political system (a system that, in the first place, allowed for his access to the position he enjoyed for so long). The relative internal peace of the period was based upon a situation of power sharing, in which caudillos kept a substantial portion of local power in exchange for their support of the central power, whose influence, even though contested, was increasing (Quintero 1994, 59–61). After that interregnum of relative stability, the situation had not essentially changed. Regional caudillos (e.g., Crespo, Hernández, Cipriano Castro) continued as the arbiters of national politics, which attested to the fact that nonstate violence still had the upper hand.

7. Upon his return from Europe Don Carlos attempts to restore the hacienda's colonial splendor, which had been seriously reduced by the calamities of the war, not to make it a model hacienda in the way that Santos Luzardo in *Doña Bárbara* or Carlos in *Peonía* attempt to do.

8. "In one of the sides one could see the foreman's lodgings and what at the time was called the *repartimiento,* a vast building, a kind of cloister with cells of various sizes that were inhabited separately by the slaves" (112).

9. In the first case I am referring to the culinary preparations for the Sunday feast, a (frustrated) celebration of the health of the hierarchical society. In the second case, I am referring to the dress rehearsals for the celebration of the feast day of Our Lady of Candelaria in Turmero.

10. "In spite of the rough and ancient appearance of the building that serves as a nest to the most beautiful lady [*castellana*] of those fertile lands, the manor [*casa solariega*] did not lack majesty. With a little effort from the imagination, the house could be very well compared to an old manor from the Middle Ages, because of its pointed gables, its thick walls, and the grates on its windows" (112).

11. El Torreón does not seem to have incorporated the latest technology of its day, as it was still using the centuries-old, animal-powered press known as the *trapiche* instead of steam-powered machinery. The hacienda is also cultivating Creole cane instead of superior varieties. Finally, unlike coffee or cocoa production, sugar

was not a product oriented toward export (in part due to its low quality), so it was destined for the production of a type of coarse brown sugar loaf (*papelón*) and liquor—products that do not exactly evoke the image of a cutting-edge form of capitalism or a cutting-edge bourgeoisie. (See Rodríguez 1986 for a historical examination of sugar production in Venezuela.) Of course, this antiquated version of capitalism is important since it justifies the lack of hunger for land that would characterize sugar production in Latin America during the nineteenth century and, consequently, the paternalism that Don Delamar shows toward peasants, since they are not really competing for scarce capital. (Rodríguez even mentions that land suitable for sugar production was reported to be fallow.)

In addition, by the mid-1820s slavery as a social institution was rather archaic. This leaves aside the mystery of how El Torreón managed to retain its slave force in one of the areas hardest hit by the independence wars (which implied the wholesale liberation or escape of slaves). In Venezuela, the slave trade ceased in the late 1700s (Pollak-Eltz 2000, 44), so the slave force working the plantation was at least a quarter-century past its prime in the case of African slaves (*negros bozales*). Had the slaves been born on the hacienda they would not have been slaves since the Ley de Libertad de Vientres ensured that all those born on the land were free. So, this agrarian utopia presents us with a world geared toward extinction. (For a historical examination of Venezuelan slavery, see Pollak-Eltz 2000.)

12. Corporeality functions in the novel as an unequivocal code, pointing to the moral condition of the person. Even though Zárate/Oliveros always acts in an irreproachable manner in front of Delamar, everybody suspects him because they "know" that something is wrong with him; the essence shines in spite of the disguises (126–27 for Clavellina and Aurora; 145 for Horacio).

13. Távora also used this metaphor in *O Cabelleira* (14).

14. This sharing of spaces between banditry and the diabolic is not new, and there is a magnificent example to prove it. In the all-out grand finale of Lewis's *The Monk* (1796), Ambrosio signs his soul over to the devil in order to avoid torture by the Inquisition (little did he know he was going to be pardoned). The devil, far from granting his request to reunite Ambrosio and Matilda (his forbidden, incestuous love), drops him in the Sierra Morena, Spain's legendary bandit country. Far from picturesque, the Sierra Morena (where the protagonist of *Manuscript Found in Saragossa* is haunted by the ghost of bandits possessed by devils) is the earthly version of hell. There the broken and pierced body of forlorn Ambrosio suffers from thirst, hunger, and exposure, birds peck his eyes out and tear his flesh, and insects swarm to drink the blood oozing from his wounds and to inject their stinging appendages into his body. Ambrosio finally dies in the seventh day of torment, drowned in an apocalyptic storm.

15. As Domingo Miliani correctly points out, Zárate's feigned omniscience reappears in Doña Bárbara, another bandit chief (2001, 97).

16. Zárate says, "Being who I am, I have no option but to follow the path on which I am now. As long as they do not kill me, I will continue being the terror of these valleys, and the threat and the nightmare to all mayors of the area. In all sincerity, I take pride in this, because there is no name more famous from Auyamal to the slopes of Cocuizas, and from the shores of Chao to the hills of San Juan" (221).

17. Silva-Beauregard felicitously points out that "the setting of the novel [Aragua] is the point in which the Llanos and the central area of the country meet. This setting has all the features of a crossroads in which two itineraries coincide, two diametrically opposing journeys." These are the journeys of Horacio Delamar, who comes from Caracas, and of Santos Zárate, who comes from the Llano (Silva-Beauregard 1994, 414).

18. Among the features of a noble robber are the fact that Zárate's career begins not with a crime but with an injustice suffered at the hands of Bustillón; that he "rights wrongs" (he saves Horacio twice, then saves Aurora and Don Carlos's honor); that he is supported by his people; that he is defeated only by treason; that he does not oppose the values of his community (agrarian patrimonialismo); and that he opposed the local tyrant (Bustillón) but is loyal to the legitimate sovereign (Páez).

19. Christianity is in many conservative rural utopias the foundation of the social order. In Zárate, this is the function of a long Sunday scene that takes place at El Torreón and at the mass in which masters and slaves share the sacrament as a place of vertical convergence (see chap. XVII, first part, "Otros tipos de nuestros viejos tiempos," and chap. XVIII, "Celos que rugen y corazones que se expanden").

20. For this same reason, Horacio "knows" that Oliveros/Zárate is not to be trusted. Oblivious to Zárate's presence at the family table, Horacio suffers an "inexplicable shock" when hearing "the strange timbre of the voice of that man" (145).

21. The novel is set in 1825, which is significant because from 1826 forward the disagreements between Páez and Bolívar/Santander and between Venezuela and Gran Colombia became more and more salient because of the resistance in Venezuela to the centralist provisions of the Constitution of Cúcuta. These disagreements eventually led in 1830 to the secession of Venezuela from Gran Colombia (Banko 1990, 59–96). The year 1825 is one in which Blanco can still vindicate Páez as the hero of an undivided national or even supranational will. From then on, even though Páez was for decades a leader of enormous prestige, he was the leader of a faction. An aged Páez is the theme of other writings by Blanco, for example "Fecha clásica" and "El jardinero de 'La Viñeta,'" collected in Tradiciones épicas y cuentos viejos.

22. In the novel, repentance belongs to the feminine sphere. In this case, it is Carmen, Zárate's common-law wife, who urges him repeatedly to repent (219, 220, 422.)

23. See the episode of the sparrow-hawk and the parrot (319–21).

Chapter 9 | Martín Fierro

1. José Hernández is the only Argentine author whose name has been applied to a particular type of scholar. A *hernandista* is a scholar whose exclusive field of specialization is Henández's work.

2. For a detailed bibliography on Hernández, see Becco 1972 and Romanos de Tiratel (2001). For a reasoned mapping of *Martín Fierro's* gigantic critical history and reception in Argentine culture, see the outstanding "Dossier de la obra" in Lois and Núñez's critical edition of the poem (2001). Within that same edition, see the essays by Rivera, Dalmaroni, Weinberg de Magis, and Bueno, who analyze particular instances of the reception of the poem (see also Prieto 1988; Ludmer 1988). For anthologies of criticism on *Martín Fierro* see Isaacson 1986 and Gramuglio and Sarlo 1993, which also provide introductory essays that aptly discuss the reception of the poem.

3. Banditry as a rhetorical trope was fairly common in the early gauchesca. The patriotic or factionalist poems by Bartolomé Hidalgo or Hilario Ascasubi frequently used the epithets "*salteador,*" "*ladrón de vacas*" or "criminal," to brand their political or military enemies (who were royalists, federalists, *oribistas,* and the Portuguese). In addition to highlighting the inveterate habit of plunder among the armies and montoneras campaigning on both sides of the Río de la Plata (Nahum 1994), it is a rhetorical procedure used liberally to de-legitimate the enemy. The disdain for private property is also used in the early gauchesca as an index of the social decomposition brought about by the civil war (see, e.g., "Diálogo patriótico interesante entre el gaucho Jacinto Chano, capataz de una estancia en las Islas del tordillo y el gaucho de la Guardia del Monte" and the "Nuevo diálogo patriótico," by Hidalgo, as well as *Paulino Lucero,* by Ascasubi). Furthermore, some of Hidalgo's pieces already express tensions between rural populations and local authorities (see "Diálogo patriótico interesante").

4. A *cielito* is a musical composition to be sung accompanied by the Spanish guitar. In the early to mid-nineteenth century Río de la Plata region, it was a genre performed by gauchos who composed cielitos with political lyrics, usually deprecating political enemies or exalting political allies.

5. For Rama, the "gauchesca was a revolutionary and political poetry product of the primary integration between the creator and a popular public, for whose leadership it is intended and whose interests it intended to further. It offers the first artistically valid image of its historical mission, that is, vividly identifying it as protagonist and agent in the history of its own self" (1976, 47). With Hernández and Lussich, this system disappears. This does not mean that it is not produced anymore, but the gauchesca will become individual lamentations and elegies, testimony that the communal system of the origins had been broken" (51). He concludes that "the poet does not consubstantiate with his public, but takes advantage of the system to

indoctrinate it with political orientations that may be alien, even contradictory to the interests of the gaucho population" (51).

6. In this respect, *Martín Fierro* is the exact opposite of *El periquillo sarniento* or *Zárate*. In the latter it was essential for the constitution of letrado identity that a clear-cut demarcation be established (at some point) between letrado and bandit, at the risk of otherwise intermingling these subject positions, which would have implied the loss of epistemological privilege (equaling a loss of the very possibility of narration).

7. Even though Sarmiento strove to create an image of rural areas as being populated exclusively by wandering gauchos (essential for the rendering of the pampas as a political vacuum, the so-called desert), the demographics of the pampas were quite complex, with large sectors of the population living sedentary lives dedicated to various forms of agriculture (Garavaglia 1999). In fact, the distinction between sedentary *paysanos* and migrant and wandering folk was quite vivid for rural inhabitants and was a source of enduring tensions within rural populations throughout the entire history of the area (Salvatore 2003). William MacCann corroborated this statement when he pointed out that "the term Gaucho is one offensive to the mass of the people, being understood to mean a person who has no local habitation, but lives a nomadic life; therefore in speaking of the poorer classes I avoid that term" (1853, 154). Later on, Lucio Mansilla established a stark distinction between paysano and gaucho: "Paysano gaucho is the individual who has a home, a permanent address, works regularly and has respect for authority, always siding with it, even against his own feelings. The true gaucho is the wandering Creole, who today is here and tomorrow is somewhere else; gambler, quarrelsome, enemy of all discipline, he avoids military service, and takes refuge among the Indians if he stabbed somebody in a fight, or joins the montonera if it appears in the area. The first one has the instincts for civilization; he imitates the inhabitant of the cities in his clothing and in his customs. The second loves tradition and hates the gringo. His luxuries are his spurs, his riding gear, his coin-studded belt, his dagger" (Mansilla 1870, 2:83–84).

8. This conflict cannot be defined simply as a class struggle, since there is no universal agreement on the characterization of the gauchos as a social class or on their situation vis-à-vis other actors in the rural world. Rodríguez-Molas (1968) provides the best example of the application of the Marxist model of class struggle to the analysis of gaucho history. Slatta (1983) argues that the gauchos constituted a class but that they lacked class consciousness (therefore, they did not articulate their struggles as a class). Lynch (1981) emphasizes the fact that instead of a model of class struggle, clientelism across classes is a model better suited to explaining the realities of the pampas. De la Fuente (2000), from the perspective of subaltern studies, connects caudillismo with class struggle, but since he tries to recover a perspective "from below," he examines motivations and perceptions among the participants of

armed insurgency that exceed both approaches (for example, the role of charisma in fashioning identities and politics).

9. For an examination of rural legislation from the colonial period forward, see Gori 1976; Rodríguez-Molas 1968; Slatta 1983; Storni 1997. For an examination of the workings of rural justice, see Salvatore 1992, 1997, 2000, and especially 2003, as well as Garavaglia 1999. For a history of social banditry in Argentina, see Chumbita 2000.

10. As in the Andean indigenist novel, the narrative proper begins only with the encroachment of capitalism or the state, disrupting a communitarian order that seems to live outside history in a sort of stasis (Cornejo-Polar 1994).

11. The fact that the poem is accompanied by an essay on the possibility of a trans-Andean route (*Memoria sobre el camino trasandino*) is a clear indication of the ideological universe in which Hernández was immersed (a philosophy of material progress classic in the liberalism of the time), as well as the audience he was targeting (Prieto 1977).

12. In historical terms, this does not mean that many regions of the country did not remain as frontier areas well into the twentieth century. Some that did remain frontier include the dry pampas (where Vairoletto, another famous social bandit, thrived), the Chaco region (theater of the saga of Mate Cosido and the Velásquez brothers, well remembered to this day), the swampy regions of the littoral (the Paraná coasts in Santa Fé and Entre Ríos) as described by Fray Mocho in *Viaje al país de los matreros* (1897) and of course Patagonia (see for example Arlt 1934 and Bayer 1972). Also, for the late history of social banditry in Argentina, see Chumbita 1999, 2000; and Carri 1968.

Chapter 10 | *Juan Moreira*

1. As Prieto (1988) points out, even though both narratives are set during roughly the same period (the third quarter of the nineteenth century, between the late 1860s and the early 1870s) Moreira's universe is much more modern than Fierro's. To begin with, Moreira's line of work implies a more thorough integration into the realities of agrarian capitalism (he carries agrarian products to the railroad that goes to Buenos Aires, to be exported abroad later). But the narrative is centered on towns (which are completely absent in *Martín Fierro*), and the gravitational pull of cities is also present, whereas that feature is missing entirely from *Martín Fierro* (travel to and from Buenos Aires is common in *Juan Moreira*). Also, the setting of the novel is clearly embedded in a geographical imaginary that is larger than that of the country or even the province (e.g., Marañón offers to help Moreira move to another province [109]). Finally, the structure of the state seems more complex and interconnected, both horizontally (with counties regularly coordinating actions against Moreira) as well as vertically (local officials and provincial authorities are constantly in contact).

2. In her brilliant book *El tiempo vacio de la ficción* (2003), Alejandra Laera, one of the few critics to analyze *Juan Moreira* from the viewpoint of Gutierrez's entire production, traces an ideological evolution from the first novel on gauchos malos (*Juan Moreira*, published in 1879) to the last (*Pastor Luna*, published in 1885). This evolution goes from an explicit indictment of the state in *Juan Moreira* to a sort of state-centered reformism in *Pastor Luna* (2003, chap. 6). This evolution is credible, well proven, and contextualized. In many ways, it seems to mirror the evolution between the two parts of *Martín Fierro*.

3. For a complete assessment of the "culture war" surrounding criollismo, see Prieto 1988 and Rubione 1983. For an analysis of the anti-moreirismo in Argentine culture see Viñas 1996.

4. For an account of some of the appropriations of Moreira as an icon during the twentieth century, see the chapter "Los Moreira" in Ludmer 1999, as well as Prieto 1988.

5. See Prieto 1988 for an illuminating study of these writers, particularly their context and the agendas that they were articulating through the use of the bandit trope.

6. These authors did not confine themselves exclusively to creating new versions of *Juan Moreira*. In fact, most of Gutiérrez's novels were adapted (as was *Martín Fierro*), with *Juan Cuello, Los hermanos Barrientos, Pastor Luna, Santos Vega*, and *Juan sin patria* being prime examples. A detailed (albeit incomplete) list of the holdings of the Biblioteca Criolla Roberto Lehmann-Nitsche in Berlin, the only place in the world with significant holdings of *folletines criollistas*, can be found in Prieto 1988.

7. Gutiérrez's gauchos malos are prone to these dubious alliances. Probably the most shocking for the modern reader is the one established by Felipe Pacheco (a.k.a. "El Tigre," hence the title of the novel *El tigre del Quequén*), who becomes the sergeant of the town partida in Moro, a bandit hideout. The justice of the peace, who is intent on pacifying the area and who is the one who names and protects El Tigre, is the major local landowner, Don Martínez de Hoz (158). This surname has a dark resonance in Argentine history. One of the forefathers of the clan was the founder of the Sociedad Rural Argentina, the organization that lives in Argentine historical memory as one of the staunchest defenders of the landowning oligarchy. One of the latest scions of the family, José Alfredo Martínez de Hoz, was minister of the economy during the 1970s, under the last dictatorship, and embodies the beginning of the end of the egalitarian dream in Argentina.

8. See the opening section of the book, where Ludmer defines her notion of "popular," as well as the intellectual tradition in which she inscribes its usage (1988,11–13).

9. Ludmer advances in this direction in her analysis of Vicenta's role as wife/traitor (1999).

10. Instead of taking place during the day, Moreira's killing occurs at night; in-

stead of having a dog, Moreira kills a dog; instead of being killed inside the courtyard while trying to climb up a wall, he is killed outside the courtyard while trying to climb down a wall; Chirino is not a cowardly and evil cop, but a good and heroic one, and he is congratulated for his actions. This divergent recounting is a common procedure in Borges's fiction, of momentous import in this particular case.

11. For an examination of voting practices in Buenos Aires during the period, see Sabato 2001.

12. Says Fierro, "I want to leave this living Hell / I am no spring chicken / And I know how to handle a spear / And among the Indians does not reach / The long arm of the Government // I know that over there the caciques / Give sanctuary to Christians / And they treat them as brothers / When they go there by their own will / Why should we be always on the run? / Let's collect our things and let's go" (199).

13. The scene at the barbershop (where Moreira, disguised as Juan Blanco, elicited opinions about himself) is telling in this respect: people may understand Moreira, but they really fear and distrust him. Moreira does not trust the people either, since he needed to question the barber about their real feelings (241).

14. "Andrés stopped and looked out: the wool warehouse was ablaze. Raging fire burst through holes in the roof and through the gates of the building. The winding flames ignited the walls as if they had intentionally been fed some inflammable substance. Little by little the entire building was being consumed. It was a huge bonfire. And the radiance of the flames could have helped distinguish, there in the woods in the back, in the paths, a vague shape, like the shadow of a man who avenges an offence and then flees the scene" (Cambaceres 1885, 175).

Chapter 11 | *Alma gaucha*

1. Martín Fierro, as well as the legendary *payador* (gaucho singer) Santos Vega, was not usually considered an example of moreirismo. When Gutiérrez first and the criollista writers later used these figures, it was considered that Fierro and Santos Vega had been unduly "degraded" (Sánchez [c. 1916] 1941, 622).

2. For a historical account of Calandria's life, see Chumbita 2000, 199–201.

3. In Europe (e.g., France, Britain, and Prussia) universal male conscription had been considered key to the creation of egalitarian "imagined communities" and to the constitution of a homogeneous citizenry, balancing service to the state with education and empowerment (thus bearing what was considered to be a clear emancipatory imprint). In Latin America conscription did not have these effects. In Latin America the armed forces (and the states that the armed forces served) were riddled with class and race conflicts that overshadowed foreign wars (which were few and far between) as the foundation for the national imaginary (foreign wars having an obvious power to make the community coalesce around a common enemy). For an illuminating analysis of the phenomenon of conscription in Latin America vis-à-vis the process of nation-state formation and for a comparison with the European and

North American experiences, see the chapter "Making Citizens" in Centeno 2002. For an anthology of the debates surrounding the 1901 conscription law, see Botana and Gallo 1997, 106–108, as well as Rodríguez-Molas 1968, 272–74.

4. The metaphor of the dispossessed by Liberal Argentina as Cruz's or Fierro's sons resonated in diverse ways. First, it is found in an almost forgotten book, *Hablan desde la cárcel los hijos de Martín Fierro: reportajes hechos en el penal de Viedma, a los más famosos bandoleros del Sud* (1933) by Rufino Marín, which is a collection of interviews with Argentine and Chilean bandits imprisoned in the Viedma penitentiary. More famously, there is the film *Los hijos de Fierro* (1972–1978) by Argentine filmmaker Fernando Solanas.

Chapter 12 | Payno

1. For example, "When traveling through Mexico, start by making your testament" (Ampère 1856, 235). See also Mme. Calderón de la Barca's *Life in Mexico during a Residence of Two Years in that Country* (1843). Other travelers' testimonies on the subject appear in Glantz 1964 and Vanderwood 1992.

2. Of course, gold is also a commodity, and it is not above the laws of commodities. But its importance in Western culture has ensured it a particular place, qualitatively different from other commodities. For this symbolic difference between money (as commodity) and gold and land as grounded values, see Barthes 1970, 39–40.

Chapter 13 | Os sertões

1. For an examination of some of the other writings on Canudos, see Elmore 2007 and Johnson 2005.

2. Da Cunha details how plants mutate in order to adapt to the weather, and their description is very similar to those of the sertanejo, since there is the same contrast between a poor appearance and a surprising resistance and resilience (127).

3. Ruin is the common fate of all human endeavors in the sertão (107, 110) as well as of nature itself (112, 139, 283–84).

Chapter 14 | Lugones

1. This is not an exception to the norm. Howard Zehr (1976) indicates that the migration of anomie from the country to the city—the former now being perceived as the locus of harmonious and stable social relations—is typical of societies undergoing rapid population growth and urbanization, internal or external migrations, and modernization of social relations, all of which characterized Argentina.

2. A similar process was taking place in Uruguay. From the last quarter of the nineteenth century on, Artigas and the artiguista experience were being revisited, and the so-called Black Legend (with Artigas as the barbarian responsible for breaking up the Provincias Unidas and for the cycle of civil wars that encompassed at least

the first postcolonial half-century) was giving way to a secular religion (*el culto artiguista*) that would redefine the Uruguayan national narrative. (For a detailed account of the creation of the artiguista cult, see Ardao 2002.) The extent of this redefinition may be seen in the famous poem "La leyenda patria," written in 1879 by Juan Zorrilla de San Martín (1855–1931), a civic piece that exalted the tradition of Uruguayan national independence. Artigas is almost completely absent from this poem. The Thirty-Three Orientals and their crusade for national emancipation occupy the narrative in its entirety. Had this omission of Artigas occurred in a poem written fifty years later, it would have been nothing short of blasphemous, in particular for the author. In fact, together with Eduardo Acevedo Díaz and Carlos María Ramírez, Zorrilla de San Martín was one of the most important proponents of alternative views on Artigas during the late nineteenth and early twentieth centuries. Both Acevedo Díaz and Zorrilla followed different paths in dealing with Artigas's bandit stint. In 1910, Zorrilla de San Martín wrote the monumental *La epopeya de Artigas*. It is monumental not only because of its length (five volumes dealing with most or all aspects of Artigas's life, career, political thinking, and significance for Uruguay and the Americas) but also because it was commissioned by the Uruguayan president in 1907 in order to present the proposals for the planned monument to Artigas to be erected in the Plaza Independencia. In *La epopeya*, banditry is significant because it is conspicuously absent. In the "Conferencia VII" (part of the first volume of the narrative), which is devoted to the history of Artigas before the 1810 Revolution, any mention of his activities outside the law is carefully erased, and Artigas becomes an enterprising "rural businessman."

Acevedo Díaz's take is different. At the same time that Sarmiento publishes *Conflictos y armonías*, which is among other things a still-furious libel against Artigas, Acevedo Díaz publishes *Ismael* (1888), part of his multivolume novelistic saga on the origins of Uruguayan nationhood. Just as Lugones did in *La guerra gaucha*, Acevedo Díaz (considered the founder of the "great" national novel in Uruguay [Ainsa 1993, 209–10]) does not deny that many of Artigas's followers were outlaws. But, as in the cases of Blanco and Lugones, the caudillo becomes the dynamic force that channels the raw energy of the multitude ("the passions and forces of the desert" and the "terrible local loves") into "the foundation of nationhood" (Acevedo Díaz 1888, 50). This is indeed the story of Ismael, the young *gaucho oriental* who is forced to become a matrero because of (as usual) an injury inflicted upon his manly honor by an arrogant and abusive Spaniard, representative of the unjust colonial order. That injury forces him to exact bloody revenge and flee to the safety of the woods (*el monte*). There he enters into a parallel, Sherwood-like society doubly devoted to subsistence and self-defense, until the call of the caudillo transforms that group of leaderless insurgents into a people. Just like Lugones, who is able to depict gaucho violence with unmatched force, Acevedo Díaz perceives how the "crumbling of the colonial edifice" engenders chaos, chaos that can be conjured only by the caudillo, who is identified with the nation-state (this is undoubtedly a "statist" version of Artigas: the narrative begins in Montevideo, not in the countryside, and begins by presenting Artigas engaged in conversation with Far Benito. Thus, the narrative chooses the lettered city (and letters, since part of the conversation is the long reading of a manuscript, part dream, part political manifesto, triggered by a reading of Rousseau) as its point of departure and its perspective on rural violence, and Artigas appears linked primarily to this lettered city, not the other way around.

3. In the celebrated taxonomy of the gauchos that Sarmiento attempts in *Facundo,* we have the minstrel or payador right before the outlaw or gaucho malo. In fact, the anecdote that Sarmiento tells places both functions into the same figure.

4. This attempt to link national traditions to the larger Western classical tradition animates other intellectuals of the period, such as Alfonso Reyes or Pedro Hénriquez Ureña.

5. Lugones's recourse to the nation as a signifier that would ground all political practice is unequivocal, hence his objection to the Jesuit experiment as analyzed in *El imperio Jesuítico* (1904). The missions were, in Lugones's view, sheer domination without hegemony, based on a "technology of the self" fashioned after monastic rule. As Lugones put it, the distance between missionaries and Indians was infinite and since there was no cultural bridge between them (and in Lugones's mind, the only cultural bridge is the nation and the leader—as far as the leader is the embodiment of the nation), the experiment in theocratic state-making was destined to fail. The missions run a destiny inverse to that of the gauchos in *La guerra gaucha.* If in the latter they go from banditry to citizens in arms, in the missions they revert to banditry (Lugones 1904, 194).

Chapter 15 | *Los de abajo*

1. See the "Declaraciones" from the Lacandon jungle and the documents compiled by García de León (1994, 1995). Collier and Lowery Quaratiello (*Basta!*) point out that 1910s zapatism had a tenuous hold in Chiapas and that the agrarian ideology characteristic of zapatism was introduced from the top down by the revolutionary state. Because of that, contemporary Chiapas zapatism had as a condition of possibility the state mediation–totalization of the concept of revolution (started by the Constitution of 1917 and its agrarian provisions) and in a second moment the heterodox interpretation-transformation by the EZLN.

2. The idea of a "Great Liberal Tradition" was inaugurated as a conscious perspective on national history during the porfiriato, which predictably considered itself the pinnacle of that tradition. The Revolution, however, rewrote this, making the porfiriato a deviation that the Revolution put on the right track (T. Benjamin 2000). In the liberal tradition, emancipation, if traced to a pre-Hispanic tradition, would be an act of justice delivered to a "Mexican nation" that pre-dated the Spanish conquest. This concept is explicitly present in the Constitution of 1824, in the work of political

thinkers such as José María Luis Mora (*México y sus revoluciones*), Fray José Servando Teresa de Mier (*La historia de la Revolución de Nueva España antiguamente Anahuac*), and Carlos María de Bustamante (*Cuadro histórico de la Revolución de la América Mexicana*), and in nineteenth-century novels by such authors as Juan Mateos (*Sacerdote y caudillo, Los insurgentes*) and Juan Díaz-Covarrubias (*Gil Gómez, el insurgente*). This "pre-Hispanic legacy" varies, since it can trace its genealogy to the Aztecs as the origin of the Mexican nation, or to the Tlaxcaltecs as the origin of the libertarian and republican traditions, or to an undefined Indian or mestizo identity.

3. Cristeros were peasant fighters who followed the banners of the Roman Catholic Church in its struggle against the revolutionary government that was intent on curbing the hold of the Church upon Mexican society during the 1920s.

4. Carlos Monsiváis defined the novel of the Mexican Revolution as a "genre of realist and symbolic intention, a method for apprehending the unhinging or the rectification of the country, an unheard-of stylistic renovation [in Mexican letters]. The genre recreates the political and military period (1910–1940) that goes from the toppling of the dictatorship of Porfirio Díaz to full institutional pacification. It is at the same time a testimonial, a denunciation, and creation." He indicates that "the first significant novel [of the genre] is from 1911 (*Andrés Pérez, maderista,* by Mariano Azuela), the first masterpiece is from 1915 (*Los de abajo,* by Mariano Azuela), and the heyday of the genre happens roughly between 1925 and 1940, even though the thematic reaches even to *Los días terrenales* by José Revueltas (1943), *Al filo del agua,* by Agustín Yáñez (1949), *Pedro Páramo* by Juan Rulfo (1955), and *La muerte de Artemio Cruz* by Carlos Fuentes (1958). During close to half a century, and notwithstanding the speed of changes, the ideas in the novel of the Revolution do not change dramatically, although artistic treatments differ considerably" (Monsiváis 1989, 724–25). Rutherford (1996, 214) rejects this inclusive definition in favor of a more restrictive one. For him, the touchstone of the genre is the *representation* of the more acute military phase of the Revolution (1910–1920). Both Rutherford and Dessau (1967) show how the genre was aesthetically influenced by most modern literary schools (e.g., French-style realism, criollismo, costumbrism, avant-garde, socialist realism, magical realism, existentialism).

5. Lamberto Popoca y Palacios exploited the analogy between revolutionaries and bandits, this time in bad faith and with a clear derogatory purpose, in his *Historia del bandalismo en el estado de Morelos. ¡Ayer como ahora! ¡1860! ¡1911! ¡Plateados! ¡Zapatistas!* (1912).

6. The novel narrates conflicts between Demetrio and Don Mónico, between villistas and huertistas, between convencionistas and constitucionalistas, between Demetrio's gang and the peasants that it victimizes, between members of the gang itself, and so forth. These conflicts converge time and again, but they are not the same. They are not even able to be inscribed in a single all-encompassing series.

7. Laclau and Mouffe used the term "*popular subject position* to refer to the posi-

tion that is constituted on the basis of dividing the political space into two antagonistic camps; and *democratic subject position* to refer to the locus of a clearly delimited antagonism which does not divide society in this way" (1985, 131).

8. Barry Carr examines the homogenizing aspect (under the sign of the popular revolutionary) of the project of the Muralists: "The notion of a single, uninterrupted continuum of revolutionary heroes is also present; for example, in David Siqueiros's mural in the Museo Nacional de Historia in Mexico City, where Emiliano Zapata is presented marching beside Francisco Madero and Venustiano Carranza" (1994, 344).

9. At the same time that I was developing this concept of the narrative of counterinsurgency, Adriana Johnson was developing similar applications in the case of Euclides da Cunha. See Johnson 2005.

10. Azuela acknowledged the extremely problematic character of his novel, since the plot connecting the scenes is at best fragmentary: "*Los de abajo*, as the primitive subtitle indicated, is a series of vignettes and scenes of the Constitutionalist Revolution, weakly tied by a novelistic plot" (Azuela 1958a, 1078).

11. I have traced a similar progression in a previous work, considered a precursor to the novel of the Mexican Revolution: *Tomochic*, by Heriberto Frías (see Dabove 2004).

12. "On a December morning, as sweet and temperate in this Tierra caliente as if it were a spring morning, the town of Yautepec woke up rejoicing, as if for a celebration. . . . Nicolás, the most honest ironsmith of Atlihuayán, was to marry the beautiful and good-hearted Pilar, the town jewel because of her character, her beauty, and her virtues" (Altamirano 1901, 327).

13. In the mural *La quema de los Judas* stones are also present: the stones that *los de abajo* throw at *los de arriba*. These were stones with a clear direction and intention, that crossed a limit (the line of clouds), that defined a mission. The small pellet in *Los de abajo* rolls down without direction or purpose (from the perspective of the mural).

14. Pablo Picatto notes a similar paradigm of representation of urban criminality in Mexico City during the same period. According to Picatto, urban purse snatchers and petty robbers (*rateros*) were central characters in the construction of the urban space and popular classes inhabiting that urban space from the point of view of power. The journalism of the period (Picatto gives as examples the newspapers *Nueva era* and *La voz de México*) refers to *rateros* as "rats" that attack in "swarms," "infestations," or "tides" (2001, 235).

15. In the novel of the Revolution that would follow *Los de abajo,* this idea of turning things upside down becomes a topic. In Rafael F. Muñoz's *Se llevaron el cañón para Bachimba*, Álvaro, when leaving the family home to follow the bola, "wanting to be like them, maybe already being like them, when leaving cut a square of red velvet to add to my saddle, and kicked a column in which there had been for many years the statue of a woman symbolizing justice, with an open book in one hand and a large

sword in the other. The marble burst when hitting the ground and I left the room stomping on it, very satisfied with myself" (84). The difference between *Los de abajo* and *Se llevaron el cañón* is in the fact that Álvaro belongs to the order he is turning upside down (it is his own house he is vandalizing). It is a gesture of rupture, but with his own past, and not with a past of domination. Therefore, it belongs to the bourgeois coordinates of the Bildungsroman and not to the narratives of peasant insurgency.

Chapter 16 | *Cesarismo democrático*

1. See Plaza 1996 for a detailed and impartial analysis of the life and works of Vallenilla Lanz.

2. See Plaza 1996 for a mapping of the many intellectual and personal relations between Vallenilla Lanz and Italian fascism, Spanish Franquism, and the right-wing movements in Portugal, Brazil, and France.

3. See "Cesarismo Democrático y Cesarismo Teocrático" (1920), an appendix to *Cesarismo democrático* that was part of the acrimonious exchange of polemics between Vallenilla Lanz and the Colombian Eduardo Santos, in which Vallenilla Lanz contrasts Venezuela and Colombia.

4. Vallenilla Lanz always maintained that he did not have Gómez in mind when he wrote *Cesarismo democrático*. In fact, the work was started before Gómez's ascension to power. However, later texts by Vallenilla Lanz, written in response to or in the context of the harsh debates sparked by *Cesarismo democrático*, link the main thesis of the work to its immediate context and the public life of the author.

5. This thesis was present in *Facundo*. Quiroga, a gaucho malo who became a caudillo, was murdered by Rosas's hired assassins because he was becoming a statesman and was starting to think about organization and constitution (Sarmiento 1845, 186).

6. This quotation is from Samuel Niño's "La guerra de independencia no fue una guerra civil" (1911), which is partially reproduced in Plaza 1996 (251), where Plaza also provides an exhaustive mapping of the debate.

7. Juan Uslar Pietri(1962) accepts the core of Vallenilla Lanz's interpretation, but he subordinates it to a nationalist interpretation.

8. The film version of *La guerra gaucha,* directed by Lucas Demare, is at the same time simpler and more complex than the narrative version upon which it is modeled. On the one hand, all traces of lawlessness are erased from the film. On the other, there are gauchos that follow the royalist cause.

Chapter 17 | *Doña Bárbara*

1. After 1924, oil exports exceeded non-oil exports, and the difference increased from then on (Coronil 1997, 117). Furthermore, the agrarian exports from the llano would represent a dwindling fraction of total agrarian exports, especially relative to

coffee, the base of the Venezuelan economy from the mid-nineteenth century to the Great Depression (Yarrington 1997).

2. Manuel Caballero cunningly compares the two forms of opposition to Gómez during the 1920s. The older form was linked to the secular model of the "invasion" (with illustrious predecessors in Miranda and Bolívar), such as the invasions attempted by Román Delgado Chalbaud, José Rafael Gabaldón, and Rafael Simón Urbina. These were easily suppressed by Gómez, now in command of a modern army for whom the insurgents were no match. The student protests of 1928, on the other hand, were an innovation within the Venezuelan political landscape that deliberately distinguished themselves from the caudillo model. This challenge dealt a severe blow to the legitimacy and public image of the caudillo, since Gómez reportedly did not know how to handle them (Caballero 1993, 273–334).

Conclusions

1. Even though his sources are mostly literary works or folklore, Hobsbawm frequently treats these narrative motifs as if they were historical facts. This has been one of the more acute criticisms directed against the classic model of the social bandit (Joseph 1990, 8). Hobsbawm has fully acknowledged the validity of this criticism (Hobsbawm [1969] 2000, 180). In this book I treated them as what they are: narrative motifs.

2. An example of invulnerability and supernatural power is Isidro Velázquez, the famous twentieth-century bandit from Chaco province in Argentina whose neckerchief pointed toward the direction from which the police came, allowing him to invariably escape persecution. His battle cry (*sapukay*) was believed to have the power to immobilize those in his pursuit (Carri 1968, 39). Even the police confirmed the supernatural powers of this bandit. A Chaco state trooper, interviewed by the *Revista Gente* in 1967, confirmed that "it is impossible [to catch Velázquez]. He has the *payé* [magic], and I am sure that if we shoot him the bullets are not going to penetrate him" (quoted in Carri 1968, 67). It is said that when the state police finally ambushed and shot him to death, they did not dare get close to him, for fear that he might rise from the dead. Another example of supernatural power is "Gauchito Gil," a bandit of the Corrientes province in Argentina who is believed to have performed a number of healings from beyond the grave. He is extensively revered in all the provinces of the Argentina littoral, and his images can be purchased at the gates of many public hospitals, primarily those that cater to the poor. Also, Isidro Velázquez's ghost, as legend goes, haunted the schoolteacher responsible for the betrayal that cost him his life. She is reputed to have gone mad because of her action.

3. Roger Bartra, in his groundbreaking *La jaula de la melancolía* follows some of these motifs well into twentieth-century Mexico (1987, 63ff.).

4. It is relevant to note that all comparisons are with nomadic peoples. There is, however, a variant of the main orientalist trope as developed by Said. It was used

more sparingly in order to characterize certain authoritarian regimes such as the one of Paraguayan dictator Francia. In this case, the analogue is Asian despotism, and more specifically the Chinese bureaucratic empire (Sarmiento 1845, 11).

5. For a careful examination of orientalism in *Facundo*, see Carlos Altamirano 1994.

6. See Prieto 1996 for an examination of the role of foreign travelers' accounts in the constitution of Argentine literature and some of its founding tropes (e.g., the *desierto*).

7. The close relationships between a new experience of temporality and the imagining of the nation-state have been famously examined by Benedict Anderson (1983, 188).

8. By the same token, the colony was for nineteenth-century liberals a sort of time interval during which America had left history, to later rejoin it (as a sort of awakening) with the wars of independence (this is the famous trope of the "Colonial Nap" or "Colonial Slumber"). This is why, in some cases, banditry and colony are considered to pertain to the same reality.

9. Though very rare, female bandit chiefs existed. However, with the exceptions of some remarks in Chumbita 2000 for the Argentine case, Vanderwood 1992 for the Mexican case, and Antônio Amaury Corrêa de Araújo (1984) for the Brazilian case, the history of female banditry in Latin America has yet to be written.

10. We see this scenario played out in *Martín Fierro, Los de abajo, Las lanzas coloradas, Zárate, El Zarco,* and the many versions of the Murieta story, among others. This defilement of the female or treason by the female is, as the legend goes, the decisive event that led Antonio Mendes Maciel, schoolteacher and shopkeeper, to become the fanatical leader of the jagunços and the reason why Pancho Villa, the most famous bandit of them all, became an outlaw in the first place.

11. These examples of feasts in alternative spaces are found in *Juan Moreira, Zárate, El Zarco, Los de abajo, ¡Vámonos con Pancho Villa!,* and *Las lanzas coloradas.*

12. Eighteenth-century England seems not to have been much different. Abbé le Blanc recounts that travelers through rural England used to set aside a specific amount of money (ten or a dozen guineas) as a tribute to highwaymen so that they might finish their journey unharmed (quoted in Seal 1996, 54).

References

Primary Sources

Acevedo Díaz, Eduardo. [1888] 1985. *Ismael*. Montevideo: Biblioteca Artigas. Colección de clásicos uruguayos.

Acevedo Hernández, Antonio. 1938. *Joaquín Murieta: drama en seis actos*. Santiago, Chile: Ercilla.

Acosta, Oscar "Zeta." [1973] 1989. *The Revolt of the Cockroach People*. New York: Vintage Books.

Aira, César. 1977. *Moreira*. Buenos Aires: Achával solo, fabricante de libros.

Alamán, Lucas. 1849–1852. *Historia de Méjico desde los primeros movimientos que prepararon su independencia en el año de 1808, hasta la época presente*. Mexico City: Imprenta de J. M. Lara.

Alberdi, Juan Bautista. [1870] 1944. *El crimen de la guerra*. Buenos Aires: Editorial Jackson.

Alegría, Ciro. [1941] 1963. *El mundo es ancho y ajeno: novelas completas*. Madrid: Aguilar.

Alencar, José de. [1870] 1999. *O gaúcho*. Porto Alegre, Brazil: L&PM.

———. [1872] 1977. *Til*. Rio de Janeiro: Livraria José Olympo Editora.

———. [1875] 1977. *O sertanejo*. Rio de Janeiro: Livraria José Olympo Editora.

Almeida, José Américo de. [1928] 1972. *A bagaceira*. Rio de Janeiro: Livraria José Olympo Editora.

———. [1935] 1979. *Coiteiros*. Rio de Janeiro: Editora Civilização Brasileira.

Altamirano, Ignacio Manuel. [1869] 1986. *Clemencia*. Mexico City: Secretaría de Educación Pública.

———. [1871] 1999. *La navidad en las montañas*. Mexico City: Editorial Porrúa.

———. [1901] 2000. *El Zarco*. Veracruz: Universidad Veracruzana.

———. 1989. *Obras completas XIX: periodismo político 2*. Mexico City: Consejo Nacional para la Cultura y las Artes.

Amado, Jorge. 1937. *Capitães da areia*. São Paulo: Livraria Martins Editora.

———. [1943] 1995. *Terras do sem fim*. São Paulo: Livraria Martins Editora.

———. 1946. *Seara vermelha*. São Paulo: Livraria Martins Editora.

Ampère, Jean. 1855. *Promenade en Amérique: États-Unis, Cuba, Mexique*. Paris: Michel Levy.

Angelis, Pedro de. 1945. *Acusación y defensa de Rosas*. Buenos Aires: Editorial La Facultad.

Apuleius. 1989. *Metamophoses*. Edited and translated by Arthur Hanson. 2 vols. Cambridge, MA: Harvard University Press.

Arinos, Afonso. [1898] 1968. *Os jagunços*. Rio de Janeiro: Philobiblion.

Arlt, Roberto. [1926] 1999. *El juguete rabioso*. Madrid: Cátedra.

———. [1934] 1997. *En el país del viento: viaje a la Patagonia (1934)*. Buenos Aires: Ediciones Simurg.

Ascasubi, Hilario. [1872] 1972. *Santos Vega, o los mellizos de la Flor: antología de la poesía gauchesca*. Edited by Horacio Jorge Becco. Bilbao, Spain: Aguilar.

Augustine, Bishop of Hippo. 1988. *The City of God against the Pagans*. Cambridge and New York: Cambridge University Press.

Azuela, Mariano. [1915/1916]. 1996. *Los de abajo*. Edited by Jorge Ruffinelli. Nanterre, France: Archivos.

———. [1960a] 1993. El novelista y su ambiente. In *Obras completas de Mariano Azuela*, volume 3. Mexico City: FCE.

———. [1960b] 1993. Precursores. In *Obras completas de Mariano Azuela*, volume 3. Mexico City: FCE.

Baptista, Pedro. 1929. *Cangaceiros do nordeste*. Parahyba do Norte, Brazil: Libraría S. Paulo.

Barrera, Carlos. [1915] 1997. *Esclavos: tragedia en tres actos y en prosa*. In *Perfil y muestra del teatro de la Revolución mexicana*, by Marcela del Río Reyes. Mexico City: Fondo de Cultura Económica.

Barreto, Lima, dir. 1953. *O cangaceiro*. Script by Rachel de Queiroz. Veracruz, Mexico: Companhia Cinematográfica Vera Cruz.

Barros, Flávio de (pictures), and Cícero Antônio de Almeida (text). 1997. *Canudos: imagens da guerra*. Rio de Janeiro: Editora Nova Aguilar.

Barroso, Gustavo. [1912] 1962. *Terra de sol: natureza e costumes do norte*. Fortaleza, Brazil: Imprensa Universitaria do Ceará.

———. [1918] 1931. *Heróes e bandidos (os cangaceiros do nordeste)*. Rio de Janeiro: Livraria Francisco Alves.

Bayer, Osvaldo. [1972] 1992. *La Patagonia rebelde I: los bandoleros*. Buenos Aires: Editorial Planeta.

Benício, Manoel. [1899] 1997. *O rei dos jagunços*. Rio de Janeiro: Editora Fundação Getulio Vargas.

Blanco, Eduardo. [1881] 1981. *Venezuela heroica*. Caracas: Ediciones de la Presidencia de la República.

———. [1882] 1997. *Zárate*. Caracas: Monte Ávila Editores Latinoamericana.

———. 1954. *Las noches del Panteón y otras obras*. Caracas: Línea Aeropostal Venezolana.

Blanco-Fombona, Rufino. [1907] 1988. *El hombre de hierro*. Caracas: Monte Ávila Editores.

Bolívar, Simón. 1939. *Proclamas y discursos del Libertador, mandados publicar por el gobierno de Venezuela, presidido por el general Eleazar López Contreras. Corregidos conforme a los originales, con la colaboración de la Señorita Esther Barret de Nazaris, y bajo la inspección de monseñor Nicolás E. Navarro y del Dr. Cristóbal L. Mendoza.* Caracas: Litografía y tipografía del Comercio.

Borges, Jorge Luis. [1974] 1985. *Obras completas.* Volumes 1 and 2. Buenos Aires: Emecé-Círculo de lectores.

———. 1996. *Obras completas.* Volumes 3 and 4. Buenos Aires: Emecé-Círculo de lectores.

———, and Betina Edelberg. [1965] 1974. *Leopoldo Lugones.* In *Obras completas en colaboración.* Buenos Aires: Emecé-Círculo de lectores.

———, and Margarita Guerrero. [1953] 1979. *El Martín Fierro.* In *Obras completas en colaboración.* Buenos Aires: Emecé.

Bunge, Carlos Octavio. 1903. *Nuestra América.* Barcelona: Henrich y Ca.

———. 1913. El derecho en la literatura gauchesca: discurso leído ante la Academia de Filosofía y Letras de la Universidad de Buenos Aires en la recepción pública. Buenos Aires: Academia de Filosofía y Letras. http://www.clarin.com/pbda/gauchesca/bunge/b-602230.htm.

Burton, Richard Francis, comp. and trans. 1897. *The Book of the Thousand Nights and a Night.* London: H. S. Nichols.

Calderón de la Barca, Madame. 1843. *Life in Mexico, during a Residence of Two Years in That Country.* London: Chapman and Hall.

Cambaceres, Eugenio. [1885] 2006. *En la sangre.* Buenos Aires: Stockcero.

Cané, Miguel, Sr. 1858. *Esther: novela original.* Buenos Aires: Imprenta de Mayo.

Carrió de la Vandera (Concolorcorvo). [1773] 1997. *El lazarillo de ciegos caminantes.* Buenos Aires: Emecé Editores.

Castellanos, Rosario. [1962] 1977. *Oficio de tinieblas.* New York: Penguin.

Clausewitz, Carl von. [1832] 1982. *On War.* London: Penguin.

Código Penal para el Distrito Federal y Territorio de la Baja-California sobre delitos de fuero común y para toda la República sobre delitos contra la Federación. 1871. Mexico City: Imprenta de Gobierno, en Palacio.

Cova García, Luis. 1955. *El bandolerismo en Venezuela (el estudio psicológico, antropológico, psiquiátrico y social del bandolero venezolano que actuó como caudillo en nuestras guerras civiles).* Alcalá de Henares, Spain: Imprenta talleres penitenciarios.

da Cunha, Euclides. [1902] 1995. *Os sertões: campanha de Canudos.* In *Obra completa.* Volume 2. Rio de Janeiro: Editora Nova Aguilar.

———. [1939] 1995. *Canudos (Diario de uma expedição).* In *Obra completa.* Volume 2. Rio de Janeiro: Editora Nova Aguilar.

———. 1995. A Nossa Vendéia. In *Artigos, fragmentos e notas.* In *Obra completa.* Volume 2. Rio de Janeiro: Editora Nova Aguilar.

Darwin, Charles. [1839] 2001. *The Voyage of the Beagle.* New York: Modern Library.

Días Fernandes, Carlos. 1914. *Os cangaceiros: romance de costumes sertanejos.* Parahyba do Norte, Brazil: Imprensa official.

Díaz Rodríguez, Manuel. [1901] 1982. *Ídolos rotos.* In *Narrativa y ensayo.* Caracas: Biblioteca Ayacucho.

———. [1902] 1982. *Sangre patricia.* In *Narrativa y ensayo.* Caracas: Biblioteca Ayacucho.

Droguett, Carlos. [1960] 1993. *Eloy.* Santiago, Chile: Editorial Universitaria.

Ebelot, Alfredo. [1889–1890] 2001. *La pampa: costumbres argentina.* Buenos Aires: Taurus.

Echeverría, Esteban. [1871] 1993. *El matadero: la cautiva.* Madrid: Cátedra.

Fernández Gama, José Bernardo. [1844] 1977. *Memórias históricas de província de Pernambuco.* Recife, Brazil: Arquivo Público estadual.

Fernández de Lizardi, José Joaquín. [1816/1830] 1996. *El periquillo sarniento.* 5 vols. Mexico City: Porrúa.

Frías, Félix. 1945. *La gloria del tirano Rosas, y otros escritos políticos y polémicos.* Buenos Aires: Jackson.

Fuentes, Carlos. 1985. *Gringo viejo.* Mexico City: FCR.

Gallegos, Rómulo. [1929] 1997. *Doña Bárbara.* Madrid: Cátedra.

Gálvez, Felipe, ed. 1987. *Extracto de la causa formada al ex coronel Juan Yáñez y sus socios: edición facsimilar del folleto de 1839.* Mexico City: Ediciones y Distribuciones Hispánicas.

Gálvez, Manuel. [1910] 2001. *El diario de Gabriel Quiroga: opiniones sobre la vida argentina.* Buenos Aires: Taurus.

García, Juan Agustín. [1900] 1986. *La ciudad indiana: Buenos Aires desde 1600 hasta mediados del siglo XVIII.* Buenos Aires: Hyspamérica.

García de León, Antonio, ed. 1994. *EZLN documentos y comunicados: 1 de enero–8 agosto de 1994.* Mexico City: Ediciones Era.

———. 1995. *EZLN documentos y comunicados: 2, 15 de agosto de 1994–29 de septiembre de 1995.* Mexico City: Ediciones Era.

García Márquez, Gabriel. [1967] 2003. *Cien años de soledad.* Madrid: Cátedra.

Ghiraldo, Alberto. 1906. *Alma gaucha.* Madrid: Renacimiento.

Glantz, Margo. 1964. *Viajes en México: crónicas extranjeras.* Mexico City: Secretaría de Obras Públicas.

Gonzales, Rodolpho. [1967] 1972. *I Am Joaquin.* Toronto: Bantam Books.

González, Juan Vicente. 1865. *Biografía de José Félix Ribas.* Paris: Casa editorial Garnier hermanos.

Guerrero, Julio. 1901. *La génesis del crimen en México: estudio de psiquiatría social.* Paris and Mexico City: Librería de la Viuda de Bouret.

———. 1905a. *Discurso inaugural de la Academia de Ciencias Sociales de México, leído por el Licenciado Julio Guerrero la noche del 29 de Mayo de 1905, en la Escuela N. Preparatoria.* Mexico City: Imprenta del Gobierno Federal.

———. 1905b. *Causas de la transformación monetaria en México*. Mexico City: Imprenta del Gobierno Federal.

Guimarães, Bernardo. [1873] 1944. *O Indio Afonso*. In *Quatro romances de Bernardo Guimarães*. São Paulo: Livraria Martins Editora.

Guimarães Rosa, João. [1956] 1986. *Grande sertão: veredas*. Rio de Janeiro: Nova Fronteira.

Güiraldes, Ricardo. [1926] 2002. *Don Segundo Sombra*. Madrid: Cátedra.

Gutiérrez, Eduardo. [1879] 1999. *Juan Moreira*. Buenos Aires: Perfil Libros.

———. [1886] 1960. *El Chacho*. Buenos Aires: Hachette.

———. 1886. *El rastreador*. Buenos Aires: N. Tommasi.

———. 1886. *Juan sin patria*. Buenos Aires: N. Tommasi.

———. 1886. *La muerte de un héroe*. Buenos Aires: N. Tommasi.

———. [1886] 1961. *Los montoneros*. Buenos Aires: Hachette.

———. 1891. *El tigre de Quequén*. Buenos Aires: L. Maucci.

———. 1899. *Los hermanos Barrientos*. Buenos Aires: N. Tommasi.

———. 1900. *Pastor Luna*. Buenos Aires: N. Tommasi.

———. 1901. *Santos Vega*. Buenos Aires: N. Tommasi.

———. 1932. *Una amistad hasta la muerte*. Buenos Aires: J. C. Rovira.

———. 1951. *Juan Cuello*. Buenos Aires: Editorial Tor.

———. 1999. *Hormiga negra*. Buenos Aires: Perfil Libros.

———, and José J. Podestá. [1886] 1986. *Juan Moreira: drama en dos actos*. In *Teatro Rioplatense (1886–1930)*, edited by Jorge Lafforgue. Caracas: Biblioteca Ayacucho.

Head, Francis Bond. [1826] 1986. *Rough Notes Taken during Some Rapid Journeys across the Pampas and among the Andes*. Buenos Aires: Hyspamérica.

Hernández, José. [1863] 1999. *El Chacho*. Rosario, Argentina: Ameghino Editora.

———. [1872/1879] 2001. *El gaucho Martín Fierro (La ida)* and *La vuelta de Martín Fierro*. Nanterre Cedex, France: Archivos.

Hudson, William Henry. [1885] 1979. *The Purple Land*. Berkeley, CA: Creative Arts Book Company.

———. [1918] 1939. *Far Away and Long Ago*. London: J. M. Dent & Sons.

Inclán, Luis G. [1865] 1984. *Astucia: el jefe de los Hermanos de la Hoja o los charros contrabandistas de la Rama: novela histórica de costumbres mexicanas con episodios originales*. Mexico City: Porrúa.

Ingenieros, José. [1903] 1962. *La sicopatología en el arte*. In *Obras completas*, volume 1. Buenos Aires: Ediciones Mar Océano.

———. 1910. *El delito y la pena ante la filosofía biológica*. Buenos Aires: Talleres gráficos de la penitenciaría nacional.

———. 1911. La psicología de Juan Moreira. *Archivos de psiquiatría y criminología* (Buenos Aires) 9:630–31.

Irving, Washington. 1975. *The Complete Tales of Washington Irving*. Garden City, NY: Doubleday.

Ker Porter, Sir Robert. 1966. *Caracas Diary, 1825–1842: A British Diplomat in a Newborn Nation*. Caracas: Instituto Otto y Magdalena Blohm.

Key Ayala, Santiago. 1920. *Eduardo Blanco y la génesis de Venezuela heroica*. Caracas: Tipografía Americana.

Lampião (Virgulino Ferreira da Silva), and Octacílio Macêdo. [1926]. *Lampião por ele mismo: entrevista en Juazeiro*. http://www.infonet.com.br/lampiao/cangaceiro.htm. Accessed September 29, 2005.

Las Casas, Bartolomé de. [1552] 2001. *Brevísima relación de la destruición de las Indias*. Madrid: Cátedra.

Lecuna, Vicente. 1923. La guerra de independencia en los llanos de Venezuela. *Boletín de la Academia Nacional de la Historia* 12(21):1017–35.

Leguizamón, Martiniano. [1896] 1977. Calandria. In *Teatro Rioplatense (1886–1930)*, edited by Jorge Lafforgue. Caracas: Biblioteca Ayacucho.

Lewis, Matthew. [1796] 1995. *The Monk*. Oxford and New York: Oxford University Press.

Llamozas, José Ambrosio. [1815] 1921. Memorial presentado al Rey en Madrid por el doctor José Ambrosio Llamozas, vicario y capellán primero del ejército de Boves. *Boletín de la Academia Nacional de la Historia* 5(17):515–27.

Lugones, Leopoldo. [1904] 1985. *El imperio Jesuítico*. Madrid: Hispamérica.

———. [1905] 1995. *La guerra gaucha*. Mexico City: CONACULTA.

———. 1915. *El ejército de la Ilíada*. Buenos Aires: Otero & Co., impresores.

———. [1916] 1972. *El payador*. Buenos Aires: Huemul.

———. [1938] 1980. *Historia de Roca*. Buenos Aires: Editorial de Belgrano.

———. [1938] 1999. *Romances del Río Seco*. Buenos Aires: Ediciones Pasco.

———. 1988. *Historia de Sarmiento*. Buenos Aires: Academia Argentina de Letras.

Lussich, Antonio. [1872] 1972. Los tres gauchos orientales. In *Antología de la poesía gauchesca*. Bilbao, Spain: Aguilar.

———. [1873] 1972. El matrero Luciano Santos. In *Antología de la poesía gauchesca*. Bilbao, Spain: Aguilar.

MacCann, William. 1853. *Two Thousand Miles' Ride through the Argentine Provinces*. 2 vols. London: Smith, Elder & Company.

Machiavelli, Niccolò. [1513] 1998. *The Prince*. Chicago and London: University of Chicago Press.

Magdaleno, Mauricio. 1937. *El resplandor, novela*. Mexico City: Ediciones Botas.

Mansilla, Lucio V. [1870] 1987. *Una excursión a los indios ranqueles*. 2 vols. Buenos Aires: CEDAL.

Marín, Rufino. 1933. *Hablan desde la cárcel los hijos de Martín Fierro: reportajes hechos en el penal de Viedma, a los más famosos bandoleros del Sud*. Buenos Aires: Librerías Anaconda.

Marlowe, Christopher. [c. 1590] 1998. *Tamburlaine the Great*. In *Doctor Faustus and Other Plays*. Oxford: Oxford University Press.

Martínez-Estrada, Ezequiel. [1948] 1983. *Muerte y transfiguración del Martín Fierro: ensayo de interpretación de la vida argentina*. 4 vols. Buenos Aires: CEDAL.

Mayer, Brantz. 1844. *Mexico as It Was and as It Is*. New York: J. Winchester, New World Press; London and Paris: Wiley and Putnam.

Mitre, Bartolomé. [1857] 1927–28. *Historia de Belgrano y de la independencia argentina*. Buenos Aires: J. Roldan.

Montalvo, Juan. [1880–1882] 1977. *Las catilinarias; El cosmopolita; El regenerador*. 3 vols. in one. Caracas: Biblioteca Ayacucho.

Montesquieu, Charles de Secondat, baron de. [1748] 1989. *The Spirit of the Laws*. Cambridge: Cambridge University Press.

Moro, Roberto, comp. 1974. *Rosas en las láminas de "El grito" y "El Grito argentino, Muera Rosas!"* Buenos Aires: A. Peña Lillo.

Muñoz, Rafael E. [1931a] 1960. *Se llevaron el cañón para Bachimba*. Volume 4, *La novela de la Revolución Mexicana*, collected by Antonio Castro Leal. Mexico City: Aguilar.

———. [1931b] 1999. *¡Vámonos con Pancho Villa!* Mexico City: Espasa-Calpe.

Navarro-Viola, Alberto. 1880, 1886. *Anuario Bibliográfico de la República Argentina*. Buenos Aires: Imprenta del Mercurio.

Neruda, Pablo. 1966. *Fulgor y muerte de Joaquín Murieta, bandido chileno injusticiado en California el 23 de julio de 1853*. Santiago, Chile: Zig-Zag.

Nina Rodrigues, Raimundo. 1939. *As collectividades anormaes*. Rio de Janeiro: Civilização Brasileira.

Nogueira Galvão, Walnice. 1974. *No calor da hora: a guerra de Canudos nos nornais (4.a expedição)*. São Paulo: Ática.

Novais-Sampaio, Consuelo, ed. 1999. *Canudos: cartas para o Barão*. São Paulo: EDUSP.

Novo, Salvador. 1948. *El Coronel Astucia y Los Hermanos de la Hoja o los charros contrabandistas: adaptación teatral de la novela de Luis Inclán*. Mexico City: Instituto Nacional de Bellas Artes.

Ocampo, María Luisa. [1929] 1997. *El corrido de Juan Saavedra*. In *Perfil y muestra del teatro de la revolución mexicana*, edited by Marcela del Río. Mexico City: FCE.

O'Leary, Daniel Florencio. 1879–88. *Memorias del general O'Leary (Narración: tomos primero y segundo)*. Caracas: Published for Simón B. O'Leary by Imprenta de la Gaceta oficial.

Páez, José Antonio. [1869] 1960. *Autobiografía*. 2 vols. N.p.: Ediciones Antártida.

Payno, Manuel. [1891] 2000. *Los bandidos de Río Frío*. Mexico City: Porrúa.

Payró, Roberto. [1910] 1991. *Las divertidas aventuras del nieto de Juan Moreira*. Buenos Aires: CEDAL.

Paz, Ireneo. 1895. *Manuel Lozada (el tigre de Alica)*. Mexico City: Imprenta, Litografía y Encuadernación de Ireneo Paz.

———. [1904] 1999. *Vida y aventuras del más célebre bandido sonorense Joaquín Murieta: sus grandes proezas en California*. Houston: Arte Público Press.

Petit, Magdalena. [1939] 1948. *Los Pincheira*. Santiago, Chile: Zig-Zag.

Piglia, Ricardo. 1997. *Plata quemada*. Buenos Aires: Planeta.

Pocaterra, José Rafael. 1990. *Memorias de un venezolano de la decadencia*. Caracas: Biblioteca Ayacucho.

Podestá, José J. [1930] 2003. *Medio siglo de farándula: memorias de José J. Podestá*. Buenos Aires: Galerna/Instituto Nacional de Teatro.

Popoca y Palacios, Lamberto. 1912. *Historia del bandalismo en el estado de Morelos: ¡Ayer como ahora! ¡1860! ¡1911! ¡Plateados! ¡Zapatistas!* Puebla, Mexico: Tipografía Guadalupana.

Potocki, Jan. 1995. *The Manuscript Found in Saragossa*. London: Viking.

Prieto, Guillermo. 1992. Grande y chispeante romance de las dos furias (Rojas y Lozada). In *Obras completas*. Mexico City: Consejo Nacional para la Cultura y las Artes.

Quesada, Ernesto. 1902. *El "criollismo" en la literatura Argentina*. Buenos Aires: Imprenta y Casa Editora de Coni Hermanos.

Radcliffe, Ann. [1794] 1988. *The Mysteries of Udolpho*. Oxford and New York: Oxford University Press.

Ramos Mejía, José María. [1899] 1972. *Las multitudes argentinas*. Rosario, Argentina: Biblioteca Vigil.

———. [1907] 1952. *Rosas y su tiempo*. Buenos Aires: La Cultura Argentina.

Reed, John. [1914] 1999. *Insurgent Mexico*. New York: International Publishers.

Rêgo, José Lins do. 1976. *Menino de engenho*. In *Ficção completa*. Petrópolis, Brazil: Editora Nova Aguilar.

Revueltas, José. [1943] 1980. *El luto humano*. Mexico City: Era.

———. [1949] 1991. *Los días terrenales*. Nanterre Cedex, France: Colección Archivos.

Rivera Indarte, José. 1946. *Tablas de sangre: es acción santa matar a Rosas*. Buenos Aires: Antonio dos Santos.

Robles, Pablo. [1891] 1982. *Los plateados de tierra caliente*. Mexico City: Premiá.

Rodriguez, Richard. 1992. *Days of Obligation: An Argument with My Mexican Father*. New York: Penguin.

Rojas, Ricardo. [1917–1923] 1948. *Los gauchescos*. Volumes 1 and 2, *Historia de la literatura Argentina: ensayo filosófico sobre la evolución de la cultura en el Plata*. Buenos Aires: Editorial Losada.

———. [1924] 1980. *Eurindia: ensayo de estética sobre las culturas americanas*. Buenos Aires: CEDAL.

Rollin Ridge, John (Yellow Bird). [1854] 1955. *The Life and Adventures of Joaquín Murieta, Celebrated California Bandit*. Norman: University of Oklahoma Press.

Romerogarcía, Manuel Vicente. [1890] 1972. *Peonía*. Caracas: Monte Avila.

Rousseau, Jean Jacques. [1762] 1967. *The Social Contract and Discourse on the Origin of Inequality*. New York: Pocket Books.

Rubione, Alfredo, ed. 1983. *En torno al criollismo: textos y polémica*. Buenos Aires: CEDAL.

Rulfo, Juan. [1955] 1992. *Pedro Páramo*. In *Toda la obra*. Nanterre Cedex, France: Archivos.

Sánchez, Florencio. 1941. *Teatro completo: veinte piezas seguidas de otras páginas del autor compliladas y anotadas por Dardo Cúneo*. Buenos Aires: Editorial Claridad.

Sarmiento, Domingo Faustino. [1845] 1977. *Facundo o civilización y barbarie*. Caracas: Biblioteca Ayacucho.

———. [1850] 1987. *Recuerdos de provincia*. Buenos Aires: CEDAL.

———. [1851] 1896. Decreto del gobernador de Salta alzándose con el poder. In *Argirópolis, capital de los estados confederados*. Volume 13, *Obras de D. F. Sarmiento*. Buenos Aires: Mariano Moreno.

———. [1852] 1997. *Campaña en el ejército grande*. Buenos Aires: Universidad Nacional de Quilmes.

———. [1867] 1896. El Chacho: último caudillo de la montonera de los Llanos. Volume 7, *Obras de D. F. Sarmiento*. Buenos Aires: Mariano Moreno.

———. [1875] 1900. Cuestiones de actualidad. In *Las doctrinas revolucionarias (1874–1880)*. Buenos Aires: Mariano Moreno.

———. [1883] 2001. *Conflictos y armonías de las razas en América*. San Justo, Argentina: Universidad Nacional de la Matanza.

———. 1899. *Práctica constitucional: primera parte*. Volume 31, *Obras de D. F. Sarmiento*. Buenos Aires: Mariano Moreno.

———. 1900a. *Práctica constitucional: segunda parte*. Volume 32, *Obras de D. F. Sarmiento*. Buenos Aires: Mariano Moreno.

———. 1900b. *Los desfallecimientos y los desvíos: política de 1880*. Buenos Aires: Mariano Moreno.

———. 1900c. *Memorias*. Volume 49, *Obras de D. F. Sarmiento*. Buenos Aires: Mariano Moreno.

———. 1909. *Viajes por Europa, Africa y América 1845–1847*. Volume 5, *Obras de D. F. Sarmiento*. Paris: Hermanos.

Schiller, Friedrich. [1795–1796] 1966. *Naïve and Sentimental Poetry; and On the Sublime: Two Essays*. New York: Ungar.

Scott, Walter. [1817] 1995. *Rob Roy*. London: Penguin.

Tatius, Achilles. *The Adventures of Leucippe and Clitophon*. Cambridge, MA: Harvard University Press.

Távora, Franklin. 1872. *Cartas a Cincinnato*. Pernambuco, Brazil: J.-W. De Medeiros, Livreiro, Editor.

———. 1876. *O Cabelleira: historia Pernambucana*. Rio de Janeiro: Typographia Nacional.

———. 1878. *O matuto*. Rio de Janeiro: Typographia Perseverança.

———. [1881] 1902. *Lourenço: cronica Pernambucana*. Rio de Janeiro: H. Garnier.

Theóphilo, Rodolfo. 1906. *Os Brilhantes*. Fortaleza, Brazil: Assis Bezerra.

Uslar Pietri, Arturo. [1931] 1993. *Las lanzas coloradas*. Edited by Domingo Miliani. Madrid: Cátedra.

Uslar Pietro, Juan. 1962. *Historia de la rebelión popular de 1814, contribución al estudio de la historia de Venezuela*. Caracas: Edime.

Valdez, Luis. 1992. *Bandido!* In *Zoot Suit and Other Plays*. Houston: Arte Público Press.

Vallenilla Lanz, Laureano. [1919] 1989. *Cesarismo democrático y otros textos*. Caracas: Ayacucho.

Varela, Félix. [1826] 1995. *Jicoténcal*. Houston: Arte Público Press.

Vizconde de Taunay. 1999. *Inocência*. São Paulo: L&PM Editores.

White, Ernest William. 1881. *Cameos from the Silver-Land, or the Experiences of a Young Naturalist in the Argentine Republic*. London: John Van Voorst.

Wordsworth, William. [1803–1807] 1932. Rob Roy's Grave. In *The Complete Poetical Works of Wordsworth*. Boston: Houghton Mifflin.

Yánez, Agustín. [1947] 1996. *Al filo del agua*. Nanterre Cedex, France: Colección Archivos.

Zorrilla de San Martín, Juan. [1910] 1985. *La epopeya de Artigas*. Montevideo: Biblioteca Artigas.

Secondary Sources

Abreu, Regina. 1998. *O enigma de* Os sertões. Rio de Janeiro: Rocco, Ministério da Cultura, Funarte.

Agamben, Giorgio. [2003] 2005. *State of Exception*. Chicago: University of Chicago Press.

Aguiar, Claudio. 1997. *Franklin Távora e o seu Tempo*. São Caetano do Sul, Brazil: Ateliê Editorial.

———. 1999. Introduçao: un romance redescoberto. Preface to *Um casamento no Arrabalde,* by Franklin Távora. Rio de Janeiro: Calibán.

Aguilar Camín, Héctor, and Lorenzo Meyer. 1994. *In the Shadow of the Mexican Revolution: Contemporary Mexican History, 1910–1989*. Austin: University of Texas Press.

Aguirre, Carlos. 2005. *The Criminals of Lima and Their Worlds: The Prison Experience, 1850–1935*. Durham, NC: Duke University Press.

Aguirre, Carlos, and Charles Walker, eds. 1990. *Bandoleros, abigeos y montoneros:*

criminalidad y violencia en el Perú, siglos XVII–XX. Lima: Instituto de apoyo agrario.

———, and Ricardo Salvatore. 2001. Introduction to *Crime and Punishment in Latin America: Law and Society since Late Colonial Times,* edited by Ricardo Salvatore, Carlos Aguirre, and Gilbert Joseph. Durham, NC, and London: Duke University Press.

Ahmad, Aijaz. 1995. Jameson's Rhetoric of Otherness and the "National Allegory." In *The Post-Colonial Studies Reader,* edited by Bill Ashcroft, Gareth Griffiths, and Helen Tiffin. London: Routledge.

Ainsa, Fernando. 1993. Eduardo Acevedo Díaz. In *Historia de la literature hispanoamericana.* Volume 2, *Del neoclasicismo al modernismo,* edited by Luis Iñigo Madrigal. Madrid: Cátedra.

Alonso, Carlos. 1990. *The Spanish American Regional Novel: Modernity and Autocthony.* Cambridge: Cambridge University Press.

Altamirano, Carlos. 1994. El orientalismo y la idea del despotismo en el *Facundo.* In *La imaginación histórica en el siglo XIX,* edited by Lelia Area and Mabel Moraña. Rosario, Argentina: UNR Editora.

Amory, Frederic. 1999. Euclides da Cunha and Brazilian Positivism. *Luso-Brazilian Review* 36:87–94.

Anna, Timothy. 1990. *The Mexican Empire of Iturbide.* Lincoln and London: University of Nebraska Press.

Andermann, Jens. 2000. *Mapas de poder: una arqueología literaria del espacio argentino.* Rosario, Argentina: Beatriz Viterbo Editora.

Anderson, Benedict. [1983] 1996. *Imagined Communities.* London: Verso.

———. 1992. El efecto tranquilizador del fratricidio: o de cómo las naciones imaginan sus genealogias. In *El nacionalismo mexicano,* edited by Cecilia Noriega Elio. Mexico City: El Colegio de Michoacán.

Andress, David. 2000. *Massacre at the Champ de Mars: Popular Dissent and Political Culture in the French Revolution.* Suffolk, England; Rochester, NY: Published for the Royal Historical Society by Boydell Press.

Appiah, Kwame Anthony. 1995. Race. In *Critical Terms for Literary Study,* edited by Frank Lentricchia and Thomas McLaughlin. Chicago: University of Chicago Press.

Araújo, Antônio Amaury Corrêa de. 1984. *Lampiño: as mulheres e o cangaço.* São Paulo: Traço Editora.

Archer, Christon. 1982. Banditry and Revolution in New Spain, 1790–1821. *Bibliotheca Americana* 1(2):59–90.

———. 1997. Politicization of the Army of New Spain during the War of Independence, 1810–1821. In *The Origins of Mexican National Politics: 1808–1847,* edited by Jaime E. Rodríguez O. Wilmington, DE: Scholarly Resources.

Ardao, Arturo. 2002. *Artigas y el artiguismo*. Montevideo: Ediciones de la Banda Oriental.

Area, Lelia, and Cristina Parodi. 1994. Escritura y silencio: el otro (?) *Facundo* de Sarmiento. In *la imaginación histórica en el siglo XIX*, edited by Lelia Area and Mabel Moraña. Rosario, Argentina: UNR Editora.

Askins, Arthur L. 1966. Franklin da Silveira Távora's *Literatura do norte*. In *Homenaje a Rodrígues-Moñino*. Madrid: Editorial Castalia.

Astesano, Eduardo. 1963. *Martín Fierro y la justicia social: primer manifiesto revolucionario del movimiento obrero argentino*. Buenos Aires: Ediciones Relevo.

Austen, Ralph A. 1986. Social Bandits and Other Heroic Criminals: Western Models of Resistance and Their Relevance for Africa. In *Banditry, Rebellion, and Social Protest in Africa*, edited by Donald Crummey. London and Portsmouth: James Curie–Heinemann.

Banko, Catalina. 1990. *Las luchas federalistas en Venezuela*. Caracas: Monte Avila.

Barkey, Karen. 1994. *Bandits and Bureaucrats: The Ottoman Route to State Centralization*. Ithaca, NY, and London: Cornell University Press.

Barnola, Pedro Pablo. 1963. *Eduardo Blanco, creador de la novela venezolana*. Caracas: Tipografía Vargas.

Barrera Bassols, Jacinto. 1987. *El bardo y el bandolero: la persecución de Santanón por Díaz Mirón*. Puebla, Mexico: Universidad Autónoma de Puebla.

Barrington, Moore. 1966. *Social Origins of Dictatorship and Democracy*. Boston: Beacon Press.

Barthes, Roland. [1957] 1995. *Mythologies*. New York: Hill and Wang.

———. [1970] 1974. *S/Z*. New York: Hill and Wang.

Bartra, Roger. 1987. *La jaula de la melancolía: identidad y metamorfosis del mexicano*. Mexico City: Grijalbo.

Baudrillard, Jean. [1990] 1999. *The Transparency of Evil: Essays on Extreme Phenomena*. London: Verso.

Bazant, Jan. 1991. From Independence to the Liberal Republic, 1821–1867. In *Mexico since Independence*, edited by Leslie Bethell. Cambridge: Cambridge University Press.

Becco, Horacio Jorge. [1972] 2001. Bibliografía Hernandiana. In *Martín Fierro*, by José Hernández [1872/1879]. Critical edition by Elida Lois and Angel Núñez. Barcelona: ALLCA XX.

Benarós, León. 1961. Eduardo Gutiérrez, una pasión de la verdad. Preface to *Los montoneros*, by Eduardo Gutiérrez. Buenos Aires: Hachette.

Benítez-Rojo, Antonio. 1996. José Joaquín Fernández de Lizardi and the Emergence of the Spanish American Novel as a National Project. *Modern Language Quarterly* 57(2):325–39.

Benjamin, Thomas. 2000. *La Revolución: Mexico's Great Revolution as Memory, Myth, and History*. Austin: University of Texas Press.

Benjamin, Walter. [1921] 1986. Critique of Violence. In *Reflections.* New York: Schocken Books.

———. 1977. *The Origin of German Tragic Drama.* London: NLB.

———. 2006. Thesis on the Philosophy of History. In *Walter Benjamin: Selected Writings, Volume 4, 1938–1940.* Cambridge, MA: Belknap Press of Harvard University Press.

Bernaldo de Quiros, Constancio. 1959. *El bandolerismo en España y México.* Mexico City: Editorial Jurídica Mexicana.

Bernucci, Leopoldo M. 2002. Preface to *Os sertões,* by Euclides da Cunha [1902]. São Paulo: Ateliê Editorial.

Beverley, John. 1987. *Del Lazarillo al sandinismo: estudios sobre la function ideological de la literature española e hispanoamericana.* Minneapolis: Prisma Institute.

———. 1999. *Subalternity and Representation: Arguments in Cultural Theory.* Durham, NC: Duke University Press.

Bhabha, Homi. [1990] 1995. DissemiNation. In *Nation and Narration,* edited by Homi K. Bhabha. London and New York: Routledge.

Billingsley, Phil. 1988. *Bandits in Republican China.* Stanford, CA: Stanford University Press.

Birkbeck, Christopher. 1991. Latin American Banditry as Peasant Resistance: A Dead-End Trail? *Latin American Research Review* 26(1):156–60.

Blanchot, Maurice. 1983. *L'écriture du desastre.* Paris: Gallimard.

Blok, Anton. 1972. The Peasant and the Brigand: Social Banditry Reconsidered. *Comparative Studies in Society and History* 14(4):494–503.

———. 1975. *The Mafia of a Sicilian Village, 1860–1960: A Study of Violent Peasant Entrepreneurs.* New York: Harper & Row.

———. 1998. Bandits and Boundaries: Robber Bands and Secret Societies on the Dutch Frontier (1730–1778). In *Challenging Authority: The Historical Study of Contentious Politics,* edited by Michael Hanagan, Leslie Page Moch, and Wayne te Brake. Minneapolis: University of Minnesota Press.

Bolet Toro, Francisco José. 1998. *Zárate:* las máscaras y los signos de la identidad nacional. *Revista de Literatura Hispanoamericana* 36:8–24.

———. 2000. *Zárate:* la nación entre idilios y ambiciones políticas. *Revista de Literatura Hispanoamericana* 41:61–82.

Borges, Dain. 1993. Puffy, Ugly, Slothful, and Inert: Degeneration in Brazilian Social Thought, 1880–1940. *Journal of Latin American Studies* 25:235–56.

———. 2001. Healing and Mischief: Witchcraft in Brazilian Law and Literature, 1890–1922. In *Crime and Punishment in Latin America: Law and Society since Late Colonial Times,* edited by Ricardo Salvatore, Carlos Aguirre, and Gilbert Joseph. Durham, NC, and London: Duke University Press.

Botana, Natalio. [1977] 1994. *El orden conservador: la política argentina entre 1880 y 1916.* Buenos Aires: Sudamericana.

———. 1994. Sarmiento and Political Order: Liberty, Power, and Virtue. In *Sarmiento: Author of a Nation,* edited by Tulio Halperín Donghi et al. Berkeley: University of California Press.

Botana, Natalio, and Ezequiel Gallo. 1997. *De la república possible a la república verdadera: 1880–1910.* Buenos Aires: Ariel.

Braudel, Fernand. [1949/1966] 1972. *The Mediterranean and the Mediterranean World in the Age of Philip II.* New York: Harper Colophon Books.

Brown, Nathan. 1990. Brigands and State Building: The Invention of Banditry in Modern Egypt. *Comparative Studies in Society and History* 32(2):258–81.

Buchbinder, Pablo. 1998. Caudillos y caudillismo: una perspectiva historiográfica. In *Caudillismos rioplatenses: nuevas miradas a un viejo problema,* edited by Noemí Goldman and Ricardo Salvatore. Buenos Aires: Eudeba.

Buffington, Robert. 2000. *Criminal and Citizen in Modern Mexico.* Lincoln: University of Nebraska Press.

Bulmer-Thomas, Victor. 1994. *The Economic History of Latin America since Independence.* Cambridge: Cambridge University Press.

Burns, E. Bradford. [1972] 1994. *Latin America: A Concise Interpretive History.* Englewood Cliffs, NJ: Prentice-Hall.

———. 1993. *A History of Brazil.* New York: Columbia University Press.

Bushnell, David, and Neill Macaulay. 1994. *The Emergence of Latin America in the Nineteenth Century.* New York: Oxford University Press.

Caballero, Manuel. 1993. *Gómez, el tirano liberal.* Caracas: Monte Avila.

Cabral de Mello, Evaldo. 1995. *A fronda dos Mazombos: nobres contra Mascates, Pernambuco 1666–1715.* São Paulo: Companhia das Letras.

Caimari, Lila. 2004. *Apenas un delincuente: crimen, castigo y cultura en Argentina, 1880–1955.* Buenos Aires: Siglo XXI.

Campbell, Leon G. 1982. Banditry and the Túpac Amaru Rebellion. *Bibliotheca Americana* 1(2):131–61.

Candido, Antônio. 1969. *Formação da literatura brasileira: 2º volume (1836–1880).* São Paulo: Livraria Martins Editora.

Carr, Barry. 1994. The Fate of the Vanguard under a Revolutionary State: Marxism's Contribution to the Construction of the Great Arch. In *Everyday Forms of State Formation: Revolution and the Negotiation of Rule in Modern Mexico,* edited by Gilbert M. Joseph and Daniel Nugent. Durham, NC, and London: Duke University Press.

Carrera Damas, Germán. 1972. *Boves: aspectos socioeconómicos de la guerra de independencia.* Caracas: Ediciones de la Biblioteca de la Universidad Central de Venezuela.

Carri, Roberto. [1968] 2001. *Isidro Velázquez: formas prerrevolucionarias de la violencia.* Buenos Aires: Colihue.

Cartwright, Cecilia Altuna. 1973. The Cangaceiro as a Fictional Character in the

Novels of Franklin Távora, Rodolfo Teófilo, and José Lins do Rêgo. Ph.D. dissertation, University of Wisconsin.

Castello, José Aderaldo. 1999. *A literatura brasileira: origens e unidade (1500–1960).* Volume 1. São Paulo: EDUSP.

Castro, Tomás de, and Antonio Alvarado. 1987. *Extracto de la causa formada al ex coronel Yáñez y socios por varios asaltos y robos cometidos en despoblado.* Mexico City: Ediciones Hispánicas.

Cella, Susana. 1992. Preface to *La guerra gaucha,* by Leopoldo Lugones [1905]. Buenos Aires: Losada.

Centeno, Miguel Angel. 2002. *Blood and Debt: War and the Nation-State in Latin America.* University Park: Pennsylvania State University Press.

Chakrabarty, Dipesh. 1997. Postcoloniality and the Artifice of History: Who Speaks for "Indian" Pasts? In *A Subaltern Studies Reader, 1986–1995,* edited by Ranajit Guha. Minneapolis: University of Minnesota Press.

Chandler, Billy Jaynes. 1978. *The Bandit King: Lampião of Brazil.* College Station and London: Texas A&M University Press.

———. 1987. Brazilian *Cangaceiros* as Social Bandits: A Critical Appraisal. In *Bandidos: The Varieties of Latin American Banditry,* edited by Richard W. Slatta. New York: Greenwood Press.

Chatterjee, Partha. [1985] 1996. *Nationalist Thought and the Colonial World: A Derivative Discourse.* Minneapolis: University of Minnesota Press.

———. 1993. *The Nation and Its Fragments: Colonial and Postcolonial Histories.* Princeton, NJ: Princeton University Press.

Chávez, Fermín. 2001. *Martín Fierro*: sus contenidos ideológicos y políticos. In *Martín Fierro,* by José Hernández [1872/1879]. Critical edition by Elida Lois and Angel Núñez. Barcelona: ALLCA XX.

Chevalier, Louis. 1973. *Laboring Classes and Dangerous Classes in Paris during the First Half of the Nineteenth Century.* New York: H. Fertig.

Chumbita, Hugo. 1999. *Ultima frontera.* Buenos Aires: Planeta.

———. 2000. *Jinetes Rebeldes: historia del bandolerismo social en Argentina.* Buenos Aires: Vergara.

Clementi, Hebe. [1980] 1994. Frontier Peoples and National Identity. In *Where Cultures Meet: Frontiers in Latin American History,* edited by David Weber and Jane Rausch. Wilmington, DE: Scholarly Resources.

Coelho Fontes, Oleone. 1999. *Lampião na Bahia.* Petrópolis, Brazil: Editora Vozes.

Cohen, Jeffrey Jerome, ed. 1996. *Monster Theory: Reading Culture.* Minneapolis: University of Minnesota Press.

Collier, George Allen, and Elizabeth Lowery Quanatiello. 1994. *Basta!: Land and the Zapatista Rebellion in Chiapas.* Oakland, CA: Food First Book, the Institute for Food and Development Policy.

Collins, Randall. 1975. *Conflict Sociology: Toward an Explanatory Science*. New York: Academic Press.

Compton, Timothy G. 1997. *Mexican Picaresque Narratives: Periquillo and Kin*. Lewisburg, PA: Bucknell University Press.

Contador, Ana María. 1998. *Los Pincheira: un caso de bandidaje social, Chile, 1817–1832*. Santiago, Chile: Bravo y Allende.

Conway, Christopher Brian. 1996. Imagining Bolívar: Mythic Representation and Official Memory in Nineteenth Century Venezuela. Ph.D. dissertation, University of California–San Diego.

Cornejo-Polar, Antonio. 1994. *Escribir en el aire: ensayo sobre la heterogeneidad sociocultural en las literaturas andinas*. Lima: Editorial Horizonte.

Corominas, Joan. 1954. *Diccionario crítico etimológico de la lengua castellana*. Bern, Switzerland: Editorial Francke.

Coronil, Fernando. 1997. *The Magical State: Nature, Money, and Modernity in Venezuela*. Chicago and London: University of Chicago Press.

Corrigan, Philip. 1994. State Formation. In *Everyday Forms of State Formation: Revolution and the Negotiation of Rule in Modern Mexico,* edited by Gilbert Joseph and Daniel Nugent. Durham, NC, and London: Duke University Press.

Costa Lima, Luiz. 1997. *Terra ignota: aconstruçao de Os sertões*. Rio de Janeiro: Civilização Brasileira.

Covarrubias Orozco, Sebastián de. [1611] 1994. *Tesoro de la lengua castellana o española*. Edited by Felipe Maldonado; revised by Manuel Camarero. Madrid: Editorial Castalia.Covo, Jacqueline. 1982. Théorie et pratique du roman nationaliste chez le Mexicain Ignacio Manuel Altamirano. In *Nationalisme et littérature en Espagne et en Amérique Latine au XIXe siècle,* edited by Claude Dumas. Lille, France: Université de Lille III.

Cros, Edmond. 1985. The Values of Liberalism in *El Periquillo Sarniento. Sociocriticism* 2:85–109.

Crummey, Donald. 1986. The Great Beast. Introduction to *Banditry, Rebellion, and Social Protest in Africa,* edited by Donald Crummey. London and Portsmouth: James Curie–Heinemann.

Cruz, Jacqueline. 1993–1994. La moral tradicional y la identidad mexicana vistas a través de los personajes femeninos de *El Zarco. In Explicación de Textos Literarios* 22(1):73–86.

Dabove, Juan Pablo. 1998. Ficción autobiográfica y letrado "nacional": sobre *El periquillo sarniento*, de J. Fernández de Lizardi. *Hispanic Culture Review* 5(12):53–67.

———. 1999. Espejos de la ciudad letrada: el "arrastraderito" y el juego como metáforas políticas en *El periquillo sarniento. Revista Iberoamericana* 65(186):31–48.

———. 2002. *Las lanzas coloradas*: vanguardia, nación y guerra. In *Las lanzas coloradas: primera narrativa,* by Arturo Uslar Pietri, edited by François Delprat. Nanterre, France: Signatarios del Acuerdo Archivos, ALLCA XX, Université Paris.

————. 2003. Mapas heterotrópicos de América Latina. In *Heterotropías: narrativas de identidad y alteridad latinoamericana,* edited by Carlos Jáuregui and Juan Pablo Dabove. Pittsburgh, PA: Instituto Internacional de Literatura Iberoamericana.

————. 2004. *Tomóchic,* de Heriberto Frías: violencia campesina, melancolía y genealogía fratricida de las naciones. *Revista de crítica literaria latinoamericana* 30(60):351–73.

Dahbour, Omar, and Micheline R. Ishay, eds. 1997. *The Nationalism Reader.* Atlantic Highlands, NJ: Humanities Press.

Danker, Uwe. 1988. Bandits and the State: Robbers and the Authorities in the Holy Roman Empire. In *The German Underworld,* edited by Richard Evans. London and New York: Routledge.

Dantas, Paulo. 1953. Franklin Távora e o romance do norte. In *O Cabeleira,* by Franklin Távora [1876]. São Paulo: Ediciones Melhoramientos.

————. 1969. *Os sertões de Euclides e outros sertões.* São Paulo: Conselho Estadual de Cultura.

Daus, Ronald. 1982. *O ciclo épico dos cangaceiros na poesia popular do nordeste.* Rio de Janeiro: Fundação Casa de Rui Barbosa, 1982.

Deans-Smith, Susan. 1992. *Bureaucrats, Planters, and Workers: The Making of the Tobacco Monopoly in Bourbon Mexico.* Austin: University of Texas Press.

de la Fuente, Ariel. 1998. "Gauchos," "Montoneros," y "Montoneras." In *Caudillismos rioplatenses: nuevas miradas a un viejo problema,* edited by Noemí Goldman and Ricardo Salvatore. Buenos Aires: Eudeba.

————. 2000. *Children of Facundo: Caudillo and Gaucho Insurgency during the Argentine State-Formation Process (La Rioja, 1853–1870).* Durham, NC: Duke University Press.

Deleuze, Gilles. [1990] 1995. *Negotiations.* New York: Columbia University Press.

————, and Félix Guattari. [1980] 1987. *A Thousand Plateaus: Capitalism and Schizophrenia.* Minneapolis: University of Minnesota Press.

————. [1991] 1994. *What Is Philosophy?* New York: Columbia University Press.

Della Cava, Ralph. 1970. *Miracle at Joaseiro.* New York: Columbia University Press.

Derrida, Jacques. [1967] 1997. *Of Grammatology.* Baltimore, MD: Johns Hopkins University Press.

Dessau, Adalbert. [1967] 1972. *La novela de la Revolución Mexicana.* Mexico City: Fondo de Cultura Económica.

Díaz, Arlene. 2001. Women, Order, and Progress in Guzmán Blanco's Venezuela. In *Crime and Punishment in Latin America: Law and Society since Late Colonial Times,* edited by Ricardo Salvatore, Carlos Aguirre, and Gilbert Joseph. Durham, NC, and London: Duke University Press.

Díaz de Ovando, Clementina. 1954. La visión histórica de Manuel Ignacio Altamirano. *Anales del Instituto de Investigaciones Estéticas.* Mexico City: UNAM.

Díaz-Ruiz, Ignacio. 2001. Ágapes, almuerzos, y "agachados" (los paladares mexicanos en Payno). In *Literatura mexicana del otro fin de siglo,* edited by Rafael Olea Franco. Mexico City: El Colegio de México, Centro de Estudios Linguisticos y Literarios.

Durkheim, Emile. [1893] 1997. *The Division of Labor in Society.* New York: Free Press.

———. [1895] 1965. *The Rules of Sociological Method.* New York: Free Press.

Eisenberg, Peter L. 1974. *The Sugar Industry in Pernambuco: Modernization without Change, 1840–1910.* Berkeley, Los Angeles, and London: University of California Press.

Eliade, Mircea. 1960. *Myth, Dreams, and Mysteries.* New York: Harper.

Elliott, Robert. 1970. *The Shape of Utopia.* Chicago: University of Chicago Press.

Elmore, Peter. 2007. Canudos: las otras escrituras. In *Os sertões*, by Euclides da Cunha [1905]. Critical edition by Leopoldo Bernucci. Nanterre, France: Colección Archivos.

Engels, Friedrich. [1845] 1958. *The Condition of the Working Class in England.* New York: Macmillan.

Englekirk, John Eugene. 1975. El descubrimiento de un narrador. In *Recopilación de textos sobre la novela de la Revolución Mexicana,* edited by Rogelio Rodríguez Coronel. Havana: Casa de las Américas.

Escalante, Evodio. 1997. Lectura ideológica de dos novelas de Manuel Altamirano. In *Homenaje a Ignacio Manuel Altamirano (1834–1893).* Xalapa, Mexico: Universidad Veracruzana.

Ewell, Judith. 1984. *Venezuela: A Century of Change.* Stanford, CA: Stanford University Press.

Facó, Rui. 1972. *Cangaceiros e fanáticos: gênese e lutas.* Rio de Janeiro: Editora Civilização Brasileira.

Fletcher, Angus. 1964. *Allegory: The Theory of a Symbolic Mode.* Ithaca, NY: Cornell University Press.

Flores Galindo, Alberto. 1990. Bandidos de la costa. In *Bandoleros, abigeos y montoneros: criminalidad y violencia en el Perú, siglos XVII–XX,* edited by Carlos Aguirre and Charles Walker. Lima: Instituto de apoyo agrario.

Foucault, Michel. [1971] 1998. Nietzsche, Genealogy, History. In *Aesthetics, Method, and Epistemology,* edited by James D. Faubion. New York: New Press.

———. [1975] 1995. *Discipline and Punish: The Birth of the Prison.* Translated by Alan Sheridan. 2nd ed. New York: Vintage Books.

Fradkin, Raúl O. 2005. Bandolerismo y politización de la población rural de Buenos Aires tras la crisis de la independencia (1815–1830). In *Nuevo mundo–mundos nuevos* 5. http://nuevomundo.revues.org/document309.html. May 3, 2005.

Franco, Jean. 1983. La heterogeneidad peligrosa: escritura y control social en vísperas de la independencia mexicana. *Hispamérica* 12(34–35):3–34

———. 2002. *The Decline and Fall of the Lettered City: Latin America in the Cold War.* Cambridge, MA: Harvard University Press.

Frazer, Christopher Brent. 1997. The Infernal Rage: Banditry and Revolution in the Mexican Bajío, 1910–1920. Ph.D. dissertation, University of Calgary.

Frega, Ana. 1998. La virtud y el poder: la soberanía particular de los pueblos en el proyecto artiguista. In *Caudillismos rioplatenses: nuevas miradas a un viejo problema*, edited by Noemí Goldman and Ricardo Salvatore. Buenos Aires: Eudeba.

Freud, Sigmund. [1912–1913] 1981. *Tótem y tabú*. In *Obras completas III*. Madrid: Editorial Biblioteca Nueva.

Gallant, Thomas W. 1999. Brigandage, Piracy, Capitalism, and State-Formation: Transnational Crime from a Historical World-Systems Perspective. In *States and Illegal Practices,* edited by Josiah McC. Heyman. Oxford and New York: Berg.

Gárate, Miriam. 1997. Argirópolis, canudos y las favelas: un ensayo de lectura comparada. *Revista Iberoamericana* 63(181):621–30.

Garavaglia, Juan Carlos. 1999. *Poder, conflicto y relaciones socials: el Río de la Plata, XVIII–XIX*. Rosario, Argentina: Homo Sapiens Ediciones.

———. 2001. El *Martín Fierro* y la vida rural en la campaña de Buenos Aires. In *Martín Fierro,* by José Hernández [1872/1879]. Critical edition by Elida Lois and Angel Núñez. Barcelona: ALLCA XX.

García-Canclini, Néstor. 1989. *Culturas Híbridas*. Mexico City: Grijalbo.

Gelman, Jorge. 1998. Un gigante con pies de barro: Rosas y los habitants de la campaña. In *Caudillismos rioplatenses: nuevas miradas a un viejo problema*, edited by Noemí Goldman and Ricardo Salvatore. Buenos Aires: Eudeba.

Genette, Gérard. 1982. *Figures of Literary Discourse*. New York: Columbia University Press.

Gerassi-Navarro, Nina. 1999. *Pirate Novels: Fictions of Nation Building in Spanish America*. Durham, NC, and London: Duke University Press.

Ghiano, Juan Carlos. 1955. *Lugones, escritor: notas para un análisis estilístico*. Buenos Aires: Editorial Raigal.

———. 1967. *Análisis de* La guerra gaucha. Buenos Aires: CEDAL.

Giddens, Anthony. 1985. *A Contemporary Critique of Historical Materialism*. Volume 2, *The Nation-State and Violence*. Oxford: Polity Press.

Gilman, Sander L. 1985. *Difference and Pathology: Stereotypes of Sexuality, Race, and Madness*. Ithaca, NY, and London: Cornell University Press.

———. 1991. *Inscribing the Other*. Lincoln: University of Nebraska Press.

Giron, Nicole. 1976. La idea de "cultura nacional" en el siglo XIX: Altamirano y Ramírez. In *En torno a la cultura nacional,* edited by H. A. Camin et al. Mexico City: Instituto Nacional Indigenista.

Glantz, Margo, comp. 1964. *Viajes en México: crónicas extranjeras (1821–1855)*. Mexico City: Secretaria de Obras Públicas.

———. 1985. Una utopía insurgente. *México en el arte* 10:44–48.

———. 1997. *Astucia,* de Luis G. Inclán, ¿novela "nacional" mexicana? *Revista Iberoamericana* 63(178–79):87–97.

———. 2003. La utopía del robo: *Los bandidos de Río Frío.* In *Heterotropías: narrativas de identidad y alteridad latinoamericana,* edited by Carlos Jáuregui and Juan Pablo Dabove. Pittsburgh, PA: Instituto Internacional de Literatura Iberoamericana.

Goic, Cedomil. 1982. La novela Hispanoamericana colonial. In *Historia de la literatura Hispanoamericana: época colonial,* edited by Luis Iñigo Madrigal. Madrid: Cátedra.

Goldman, Noemí. 1998. Los orígenes del federalismo rioplatense. In Volume 3 of *Nueva historia argentina,* edited by Noemí Goldman. Buenos Aires: Editorial Sudamericana.

———, and Ricardo Salvatore, eds. 1998. *Caudillismos rioplatenses: nuevas miradas a un viejo problema.* Buenos Aires: Eudeba.

Gomes de Almeida, José Mauricio. 1981. *A tradição regionalista no romance Brasileiro (1857–1945).* Rio de Janeiro: Achiané.

González Echevarría, Roberto. 1985. Doña Bárbara Writes the Plain. In *The Voice of the Masters: Writing and Authority in Modern Latin American Literature.* Austin: University of Texas Press.

———. [1990] 1998. *Myth and Archive.* Cambridge: Cambridge University Press.

Gori, Gastón. 1976. *Vagos y malentretenidos: aporte al tema hernandiano.* Buenos Aires: Rodolfo Alonso.

Gott, Richard. 2000. *In the Shadow of the Liberator: Hugo Chávez and the Transformation of Venezuela.* London: Verso.

Graham, Richard. 1990. *Patronage and Politics in Nineteenth-Century Brazil.* Stanford, CA: Stanford University Press.

Gramuglio, María Teresa, and Beatriz Sarlo, eds. 1993. *Martín Fierro y su crítica, antología.* Buenos Aires: CEDAL.

Grudzinska, Grazyna. 1982. Teoría y práctica del nacionalismo literario en Ignacio M. Altamirano. In *Nationalisme et littérature en Espagne et en Amérique Latine au XIXe siècle,* edited by Claude Dumas. Lille, France: Université de Lille III.

Guerra, François-Xavier. 2003. Forms of Communication, Political Spaces, and Cultural Identities in the Creation of Spanish American Nations. In *Beyond Imagined Communities: Reading and Writing the Nation in Nineteenth-Century Latin America,* edited by Sara Castro-Klarén and John Charles Chasteen. Washington, DC: Woodrow Wilson Center Press; Baltimore, MD: Johns Hopkins University Press.

Guha, Ranajit. [1983] 1999. *Elementary Aspects of Peasant Insurgency in Colonial India.* Durham, NC: Duke University Press.

———. 1988. The Prose of Counter-Insurgency. In *Selected Subaltern Studies,* edited by Ranajit Guha and Gayatri Chakravorty Spivak. New York: Oxford University Press.

Guy, Donna. 1991. *Sex and Danger in Buenos Aires: Prostitution, Family, and Nation in Argentina*. Lincoln: University of Nebraska Press.

Habermas, Jurgen. [1973] 1975. *Legitimation Crisis*. Boston: Beacon Press.

Hale, Charles A. 1968. *Mexican Liberalism in the Age of Mora, 1821–1853*. New Haven, CT, and London: Yale University Press.

Hall, Stuart. 1997. The Spectacle of the 'Other.' In *Representation: Cultural Representation and Signifying Practices*, edited by Stuart Hall. London: Sage.

———. 2000. Culture, Community, Nation. In *Representing the Nation: A Reader: Histories, Heritage and Museums*, edited by David Boswell and Jessica Evans. London: Routledge.

Hallstead, Susan. 2005. FashionNation: The Politics of Dress and Gender in Nineteenth Century Argentine Journalism, 1829–1880. Ph.D. dissertation, University of Pittsburgh.

Halperín Donghi, Tulio. [1967] 1997. *Historia contemporánea de América Latina*. Buenos Aires: Alianza Editorial.

———. [1972] 2002. *Revolución y guerra: formación de una elite dirigente en la Argentina criolla*. Buenos Aires: Siglo XXI.

———. 1982. *Guerra y finanzas en los orígenes del estado Argentino (1791–1850)*. Buenos Aires: Eudeba.

———. 2003. Argentine Counterpoint: Rise of the Nation, Rise of the State. In *Beyond Imagined Communities: Reading and Writing the Nation in Nineteenth-Century Latin America*, edited by Sara Castro-Klarén and John Charles Chasteen. Washington, DC: Woodrow Wilson Center Press; Baltimore, MD: Johns Hopkins University Press.

Hamnet, Brian. 1986. *Roots of Insurgency: Mexican Regions, 1750–1824*. Cambridge: Cambridge University Press.

Hardt, Michael, and Antonio Negri. 1994. *Labor of Dionysus: A Critique of the State-Form*. Minneapolis: University of Minnesota Press.

———. 2000. *Empire*. Cambridge, MA: Harvard University Press.

———. 2004. *Multitude: War and Democracy in the Age of Empire*. New York: Penguin Press.

Harries, Jill. 1999. *Law and Empire in Late Antiquity*. Cambridge: Cambridge University Press.

Haslip-Viera, Gabriel. 1999. *Crime and Punishment in Late Colonial Mexico City, 1692–1810*. Albuquerque: University of New Mexico Press.

Hayden, Tom, ed. 2002. *The Zapatista Reader*. New York: Avalon Publishing Group.

Herlinghaus, Hermann. 2000. *Modernidad heterogénea: descentramientos hermenéuticos desde la comunicación en América Latina*. Caracas: Centro de Investigaciones Post-Doctorales.

Heyman, Josiah McC., ed. 1999. *States and Illegal Practices*. Oxford and New York: Berg.

————, and Alan Smart. 1999. States and Illegal Practices: An Overview. In *States and Illegal Practices*, edited by Josiah McC. Heyman. Oxford and New York: Berg.

Hidalgo, Bartolomé. 1972. Diálogo patriótico interesante. In *Antología de la poesía gauchesca*, edited by Jorge Becco. Madrid: Aguilar.

Hobsbawm, Eric. [1959] 1965. *Primitive Rebels*. New York: Norton Library.

————. [1969] 1981. 3rd ed. *Bandits*. New York: Pantheon Books.

————. [1969] 2000. 4th ed. *Bandits*. New York: Pantheon Books.

————. 1973. The Rules of Violence. In *Revolutionaries: Contemporary Essays*, by Eric Hobsbawm. New York: Random House.

————. [1983] 1984. Preface to *Bandoleros, gamonales y campesinos: el caso de la violencia en Colombia*, by Gonzalo Sánchez and Donny Meertens. Bogotá: El Ancora.

————. 1988. Review of *Bandidos: The Varieties of Latin American Banditry*, edited by Richard W. Slatta. *Hispanic American Historical Review* 68(1):135–36.

————. 1992. Introduction: Inventing Traditions. In *The Invention of Tradition*, edited by Eric Hobsbawm and Terence Ranger. Cambridge: Cambridge University Press.

Horsley, Richard, and John S. Hanson. 1985. *Bandits, Prophets, and Messiahs: Popular Movements in the Time of Jesus*. Minneapolis, Chicago, New York: Winston Press.

Iñigo Madrigal, Luis. 1993. José Joaquín Fernández de Lizardi. In *Historia de la literatura Hispanoamericana II: del Neoclasicismo al Modernismo*, edited by Luis Iñigo Madrigal. Madrid: Cátedra.

Isaacson, José. 1986. *Martín Fierro: cien años de crítica*. Buenos Aires: Plus Ultra.

Izard, Miguel. 1981. Ni cuatreros ni montoneros: llaneros. *Boletín Americanista* 31:83–142.

————. 1982. Oligarcas temblad, viva la libertad: los llaneros del Apure y la Guerra Federal. *Boletín Americanista* 32:227–77.

————. 1983. Sin domicilio fijo, senda segura, ni destino conocido: los llaneros del Apure a finales del periodo colonial. *Boletín Americanista* 33:13–83.

————. 1984. Ya era hora de emprender la lucha para que en el ancho feudo de la violencia reinase algún día la justicia. *Boletín Americanista* 34:75–125.

————. 1987. Sin el menor arraigo ni responsabilidad: llaneros y ganadería a principios del siglo XIX. *Boletín Americanista* 37:109–42.

————. 1988. Cimarrones, cuatreros e insurgentes. In *Los llanos: una historia sin fronteras*. Bogotá: Academia de Historia del Meta.

————, and Richard Slatta. 1987. Banditry and Social Conflict on the Venezuelan Llanos. In *Bandidos: The Varieties of Latin American Banditry*, edited by Richard W. Slatta. New York: Greenwood Press.

Jackson, Joseph Henry. 1955. Introduction to *The Life and Adventures of Joaquín Murieta, the Celebrated California Bandit*, by Yellow Bird (John Rollin Ridge) [1854]. Norman: University of Oklahoma Press.

Jameson, Fredric. 1981. *The Political Unconscious: Narrative as a Socially Symbolic Act.* Ithaca, NY: Cornell University Press.

———. 1986. Third-World Literature in the Era of Multinational Capitalism. *Social Text* 15:65–88.

Jáuregui, Carlos A. 2006. *Canibalia: canibalismo, calibanismo, antropofagia cultural y consumo en América Latina.* Havana: Fondo Editorial Casa de las Américas.

Jitrik, Noé. 1960. *Leopoldo Lugones, mito nacional.* Buenos Aires: Palestra.

———. [1971] 2001. El tema del canto en el *Martín Fierro*, de José Hernández. In *Martín Fierro*, by José Hernández [1872/1879]. Critical edition by Elida Lois and Angel Núñez. Barcelona: ALLCA XX.

Johnson, Adriana. 2005. Subalternizing Canudos. *MLN* 120(2):355–82.

Johnson, Alan. 2000. Labeling Theory. In *The Blackwell Dictionary of Sociology.* Malden, MA: Blackwell Publishers.

Jones, David. 1986. *History of Criminology: A Philosophical Perspective.* New York, Westport, CT, and London: Greenwood Press.

Jonson, H. B. 1985. The Portuguese Settlement of Brazil, 1500–1580. In *The Cambridge History of Latin America.* Volume 1, *Colonial Latin America*, edited by Leslie Bethell. Cambridge: Cambridge University Press.

Joseph, Gilbert M. 1990. On the Trail of Latin American Bandits: A Reexamination of Peasant Resistance. *Latin American Research Review* 25(3):7–54.

———. 1991. "Resocializing" Latin American Banditry: A Reply. *Latin American Research Review* 26(1):161–73.

———. 1994. Rethinking Mexican Revolutionary Mobilization: Yucatán's Seasons of Upheaval, 1909–1915. In *Everyday Forms of State Formation: Revolution and the Negotiation of Rule in Modern Mexico,* edited by Gilbert M. Joseph and Daniel Nugent. Durham, NC, and London: Duke University Press.

———. 2001. Introduction to *Crime and Punishment in Latin America: Law and Society since Late Colonial Times,* edited by Ricardo Salvatore, Carlos Aguirre, and Gilbert Joseph. Durham, NC, and London: Duke University Press.

———, and Daniel Nugent, eds. 1994. *Everyday Forms of State Formation: Revolution and the Negotiation of Rule in Modern Mexico.* Durham, NC, and London: Duke University Press.

Kattra, William H. 1993. *Sarmiento de frente y perfil.* New York: Peter Lang.

Katz, Friedrich. 1998. *The Life and Times of Pancho Villa.* Stanford, CA: Stanford University Press.

Knight, Alan. 1985. El liberalismo mexicano desde la Reforma hasta la Revolución (una interpretación). *Historia Mexicana* 35(1):59–92.

———. 1986. *The Mexican Revolution.* 2 vols. Cambridge: Cambridge University Press.

———. 1994. Weapons and Arches in the Mexican Revolutionary Landscape. In *Everyday Forms of State Formation: Revolution and the Negotiation of Rule in Mod-*

ern Mexico, edited by Gilbert M. Joseph and Daniel Nugent. Durham, NC, and London: Duke University Press.

Krispín, Karl. 1997. Preface to *Zárate,* by Eduardo Blanco [1882]. Caracas: Monte Ávila Editores Latinoamericana.

Laclau, Ernesto. 1996. *Emancipation(s).* London: Verso.

———. 2000. Identity and Hegemony. In *Contingency, Hegemony, Universality: Contemporary Dialogues on the Left,* edited by Judith Butler, Ernesto Laclau, and Slavoj Žižek. London: Verso.

———, and Chantal Mouffe. [1985] 1999. *Hegemony and Socialist Strategy.* London: Verso.

Laera, Alejandra. 2004. *El tiempo vacio de la ficción: las novelas argentinas de Eduardo Gutiérrez y Eugenio Cambaceres.* Buenos Aires: Fondo de Cultura Económica de Argentina.

Lamnek, Siegfried. [1977] 2002. *Teorías de la criminalidad: una confrontación crítica.* Mexico City: Siglo XXI.

Lane, Frederic C. 1979. *Profits from Power: Readings in Protection Rent and Violence-Controlling Enterprises.* Albany: State University of New York Press.

Leal, Luis. 1974. Picaresca hispanoamericana de Oquendo a Lizardi. In *Estudios de literatura hispanoamericana en honor a José J. Arrom,* edited by Andrew P. Debicki and Enrique Pupo-Walker. Chapel Hill: Publications of the Department of Romance Languages, University of North Carolina.

———. 1977. Picaresca hispanoamericana de Oquendo a Lizardi. In *Estudios de literatura hispanoamericana en honor a José J. Arrom.* Chapel Hill: Publications of the Department of Romance Languages, University of North Carolina.

———. 1999. Introduction to *Vida y aventuras del más célebre bandido sonorense Joaquín Murieta: sus grandes proezas en California,* by Ireneo Paz [1904]. Houston: Arte Público Press.

Lechner, Norbert. 1995. A Disenchantment Called Postmodernism. In *The Postmodernism Debate in Latin America,* edited by John Beverley, José Oviedo, and Michael Aronna. Durham, NC: Duke University Press.

LeGrand, Catherine. 1986. *Frontier Expansion and Peasant Protest in Colombia, 1830–1936.* Albuquerque: University of New Mexico Press.

Leps, Marie-Christine. 1992. *Apprehending the Criminal: The Production of Deviance in Nineteenth-Century Discourse.* Durham, NC, and London: Duke University Press.

Levi, Margaret. 1988. *Of Rule and Revenue.* Berkeley: University of California Press.

Levine, Robert M. 1992. *Vale of Tears: Revisiting the Canudos Massacre in Northeastern Brazil, 1893–1897.* Berkeley: University of California Press.

Lewin, Linda. 1979. Oral Tradition and Elite Myth: The Legend of Antônio Silvino in Brazilian Popular Culture. *Journal of Latin American Lore* 5(2):157–202.

———. 1987. The Oligarchical Limitations of Social Banditry in Brazil: The Case of the "Good" Thief Antônio Silvino. In *Bandidos: The Varieties of Latin American Banditry,* edited by Richard W. Slatta. New York: Greenwood Press.

Lois, Elida, and Angel Núñez, eds. 2001. *Martín Fierro: edición crítica.* By José Hernández [1872/1879]. Barcelona: ALLCA XX.

Lombardi, John. 1982. *Venezuela: The Search for Order, the Dream of Progress.* New York and Oxford: Oxford University Press.

López Cámara, Francisco. 1967. *La estructura social y económica de México en la época de la reforma.* Mexico City: Siglo XXI.

Lozano-Armendares, Teresa. 1987. *La criminalidad en la ciudad de México, 1800–1821.* Mexico City: Universidad Nacional Autónoma de México, Instituto de Investigaciones Históricas.

Ludmer, Josefina. 1988. *El género gauchesco: un tratado sobre la patria.* Buenos Aires: Sudamericana.

———. [1994] 1999. Los escándalos de Juan Moreira. Introduction to *Juan Moreira,* by Eduardo Gutiérrez [1879]. Buenos Aires: Perfil Libros.

———. 1999. *El cuerpo del delito: un manual.* Buenos Aires: Perfil Libros.

Luna, Félix. 1966. *Los caudillos.* Buenos Aires: A Peña Lillo Editor.

———. 2000. *Conflictos en la Argentina Próspera: de la Revolución del Parque a la restauración conservadora.* Buenos Aires: Planeta.

Lunenfeld, Marvin. 1970. *The Council of the Santa Hermandad: A Study of the Pacification Forces of Ferdinand and Isabella.* Coral Gables: University of Miami Press.

Lynch, John. [1981] 1997. *Juan Manuel de Rosas: 1829–1852.* Buenos Aires: Emecé Editores.

———. 1992. *Caudillos in Spanish America.* Oxford: Clarendon Press, 1992.

MacLachlan, Colin M. 1974. *Criminal Justice in Eighteenth-Century Mexico: A Study of the Tribunal of the Acordada.* Berkeley, London, Los Angeles: University of California Press.

Magdaleno, Mauricio. 1948. El perenne verdor de Astucia. In *El Coronel Astucia y Los Hermanos de la Hoja o los charros contrabandistas: adaptación teatral de la novela de Luis Inclán,* adapted by Salvador Novo. Mexico City: Instituto Nacional de Bellas Artes.

Mallon, Florencia. 1983. *The Defense of Community in Peru's Central Highlands: Peasant Struggle and Capitalist Transition, 1860–1940.* Princeton, NJ: Princeton University Press.

———. 1994. *Peasant and Nation: The Making of Postcolonial Mexico and Peru.* Berkeley: University of California Press.

Mansour, Mónica. 1996. Cúspides inaccesibles. In *Los de abajo,* by Mariano Azuela [1915/1916]. Edited by Jorge Ruffinelli. Nanterre Cedex, France: Archivos.

Maravall, José Antonio. 1987. *La literatura picaresca desde la historia social.* Madrid: Taurus.

Marotti, Giorgio. 1988. *Santi e banditti nel romanzo brasiliano.* Rome: Bulzoni.

Márquez Rodríguez, Alexis. 1990. *Historia y ficción en la novela venezolana*. Caracas: Monte Avila Editores.

Martin, Gerald. 1989. *Journeys through the Labyrinth*. London: Verso.

Martin, Norman Francis. 1957. *Los vagabundos en la Nueva España, siglo XVI*. Mexico City: Editorial Jus.

Martínez Luna, Esther. 2001. Astucia, tesoro de la lengua y mural de costumbres mexicanas. In *Astucia: el jefe de los Hermanos de la Hoja o los charros contrabandistas de la Rama: novela histórica de costumbres mexicanas con episodios originales*, by Luis Inclán [1865]. Mexico City: Océano.

Martins, Wilson. 1977. *História de inteligência Brasileira*. Volume 3, 1855–1877. São Paulo: Editora Cultrix.

Matthews, Robert Paul. 1977. *Violencia rural en Venezuela, 1840–1858: antecedentes socio-económicos de la guerra federal*. Caracas: Monte Ávila.

McAdam, Doug, John McCarthy, and Mayer Zald. 1996. Introduction: Opportunities, Mobilizing Structures, and Framing Processes: Toward a Synthetic, Comparative Perspective on Social Movements. In *Comparative Perspectives on Social Movements: Political Opportunities, Mobilizing Structures, and Cultural Framings*. Cambridge: Cambridge University Press.

Mello, Federico Pernambucano de. [1985] 2004. *Guerreiros do sol: o banditismo no nordeste do Brasil*. Recife, Brazil: A girafa.

Melossi, Dario. [1990] 1992. *El estado del control social: un estudio sociológico de los conceptos de estado y control social en la conformación de la democracia*. Mexico City: Siglo XXI.

Menton, Seymour. [1988] 1996. Texturas épicas de *Los de abajo*. In *Los de abajo*, by Mariano Azuela [1915/1916]. Edited by Jorge Ruffinelli. Nanterre Cedex, France: Archivos.

Meyer, Jean. 1984. *Esperando a Lozada*. Zamora, Mexico: El Colegio de Michoacán.

———. 1989. *La tierra de Manuel Lozada*. Guadalajara, Mexico: Universidad de Guadalajara.

Miliani, Domingo. 2001. Introduction to *Doña Bárbara*, by Rómulo Gallegos [1929]. Madrid: Cátedra.

Monsiváis, Carlos. 1989. No con un sollozo, sino entre disparos (notas sobre cultura mexicana 1910–1968). *Revista Iberoamericana* 55:148–49.

———. 1997. Manuel Payno: México, novela de folletín. In *Del fistol a la linterna, Homenaje a José Tomás de Cuéllar y Manuel Payno, en el centenario de su muerte*, edited by Margo Glantz. Mexico City: UNAM.

———. 1999. *El Zarco*: los falsos héroes y los verdaderos héroes románticos. In *El Zarco*, by Ignacio Altamirano [1901]. Mexico City: Editorial Océano.

Monterde, Francisco. 1973. *Mariano Azuela y la crítica mexicana*. Mexico City: Sep / Setentas.

Moore, Barrington. 1966. *Social Origins of Dictatorship and Democracy: Lord and Peasant in the Making of the Modern World.* Boston: Beacon Press.

Mora Escalante, Sonia. 1993–1994. Le picaresque dans la construction du roman hispano-americain: le cas du *Periquillo. Études Litteraires* (Quebec) 26(3):81–95.

Moraña, Mabel. 1984. *Literatura y cultura nacional en Hispanoamérica (1910–1940).* Minneapolis, MN: Institute for the Study of Ideologies and Literatures.

———. 1997a. *El periquillo sarniento* y la ciudad letrada. In *Políticas de la escritura en América Latina.* Caracas: Excultura.

———, ed. 1997b. *Ángel Rama y los estudios latinoamericanos.* Pittsburgh, PA: Instituto Internacional de Literatura Iberoamericana.

Moreta, Salustiano. 1978. *Malhechores-Feudales: violencia, antagonismos y alianzas de clases en Castilla, siglos XII–XIV.* Madrid: Ediciones Cátedra.

Moro, Roberto, comp. 1974. *Rosas en las laminas de "El Grito" y "El Grito arjentino, Muera Rosas!"* Buenos Aires: A. Peña Lillo.

Morón, Guillermo. 1964. *A History of Venezuela.* London: Allen & Unwin.

Myers, Jorge. 1995. *Orden y virtud: el discurso republicano en el régimen rosista.* Buenos Aires: Universidad Nacional de Quilmas.

Nahum, Benjamin. 1994. *Manual de historia uruguaya.* Montevideo: Ediciones de la Banda Oriental.

Negri, Antonio. 1999. *Insurgencies: Constituent Power and the Modern State.* Translated by Maurizia Boscagli. Minneapolis: University of Minnesota Press.

Nietzsche, Friedrich. [1887] 1994. *On the Genealogy of Morality and Other Writings.* Cambridge: Cambridge University Press.

Nouzeilles, Gabriela. 2000. *Ficciones somáticas: naturalismo, nacionalismo y políticas médicas del cuerpo (Argentina 1880–1910).* Rosario, Argentina: Beatriz Viterbo.

Novais Sampaio, Consuelo. 1999. Canudos: a construção do medo. In *Canudos: cartas para o Barão,* edited by Consuelo Novais Sampaio. São Paulo: EDUSP.

Novo, Salvador. 1984. Preface to *Astucia: el jefe de los Hermanos de la Hoja o los charros contrabandistas de la Rama: novela histórica de costumbres mexicanas con episodios originales,* by Luis G. Inclán [1865]. Mexico City: Porrúa.

Olea Franco, Rafael, ed. 2001. *Literatura mexicana del otro fin de siglo.* Mexico City: El Colegio de México, Centro de Estudios Linguisticos y Literarios.

O'Malley, Pat. 1979. Social Bandits, Modern Capitalism, and the Traditional Peasantry: A Critique of Hobsbawm. *Journal of Peasant Studies* 6(4):489–501.

Onega, Gladys. 1969. *La inmigración en la literatura argentina, 1880–1910.* Buenos Aires: Galerna.

Ortiz, Fernando. 1995. *Los negros curros.* Havana: Editorial de Ciencias Sociales.

Osorio, Nelson. 1995. Doña Bárbara. In *Diccionario enciclopédico de las letras de América Latina.* Caracas: Monte Avila.

Oszlak, Oscar. 1982. *La formación del estado Argentino.* Buenos Aires: Editorial de Belgrano.

Palacios Herrera, Oscar. 1989. *Dionisio Cisneros, el último realista*. Caracas: Academia Nacional de la Historia.

Palti, Elías José. 1994. Literatura y política en Ignacio M. Altamirano. In *La imaginación histórica en el siglo XIX*, edited by Lelia Area and Mabel Moraña. Rosario, Argentina: UNR Editora.

————. 1997. Legitimacy and History in the Aftermath of Revolutions (Latin America, 1820–1910): A Journey through the Fringes of Liberal Thought. Ph.D. dissertation, University of California–Berkeley.

————. 2004. Los poderes del horror: *Facundo* como epífora. *Revista Iberoamericana* 70(207):521–44.

Paredes, Américo. [1958] 1998. *With His Pistol in His Hand: A Border Ballad and Its Hero*. Austin: University of Texas Press.

————. 1960. Luis Inclán: First of the Cowboy Writers. *American Quarterly* 12(1):55–70.

Paul Arranz, María del Mar. La novela de la Revolución Mexicana y la revolución en la novela. *Revista Iberoamericana* 65(186):49–57.

Paz Sánchez, Manuel de, et al. 1993. *El bandolerismo en Cuba (1800–1933): presencia canaria y protesta rural*. Santa Cruz de Tenerife, Spain: Centro de Cultura Popular Canaria.

Perez, Louis A., Jr. 1989. *Lords of the Mountain: Social Banditry and Peasant Protest in Cuba, 1878–1918*. Pittsburgh, PA: University of Pittsburgh Press.

Pérez Perdomo, Rogelio. 1990. *La organización del estado en Venezuela en el siglo XIX (1830–1899)*. Caracas: Ediciones IESA.

Phillips, Dretha M. 1987. Latin American Banditry and Criminological Theory. In *Bandidos: The Varieties of Latin American Banditry*, edited by Richard W. Slatta. New York: Greenwood Press.

Picatto, Pablo. 2001. *City of Suspects: Crime in Mexico City, 1900–1931*. Durham, NC: Duke University Press.

Pino Iturrieta, Elías. 1988. Ideas sobre un pueblo inepto: la justificación del gomecismo. In *Juan Vicente Gómez y su época*, edited by Elías Pino Iturrieta. Caracas: Monte Ávila.

Pinto Rodríguez, Jorge. 1991. El bandolerismo en la frontera, 1880–1920: una aproximación al tema. In *Araucania*, edited by Sergio Villalobos and Jorge Pinto Rodríguez. Concepción, Chile: Ediciones Universidad de la Frontera.

Pivel-Devoto, Juan. 1950. De la leyenda negra al culto artiguista. *Marcha*, June 23.

Plaza, Elena. 1996. *La tragedia de una amarga convicción: historia y política en el pensamiento de Laureano Vallenilla Lanz (1870–1936)*. Caracas: UBV.

Pollak-Eltz, Angelina. 2000. *La esclavitud en Venezuela: un estudio histórico-cultural*. Caracas: Universidad Católica Andrés Bello.

Porras Cruz, Jorge Luis. 1976. *Vida y obra de Luis G. Inclán*. Río Piedras, PR: Editorial Universitaria.

Portinaro, Pier Paolo. [1999] 2003. *Estado: léxico de política*. Buenos Aires: Nueva Visión.

Poumier-Taquechel, Maria. 1986. *Contribution à l'étude du banditisme social à Cuba*. Lille, France: Atelier National.

Prassel, Frank Richard. 1993. *The Great American Outlaw: A Legacy of Fact and Fiction*. Norman: University of Oklahoma Press.

Pratt, Mary Louise. 1992. *Imperial Eyes: Travel Writing and Transculturation*. London and New York: Routledge.

Prieto, Adolfo. [1977] 2001. La culminación de la poesía gauchesca. In *Martín Fierro*, by José Hernández [1872/1879]. Critical edition by Elida Lois and Angel Núñez. Barcelona: ALLCA XX.

———. 1988. *El discurso criollista en la formación de la Argentina moderna*. Buenos Aires: Sudamericana.

———. 1996. *Los viajeros ingleses y la emergencia de la literatura argentina, 1820–1850*. Buenos Aires: Sudamericana.

Putnam, Samuel. 1995. Translator's introduction to *Rebellion in the Backlands*, by Euclides da Cunha [1902]. Cambridge: Picador.

Queiroz, Maria Isaura Pereira de. 1968. *Os cangaceiros, les bandits d'honneur brésiliens*. Paris: Julliard.

Quintero, Inés. 1994. El sistema político guzmancista (tensiones entre el caudillismo y el poder central). In *Antonio Guzmán Blanco y su época*, edited by Inés Quintero. Caracas: Monte Ávila.

Rama, Ángel. 1976. *Los gauchipolíticos rioplatenses*. Buenos Aires: Calicanto.

———. 1984. *La ciudad letrada*. Hanover, NH: Ediciones del Norte.

Ramos, Julio. 1989. *Desencuentros de la modernidad en América Latina: literatura y política en el siglo XIX*. Mexico City: FCE.

Renan, Ernst. [1890] 1990. What Is a Nation? In *Nation and Narration*, edited by Homi K. Bhabha. London: Routledge.

Reyes Abadie, Washington. [1974] 1986. *Artigas y el federalismo en el Río de la Plata*. Buenos Aires: Hyspamérica.

Rivera, Jorge. 1967. *Eduardo Gutiérrez*. Buenos Aires: CEDAL.

Robert, Marthe. 1970. *Kafka*. Buenos Aires: Paidós.

———. 1977. *The Old and the New: From Don Quixote to Kafka*. Berkeley: University of California Press.

Rock, David. 1987. *Argentina, 1516–1987: From Spanish Colonization to Alfonsín*. Berkeley: University of California Press.

Rodríguez, José Angel. 1986. *Los paisajes neohistóricos cañeros en Venezuela*. Caracas: Academia Nacional de la Historia.

Rodríguez-Molas, Ricardo. [1968] 1982. *Historia social del gaucho*. Buenos Aires: CEDAL.

Rohlfes, Laurence. 1983. Police and Penal Correction in Mexico City, 1876–1911:

A Study of Order and Progress in Porfirian Mexico. Ph.D. dissertation, Tulane University.

Romanos de Tiratel, Susana. 2001. Bibliografía 1972–2001. In *Martín Fierro,* by José Hernández [1872/1879]. Critical edition by Elida Lois and Angel Núñez. Barcelona: ALLCA XX.

Rothert, Otto A. 1996. *The Outlaws of Cave-in-Rock: Historical Accounts of the Famous Highwaymen and River Pirates Who Operated in the Pioneer Days upon the Ohio and Mississippi Rivers and over the Natchez Trace.* Carbondale: Southern Illinois University Press.

Rubin, Jeffrey. 1997. *Decentering the Regime: Ethnicity, Radicalism, and Democracy in Juchitán, Mexico.* Durham, NC, and London: Duke University Press.

Rubione, Alberto, ed. 1983. *En torno al criollismo: textos y polémica.* Buenos Aires: CEDAL.

Ruffinelli, Jorge, ed. 1996a. *Los de abajo,* by Mariano Azuela [1915/1916]. Critical edition. Nanterre Cedex, France: Archivos.

———. 1996b. La recepción crítica de *Los de abajo.* In *Los de abajo,* by Mariano Azuela [1915/1916]. Critical edition by Jorge Ruffinelli. Nanterre, France: Archivos.

Ruiz, Bladimir. 2000. Creando la nación: tradición, genealogías y modernización en la literatura del siglo XIX en Venezuela. Ph.D. dissertation, University of Pittsburgh.

Ruiz-Barrionuevo, Carmen. 1997. Introduction to *El periquillo sarniento.* By José Joaquín Fernández de Lizardi [1816]. Madrid: Cátedra.

Rutherford, John. 1996. The Novel of the Mexican Revolution. In *The Cambridge History of Latin American Literature,* volume 2, edited by Roberto González-Echevarría and Enrique Pupo-Walker. Cambridge: Cambridge University Press.

Sabato, Hilda. 2001. *The Many and the Few: Political Participation in Republican Buenos Aires.* Stanford, CA: Stanford University Press.

Said, Edward. [1978] 1994. *Orientalism.* New York: Vintage Books.

———. 1993. *Culture and Imperialism.* New York: Vintage Books.

Salas, Horacio. 1996. *El centenario: la Argentina en su hora más gloriosa.* Buenos Aires: Planeta.

Salessi, Jorge. 1996. *Médicos maleantes y maricas: higiene, criminología y homosexualidad en la construcción de la nación argentina.* Rosario, Argentina: Beatriz Viterbo Editora.

Salomón, Noel. 1965. La crítica del sistema colonial de Nueva España en *El periquillo sarniento. Cuadernos Americanos* 24:167–79.

Salvatore, Ricardo. 1992. Criminology, Prison Reform, and the Buenos Aires Working Class. *Journal of Interdisciplinary History* 23(2):279–99.

———. 1997. Los crímenes de los paisanos: una aproximación estadística. *Anuario IEHS* 12:91–100.

———. 2000. The Crimes of Poor "Paysanos" in Mid-Nineteenth-Century Buenos Aires. In *Reconstructing Criminality in Latin America,* edited by Carlos Aguirre and Robert Buffington. Wilmington, DE: Scholarly Resources.

———. 2001. Death and Liberalism: Capital Punishment after the Fall of Rosas. In *Crime and Punishment in Latin America: Law and Society since Late Colonial Times,* edited by Ricardo Salvatore, Carlos Aguirre, and Gilbert Joseph. Durham, NC, and London: Duke University Press.

———. 2003. *Wandering Paysanos: State Order and Subaltern Experience during the Rosas Era.* Durham, NC: Duke University Press.

———, Carlos Aguirre, and Gilbert Joseph, eds. 2001. *Crime and Punishment in Latin America: Law and Society since Late Colonial Times.* Durham, NC, and London: Duke University Press.

Sampson, Steven. 2003. "Trouble Spots": Projects, Bandits, and State Fragmentation. In *Globalization, the State, and Violence,* edited by Jonathan Friedman. London: Altamira Press.

Sánchez, Gonzalo, and Donny Meertens. [1983] 1984. *Bandoleros, gamonales y Campesinos: el caso de la violencia en Colombia.* Bogotá: El Ancora.

Scardaville, Michael C. 2000. (Hapsburg) Law and (Bourbon) Order: State Authority, Popular Unrest, and the Criminal Justice System in Bourbon Mexico City. In *Reconstructing Criminality in Latin America,* edited by Carlos Aguirre and Robert Buffington. Wilmington, DE: Scholarly Resources.

Scavino, Dardo F. 1993. *Barcos sobre la pampa: las formas de la guerra en Sarmiento.* Buenos Aires: Ediciones El Cielo Por Asalto, Imago Mundi.

Schartzman, Julio. 2001. El gaucho letrado. In *Martín Fierro,* by José Hernández [1872/1879]. Critical edition by Elida Lois and Angel Núñez. Barcelona: ALLCA XX.

Schmidt, Friedhelm. 2000. Literaturas heterogéneas y alegorías nacionales: ¿paradigmas para las literaturas poscoloniales? *Revista Iberoamericana* 66(190):175–85.

Schmitt, Carl. [1922/1934] 1985. *Political Theology: Four Chapters on the Concept of Sovereignty.* Cambridge, MA, and London: MIT Press.

———. [1932] 1976. *The Concept of the Political.* New Brunswick, NJ: Rutgers University Press.

Schwartz, Rosalie. 1982. Bandits and Rebels in Cuban Independence: Predators, Patriots, and Pariahs. *Bibliotheca Americana* 1(2):91–130.

———. 1989. *Lawless Liberators: Political Banditry and Cuban Independence.* Durham, NC, and London: Duke University Press.

Schwarz, Roberto. [1973] 1992. Misplaced Ideas: Literature and Society in Late-Nineteenth-Century Brazil. In *Misplaced Ideas: Essays on Brazilian Culture.* London and New York: Verso.

———. 1995. National by Imitation. In *The Postmodernism Debate in Latin America,* edited by John Beverley, José Oviedo, and Michael Aronna. Durham, NC: Duke University Press.

Scott, James. 1985. *Weapons of the Weak: Everyday Forms of Peasant Resistance*. New Haven, CT, and London: Yale University Press.

———. 1990. *Domination and the Arts of Resistance: Hidden Transcripts*. New Haven, CT: Yale University Press.

Scrunton, Roger. [1982] 1996. *Dictionary of Political Thought*. London: Macmillan.

Seal, Graham. 1996. *The Outlaw Legend: A Cultural Tradition in Britain, America, and Australia*. Cambridge: Cambridge University Press.

Shaw, Brent. 1984. Bandits in the Roman Empire. *Past and Present* 105:3–52.

Shumway, Nicolas. 1991. *The Invention of Argentina*. Berkeley: University of California Press.

Silva-Beauregard, Paulette. 1994. Dos caras, un retrato y la búsqueda de un nombre: el letrado ante la modernización en *Zárate* de Eduardo Blanco. In *Esplendores y miserias del siglo XIX*, edited by Beatriz González Stephan, Javier Lasarte, Graciela Montaldo, and Maria Julia Daroqui. Caracas: Monte Avila Editores.

Singelmann, Peter. 1975. Political Structure and Social Banditry in Northeast Brazil. *Journal of Latin American Studies* 7(2):59–83

———. 1991. Establishing a Trail in the Labyrinth. *Latin American Research Review* 26(1):152–55.

Slater, Candace. 1989. *Stories on a String: The Brazilian Literatura de Cordel*. Berkeley: University of California Press.

Slatta, Richard. 1980. Rural Criminality and Social Conflict in Nineteenth-Century Buenos Aires Province. *Hispanic American Historical Review* 60(3):450–72.

———. 1983. *Gauchos and the Vanishing Frontier*. Lincoln and London: University of Nebraska Press.

———, ed. 1987. *Bandidos: The Varieties of Latin American Banditry*. New York: Greenwood Press.

———. 1991. Bandits and Rural Social History: A Comment on Joseph. *Latin American Research Review* 26(1):145–51.

———. 1994. Banditry. In *Encyclopaedia of Social History*, edited by Peter Stearns. New York: Garland.

Sol, Manuel. 2000. Estudio preliminar. In *El Zarco*, by Ignacio Manuel Altamirano [1901]. Xalapa, Mexico: Instituto de Investigaciones Lingüístico-Literarias, Universidad Veracruzana.

———. 2001a. Estructura y significado en *Astucia. El Jefe de los Hermanos de la Hoja o los charros contrabandistas de la Rama*, de Luis Inclán. *Texto Crítico* 5(9):57–71.

———. 2001b. El habla en *Astucia*, de Luis Inclán. In *Literatura mexicana del otro fin de siglo*, edited by Rafael Olea Franco. Mexico City: El Colegio de México, Centro de Estudios Linguisticos y Literarios.

Solanas, Fernando. 1972–1978. *Los hijos de Fierro.* Buenos Aires: Argentina Sono Film.

Solares Robles, Laura. 1999. *Bandidos somos y en el camino andamos: bandidaje, caminos y administración de justicia en el siglo XIX. 1812–1855. El caso de Michoacán.* Morelia, Mexico: Instituto Michoacano de Cultura e Instituto de Investigaciones Dr. José Luis María Mora.

Sommer, Doris. 1991. *Foundational Fictions: The National Romances in Latin America.* Berkeley: University of California Press.

———. 1993. Irresistible Romance: The Foundational Fictions of Latin America. In *Nation and Narration,* edited by Homi K. Bhabha. London and New York: Routledge.

Sorensen Goodrich, Diana. 1996. *Facundo and the Construction of Argentine Culture.* Austin: University of Texas Press.

Spell, Jefferson Rea. 1963. A Textual Comparison of the First Four Editions of *El Periquillo Sarniento. Hispanic Review* 31(2):134–47.

———. 1971. *Bridging the Gap.* Mexico City: Libros de México.

Spivak, Gayatri Chakravorty. 1988. Subaltern Studies: Deconstructing Historiography. In *Selected Subaltern Studies,* edited by Ranajit Guha and Gayatri Chakravorty Spivak. New York: Oxford University Press.

———. 1997. Translator's preface to *Of Grammatology,* by Jacques Derrida. Baltimore, MD, and London: Johns Hopkins University Press.

Spraggs, Gillian. 2001. *Outlaws & Highwaymen: The Cult of the Robber in England from the Middle Ages to the Nineteenth Century.* London: Pimlico.

Staples, Anne. 2001. *Los bandidos de Río Frío* como fuente primaria para la historia de México. In *Literatura mexicana del otro fin de siglo,* edited by Rafael Olea Franco. Mexico City: El Colegio de México, Centro de Estudios Linguisticos y Literarios.

Stavans, Ilan. 1995. *Bandido: Oscar "Zeta" Acosta and the Chicano Experience.* New York: Icon Editions.

———. 1996. *Hispanic Condition: Reflections on Culture and Identity in America.* New York: Harper Collins.

Stolley, Karen. 1994. Lazos de familia: el problema de la genealogía en la obra de Lizardi. In *La imaginación histórica en el siglo XIX,* edited by Lelia Area and Mabel Moraña. Rosario, Argentina: UNR Editora.

Storni, Carlos Mario. 1997. *Investigaciones sobre la historia del derecho rural argentino: españoles, criollos, indios y gauderios en la llanura pampeana.* Buenos Aires: Instituto de Investigaciones de Historia del Derecho.

Svampa, Maristella. 1994. *El dilema argentino: civilización o barbarie. De Sarmiento al revisionismo peronista.* Buenos Aires: Ediciones el cielo por asalto.

———. 1998. La dialéctica entre lo nuevo y lo viejo: sobre los usos y nociones del caudillismo en la Argentina durante el siglo XIX. In *Caudillismos rioplatenses: nuevas miradas a un viejo problema*, edited by Noemí Goldman and Ricardo Salvatore. Buenos Aires: Eudeba.

Taylor, William. 1982. Bandit Gangs in Late Colonial Times: Rural Jalisco, Mexico, 1794–1821. *Bibliotheca Americana* 1(2):29–59.

———. 1988. Banditry and Insurrection: Rural Unrest in Central Jalisco, 1790–1816. In *Riot, Rebellion, and Revolution: Rural Social Conflict in Mexico*, edited by Friedrich Katz. Princeton, NJ: Princeton University Press.

———. 1996. *Magistrates of the Sacred: Priests and Parishioners in Eighteenth-Century Mexico*. Stanford, CA: Stanford University Press.

Teskey, Gordon. 1996. *Allegory and Violence*. Ithaca, NY, and London: Cornell University Press.

Thompson, E. P. 1974. Patrician Society, Plebeian Culture. *Journal of Social History* 7(4):382–405

———. 1975. *Whigs and Hunters: The Origins of the Black Act*. New York: Pantheon Books.

Thomson, Guy, and David LaFrance. 1999. *Patriotism, Politics, and Popular Liberalism in Nineteenth-Century Mexico: Juan Francisco Lucas and the Puebla Sierra*. Wilmington, DE: Scholarly Resources.

Thomson, Janice. 1994. *Mercenaries, Pirates, and Sovereigns: State Building and Extraterritorial Violence in Early Modern Europe*. Princeton, NJ: Princeton University Press.

Thornton, Bruce. 2003. *Searching for Joaquín: Myth, Murieta, and History in California*. San Francisco: Encounter Books, 2003.

Tilly, Charles. 1975a. Foreword to *The Mafia of a Sicilian Village, 1860–1960: A Study of Violent Peasant Entrepreneurs*, by Anton Blok. New York: Harper & Row.

———. 1975b. Reflections on the History of European State-Making. In *The Formation of National States in Western Europe*, edited by Charles Tilly. Princeton, NJ: Princeton University Press.

———. 1975c. Western State-Making and Theories of Political Transformation. In *The Formation of National States in Western Europe*, edited by Charles Tilly. Princeton, NJ: Princeton University Press.

———. 1985. War Making and State Making as Organized Crime. In *Bringing the State Back*, edited by Peter B. Evans, Dietrich Rueschemeyer, and Theda Skocpol. Cambridge: Cambridge University Press.

———. 1994. Afterword: Political Memories in Space and Time. In *Remapping Memory: The Politics of Time Space*, edited by Jonathan Boyarin. Minneapolis and London: University of Minnesota Press.

Todorov, Tzvetan. 1965. *Théorie de la littérature: textes des formalistes russes réunis, présentés et traduits par Tzvetan Todorov*. Paris: Éditions du Seuil.

————. [1984] 1999. *The Conquest of America: The Question of the Other.* Norman: University of Oklahoma Press.

Torres, María Inés de. 1997. Construir la nación desde la(s) periferia(s): sujetos letrados y sujetos criollos en el Uruguay del siglo XIX. Ph.D. dissertation, University of Pittsburgh.

————. 2000. Discursos fundacionales: nación y ciudadanía. In *Uruguay: imaginarios culturales: desde las huellas indígenas a la modernidad,* edited by Mabel Moraña and Hugo Achugar. Montevideo: Trilce; Pittsburgh, PA: Instituto Internacional de Literatura Iberoamericana.

Torres Molina, Ramón. 1997. *El federalismo del interior (1810–1869).* Buenos Aires: Ediciones al margen.

Urbaneja, Diego Bautista. 1988. El sistema político gomecista. In *Juan Vicente Gómez y su época,* edited by Elías Pino Iturrieta. Caracas: Monte Avila.

Valenzuela Márquez, Jaime. 1991. *Bandidaje rural en Chile central: Curicó, 1850–1900.* Santiago, Chile: Dirección de Bibliotecas, Archivos y Museos.

Vanderwood, Paul. 1982. Social Banditry. *Bibliotheca Americana* 1(2):1–28.

————. 1987. Nineteenth-Century Mexico's Profiteering Bandits. In *Bandidos: The Varieties of Latin American Banditry,* edited by Richard Slatta. New York: Greenwood Press.

————. 1992. *Disorder and Progress: Bandits, Police, and Mexican Development.* Wilmington, DE: Scholarly Resources.

Van Praag Chantraine, Jacqueline. 1979. *El periquillo sarniento:* un pícaro criollo. In *La picaresca: orígenes, textos, estructuras,* edited by Manuel Criado de Val. Madrid: Fundación Universitaria Española.

Van Young, Eric. 1997. Agustín Marroquín: The Sociopath as Rebel. In *The Human Tradition in Modern Latin America,* edited by William H. Beezley and Judith Ewell. Wilmington, DE: SR Books.

————. 2001. *The Other Rebellion: Popular Violence, Ideology, and the Mexican Struggle for Independence, 1810–1821.* Stanford, CA: Stanford University Press.

————. 2005. Crime as Rebellion and Rebellion as Crime. Unpublished manuscript.

Viana Moog, Clodomir. [1954] 1994. Bandeirantes and Pioneers. In *Where Cultures Meet: Frontiers in Latin American History,* edited by David Weber and Jane Rausch. Wilmington, DE: Scholarly Resources.

Vidal, Hernán. 1985. *Socio-historia de la literatura colonial Hispanoamericana: tres lecturas orgánicas.* Minneapolis, MN: Institute for the Study of Ideologies and Literature.

Viñas, David. 1973. *La crisis de la ciudad liberal.* Buenos Aires: Editorial Siglo XX.

————. 1982. *Literatura Argentina y realidad política.* Buenos Aires: CEDAL.

————. 1994. Sarmiento: Madness or Accumulation. In *Sarmiento, Author of a Nation,* edited by Tulio Halperín Donghi. Berkeley: University of California Press.

———. 1996. *Literatura Argentina y política.* 2 vols. Buenos Aires: Editorial Sudamericana.

———. 2001. José Hernández, del indio al trabajo y a la conversión. In *Martín Fierro,* by José Hernández [1872/1879]. Critical edition by Elida Lois and Angel Núñez. Barcelona: ALLCA XX.

Viqueira Albán, Pedro. 1987. *¿Relajados o reprimidos? diversiones públicas y vida social en la ciudad de México durante el Siglo de las Luces.* Mexico City: FCE.

Vogeley, Nancy. 1983. Mexican Newspaper Culture on the Eve of Mexican Independence. *Ideologies and Literature* 4(17):358–77.

———. 1987. The Concept of the People in *El Periquillo Sarniento. Hispania* 70(3): 457–67.

———. 2001. *Lizardi and the Birth of the Novel in Spanish America.* Gainesville: University Press of Florida.

Wald, Elijah. 2001. *Narcocorrido: A Journey into the Music of Drugs, Guns, and Guerrillas.* New York: Rayo.

Warren, Richard. 2000. Mass Mobilization versus Social Control: Vagrancy and Political Order in Early Republican Mexico. In *Reconstructing Criminality in Latin America,* edited by Carlos Aguirre and Robert Buffington. Wilmington, DE: Scholarly Resources.

Weber, David, and Jane Rausch, eds. 1994. *Where Cultures Meet: Frontiers in Latin American History.* Wilmington, DE: Scholarly Resources..

Williams, Raymond. 1973. *The Country and the City.* New York: Oxford University Press.

———. 1977. *Marxism and Literature.* Oxford: Oxford University Press.

———. 1991. Base and Superstructure in Marxist Cultural Theory. In *Rethinking Popular Culture: Contemporary Perspectives in Cultural Studies,* edited by Chandra Mukerji and Michael Schudson. Berkeley: University of California Press.

Wilson, Stephen. 1988. *Feuding, Conflict, and Banditry in Nineteenth-Century Corsica.* Cambridge: Cambridge University Press.

Woll, Allen L. 1987. Hollywood Bandits, 1910–1981. In *Bandidos: The Varieties of Latin American Banditry,* edited by Richard W. Slatta. New York: Greenwood Press.

Womack, John, Jr. [1968] 1970. *Zapata and the Mexican Revolution.* New York: Vintage Books.

Yarrington, Doug. 1997. *A Coffee Frontier: Land, Society, and Politics in Duaca, Venezuela, 1830–1936.* Pittsburgh, PA: University of Pittsburgh Press.

Zaragoza-Rovira, Gonzalo. 1996. *Anarquismo argentino, 1876–1902.* Madrid: Ediciones de la Torre.

Zehr, Howard. 1976. *Crime and the Development of Modern Society: Patterns of Criminality in Nineteenth-Century Germany and France.* Totowa, NJ: Rowman and Littlefield.

Ziems, Ángel. 1988. Un ejército de alcance nacional. In *Juan Vicente Gómez y su época*, edited by Elías Pino Iturrieta. Caracas: Monte Avila.

Zorroaquín-Becú, Horacio. 2001. Alberdi y Hernández. In *Martín Fierro*, by José Hernández [1872/1879]. Critical edition by Elida Lois and Angel Núñez. Barcelona: ALLCA XX.

Index

371